Persuasive Transactions

Persuasive

Transactions

Persuasive

Transactions

STEPHEN W. LITTLEJOHN

Humboldt State University

DAVID M. JABUSCH

University of Utah

SCOTT, FORESMAN AND COMPANY

Glenview, Illinois   London, England

Library of Congress Cataloging-in-Publication Data

Littlejohn, Stephen W.
  Persuasive transactions.

  Includes bibliographies and index.
  1. Persuasion (Rhetoric)   2. Communication.
I. Jabusch, David M.   II. Title.
P301.5.P47L58   1987   808   86-27954
ISBN 0-673-15987-6
123456-MPC-919089888786

Acknowledgments and photo credits begin on page 333, which is a legal extension of the
copyright page.

Preface

Persuasive Transactions is a text for undergraduate persuasion courses. It emphasizes theory and analysis and treats practice in this conceptual context. The book is based on four premises.

First, persuasion is a transactional, rule-governed process by which communicators jointly enact outcomes relevant to their aims. This perspective is established and explained early in the text and is integrated throughout.

Second, persuasion occurs in all communication contexts. The book is therefore organized into three parts. Part 1 sets out general theoretical directions, while Part 2 explores personal contexts of persuasion, including interpersonal relationships, groups and organizations, and negotiation. Part 3 discusses public contexts, including public advocacy, mediated persuasion, campaigns, and social movements.

Third, persuasion is best understood through an eclectic approach combining social science research, rhetorical scholarship, and personal insight. The material in the text draws from all of these. The book aims not to prescribe a universal set of principles, but to enable the student to adapt to a variety of sociocultural settings and to understand variation in persuasive practices. Insights from various research traditions and the authors' personal experiences are useful toward this end. More specifically, the book attempts to integrate insights of thinkers from Aristotle to Abraham Maslow, with concepts such as emotion (which receive little mention in recent discussions of persuasion), along with the best of modern persuasion and argumentation theory and research.

Finally, persuasive competence involves a blend of theoretical understanding, sensitivity, and skill. Pedagogically, competence is achieved by the study of theory, application of theory in analysis of experience, and practice. A good textbook works in concert with effective instruction, and this text is designed to present theory, to suggest ways in which that theory can help students understand experience through the use of both fictional and real-world examples and cases, and to provide ideas for student exercises.

Special thanks go to several individuals who provided essential assistance in the creation of this book, among them Janis Wright and Jackie Byrd. At Scott, Foresman, Barbara Muller guided the early stages of the manuscript, and Kathy Lorden and Carol Leon saw the text through editing and production. We acknowledge the assistance of our reviewers: Professor Glen Clatterbuck, Miami University; Professor William Seiler, University of Nebraska; and Professor David Vancil, Colorado State University. Thanks, too, to Professor Bruce Gronbeck, University of Iowa, for his helpful suggestions on fine-tuning the manuscript.

This project has become a major instrument in our own learning, and we hope the students gain at least a fraction of what we have learned in its preparation.

Stephen W. Littlejohn
David M. Jabusch

Contents

Persuasive Transactions

Part 1

Basic Concepts of Persuasion

1 / Communication and Persuasion

Open any national news magazine. As you read the summary of the week's events, see how many contemporary affairs involve influence through communication. Georgia prison officials argue for more effective forms of incarceration. A television evangelist is considering running for the office of President of the United States. The government of South Africa struggles to justify its case in the face of increasing opposition to apartheid. The Secretary of the Navy pushes for new ports in different locations. Now look between the articles. Persuasion abounds. An inserted card urges educators to subscribe to the magazine for their students. A luxury hotel in Washington, D.C., tries to lure you with descriptions of gourmet meals and spacious suites. A spate of political cartoons grabs your attention. Reviewers tell you why you should or should not read particular books. Employers advertise job openings, and real estate firms push property.

The 1980s in America is a time of profound and pervasive choices, and there is seemingly no end to advocates on all sides of the issues. These advocates define the issues and present the options, attempting to create stability or change.

Indeed, persuasion is today the keynote of public decision making in our society. It is one of the most important means of creating and affecting choice in both public and private life. It marks media communication, workplace interaction, and family relations. Persuasion is a natural and unavoidable part of our human condition.

It is no wonder, then, that social scientists have long been fascinated with influence and persuasion. Scholars in psychology, sociology, political science, and communication have been especially interested in processes by which individuals are influenced by others and by messages. The study of persuasion, too, has had profound practical implications, not only for those who would influence, but for all of us who are influenced. The question is never whether to participate in persuasion, for social life in modern societies is impossible without it. Rather, the most important questions involve how and when influence takes place and the manner in which individuals participate responsibly in this process. These questions of process and responsibility are the theme of this book.

/ *Perspectives on the Study of Persuasion*

Persuasion has been studied in a variety of ways. These approaches can be narrowed down to four general perspectives, each representing a major way in which scholars have come to understand persuasion. They are the transmissional perspective, the behavioristic perspective, the interactional perspective, and the transactional perspective.[1]

/ *Transmissional perspective*

The earliest perspective on persuasion stressed the sending and receiving of messages. In this view, persuasion is seen primarily as an act of transmitting information and manipulating the person who is to be persuaded. The transmissional perspective follows a linear model of communication: transmitter→ message→receiver. In his recent book on persuasion, Robert B. Cialdini illustrates the perspective quite clearly:

> There is a group of people who know very well where the weapons of automatic influence lie and who employ them regularly and expertly to get what they want. They go from social encounter to social encounter requesting others to comply with their wishes; their frequency of success is dazzling. The secret of their effectiveness lies in the way they structure their requests, the way they arm themselves with one or another of the weapons of influence that exist within the social environment. To do this may take no more than one correctly chosen word that engages a strong psychological principle and sets an automatic behavior tape rolling within us. And trust the human exploiters to learn quickly exactly how to profit from our tendency to respond mechanically according to these principles.[2]

Not all transmissional discussions of persuasion depict the process in such strong terms. For example, a productive line of research in the communication field has dealt with "compliance-gaining strategies."[3] Although the concept behind this work is quite transmissional, it has made an important contribution and is incorporated, in a reconceptualized fashion, later in this book.

The transmissional perspective usually aims to teach people how to package and deliver persuasive messages. In the writings on persuasion, the transmissional approach has been largely responsible for "how-to" material. Such writings tell us what to say and how to say it in order to be effective persuaders. The primary weakness of the transmissional approach is that it tends to be prescription-oriented and manipulative. As we shall see in the coming pages, persuasion is not best conceived as something one person does *to* another.

/ Behavioristic perspective

The approach to the study of communication that stresses the effects of communication on behavior is the behavioristic perspective. In it, behavior in communication with others is seen as a response to various stimuli. Messages as stimuli are treated as causes and their behavioral responses as effects. In other words, this perspective stresses the impact of messages on people. What do people do as a consequence of being exposed to a message? How do their attitudes, beliefs, values, opinions, and behaviors change? These questions are the focus of the behavioristic perspective.

Because of its emphasis on behavior—on observable effects—this perspective has been very influential in research and theory on persuasion. Wallace C. Fotheringham, for example, defines *persuasion* from the behavioristic perspective as "that body of effects in receivers, relevant and instrumental to source-desired goals, brought about by a process in which messages have been a major determinant of those effects."[4] This definition stresses the behavioral outcomes of communication as the key to understanding persuasion.

Although behavioristic research and theory has been useful in helping to understand persuasion—and we make use of much of it here—it is now generally believed inadequate by itself to provide a comprehensive picture of persuasion because it fails to capture the process of what people do together when persuasion occurs.

/ Interactional perspective

The third approach to persuasion seen in the writings on communication is the interactional perspective. This view sees communication as an event in which individuals respond sequentially to one another. One person's response affects another person's, which in turn affects the first person's again. Communication thus is like a ping pong game. Although this approach also stresses communication effects, it recognizes that responding is mutual and interpersonal. A recent and influential survey of literature on persuasion expresses the interactional perspective in this way:

> Here we are suggesting an even broader conceptual outlook that views all parties to a persuasive transaction as *changeable* and *interactive* rather than conceiving of persuasion as a process whereby the persuader(s) *act* and the target(s) *react*.[5]

Little traditional work on persuasion incorporates the interactional perspective, although we make use of it in this book when discussing the interpersonal and organizational arenas of persuasion.

These three perspectives on persuasion are not necessarily inconsistent with one another. Rather, they represent different angles from which to view the process; they differ in focus, not necessarily in substance. Each of these perspectives has contributed in its own right to our understanding of communication and persuasion. However, we believe that the study of communication—and of persuasion in particular—is better served by a fourth, more complete perspective, which builds on these first three.

/ Persuasion as Transaction

Consider these situations. An overweight person, wanting to slim down, seeks the help of a psychologist who is a specialist in behavior modification. Another person, a heavy smoker, has been advised by a physician to quit smoking or face some serious medical problems. The smoker reads a book designed to motivate people to quit smoking by offering specific suggestions for doing so. A married couple is having difficulty resolving issues in their marriage. To improve the quality of their relationship would require changes in the behavior of both parties. They attend a weekend marriage enrichment workshop.

In each of these cases, who is the persuader and who the persuadee? Which acts—seeking behavior modification or offering it, reading a book or writing it, attending a workshop or conducting it—constitute persuasion? The answer is not clear. The three perspectives on persuasion already discussed are inadequate to explain these situations. For example, the behavioristic perspective would enable us to look at the behavior changes in the participants, but would be weak in helping us understand the give-and-take nature of these situations. The transmissional perspective would help us focus on the messages that were sent and received in these situations, but would confuse us when we tried to designate who is persuading whom. Finally, the interactional perspective would enable us to see the interdependency of responses in these situations, but would not be very useful in showing us how people are acting in accord with interpretations of context. Further, the subtle, frequently unobservable cognitive activity of communicators in the more traditional "receiver" role are even more difficult to understand using these perspectives.

For these reasons, we prefer the *transactional perspective* to the study of communication and persuasion.[6] The focus of this approach is shared meaning and coordinated action. It is based on the assumption that people do more than respond to messages; they actively create meanings and coordinate their actions, and they do so by producing, exchanging, and acting on messages. In any genuine transaction, as in a store purchase, each party must actively give something; receiving or responding alone is not enough. Persuasion is like that: its outcome of shared meaning and coordinated action depends upon the active participation of everyone involved. We do not deny that people sometimes respond passively, that they occasionally communicate mindlessly, as from a script. However, the bulk of important communication in society involves active engagement.

Persuasion from a transactional perspective therefore is a joint process. It is not something that one person does to another, or even that people take turns doing to each other. Rather, it is a process actively created by its participants through symbolic interaction with one another. It requires the use of symbols in a social process of creating meaning and coordinating action.

In this view of communication, both parties give and both take, creating something new in the exchange. Through giving and taking, a *transaction* is created. The exchange is merely the means by which something else is created, perhaps the bonding of the relationship. The important characteristic of the transactional outcome is that it is only possible because both parties acted together in its creation.

/ The Concept of Persuasion

/ The problem of definition

Persuasion has been defined in a variety of ways, depending on the perspective taken. The transmissional perspective yields definitions that emphasize transfer or one-way action. The behavioristic perspective accents effects. The interactional perspective leads to definitions that highlight reciprocity. However, it would be fruitless to label any the "true" or best definition of persuasion. Definitions serve only to make useful distinctions. Before defining *persuasion* for ourselves, let us examine some characteristics of persuasion that most definitions espouse in one form or another.[7]

1. *Persuasion results in some change or effect* in either the behavior or cognitive system of one or more participants. In a murder case, for example, the crime charged can only be attempted murder until the victim dies. So persuasion remains only an attempt until an effect can be identified. (We take the generic term for people effecting change among one another to be *influence*. As we shall see, not all influence involves persuasion.)

Persuasion may involve a new behavior, a modified attitude, an altered value, a changed level or arousal, or merely a different situational orientation toward self, others, ideas, or things. The change need not be, and usually is not, profound, but it must involve a modification—temporary or enduring—in one's orientation toward some aspect of the world.

The change may be in oneself, the other person, or both, and therefore involves sender and receiver purposes. *Compliance-seeking* is the attempt to change another person or oneself by a communication transaction. *Compliance-responding* is the actual change undertaken in response to the transaction. For example, a weight-loss specialist tours the country giving speeches on the dangers of obesity, seeking the compliance of overweight people. Fat people, themselves concerned about their overweight, look for a solution, attend one of the lectures, and subsequently lose weight.

/ **Public pressure persuaded the makers of Coca-Cola to bring back the original version of the soft drink.**

2. *Persuasion involves choice.* We undertake some of our actions because we are forced to do so. Others are more freely chosen. Still others are based on limited choice. When we act on the basis of our perceptions and evaluations of the situation—our internal predispositions or orientations—we are making choices to follow certain courses of action over others. When we act solely on the basis of outside pressures without regard to personal orientations, we are not acting on the basis of choice. Choice is therefore important for distinguishing persuasion from coercion. If someone pulls a gun on you and you hand over your money, your compliance is probably not a result of persuasion. Likewise, when you carry out a trivial social activity prescribed by etiquette or expected behavior—such as holding the door for an elderly person—persuasion is probably not the relevant process behind your action. Since real choice is almost impossible to assess, the *perception of choice* on the part of the changing person is the key to whether persuasion is occurring.

3. *Persuasive communication is a process.* Without communication, influence is exerted through physical force. Prisoners are incarcerated, slaves are chained, and children are picked up and placed in their car seat. Although all of these acts communicate something, compliance is not a consequence of the communication.

Communication is the attempt to share meaning and coordinate actions by message transaction and is, by definition, an interpersonal symbolic act. Therefore, when we say that persuasion is communication, we mean that it is interpersonal, that it involves transaction among two or more individuals. This definition also stresses the symbolic nature of persuasion, focusing on its involvement with messages and meanings, an idea covered in greater detail in the next chapter. We acknowledge the view that people can persuade themselves outside communication with others, but such a definition expands the concept too far to include almost anything psychological. We therefore prefer to think of persuasion as an interpersonal communication event.

Our definition, then, includes these three criteria but frames them in a transactional way: **Persuasion is communication in which two or more individuals act together to bring about an outcome of change.** This definition treats persuasion as a generic concept covering either the process of communication leading to change or the outcome of that process. The term *persuasive communication* is useful to designate the process in contrast with persuasion as outcome.

/ Persuasive communication

We define *persuasive communication* as that communication occurring in situations where people intend to affect personal choices. Persuasion itself is the change that results from this process, but the desired outcome need not occur for persuasive communication to take place. In addition to the three characteristics of persuasion discussed above, this definition involves a fourth concept, *intention.*

In the process of communication, some outcomes are anticipated, even planned, and others are not. Although some communication may lead to inadvertent outcomes, persuasive communication is by definition purposive; it has a planned outcome. The purpose of persuasive communication is persuasion. When communicators desire personal change in themselves or others and communicate so as to achieve it, persuasive communication is occurring. When such communication leads to the intended outcome, persuasion itself is that outcome.

Suppose, for example, that Cindy and Claire are chatting over lunch one day for no other purpose than to fill time and enjoy each other's company. Cindy tells Claire about some entertaining movies she has recently seen, and Claire, realizing she has not been to the show in weeks, decides to take in one of Cindy's favorites that very evening. Is this persuasive communication? It is not in our view, because neither Cindy nor Claire intended influence to occur. Now suppose that Cindy has recognized that Claire has been a virtual recluse for weeks and thinks she should get out and enjoy herself. She deliberately talks up movies with Claire in an attempt to get her to go see some of them. Or suppose that Claire herself feels bored and wonders how to pep up her life a bit. She takes Cindy out to lunch in hopes that Cindy will give her some kind of guidance. We would identify these latter situations as persuasive communication because one or both parties wanted to achieve change.

1 The Nature of Persuasion

We have seen that persuasion is a transactional communication process. Let us now discuss six characteristics that further elaborate the nature of persuasion.

1. *Persuasive communication is a process, not a product.* We can easily examine the residues of persuasion—written documents, tapes, films, objects, speeches, letters, and a host of other forms. We can also look at the mechanisms of persuasion, its wires, apparatuses, microchips, transistors, transmitters, sensors, and more. But these artifacts and mechanisms are only products. Persuasive communication itself is an event; it happens. In short, it is a process.

Process involves three dynamics, the first of which is *change.*[8] Persuasion is never static; it never recurs exactly the same way. When we examine a persuasion event, therefore, we are seeing something unique: it may be similar—sometimes very similar—to other events, but never the same. In a political campaign, for example, a candidate may give essentially the same speech to similar audiences time after time, but each event is different from the others in various ways. For one, different audiences respond in different ways.

The second aspect of process is the *interrelatedness of events.* You cannot legitimately treat one part of a communication event as if it were independent from the others. The crowd reaction at a political rally, for example, depends in part on the setting, the speech, and the speaker. These, in turn, are all affected by the audience reaction itself. The speaker's mood may affect the speech delivery, but the delivery, in turn, will affect the speaker's mood. And so it goes among all the elements of the process. We prefer to think of persuasion as a system in which all of the elements relate to each other.

Finally, persuasion involves *simultaneous action.* Although many models treat persuasion as if it were linear, occurring one step at a time, most persuasion events consist of acts that overlap and occur simultaneously. As the politician speaks, the audience responds; they may shout, cheer, mill about, and talk to each other, even as the speaker is delivering the address.

2. *Persuasion is inseparable from its context.* The situation in which persuasion occurs affects the events comprising the transaction. Likewise, communication transactions themselves affect the environment. Always, then, persuasion and context go hand in hand. Contexts consist of three parts.

First, every persuasion transaction has a *historical background.* The event, including the meanings, responses, and actions of the participants, arises in part from what has happened before. Likewise, each transaction becomes part of the historical backdrop of future persuasion. We are referring here not only to world history, though the times in which we live can exert a mighty influence on events. We are also referring to the personal experience of the participants and the history of the relationships among them. For example, a communication transaction in a family occurs within the patterns of interaction that have gone before and the individual experiences of family members inside and outside the family itself.

/ **The three contexts of persuasion—historical, socio-cultural, and physical—
affect the persuasive communication.**

Second, each persuasion event occurs in a *social and cultural context*. This
aspect of context consists of the people and their meanings, norms, values, roles,
and rules. Consequently, good family therapists understand a particular conversation between members of a family within the context of the family system
itself. How does this family operate? What are the role divisions and distribu-
tions of power? What rules are used by members of this family to interpret and
to act within the family setting? Two different married couples could have very
similar conversations, but their words could hold entirely different meanings,
depending upon the socio-cultural factors of the family context. There is always
more to an interaction than just what is heard.

Finally, the *physical setting* is an important element of persuasion context.
Persuasion events must occur in a place, and that place can influence how the
event is played out by the participants. Communicators often use very different
interactional rules in different settings. Thus children who may be little mon-
sters at home sometimes seem so angelic in someone else's house. (Actually, we
know a few adults in the same category!) Physicians, realtors, and other professional communicators watch for the influence of their offices on clients.

These contexts—historical, socio-cultural, and physical—are usually interrelated. The place, including its character, is partially a product of the socio-cultural and historical contexts. The socio-cultural context cannot be separated
from history and is manifest in part by the physical context in which the communication occurs. Neither is history isolated; rather, it reflects a continuum of
cultural and physical experiences.

3. *Persuasion is personally and socially functional.* Symbolic interaction is an essential feature of humanity. It is our primary way of adapting to and accommodating our environment. It enables us to think and to regulate behavior. Consider the simple act of filling out an employment form. In asking for work, one is not only seeking to meet the immediate objective of getting a job, but is also reinforcing the self-image, obligating the employer to respond, and perhaps accomplishing an array of other functions. Communication, beyond serving the selfish objectives of those who give speeches, write poems, undergo counselling, or participate in any of the innumerable other forms of communication, functions in a broader sense to make us what we are. It is not something we can choose to do or not to do; we must communicate.[9]

Persuasion too is a natural part of being human. One popular point of view in the "me-decade" of the seventies was that persuasion is wrong, that people have no business trying to change others. That notion, however, is unrealistic. People often try to influence others, and they often seek to be influenced themselves. We conceive of persuasion as change brought about by two or more people in search of new alternatives. It is the outcome of dialogue among persons who seek or resist change. This dialogue is continual because it is necessary for personal and social growth and maintenance.

4. *The factors of persuasion are many.* A common myth is that persuasion results from the use of a few simple gimmicks, that being persuasive means knowing just the right strategy. No wonder persuaders are often frustrated! There is no trick to persuasion. It is the outcome of many personal, social, and cultural variables, which are discussed in some detail in Chapter Four. We do not mean that message strategies are unimportant, but no formula will guarantee success. Some persuaders look for the right button to press, for a magical machine that will bring about the desired response from others. Although a persuader's strategies are important in bringing about change, these alone are never solely responsible for any change that might occur. Readers looking for simple solutions to persuasion problems will not find them in this book.

5. *People are actively involved in their own change.* Another myth is that persuasion is something someone does to someone else. This myth sees persuasion as a passive response to an active attempt to influence. We know that people are actively involved in their own persuasion.[10] A person not open to change will not change regardless of the strategies employed by others, unless, of course, those strategies involve coercion or physical force.

Conversely, when change does occur, it results in part from the active information processing of the changed person. As we will see in the next chapter, persuasion occurs because individuals anticipate the consequences of changed orientations. Human beings have an amazing ability to reward and punish themselves and actively change behaviors using reinforcements they themselves set up. Consider religious conversion as an example. Conversion is the coming together of a need and an opportunity. The convert anticipates rewards in the new religion that will overcome problems not solved by other alternatives. In a sense, then, people persuade themselves. Those seeking compliance can structure information in such a way as to facilitate this process, but it is the information processing within the receiver that actually leads to the change.

6. *Participants in persuasion are interdependent.* If you check your uncritical image of persuasion, you probably see one person manipulating someone else. You may think of persuasion strictly as gaining compliance. Parents get their children to behave. Advertisers get people to buy. Preachers win converts. Politicians win votes. Most of us operate by this myth much of the time. In fact if our attempts at persuasion yield outcomes different from those we want, we often blame ourselves for not being good enough "persuaders."

However, if you reflect a moment, you will see that persuasion is more complex than this simple notion implies. It is not strictly something one person does to another. People engage one another in persuasion. They enter the transaction together, each contributing to whatever outcome results. Most parents understand—and many childless couples never realize—that no method of discipline always works with their children. Children often respond as their parents desire, but they do so when they themselves see reason to do so. When they comply, they are responding in part to the control of the parent and in part to their own desire for guidance, reward, or avoidance of punishment. Often parents make adjustments themselves meet the apparent objectives of their children. The result of a parent's attempt to change the child is often a change in the parent!

Advertisers, too, respond to the public. Does the public buy because of what the advertiser says, or is the advertiser responding to the wants of the public? Probably both are operating. Preachers rarely convert secure nonbelievers. People are affected by religious speakers when they themselves either already believe and seek reinforcement or are insecure in their own beliefs and desire change. In the political arena, we cannot be certain that the candidate really wins many votes directly. In fact, candidates themselves often change considerably in order to appeal to the voters.

In these examples, it is not always clear who is "persuading" whom. Of course, communicators do not always have equal influence in any persuasion situation. Influence is rarely balanced, but almost always some influence flows both ways. In the next chapter, we discuss this idea of distribution of influence in more detail.

/ Functions and Arenas of Persuasion

/ The functions of persuasion

Persuasion is an important instrument in the establishment, maintenance, and change of personal and social orientations. Here we discuss three major functions of persuasion in society: it regulates social interaction, it enables conflict to be managed, and it serves to disseminate information and innovation.

/ **Rank-and-file members persuasively communicate their needs to their representatives, and labor negotiators convince the membership that they will represent their interests fairly.**

/ *Regulating social interaction.* The first, and perhaps primary, function of persuasion is to regulate social interaction.[11] It does so by establishing, maintaining, and changing rules. By affecting rule choice, persuasive messages can set up new patterns of interaction or change old ones. This may mean changing who talks with whom, what they talk about, and the manner in which they interact. If, for example, you are persuaded to join a particular cause, you will begin paying attention to different messages in the media, going to meetings you did not formerly attend, and speaking with people in somewhat different terms than you would have used before the new commitment was made.

/ *Managing conflict.* Another function of persuasion is conflict management. Conflict management involves careful definition of problems, the attempt to understand others' points of view, creative generation of solutions that meet a variety of objectives, and the development of respect and trust. Persuasion enters all of these aspects of conflict management.[12] People influence each others' definition of the problem; they create the desire on the part of others to understand their own point of view; they argue over solutions; they open themselves to change as appropriate. Negotiation, for example, is a means of resolving conflicts between disputing parties. In negotiation, persuasion abounds, and the parties agree to live with the outcome.

/ *Disseminating ideas.* Finally, persuasion functions to disseminate ideas, opinions, and innovations. A long history of research demonstrates that people do not suddenly adopt new ideas. Rather, innovations, be they new ways of thinking, new beliefs, or new practices, come to be accepted through persuasive communication.[13] Persuasion, then, is a channel for change in society. Apart from the fact that it helps individuals and groups achieve their individual objectives, persuasion operates in a broader sense in society in this dissemination process. Physicians, farmers, business people, and others come to adopt practices in part because of this dissemination process.

/ The arenas of persuasion

Consider a sports arena. Imagine a large stadium in which people come to watch a game. On the field, players move together one on one and team against team. In the stands, people talk, mill about, eat, and engage in a variety of other behaviors, some of which are focused on the game and some of which are not. Yet, despite the variety of activity going on at a sporting event, any informed person could tell you what is happening and define it as a football, basketball, or soccer game. Communication in society is something like the happenings in a sports arena. People communicate with one another one on one, in groups, and in organizations; a variety of activities are going on in the social arena; yet enough structure exists to identify what is happening.

Actually, a sporting event includes a number of arenas. We could, for example, look at the very small arena of two players engaging one another. To them, at that moment, the relevant action seems limited to their encounter; yet, either would tell you that what is happening there is affected by and affects the entire team, the game, and the event as a whole. Or, we could broaden the arena to take into account what the team is doing. Again the team has its own world, but that world affects and is affected by the bigger stadium and what is happening there. Finally, we can step way back, as from a helicopter flying overhead, and view the entire stadium, the people as a mass, and the event as a whole.

Communication arenas, too, can be expanded or contracted depending upon one's perspective. For purposes of discussion, we divide persuasion into two general arenas, the interpersonal and the public.

/ Interpersonal arena.
The interpersonal arena of persuasion accents relationship. Here we are interested in the ways people interact to establish, maintain, and change their relationships with other people. Much of the talk encountered in a busy day occurs in this arena: it involves one person engaging another on some subject of importance. For example, when a welfare eligibility worker meets to talk with a client in the welfare office, the focus will probably be on the two of them together, and much of what happens will establish a relationship between them. The worker needs information about the client, and the client wishes to achieve a fair level of support. Initially, at least, the eligibility worker may want to influence the client to become self supporting or produc-

tive in some way, while the client may want the worker to know that he is as productive as possible at this point in his life, but still cannot be self supporting.

Interpersonal persuasion occurs in a variety of settings, one of which is the organization. Organizational persuasion necessarily includes the interpersonal, but it also involves the participant's awareness of and relationship to a larger group. The welfare worker is constrained, in part, by the policies of the department and the procedures established by the eligibility section, and communicates from within a role which is established by the organization. The audience is not just the client, but also the supervisor, who may require a report of all meetings with clients. The client too is part of this organizational structure. Needs are assessed on the basis of rules of eligibility, and the role of client determines in part when he can visit the welfare department, how appointments are made, and how long conferences can last.

Part 2 of this book deals with the interpersonal arena. It includes chapters on persuasion in relationships, persuasion in organizations, and negotiation and mediation.

/ Public arena.   When we move to the public arena, we take a larger scope of activity and a larger number of people into consideration, although we do not give up interpersonal processes. The welfare eligibility worker and client, for example, may both be part of the audience for a social movement to reduce welfare costs to the taxpayer. The movement may involve carefully orchestrated campaigns using public meetings, speeches, media advertising, and other forms of persuasion to accomplish social change. The threat of welfare reductions, in this particular case, may cause our worker to lose his job and the client to lose benefits. The nature of their interaction on the interpersonal level can even be influenced by these social pressures.

Part 3 of the book looks at the public arena in more detail, discussing, among other subjects, mass communication and media, advertising, public advocacy, and campaigns and movements.

/ Ethical Responsibility in Persuasion

Ethical responsibility is the willingness and ability to act on the basis of moral choice. It is the active consideration of appropriate conduct. Ethics is no simple matter; an entire branch of philosophy has emerged to deal with its complexities. One of the reasons ethics is not simple is that there is no agreement on what constitutes ethical behavior, although numerous positions have been asserted.

One of the differences you will see among ethical positions is that between the universalist and the relativist. *Universal ethics* claims that certain values or norms of conduct should always be followed, that certain standards are overriding and universal. Universalists might say, for example, that one must never lie. Another form of universalist thought lies on a more abstract level, claiming certain universal principles such as the need to respect the dignity of each individual human being.

At the opposite extreme is *relative ethics.* This position claims that there should be no universal standards of behavior, that context and culture are all-important in determining ethically appropriate conduct. In some circumstances, for example, lying is ethical and truth telling wrong, says the relativist. On the more abstract level, the relativist would claim that there are no universal principles. For example, in response to the claims that individual dignity should always be respected, the relativist might say that in many cultures, the needs of the person are considered subordinate to those of the group and to act otherwise in such cultures would violate a sacred and time-honored way of being. It is possible, of course, to take a position in the middle, claiming that some standards or principles are universal but that much of our conduct must be guided by contextual factors.

Another difference you will see among ethical positions is that between *ends-oriented* and *means-oriented* approaches. Many people make moral choices on the basis of the expected outcome. If the outcome is good, the means are unimportant. The ends justify the means. The alternative position looks primarily at means, basing conduct on the propriety of actions, not on their results. For example, an individual who bases ethical decisions on outcomes might lie to a friend to avoid hurting the friend's feelings. In contrast, a means-oriented individual might tell the truth because of a belief that lying is wrong, or wrong under the circumstances at hand. It is possible, though often difficult, to be both means- and ends-oriented in one's ethics.

Communication and persuasion almost always demand ethical choice. Recognizing that several ethical positions are defensible, we wish to share our position, which we think is particularly relevant to communication and also consistent with the transactional perspective.

We begin with the premise that one should communicate in such a way as to maximize shared responsibility for the outcome of the transaction. This premise is ends-oriented in that it aims to achieve the best possible outcome for all the participants in a transaction. However, it is also means-oriented because it recognizes the importance of two principles of conduct that motivate a desire for shared responsibility. These principles are caring and openness.

Caring is concern for the well-being of self and others. It involves a feeling that what happens to others is as important as what happens to self. It is the spirit of good will. *Openness* is a willingness to share information with others and, conversely, an interest in the disclosures of other people. It is, in short, a spirit of honesty.

Figure 1.1 illustrates how these two principles can fit together.[14] Four ethical positions are possible from their combination: irresponsibility, unshared responsibility, abdicated responsibility, and ethical responsibility. Lack of caring

Caring

		High	Low
		Concern for consequences and well-being of participants	Lack of concern for consequences and well-being
High	Sharing information completely and honestly	***Ethical responsibility*** Communicators share responsibility for determining the consequences of the transaction.	***Abdicated responsibility*** Communicator refuses to assume responsibility for the consequences, leaving total responsibility up to the other communicator.
Low	Withholding or distorting information	***Unshared responsibility*** Communicator assumes total responsibility for consequences of the transaction, allowing the other communicator no opportunity to share responsibility.	***Irresponsibility*** Communicator refuses to assume responsibility and withholds the opportunity for the other communicator to have control.

Openness (row label, left side: High / Low)

/ FIGURE 1.1 Model of Responsibility

and openness leads to irresponsible behavior. The communicator does not care about the outcome and is closed, preventing the other party from participating as a full partner in the decision. The outcome from such a transaction is apt to be a disaster for the receiving party.

Caring without openness is characteristic of unshared responsibility. Here the communicator cares about the well-being of the other, but is unwilling to empower the other person by honest sharing of information. This is a common position in communication, especially in traditional approaches to persuasion.

It is strictly outcome-oriented and assumes that one's own perspective is so important that the other person should not be allowed a chance to enter equally into the transaction. Sometimes this stance is necessary, as in communicating with a child, but much of the time it is undesirable.

The opposite position is one of openness without caring. It is characteristic of blatantly hurtful communication in which the consequences of revealing information are not considered. Such communication abdicates responsibility for the outcome of the transaction. It is not a common ethical stance in persuasion because it is oriented neither at change in oneself nor the other. Such communication is not usually intended to influence.

We think people should operate with caring and openness most of the time. Such ethical responsibility promotes shared outcome. It recognizes that persuasion is a transaction and that change is a consequence of joint decision and action. It does not deny the importance of compliance-seeking, but it permits full participation in the compliance process.

Most of the time you will probably have to choose between persuading with unshared responsibility and persuading with shared responsibility. Almost always, we think, you will care enough to want a positive outcome for yourself and others. The typical sales situation illustrates these two common ethical choices. Although irresponsible behavior, with low caring on the part of the salesperson, can certainly be found, most people who make a living in the sales field really do care about the well-being of the buyer. But they are not always willing to be open with clients. The question is whether to treat the buyer as an equal partner in the transaction and possibly lose the sale, or to follow the belief that you know best and will do all you can to ensure that the purchase is made.

All of us have been in this choice situation many times, whether in selling or in some other aspect of life. We once knew an insurance agent, whom we offhandedly referred to as an "insurance salesman." He corrected us at once. A salesperson, he explained, has but one objective: to close the deal and make the commission. All that is said and done with the client aims at that end. An agent, on the other hand, has the best outcome for the client as an objective and sees his or her role as acting on behalf of the client. The agent attempts to provide as much information as possible, so that the agent and client together can come to a mutually agreed-upon closure.

/ Achieving Competence in Persuasion

At the end of each chapter in this book, you will find a section designed to help you improve your competence in persuasion. We think achieving competence in any aspect of social life, like persuasion, is a complicated matter, and we take a little space at this point to discuss our orientation toward it.

Competence is sometimes equated with proficiency, or the ability to get a job done effectively. Although competence involves proficiency, we believe it is more, for effective persuasion is not just the achievement of a favorable outcome for oneself. Persuasive competence means behaving in such a way as to increase the likelihood that the best possible outcome will be achieved by all who are concerned with the transaction. Because effectiveness involves more than simply winning compliance, competence is a more complicated matter than exercising know-how.

/ Dimensions of persuasive competence

Persuasive competence is not largely different from communication competence, which is the ability to exchange messages so as to increase shared meaning and coordination with others. Persuasive competence, therefore, refers to the establishment of coordinated interaction that brings about constructive and desired change. It consists of three factors.

1. *Persuasive competence involves cognitive understanding.* This dimension of competence is knowledge of the process of communication as it is being played out in the transaction of the moment. In persuasion it involves an understanding of how and why change occurs. It means knowing the effects of personal, social, cultural, and situational factors. It is an awareness of the role of message strategies, and a sense of their limitations as well. In short, cognitive understanding is the critical thought that can lead to more effective participation in persuasion.

For example, a competent campaign manager for a political candidate has an understanding of how communication occurs and what factors of persuasion operate in various situations. The campaign manager understands the complexity of persuasion and the ways in which people's meanings, rules, roles, and values affect their choices. This person knows that persuasion is largely a process of information processing, in which messages are designed to provide insights into the candidate's style, experience, and positions, and that people will integrate that information into a complex web of already-existing predispositions.

2. *Persuasive competence involves interpersonal sensitivity.* Knowledge of communication alone is not sufficient to claim competence. It also involves a subtle but strong set of sensitivities. The competent communicator is aware of the needs and feelings of others and of self. Sensitivity also involves an awareness of the demands of the situation. In persuasion, sensitive communicators are able to read cues that tell them when the time is right for compliance seeking and what strategies are best under the personal, social, cultural, and physical circumstances. In large measure, sensitivity consists of attentiveness to feedback, interpersonal caring, and self-awareness.

Thus the campaign manager, in addition to knowing something about the process of persuasion, has an ability to sense the moods of people, not only in the campaign staff, but in the public as well. He or she is able to detect with some accuracy how people are feeling and the ways in which events affect responses relevant to the campaign goal.

3. *Persuasive competence involves communication skills.* Skills are learned capacities to use various tactics effectively for the achievement of immediate objectives. They consist of the trained ability to manipulate the body and voice and to operate facilely on ideas and concepts. Skilled communicators speak, listen, read, and write well. Although skills by themselves do not constitute competence, they are an essential element which, combined with understanding and sensitivity, can lead to a constructive persuasive outcome.

Good campaign organizations consist of people with a variety of important communication skills, including, for example, writing, conducting meetings, operating television and film equipment, listening, and a host of others. Within the realm the job of running the campaign, an effective campaign manager will be able, minimally, to speak and listen well, to write easily and in a readable fashion, and to read quickly and with high comprehension. The campaign manager will also have skills of translating ideas into practical discourse, to demonstrate points, to organize tasks, and many more.

/ Theory / Practice / Analysis

The ultimate purpose of this text is to help you improve your competence in persuasion. This book paints a large picture that emphasizes all of the factors of competence discussed above. In order to achieve competence in its fullest sense, you will need to use a three-fold approach. First, you must study principles, derived from theory. *Theory* consists of explanations of the process of persuasion. A *principle* is a generalization that helps us understand something about persuasion. Principles obviously assist understanding, but in directing attention to certain aspects of the process, they also help one to become more sensitive and skilled. To the extent that principles help one understand the importance of values and individual human choice, they can also have an impact on ethical responsibility. At the end of each chapter, you will find a list of what we consider to be the most important principles of the chapter under the heading "Theory." This section is essentially a brief summary of the main points of the chapter.

Second, to develop persuasive competence, you must practice. *Practice* is experience. It may be guided and structured, as in a persuasion course, or natural, as in everyday life. Your persuasion course will probably involve practice of some kind: you may work on in-class assignments, or complete projects outside class, or both. As part of the competence section at the end of each chapter, we have listed a variety of exercises you can do under the heading of "Practice." These exercises are designed to have you try out the various ideas included in the chapter.

We are all practicing persuaders, but practice by itself is not sufficient to develop competence. Rather, to have persuasive competence, you must bring principles and practice together through analysis. *Analysis* is the careful examination of practice by applying theoretical principles. It can result in improved practice, modified theory, or both. Analysis can take many forms. In everyday life we often analyze what we do or observe. How often, for example, have you reconsidered a conversation in your mind after it actually occurred? People operate by implicit principles. Everybody has theories on which they rely, even though these are not necessarily learned at a college or university in the context of scholarly research. People become more competent because they actively bridge theory and practice by analysis. Neither thoughtless experience nor groundless principle can make you more competent, but put principles together with experience, and you are well on your way. The third section at the end of each chapter, under the heading "Analysis," includes activities that require you to examine persuasion experiences by applying principles.

Obviously, the quality of the theories we use to produce principles is extremely important. We certainly are not implying that analysis can be based on any theory at all. Researchers undertake studies to improve our theoretical understanding of persuasion. Although we include our own experience, this book is based largely on theories of persuasion derived from this kind of research. We hope that the analysis you are able to undertake with these principles will enable you to improve your competence in persuasion to the maximum extent possible.

The purpose of many college communication courses, including most persuasion courses, is to bring together these three elements—principles (theory), practice, and analysis—for the accelerated development of competence. Analysis and practice in such courses may take the form of criticism, group discussion, observational activities, or other structured experiences leading to the application of principles. In more advanced courses, it may involve actual research. What this kind of instruction actually provides is a "kit of tools" for you to use in the variety of persuasion situations in which you will find yourself. Analysis does not follow any set pattern, but is done on the basis of what you judge to be necessary at any given time.

The theory-practice-analysis cycle can affect all four dimensions of competence, as illustrated in Figure 1.2.[15] The chapters of this text are organized around this model. Each chapter presents principles relevant to an aspect of persuasion. At the end of each chapter is a set of activities for analysis and practice.

To get an idea of what to expect in the competence sections at the end of each chapter, look at the three sections below. "Theory" provides a summary of the important ideas in Chapter 1, "Practice" suggests some activities to put these concepts to work, and "Analysis" lists some thought-provoking exercises for the careful examination of these concepts in actual experience.

Theory

1. Communication and persuasion are important parts of human life.

2. The transactional perspective holds the greatest potential for understanding the process of persuasion.

3. As a transaction, persuasive communication is conceived as a process, inseparable from context, that has important personal and social functions.

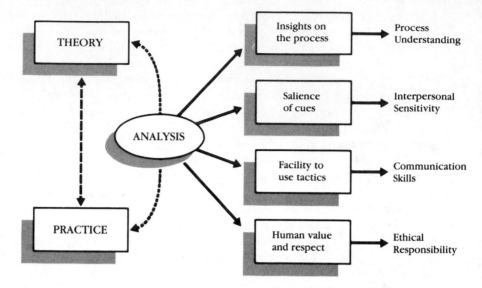

/ FIGURE 1.2 The Development of Communication Competence

4. *Persuasion* is defined as communication in which two or more individuals act together to bring about an outcome of change.

5. The basic assumptions of persuasion are that factors of persuasion are many, people are actively involved in their own change, and participants in persuasion are interdependent.

6. Persuasion occurs in interpersonal and public arenas.

7. Ethical responsibility involves sharing the responsibility for the outcome of the persuasive transaction.

Practice

1. With a partner, agree upon a situation in which you can play the role of communicators. The situation might involve discussing an important idea, solving a relationship problem, resolving a conflict, selling some goods, or any other. Each of you take a role and play through the situation in two ways. First, both persons should try to take all the responsibility for the outcome of the persuasion. Be as manipulative and closed as possible in an attempt to get your partner to comply. Next, play the situation in such a way that responsibility for the outcome is shared. In this mode, be as open as possible. After the exercise, discuss the results.

2. Develop an advertising campaign that deliberately takes process, context, and function into account. Discuss the way in which you would have approached the assignment differently if you had assumed instead that persuasive communication is a product, not a process; that context is unimportant; and that the only function of the campaign is to sell your product.

Analysis

1. Interview a professional persuader, such as a politician, preacher, salesperson, or attorney. Find out as much as possible about the individual's sensitivity, skill, ethics, and understanding of process, and how these enter into his or her communication decisions.

2. Think about a persuasive situation in which you have recently been involved. Write a paper outlining the ways in which it was affected by context, including history, socio-cultural factors, and physical place.

3. Attend a public meeting in which an important issue is being discussed. Take some time to read about the issue before going to the meeting. At the meeting, listen carefully to the persuasion of the participants. Try to determine to what extent people are behaving in a caring and open manner. To what extent is responsibility for the outcome of the meeting being shared? Would you say that the individuals are communicating in an ethically responsible fashion? Why or why not?

Notes

[1]These perspectives are discussed in greater depth in David M. Jabusch and Stephen W. Littlejohn, *Elements of Speech Communication* (Boston: Houghton Mifflin, 1981), pp. 12–25.

[2]Robert B. Cialdini, *Influence: Science and Practice* (Glenview, IL: Scott, Foresman, 1985), pp. 10–11.

[3]This literature is summarized by Lawrence R. Wheeless, Robert Barraclough, and Robert Stewart, "Compliance-Gaining and Power in Persuasion," in *Communication Yearbook 7*, ed. Robert N. Bostrom (Beverly Hills: Sage Publications, 1983), pp. 105–145.

[4]Wallace C. Fotheringham, *Perspectives on Persuasion* (Boston: Allyn and Bacon, 1966), p. 7.

[5]Gerald R. Miller, Michael Burgoon, and Judee K. Burgoon, "The Functions of Human Communication in Changing Attitudes and Gaining Compliance," in *Handbook of Rhetorical and Communication Theory,* ed. Carrol C. Arnold and John Waite Bowers (Boston: Allyn and Bacon, 1984), p. 456.

[6]The transactional approach to communication was perhaps first introduced by Dean C. Barnlund, "A Transactional Model of Communication," in *Language Behavior: A Book of Readings,* ed. Johnny Akins et al. (The Hague: Mouton, 1970), pp. 53–71.

[7]For a summary of definitions of *persuasion,* see Mary John Smith, *Persuasion and Human Action: A Review and Critique of Social Influence Theories* (Belmont, CA: Wadsworth Publishing, 1982), pp. 4–7.

[8]This discussion of process relies heavily on Leonard Hawes, "Elements of a Model for Communication Processes," *Quarterly Journal of Speech,* 59 (1973): 11–21.

[9]For a fuller discussion of communication functions, see Frank E. X. Dance and Carl Larson, *The Functions of Human Communication* (New York: Holt, 1976).

[10]This idea of human involvement and responsibility reflects "new paradigm" thinking in the social sciences. Recent examples of this line of thought can be found in John Shotter, *Social Accountability and Selfhood* (Oxford: Basil Blackwell, 1984); Ron

Harre, *Personal Being* (Cambridge: Harvard University Press, 1984); and Kenneth Gergen, *Toward Transformation in Social Knowledge* (New York: Springer-Verlag, 1982).

[11]The regulatory function of communication is discussed in fuller terms by Dance and Larson, *Functions.*

[12]The role of persuasion in conflict has been explored by Herbert Simons, "The Carrot and the Stick as Handmaidens of Persuasion in Conflict Situations," in *Perspectives on Communication in Social Conflict,* ed. Gerald R. Miller and Herbert Simons (Englewood Cliffs, NJ: Prentice-Hall, 1974), pp. 172–205.

[13]The role of interpersonal communication in the dissemination of innovations is more thoroughly discussed in Everett M. Rogers and F. Floyd Shoemaker, *Communication of Innovations, A Cross-Cultural Approach* (New York: Free Press, 1971); and Everett M. Rogers and D. Lawrence Kincaid, *Communication Networks* (New York: Free Press, 1981).

[14]Jabusch and Littlejohn, *Elements,* p. 9.

[15]This model of competence is developed in Stephen W. Littlejohn and David M. Jabusch, "Communication Competence: Model and Application," *Journal of Applied Communication Research,* 10 (1982): 29–37.

2/ Interpretation and Action in Persuasion

The major illness of a United States President is always a serious national concern. So when President Ronald Reagan was told, after his minor surgery for removal of polyps in the large intestine, that a large mass had been discovered deep in the colon, the White House had cause to worry. Reagan and his staff were informed that the growth had a 50-50 chance of being cancerous. Major surgery was scheduled.

The President and his advisers had more to worry about than his personal health. How would the illness be perceived by the public? What would surgery mean to the President's credibility as a strong and healthy leader? How would national security be affected? More than answering these questions, however, decisions had to be made about how to handle the situation. How much information should be released to the public? What should the President say, and what should be left to Press Secretary Larry Speakes and to the medical team to report?

The communication problem accompanying the health ordeal turned out to be of immense importance. It involved a major set of interpretations, followed by carefully planned actions, to persuade the American public and foreign leaders that little was amiss in American leadership.

We know from the last chapter that persuasive communication involves changing one's orientation to some aspect of reality. In this chapter we explain the role of interpretation and action in that process. We introduce the concept of cognitive system, show how that system provides a set of rules, and discuss ways in which communication is a process of coordinating interpretation and action. Chapter 3 discusses the cognitive system in greater detail, and Chapter 4 considers the processes by which persuasion occurs.

The participants in any communication transaction have an important task to accomplish: they must coordinate their actions so that what they are doing seems to make sense.[1] Sometimes they succeed, and sometimes not. The essential problem of communicators—including those engaged in persuasion—is to move from their own personal orientations to a system that involves all of the communicators in coordinated joint action. This is not always easy, and in persuasion it can be especially difficult because of the diversity of objectives held by the various communicators in the transaction.

/ Elements of Cognition

Communicators do not approach persuasion empty-handed. They enter a transaction with a full kit of tools. Just as a carpenter begins any job with tools and materials, communicators also have resources, which, as a group, are called the *cognitive system.* The cognitive system is a person's way of thinking, of ordering the world at a given moment. It is dynamic, and although it has continuity from moment to moment, it is constantly changing, growing, and developing. Each encounter with the world, especially one involving communication, returns something new to the cognitive system.[2]

/ Concepts: The building blocks of cognition

In its most fundamental terms, the cognitive system consists of elements called concepts. A *concept* is a group of things associated with one another because of certain common characteristics. The group is symbolized by a name or label, which is used to think about and communicate the concept. Concepts are constructions of an individual's cognitive system, and although concepts may be shared with many other people, they are fluid and vary from person to person and group to group. In other words, the thing being conceptualized does not determine its meaning; what is defined as a concept depends upon the individual's perception of the moment.

We illustrate concepts in our classes with a simple exercise. We ask each student to select an object from pocket, purse, briefcase, or elsewhere and to put it on a table in the middle of the room. An interesting and varied group of objects results. Then we have a student come to the table and sort the objects. The task is simple. For example, a student might put metal objects in one pile, wooden objects in another, plastic things in another, and cloth elsewhere. In this example, materials are used as the concepts to sort the objects. Then another student is called up. He or she might sort the object according to function. Another student might choose size. Another color. We push the students to repeat the exercise until they have to think about new concepts with which to sort the pile of possessions. No object belongs objectively and purely to any one category; all categories are valid and potentially useful. How one perceives an object at any given moment depends upon the conceptualization in operation at that time.

Our systems of concepts naturally consist of associations among objects, but they also involve feelings, ideas, and other intangible elements. The conceptual system involves association and symbolization, and the resulting meanings affect our ways of thinking and acting.

/ Cognition and information processing

The cognitive system, then, determines what one "knows"—what is remembered, what is valued, what is believed, and what is felt. The cognitive system is a complex web of concepts and relations among them that enable an individual to process information. When a communicator encounters information in the form of experiences or messages, he or she will assimilate that information into the cognitive system. Information is not just brought in, but is organized into a complex conceptual framework. Your previous experience affects how you think at any given time. What you attend to, what you perceive, what you remember, and how you organize an experience depends upon the make-up of your system. In the next chapter, we discuss in much more detail what comprises the cognitive system and how it is organized; then in Chapter 4, we cover the various ways in which that system changes.

When you speak or act in some way, you draw upon your kit of tools to determine just how that action will proceed. When you observe the actions of others and listen to what they have to say, you again use your cognitive resources to come to an understanding of what is meant. These are information-processing tasks. In persuasion, information processing is used to establish when persuasion should be undertaken, how to approach it, and what adjustments are to be made during the transaction itself.

We do not mean to imply here that every action and interpretation is consciously thought out. Often we are unaware of our actions and interpretations as they are happening. In these instances, we are behaving according to a script or program that guides our behavior. That script is itself deeply embedded in the cognitive system, and the organization of the system in large measure determines what script is chosen and how it will be played out. When a problem or unexpected response is encountered, we may abandon the script, think through the situation, and become very conscious of our information processing at that moment. You know, for example, how carefully and consciously you attend to certain advertisements when you are thinking about making a major purchase. Much persuasion is like that; it demands attention and conscious thought.[3]

/ Cognitive organization and symbolic interaction

How, then, do people use the cognitive system to process information? We know that human beings are equipped from birth with a huge cerebral cortex that makes complex cognitive processing possible. Our most important capability is symbolization. We use stimuli to represent things other than themselves. We can view the structures of the world in many different ways, manipulating our images and working with images by operating on symbols. Language is the most pervasive and complex system of symbols used in cognition; but, of course, humans use a variety of other kinds of nonverbal symbols as well, including objects, motions, and space. Meanings are what symbols come to represent for us in terms of their referents, feelings, and experiences.

Concepts, then, are important, but equally important are the relationships or connections among the concepts in the system. The cognitive system is organized through its conceptual connections; concepts are not discrete elements, but sets of overlapping cognitions. Frankly, socio-behavioral scientists do not really know how the human cognitive system is organized, but they do have some good hypotheses. Perhaps the most popular idea of cognitive organization is one of hierarchy. People organize their thoughts in terms of elaborate levels of abstraction. Smaller or more concrete concepts are organized into larger, more encompassing ones. These categories are interconnected in such a way as to create a web or network of elements.[4] In Chapter 3, we discuss the nature of this network in more detail. What makes people different from one another is that they put their concepts together in different ways.

Let us look at two examples. The first is a possible cognitive organization for a feminist. Such a woman might tell us that she values individual human freedom of choice. That would be a very central concept and would be at the hub of many of her thoughts about women and men. Figure 2.1 illustrates in simplified form a possible pattern of several cognitive elements in this person's system. The second example is the cognitive system of a traditional woman (Figure 2.2). Note the way in which more concrete elements relate to more abstract ones to create a hierarchy. This woman might tell us that she values her defined role as wife and mother above all. You can see that this person has a very different orientation toward the world than the feminist because of her drastically different cognitive organization. These two women would define femininity differently, have different attitudes toward parenting, and seek very different goals.

Our experience in life, especially our interactions with other people, in large measure determine how we think. Meanings, which are embedded in the organization of the cognitive system, are an outcome of symbolic interaction with others. Meaning does not reside in the symbol itself, nor is meaning given naturally in any situation; people assign meanings on the basis of the cognitive system, which in turn is affected by interactions with others. Therefore, human conduct is affected by an important circle: communication both affects and is affected by the cognitive system.[5] As professors, for example, we know that our teaching affects how we think, but our thinking, in turn, affects what and how we teach.

/ The problem of multiple meanings

As we have seen, one view of cognitive organization involves hierarchy, or the relative ordering of thoughts, feelings, beliefs, and values. If this view is correct, our thoughts and actions will usually be linked to several levels in the cognitive hierarchy. Thus, an individual can be operating on the basis of several meanings

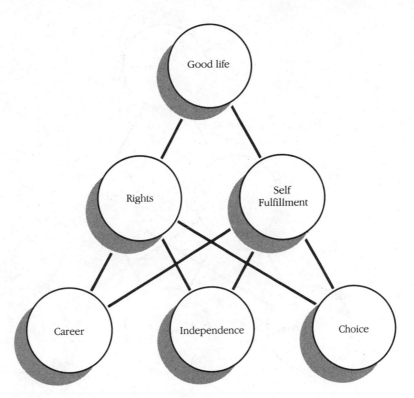

/ FIGURE 2.1 Simplified Cognitive System of a Feminist

at once, each linked to a different part of the cognitive system. How can this be true?

Imagine that a traditional woman is confronted with a financial crisis in the family. Perhaps her husband has been laid off, and the family income stops. Imagine further that the wife knows that she can get a job with her uncle's firm as a clerk. Should she go to work or not? Her value of being a wife, mother, and homemaker tells her not to; but her belief in family happiness and security tells her she must. Employment means two different things to her. Within the context of her self image as homemaker, she takes employment as a "giving-up" of something important; within the context of her belief in the happiness and security of the family, she takes it to be "providing something important." Such a dual meaning is common. Whenever you are ambivalent about something, or have internal conflict, you experience inconsistent meanings from different parts of your cognitive system.

This condition of multiple meanings is important because it provides people with choice. How you interpret a state of affairs and what you decide to do about it are not tightly determined by a rigidly organized cognitive system. People do have various avenues of interpretation and action available to them, and

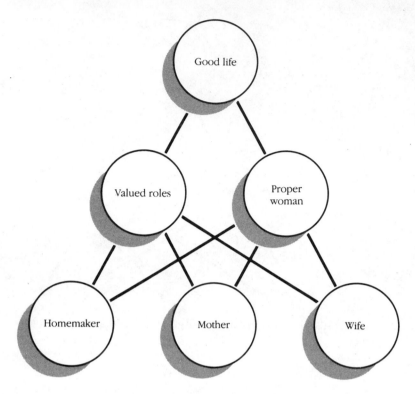

/ **FIGURE 2.2** Simplified Cognitive System of a Traditional Woman

they do make choices within a range of options. Choice is never totally free; we are bound to a certain extent by the general parameters of the cognitive system, which are determined by our previous history of interaction. But the cognitive system still enables us to go in a number of directions. In the example above, the woman can go to work or not, and she finds ample reason for doing either.

/ Cognition and Action

/ Using rules in communication

What governs the meanings that are employed by individuals in a communication transaction? Our cognitive systems provide us with rules that we use to guide our actions. Two kinds of rules are used: interpretation rules and action rules.

/ Interpretation rules.
Interpretation rules are those used to determine what an action or statement should be taken to mean. These rules tell us what someone's statement should count as or how it should be interpreted. For example, if

/ **In established relationships, interpretation and action rules mesh well and persuasive communication proceeds smoothly.**

someone says, "I'm thirsty," you might take the sentence to be a simple statement of fact, a request for a drink of water, an ironic remark, or a comment on your relationship. Sometimes interpretation is more difficult. Think of a time when you said something important to a friend only to be greeted with silence. How did you interpret that silence? Did your friend hear you? Did he choose to ignore your point? Did he wish to tell you by silence that your point was silly? Was he thinking about your idea? In trying to figure out your friend's response, you dipped into your kit of tools and chose a set of rules to interpret that action.

/ *Action rules.*   The second kind of rule is the action rule. This is a guideline for responding or acting. It tells you how you should behave or what you should say in a transaction with another person. When your friend remained silent after you spoke, what did you do next? Did you repeat the statement? Did you wait for a response? Did you ignore his silence and change the subject? Did you chastise him for ignoring you? Again, your behavior depended on what action rules you chose to use at that moment.

To illustrate interpretation and action rules, let us consider the various ways in which employees treat a company magazine or newsletter. Some interpret the periodical as useful, valid information and respond by careful reading. Others see it as public relations propaganda, and throw it away. Some employees may consider the house organ as an intrusion and nuisance, as just another piece of paper in a tall pile, and set it aside. Still others think of it as an interesting bit of news and photography to be glanced at during lunch or on the bus going home. In each of these instances, the interpretation rules tell the employee what to *think* about the magazine (useful, propaganda, intrusive, news), and the action rules tell the employed what to *do* about it (read it, throw it away, and so on).

This discussion of rules may seem terribly rational and conscious. Much of the time interpretation and action are rational. We certainly do pick through the kit of tools when we encounter a problem in communication that demands special attention. However, it is also true that much of the time we operate on automatic pilot. We are not always consciously aware of what we are saying and doing, and although we are always interpreting others, we are not always aware of those interpretations at the time of the transaction. This state of affairs does not mean that we are relying on rules any less. The scripts or programs on which we rely in these seemingly out-of-awareness situations come fully equipped with interpretation and action rules. The scripts, too, are part of the kit of tools. Have you ever followed rather automatic and standard patterns of behavior with another person only to discover that the expected response according to the script did not follow? At that moment you interrupted the script, plugged in your conscious processing, and thought through your choice of rules in a much more deliberate fashion.

Interpretation rules and action rules are closely associated. You choose action rules in part on the basis of your interpretations of what is going on. In essence, the cognitive system supplies you with a set of rules for understanding what is happening, then gives you corresponding action rules to guide what you will do about it. If you interpret your friend's silence to be rejection, you will behave very differently than if you take the silence to mean contemplation. Much of the time, especially in ritualized or mundane communication, people have no trouble interpreting and acting on the actions of others. Where a relationship is established or where expectations are shared, people's rules may mesh well and interpretation and action flow without difficulty. In fact in these moments, we probably do rely on scripts and programmed behavior.

Before we discuss in more detail how people coordinate their actions in communication and persuasion, let us take a closer look at the origins of interpretation and action rules. We already know that these rules are deeply rooted in the organization of a person's cognitive system. We also know that a variety of rules may be available in the person's kit of tools for use in a given situation because of the variety of meanings that the cognitive system holds for that situation. Thus, when faced with the need to interpret and act, the individual will fall back on the cognitive system to guide the choice of rules.

/ Levels of cognition

The conceptual system is organized into a variety of levels, or contexts, which provide cognitive anchors. Although a variety of levels operate, four are especially important in communication and persuasion. These are culture, self-image, relationship, and episode.

/ Culture.
The level of culture is general group values, norms, and world views. Often we act from a keen awareness of the requirements of the larger

community to which we identify. For example, an individual's response of silence will be taken to mean very different things from the standpoint of the Japanese, Native American, and Anglo-American cultures. Since silence is somewhat uncomfortable for many Anglo-Americans, it is often interpreted as rejection. That would not be the case among Native Americans, who would probably take a silent response to mean thought and reflection. Within the Japanese culture, a silent response might be interpreted as reserve or proper deference. Culture may or may not operate in a given transaction. For some people it is almost always the most important cognitive level; for others it rarely is.

/ Self-image. The second cognitive level is the self-image. Here the individual's conception of the self—"What kind of person am I?"—may be the predominant force in choosing rules. If your self-image of being a careful and good communicator is very strong, you may act on the basis of a rule such as, "If my partner is silent, ask why."

/ Relationship. Often the third cognitive level, relationship, is highly salient as a context in a given transaction. When this is the case, you will probably base your interpretations and actions on the perception of what is right for the relationship. If you know from past experience that your friend always responds quickly when he is interested, you may take his silence to indicate a lack of interest and respond by trying to make your idea seem more attractive.

/ Episode. Finally, one is guided by what is supposed to happen in the particular episode being enacted. If your partner's silent response occurs in the episode of getting off to work in the morning, you might interpret it to mean that he is distracted. If it occurs in the episode of getting ready for bed at night, you might take it to mean that he is tired. If it occurs in the episode of heavy intellectual talk, you might take it to mean that he is thinking and wants time to formulate an answer.

/ The hierarchy of contexts. These contexts, culture, self-image, relationships, and episode, can be arranged in a hierarchy. They are not independent, but are used to understand one another (see Figure 2.3). For example, the self-image may depend in part on culture. The perception of a relationship may depend upon both culture and self-image. One's interpretation of an episode is often dependent on all the other three. The order in the hierarchy depicted in Figure 2.3, however, is not set. People have the ability to shuffle the hierarchy around, and the ladder of effects of one person may be entirely different from that of another. Sometimes, for example, the self-image is context for understanding a relationship; sometimes it is the other way around. Sometimes an episode is understood within the context of the relationship; other times, the relationship seems a function of episode. Likewise, all of these contexts of meaning do not operate all the time. Sometimes one is especially strong and the

/ **FIGURE 2.3**   Hierarchy of Contexts

others hardly operate at all. On other occasions, however, several of the contexts are operating on one's interpretation of an event.

/ Causal and practical forces

It should be apparent from the foregoing discussion that the perceived importance of a particular context or level within the cognitive system is important in guiding the choice of rules for interpreting and acting. A second important factor in this choice is the person's sense of whether action seems necessary because of the demands of prior conditions or whether action is necessary because it will achieve a future state. We call the rules arising out of the perceived press of prior conditions *causal* because individuals invoke them out of a sense that their behavior is being caused. If you respond to your friend's silence by crying, you might explain, "I couldn't help it; I'm just a very sensitive person." Or perhaps you respond to the silence by being silent yourself. Here you might say that your relationship requires you to wait patiently while the other person has a chance to think about what he wants to say. In both of these examples, causal rules guided your actions.

Often, however, we do not act out of a sense of the press of prior conditions. We choose to be strategic in our actions, to behave in ways we think will achieve an objective in the future. We call such rules *practical*. Suppose you respond to your friend's silence by badgering him. How would you explain that? If you badgered to get your friend to give you a verbal response, you would be choosing a rule on the basis of achieving an objective. If you responded by leaving the room, you might explain, "I wanted him to know that I won't put up with such

/ Persuasion abounds in an editorial meeting as a newspaper's editors decide which stories and photographs to run.

behavior," implying the attempt to achieve compliance from your friend. Can a rule choice be both causal and practical? Of course. Many of our actions are both pushed by perceived causes and pulled by desired outcomes.

In summary, then, people choose their rules for communication on the basis of a context and causal or practical force. Within the constraints of the contextual level and forces, one makes a choice of rules to interpret and to govern action in a given transaction.

Persuasion puts special demands on communicators. In persuasion, the communicators desire change, and they communicate in ways to achieve it. Interpretation and action rules are therefore chosen in part to facilitate this objective. Almost always, compliance seekers are strongly influenced by practical forces in choosing rules of action. Those rules will be strongly anchored in a context or set of contexts. Will compliance lead to change in the way in which the episode is carried out in the future, will it affect the relationship, does it have implications for the self-concept, or is it intended to make changes in cultural perceptions or behaviors?

Consider, for example, how important action rules are to a campaign planner, who must get the greatest possible effect out of a limited budget. The campaign planner might have to consider the available skills of the staff; the money available for travel, publications, and entertainment; the timeline of the campaign; and a host of other factors. Each decision is guided by an action rule or set of rules that attempt to maximize persuasive outcome within the constraints of a finite set of resources. This example illustrates that the communicator, in this case the campaign manager, is rarely constrained by a single rule, but has choices of available actions.

Those who respond by complying also interpret the situation. If you want to change how you behave in particular episodes, your feelings about a relationship, your self-image, or cultural orientation, you will probably choose rules that enable you to respond with compliance. If you resist change, your rules will provide a pressure not to comply. How one interprets the actions of the compliance seeker also depends upon one's compliance-responding intentions. If you want to change, you probably take another's attempt to influence you as a friendly and cooperative act. If not, you might interpret that behavior as intrusive, manipulative, or perhaps irrelevant.

/ Dimensions of Cognition

Thus far we have described the cognitive system as an organized set of concepts that provide rules for interpreting and acting. In addition, the cognitive system consists of dimensions or factors that run throughout the conceptual structure. Concepts constitute the elements of the system; dimensions provide a set of variables that can be used to characterize these elements. They are, in other words, qualities with which cognition can be understood. Because of their importance, the dimensions of cognition are the main topic of the next chapter. Here we provide a preview.

The first dimension of the cognitive system is the *reality dimension*. It is the aspect of cognition that provides a set of beliefs as to what is real. It is one's way of organizing the world of experience. It also provides a set of guidelines on how one should act. It includes our beliefs, attitudes, and orientations to issues. The second dimension is *arousal*. The arousal dimension is used to characterize the emotional response and govern one's feelings about experiences. Third, the *goal dimension* arises out of the values and perceived needs embedded in the cognitive structure. It provides a set of guidelines for behavior and action. Finally, the *relationship dimension* is used to describe ways in which the system informs us about ourselves in relation to other people. When the cognitive system processes information about the structure of experience, the reality dimension is at work. When it helps us define our feelings and emotional response, the arousal dimension is operating. When we make decisions about how to behave or what we want to achieve, the goal dimension comes into play, and when we interpret our interactions with others, the relationship dimension operates.

Clearly, these dimensions are not independent from one another. They are merely different ways to look at the complexity of information processing. They operate simultaneously and affect one another. A given action is not merely the establishment of reality, arousal, goal-directedness, or relationship definition, but is probably a combination of some, if not all, of these. Dimensions are like angles from which to view information processing. As such they provide another important way to understand how people think when they interpret and act.

/ Coordinating Meanings and Actions

/ The problem of coordination

Obviously the choice of communication rules has implications for interaction. Rules chosen by one participant may not resemble those of other participants. In fact, the logic of the rules chosen by one person may be at odds with that of the other. Further, one's actions in communication require interpretation of the other's actions. Consider the following example.

Imagine a professor and student discussing the possibility of a make-up test. The professor thinks the student didn't take the examination because he wasn't prepared, and decides to lower the student's grade. The student, on the other hand, believing that he has an adequate excuse, seeks an opportunity to demonstrate his knowledge. He begins the conversation by saying, "I'm sorry I couldn't be in class on exam day. When can I make up the test?" How will the professor interpret this statement? From the perspective of the rules with which she enters the transaction, she takes this statement as impertinence. She responds, "Why should I give you a special favor?" The student doesn't think this is a special favor and takes the professor's reaction as prejudice. In this case the communicators have very different interpretation rules. Further, the logics of their rule systems are incompatible. Both are perfectly reasonable in their own ways, but together they do not constitute a coherent communication system.

This is a coordination problem. Coordination often comes quickly and easily. Sometimes the coordination is easily accomplished because the communicators are operating on a shared set of expectations; sometimes it arises because, although the communicators entered the transaction with different expectations, they quickly achieve a common logic through trial and error. At other times, however, communicators struggle to achieve coordination and fail.

Ideally, communicators are comfortable with a transaction when they believe it is coherent. Their expectations of how the other person will respond are fulfilled. Coordination is not necessarily a matter of shared meanings; the communicator's interpretation and action rules do not have to be the same, but they must mesh, so that one's actions seem to follow naturally from the other's. When this happens, we say that coordination is achieved. In an ongoing relationship, when the pattern is so well coordinated that it happens the same way over and over again, we say that the pattern is *enmeshed*. The process of coordination is illustrated in Figure 2.4.[6] Each person's action is interpreted and acted upon by the other. Interaction is thus a sequence of interpretation-action cycles.

Let's return to our example of the professor and the student. If the student sticks to his original rule choice, forcing him to interpret the professor's question as insensitive he will repeat the question, perhaps in the form of a demand. If the professor is equally inflexible, the pattern could accelerate to a shouting match. Most of the time, however, communicators come to realize through trial

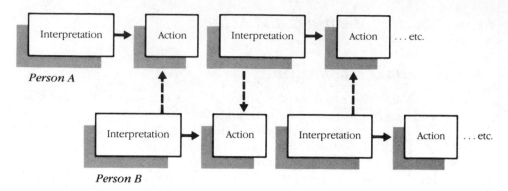

Person A

Person B

/ FIGURE 2.4 The Coordination of Interaction

and error that something strange is going on, that the interaction lacks coordination. At that point, meanings change, and one or both communicators alter their interpretations and actions.

The student in the example above, for instance, may change his interpretation of the professor's statement, now believing she just wasn't aware of his problem. Such an interpretation would prompt further explanation: "Oh, but I was sick." At this point, the professor may go in any number of directions. If she interprets the statement as an excuse, the logic of her system has not changed, and coordination may not be achieved. If, however, she interprets the statement as legitimate cause beyond the student's control, she will probably respond with something like, "Oh, why didn't you say so before?" Now the transaction seems headed in the right direction.

Rules are important in communication; how you deal with rules may help or hinder your effectiveness as a communicator. People who are unable to interpret the rules of others or have an inadequate repertoire of rules from which to draw when responding to other people are usually unable to accomplish much in their daily interactions. One of the signs of communication competence is the ability to move in and out of a variety of communication situations with ease, adapting to the rule systems of others.

Enmeshment is desirable in cases where it leads to a comfortable mode of operation that allows the communicators to relax and talk without difficulty. However, coordination does not always feel good. Sometimes we get ourselves into patterns that we do not like, but the logic of the interaction is so strong that we do not know how to break out of them. In that case enmeshment is undesirable because it prevents the participants from making choices and changing the nature of their communication. Such a system is known as an *unwanted repetitive pattern* (that's right, URP).

Clearly, when individuals enter a transaction with very different rules, some change must occur in the rule structure of one or both in order for coordination to be achieved. We think that this change is often the basis for persuasion. In the example of the student and teacher above, the student has achieved a persuasive aim if the instructor comes to interpret his statement of illness as legitimate reason to miss the exam and responds by allowing him to take a late test without penalty.

/ Coordination and persuasion

In Chapter Four we discuss several factors of persuasion. That chapter deals with how cognitive change can occur through learning, perception, and tension reduction. In each of these cases, the cognitive system changes, either momentarily or more permanently, enlarging or making possible a different rule repertoire. When people change as a result of persuasion, they are led to choose different rules of interpretation, action, or both. In the case of the unwanted repetitive pattern, the communicators may seek change. They desperately want to have a modified rule structure so that their choices are enlarged, and they may seek the intervention of an outsider or struggle between themselves to try out different ways of responding. This too is persuasion.

Our discussion of rules may seem relevant only to interpersonal, face-to-face interaction. Actually, it applies equally well to all forms of communication. Whenever a communicator prepares a message, that action must proceed on the basis of the interpretation and action rules of the moment. That is why we think the rules perspective is especially helpful to understanding persuasion in all settings.

Consider, for example, the care with which political campaign organizations treat poll results. Politicians employ entire organizations to poll the public on their opinions of a variety of issues in an attempt to interpret the actions of the voters. The campaign planners prepare positions on issues that appeal to what is thought to be important to the public or a significant subset of the public. Voters, on the other hand, respond to the expressed positions of the candidate in their talk, in their responses to polling questions, and in their votes. The interaction model presented in Figure 2.4 (p. 38) can apply to this society-wide coordination problem just as it fits interpersonal communication.

The late Hubert H. Humphrey lost the 1968 presidential election by a hair. He struggled in vain for weeks during the campaign on the issue of the Vietnam war. His problem was that he could not achieve coordination with the increasing opposition to the war because of his need to be consistent with the position of the current administration, in which he was vice-president. Late in the campaign, he switched from the expected hawkish position to a politically expedient dovish one. Many analysts believe, however, that this change only hurt him because it was interpreted by many voters as a crass political move; indeed, it may have cost him the election.

Various groups in society also have the problem of achieving coordination through communication. The case of the New Christian Right is a good example. This large, politically conservative group has been struggling to win converts to a strong belief system about God, the nation, and certain political issues. It has become embroiled in a particularly frustrating controversy with more liberal segments of society. The two groups are trapped in an unwanted repetitive pattern, in which the position of each is taken as evidence that one's own position is right.[7]

Another misunderstanding that may have arisen in the above discussion of rules is that persuasive transactions always begin with one party assuming the role of persuader and the other that of persuadee. Persuasion situations are usually not that simple. Let's examine this knotty problem of the distribution of influence in persuasion.

/ The Distribution of Influence in Persuasion

Earlier we wrote that persuasion can be conceived of as compliance seeking and compliance responding.[8] Compliance seeking is attempting to achieve change in others, while compliance responding is changing in response to the desires of others. Basically, persuasion transactions take one of three configurations: conflict and negotiation, dominance and submission, and problem solving. These arise from various degrees of compliance-seeking and compliance-responding intentions on the part of the communicators (see Figure 2.5).

Perhaps the most common conception of persuasion is one in which one party is dominant and attempts to influence, and the other party is submissive and complies. Although this conception is neat, it is not very typical. More often, both parties intend to influence the other. This is the classic conflict situation. Persuasion is so closely tied to conflict that it is part of the same process.[9] Conflict is marked by attempts to persuade, and persuasion itself is frequently the outcome of conflict. In fact, conflict can be defined as a struggle for influence. One party may or may not end up with greater influence than the other.

Another situation that frequently occurs is that both parties are in search of new alternatives and would be open to influence, but neither initially asserts influence. Such a situation leads to discussion of alternatives and mutual problem solving, although the participants probably will attempt to influence one another eventually.

In actual life, these three communication situations wax and wane, one leading to another. Persuasion cannot be separated from context. Rarely can an attempt to influence be isolated from the stream of communication events. Almost always, problem solving leads to conflict, sometimes mild, sometimes severe. In searching for alternatives, one of the problem solvers becomes committed to a particular solution and attempts to elicit the compliance of the other. If the other party is ready to submit, a dominance-submission situation ends the problem solving. On the other hand, the second party may become committed to another solution, resulting in negotiation. Events could also happen in the opposite direction: what begins as conflict turns into problem solving, evolving later into dominance-submission, as the communicators realize that their original positions are flawed and together seek new alternatives. In short, persuasion, like all communication, is transaction and involves the give-and-take of all participants.

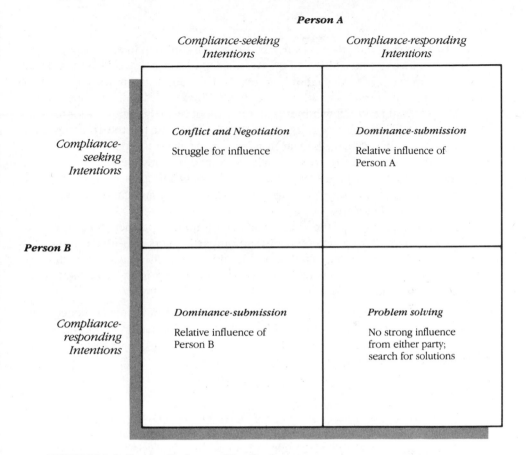

/ FIGURE 2.5 Types of Influence Distribution

/ *Theory* / *Practice* / *Analysis*

Theory

1. The basic resource of all communication is the cognitive system.

2. The cognitive system provides rules for interpretation and action, which are used by individuals in communication and persuasion.

3. The primary problem of all communication and persuasion is coordination of rules.

4. Influence can be distributed in a variety of ways in a transaction, but almost always it will change from moment to moment as the transaction progresses.

Practice

1. In a group of four, discuss various subjects of common interest. Choose one of the topics to be the subject of the persuasion exercise. Have each member of the group prepare to engage in persuasion role-play with another member of the group. The group should then be divided into two dyads. Each member of the dyad should take a few minutes to think about his or her strategy for the persuasion, emphasizing the cultural level of context. During the role-plays, the participants should base their arguments primarily on the norms, values, and belief structures of a culture to which the couple strongly identify. This culture could be ethnic, religious, or some other large-group affiliation. The participants should also try to respond to the persuasive communication of their partners in terms of culture.

The exercise should then be repeated with another partner from the group, this time emphasizing statements based on participants' self-images. After the two role-plays, the group as a whole should discuss the ways in which one's approach to persuasion changes depending upon the context being used. What other approaches would you have preferred to take and why?

2. Prepare two versions of a persuasive speech for two different audiences with which you are quite familiar. How did you adapt the speeches to the interpretation rules of the audience? What action rules did you use to formulate your arguments?

Analysis

1. Consider an ongoing conflict in which you have been engaged for a time. Carefully think about how you have processed information in the transactions that have been part of this struggle. What does this analysis reveal to you about your cognitive system? What levels of cognition have been operating in your interpretations and actions in these episodes? To what extent have you been operating out of causal or practical force?

2. Repeat the above exercise with a conflict that you are not personally part of but that involves people you know. Carefully observe the transactions of the participants in this conflict and interview the communicators to ascertain their interpretation and action rules. What does your analysis reveal about the cognitive operations of the participants in the conflict?

3. Choose a public controversy of interest. Gather as many public statements by the advocates on both sides of the controversy as possible and review this discourse to discover the patterns of response involved. What does each side claim? How does each side answer the charges and claims of the other? After doing background reading on the groups involved in the conflict, write an analysis that provides your best interpretation of the rules used by the parties in their communications and discusses the extent to which you believe the groups' actions are coordinated with one another.

Notes

[1]This discussion of communication is based on the theory of the Coordinated Management of Meaning as presented in W. Barnett Pearce and Vernon Cronen, *Communication, Action, and Meaning* (New York: Praeger, 1980).

[2]For a more complete discussion of the cognitive system and persuasion, see R. Petty, T. Ostrom, and T. Brock, *Cognitive Responses in Persuasion* (Hillsdale, NJ: Erlbaum, 1980); and M. E. Roloff and C. R. Berger, *Social Cognition and Communication* (Beverly Hills, CA: Sage Publications, 1982).

[3]The problem of awareness in persuasion is discussed in detail by Michael Roloff, "Self-Awareness and the Persuasion Process," in *Persuasion: New Directions in Theory and Research* (Beverly Hills: Sage, 1980).

[4]See, for example, Harold M. Schroder, Michael S. Driver, and Siegfried Streufert, *Human Information Processing: Individuals and Groups Functioning in Complex Social Situations* (New York: Holt, Rinehart and Winston, 1967).

[5]This is the position of symbolic interactionism. See *Symbolic Interaction,* ed. Jerome G. Manis and Bernard N. Meltzer (Boston: Allyn and Bacon, 1978).

[6]Adapted from Pearce and Cronen, *Communication,* p. 174.

[7]For a discussion of this case see W. Barnett Pearce, Stephen W. Littlejohn, and Alison Alexander, "Ideological Conflict and Reciprocated Diatribe: The New Christian Right and the Humanist Response," *Communication Quarterly,* in press.

[8]These concepts are discussed in detail by Mary John Smith, "Cognitive Schemata and Persuasive Communication: Toward a Contingency Rules Theory," in *Communication Yearbook 6* (Beverly Hills: Sage Publications, 1982), p. 338.

[9]The connection between persuasion and conflict is discussed by Herbert Simons, "The Carrot and Stick as Handmaidens of Persuasion in Conflict Situations," in *Perspectives on Communication in Social Conflict,* ed. G. R. Miller and H. W. Simons (Englewood Cliffs, NJ: Prentice-Hall, 1974), pp. 172–205.

3 / Persuasion and the Individual

You are driving home after a tough day at work. Several irritating problems have left you uptight. A car cuts in front of you, forcing you to brake slightly. You notice that the dress and grooming of the driver suggest cultural values considerably different from your own. The automobile carries two bumper stickers—one for a political candidate you despise, the other for a cause you oppose. You angrily honk your horn and mutter, "Stupid careless roadhog! Does he think he owns the highway?"

The next day you have been productive at work and have received several compliments for your efforts. Driving home, you notice a car signaling its desire to shift to your lane. You are attracted by the looks of the driver. A bumper sticker supporting a cause you favor is prominently displayed. Although traffic is bumper to bumper, you slow down, smile, and motion for the driver to cut over in front of you.

What was the difference inside you which resulted in virtually opposite responses to almost identical circumstances? Obviously very different things were going on. We call the complex interaction of several factors your *cognitive system*.

/ Dimensions of the Cognitive System

As defined in Chapter 2, the cognitive system is a set of concepts that guide a person's understanding and acting in the world. It is, in short, the basis for an individual's information processing. Our cognitive system guides the rules by which we think and guides what we do about what we think. Recall from the last chapter that the cognitive system consists of a dynamic and complex network of elements. We discussed in that chapter, in general terms, how the cognitive system is used as a kit of tools in communication. More precisely, then, what characterizes the kit of tools? This chapter explores that question.

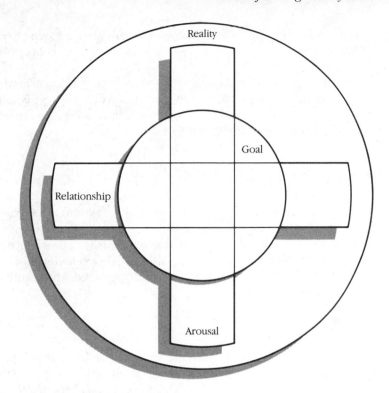

/ FIGURE 3.1 Dimensions of the Cognitive System

Four dimensions characterize the cognitive system. The *reality dimension* is made up of those elements that guide one's sense of what is real or probable (or not real/probable). In a sense, all cognition is based on beliefs about issues of one sort or another; thus, the elements of the reality dimension are the foundation of the cognitive system. The *goal dimension* consists of those elements that guide one's sense of what is desirable (or not desirable). The elements of the goal dimension tell us what to seek and what to avoid. The *arousal dimension* constitutes a somewhat undifferentiated readiness to receive and process messages on the one hand, and to yield to those messages on the other. Finally, the *relationship dimension* are those elements that guide our sense of connectedness to other people.

As Figure 3.1 illustrates, these four dimensions are not discrete parts, but constitute an organization of the cognitive system that emphasizes commonality and interrelationship. In other words, a given element in one's system may be affected by any combination of these dimensions.

Recall, for example, the illustration in the last chapter of the traditional woman. We depicted a web of concepts in which homemaker, mother, and wife are interpreted as good and proper. These concepts and their relations to one another involve *arousal,* a sense of *reality,* a set of *goals,* and a perception of *relationships.* Our purpose in this chapter is not to deal with individual cognitive elements or concepts (such as homemaker, mother, and wife), but with the dimensions that affect interrelatedly the entire system of concepts (the traditional woman).

These dimensions also overlap with one another. For example, what arouses a person depends in part on his or her conception of reality, goals, and relationships; what is considered real is, in part, a matter of arousal and involves goals and relationships (see again Figure 3.1).

/ The Reality Dimension

Perhaps the most basic dimension of the cognitive system is the reality dimension. Reality—what is believed to be factual—constitutes the focus of much of the raw material of the entire system. It is the basis for one's concepts and the relations among them. The elements of this dimension focus on what is "real" or probable and how the world is packaged or organized. The reality dimension provides a belief structure.

/ Beliefs

A *belief* is a datum about the universe which an individual accepts. Rokeach defines *belief* very broadly as "any simple proposition, conscious or unconscious, inferred from what a person says or does, capable of being preceded by the phrase 'I believe that. . . .'."[1] Thus, a person who says, "*I believe that* Professor Jones is an easy grader" or "*I believe that* cigarette smoking causes lung cancer" is expressing a belief.

Beliefs can be distinguished as statements of knowledge, opinion, and faith. A person may say, "I believe [know] the sun will rise tomorrow, I believe [opinion] radiation is dangerous to your health, and I believe [have faith] there is a God." Other theorists place emphasis on the *degree* of probability people place on beliefs.[2] Thus an individual may believe that the earth is round and that it will rain tomorrow, but will attribute different strengths or probabilities to those beliefs.

Further, although all of the foregoing statements of belief sound like "facts" and may be accepted by individuals as such, both Rokeach and Simons imply that beliefs are *propositions* or *claims* people accept or *judgments* people make or accept which may or may not have any basis in "objective reality."[3]

/ Belief salience.
Beliefs vary in their *salience*. That is, some beliefs are simply more important to us than others. Further, the importance of a belief can vary for the same individual over time and context. Both of us have experienced the anguish of divorce. At the time of our divorces, beliefs related to marriage and divorce laws, noncustodial parenting, and living singly were important to us to the point of preoccupation. Since both of us have experienced the joy and challenge of remarriage, an entirely different set of beliefs related to a variety of

issues have become more important to us and occupy more of our conscious thought. This does not mean we have abandoned our beliefs regarding divorce. They are simply not as important or influential a part of our cognitive system as they once were.

/ *Organization of beliefs.* Perhaps the most obvious relationship within the reality dimension of the cognitive system is the way beliefs cluster at different levels of specificity. That is to say, beliefs at a certain level of specificity can make up a more comprehensive belief, which in turn relates to equally comprehensive beliefs, which constitute an even more comprehensive belief or attitude.

As an example let us consider the issue of deploying the MX missile on a "race track" on the Utah-Nevada border. Certainly a person could have a great many beliefs about the plan, including the following:

   I. The race track basing mode will destroy thousands of square miles of range land.
      A. Range land supports many domestic animals.
         1. Ranchers' livelihood depends on domestic animals.
         2. Consumers' food is based on domestic animals.
            a. A scarcity of grazing animals will cause the price of meat to rise.
      B. Range land supports many wild animals.
         1. We are all dependent on other life forms.
         2. Wild animals are to be appreciated and enjoyed.

   II. The race track basing mode will consume huge quantities of water.
      A. Water is already scarce in the desert Southwest.
      B. Water is necessary to life.
      C. Water is necessary to further development of the area.

   III. The race track basing mode will create many new jobs.
      A. New jobs will attract many new people to the area.
         1. New people will be different in life-style from the local people.
         2. More people will compete for precious resources.
         3. More people will require services.
         4. More people will create social ills.
            a. The crime rate will go up.
            b. Pollution will increase.
            c. Gambling and prostitution will increase.
            d. Religious values will be diluted.
      B. New jobs will improve the economy.
         1. They will attract other businesses to the area.
         2. They will cause property values to increase.
         3. They will attract new capital to the area.
         4. They will create new markets for a variety of goods.
      C. New jobs will prevent young people from leaving the area.

The example could be extended almost indefinitely. From this brief outline, however, you can see that smaller beliefs cluster into larger and larger beliefs.

/ *Beliefs and rationality.* Argumentation theorists have made an important contribution to our understanding of how beliefs are acquired, organized, and used to draw further inferences. According to this tradition, the essence of the reality dimension of the cognitive system is the *probability* of our beliefs as determined by concrete data and the reasoning process whereby we draw inferences and make claims from those data. It attempts to explain how people decide and act upon inferences or arguments which they receive or which they generate for themselves. Indeed, some persuasion theorists claim that the predominant generative force in persuasion is that of the arguments or reasons people generate in a process of self-persuasion.[4]

Despite differences of opinion as to the relative importance of rationality, theorists since Aristotle have recognized people's ability to behave on a rational basis as a significant dimension of their cognitive system and an important determinant of their behavior. For centuries, mainstream Western thought has been dominated by a way of knowing characterized by empiricism, rationalism, and instrumentalism. The belief system is thought to be based on careful observation (empiricism), reasoning (rationalism), and consideration of practical outcomes (instrumentalism).[5] This kind of thinking emphasizes the need to base one's beliefs on evidence in the form of direct observation or expert authority. Reasoning is analyzed for fallacies, and evidence is tested for validity. Value is assigned to the outcomes of one's beliefs and actions, such that abstract ideas are less valued than ideas with practical impact. Although college communication classes often teach this kind of thinking as a basis for the belief system, it is by no means the only way of structuring knowledge. Much belief is based on intuition, sign, superstition, cultural morals, divine authority, and other forms. The Western model is useful in many of the situations in which contemporary people must live and work, but it is not the only model for all people at all times. In fact, to employ such thinking might be counterproductive in many situations.

According to Western thought, then, human rationality is rooted in two basic processes: (1) observation, or the accumulation of information or data, and (2) the reasoning process whereby we draw inferences, arrive at conclusions, or make claims on the basis of that information or data. Let us examine each of these processes and how they contribute to the development and organization of beliefs in our cognitive systems.

Observation: the accumulation of data. Many beliefs about what we think we know are based upon observation, either our own or that of others. It is by our own observations or the reports and stories of others that we accumulate the raw data from which we reason or generate arguments.

When we speak of observation, it sounds like we are describing a process whereby our sense organs, like biological recording devices, assimilate and record everything that is going on around us. Observation can better be viewed as a complex interaction between the outside world and our cognitive system, which is only mediated by our sensory organs. That is, our five senses do not record every stimulus they encounter, nor does our brain record or recall every piece of information it receives with equal efficiency.

Perhaps you have had the experience of attending a concert and recording it while you listened. Sometime later you listened to the recording and were surprised at the variety of sounds (a passing aircraft or a barking dog) recorded that you did not notice at the time. In focusing on the concert, you had filtered out sounds that would have intruded on your enjoyment.

Not only are our observations filtered by our sense organs and stored selectively by our brain, but our cognitive system actually influences the way we perceive the outside world and what we perceive. Our knowledge, beliefs, attitudes, values, needs, and emotions actually dictate what we will perceive and remember at any given time.

Have you ever been on a nature walk with a naturalist? The person whose cognitive system contains more information actually sees and hears a greater number of different animals, birds, trees, flowers, or rock formations than the novice. The interaction between our cognitive system and our perceptions is an important issue in persuasion theory and will be discussed in greater detail in Chapter 4. It is enough to say here that our observations are all subjective or selective to some degree.

If we depended only upon our own observations for our reasoning, however, we would lead very limited lives. Schools and libraries would become obsolete and we would be literally doomed to re-invent the wheel, electric light bulb, and airplane. No, much of what we know is based upon the observations, discoveries, and constructions of others.

Early in our lives we depend heavily on the observations or experiences of our parents, teachers, or religious leaders. Later in life we grow to become more critical of "authority," but we must still depend in varying degrees on observations reported to us by friends, professionals, scientists, and journalists. How we evaluate and use the observations of others will be discussed later in this book.

We have seen, then, that our own observations and the observations of others, however selective, subjective, or distorted, produce the raw material or data which forms the basis of our rationality. Let us now turn to the kinds of data these observations produce.

Kinds of data. Traditionally the data produced by people's observations have been classified in different ways. We will discuss examples, statistics, testimony, and analogies.

Examples and *statistics* constitute essentially the same kind of data. Examples are beliefs about instances of a particular phenomena from which we tend to generalize. For instance, a person may observe one or more instances of small business failures and draw an inference from those examples. Statistics are beliefs which summarize numerous related examples or instances, typically expressed in numerical form. Thus, a professor expresses the numerous grades on an examination by computing the class average. Examples and statistics may be selected (sampled) or observed selectively in ways that could produce some-what different (though still "rational") inferences, claims, or conclusions.

A second kind of data we use in the process of building a belief system is *testimony.* As we will see in our discussion of source credibility, we tend to rely more heavily on sources we trust because of their competence or integrity. Many of our early beliefs are inferences which we accept on the basis of the claims of our parents, teachers, or other authority figures. For instance, how often have you heard this kind of dialogue:

Daughter: "Will I ever grow up and be independent like you?"
Mother: "Of course you will, dear."
Daughter: "How do you know?"
Mother: "Trust me."

As we become more educated and experienced we learn to make finer dis-criminations about authority by assessing the *degree* of their authority. We will give you some tools for assessing authority later in this book.

A third type of data or information from which we reason is the *analogy.* An analogy is an extended comparison of two parallel cases or instances. Two prob-lems can be compared in order to better understand them and draw inferences about them, as on the button reading, "*El Salvador* is Spanish for *Vietnam.*" Analogies are frequently used to evaluate solutions which have not been tried, such as, "Socialized medicine in the United States would be like that in Great Britain."

Analogic data have often been criticized by traditional argumentation the-orists, but we find that using analogies as data for drawing inferences is not only unavoidable but can be desirable. Placing two objects or other phenomena side by side for paired comparison is the very basis of measurement. In fact, given the tendency of the cognitive system to group or classify observations, analogic thinking is unavoidable. All statistical, correlational studies are basically ana-logic. Much of our intrapersonal decision making is based upon choosing one item over another or one option over another. Even the much maligned figura-tive analogy can be a reasonable basis for inferences if the essential variable is contained in the analogy.

Reasoning.   The second basic process which contributes to the develop-ment of beliefs in our cognitive systems is reasoning. *Reasoning* is the mental process whereby we draw inferences and conclusions and make claims on the basis of data. In a sense it is a process of progressing from those components in our observations or our cognitive system which are more probable to those which are less probable.

Traditionally, reasoning has been viewed as two interrelated subprocesses, induction and deduction. *Induction* is the process by which we reason from specific data to generalizations. For instance, when scientists experiment with animals, they try their procedure on hundreds of guinea pigs, dogs, or sheep in order to draw a generalization such as "cigarette smoking increases your chance of contracting lung cancer or heart disease." Most beliefs which represent what we think we know are arrived at inductively. For example, you may read in a newspaper that someone was killed in a motorcycle accident. Later, when driving, you may shift lanes and nearly miss a motorcyclist in your blind spot. Still later you read an insurance company's study which indicates a higher mortality rate for cyclists than for people riding other vehicles. From these specific observations you may conclude that riding a motorcycle can be dangerous.

Deduction is the process of drawing inferences and conclusions or making claims about a specific case or phenomena on the basis of an accepted generalization. Thus, if you accept the generalization that riding a motorcycle is dangerous to human beings, you will conclude that motorcycle riding would be dangerous to you or to any other individual human being.

In his *Rhetoric,* Aristotle described deductive reasoning in persuasive communication as the *enthymeme,* which has three distinguishing characteristics. First, it usually has a part or parts missing. Thus, in making our deduction, we do not have to state the obvious, "*You are a human being, therefore* motorcycle riding . . . ." Second, an enthymeme is based upon probabilities, not certainties. Motorcycle riding only increases the likelihood that you will be injured; that outcome is by no means certain. Finally, people reasoning together supply the missing parts. You no doubt accepted the premise, "I am a human being," whether consciously or not.

Induction and deduction are closely related. The generalization from which deduction progresses is usually established by induction. In our example, the generalization "Motorcycle riding can be dangerous to human beings" is both the conclusion of our induction and the starting point of our deduction. Further, in both induction and deduction, you continually move from that which is more probable to that which is less probable, that is, (1) an *observed* relationship between motorcycle riding and injury in several newspaper reports and the insurance study, (2) a generalization about the chances of human beings getting hurt, and (3) a prediction about an individual human being.

Although illustrative, there are two disadvantages to the foregoing traditional approach to the analysis of the reasoning process. First, it is somewhat cumbersome, since most people don't supply all of those connecting parts when they're developing beliefs, let alone communicating. Second, it does not provide for people's reasoning directly from the specific to the specific, directly from authoritative data, or other variations from the traditional model.

A contemporary philosopher, Stephen Toulmin,[6] has provided a useful model for analyzing reasoning in a greater variety of forms. Toulmin begins with the basic process of making *claims* on the basis of particular *data*. Rieke and Sillars broaden the concept of data to "grounds."[7] In the case of motorcycle riding, data are contained in newspaper accounts and the insurance report and the claim is that motorcycle riding is dangerous to your health.

Toulmin next posits a connection between the data and claim which he labels the *warrant*. In the above case the unstated warrant would be "The insurance company's sample is representative of all cyclists." If it were not representative, of course, the claim would not follow from the data. If a person

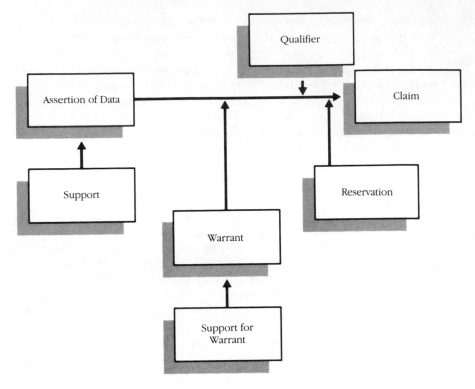

/ FIGURE 3.2 Toulmin's Model

doesn't believe either the data or the warrant, further concrete support may be required to establish that the insurance company did in fact establish the connection between motorcycle riding and injury and that it used a representative sample.

In addition to the basic data-warrant-claim relationship Toulmin's model also provides for a *qualifier* or statement of the probability or likelihood of the claim. The insurance study of motorcycle fatalities will be expressed in statistical probabilities and a person's claim would include modifiers like "more likely." In any case most people have some notion of the likelihood of their claims as they are thinking and talking together.

Finally Toulmin claims that people may attach *reservations* to their reasoning. Reservations account for possible intervening variables, extenuating circumstances, or exceptional cases. Hence, you may develop the belief that riding a motorcycle is dangerous unless you drive more carefully, avoid heavy traffic, and wear a helmet. See Toulmin's model in diagram form above.

Now that we have seen how people accumulate data and have examined the process of reasoning, let's look at the two together. First, when the data are examples and statistics, the claim is the generalization and the warrant is the assertion that the examples or statistics are representative of the class to which you are generalizing. Thus if the Soviets had broken fifty out of fifty-two treaties with the U.S. (assertion of data), you might generalize (claim) that the Soviets probably (qualifier) cannot be trusted to honor their treaties with the U.S., assuming that the Soviets are consistent in their dealings with the U.S. (warrant) unless it is in their best interests to keep an agreement (reservation).

When the data are from authority, the claim follows from the quotation of that authority (data) and the warrant is the assertion of the credibility of the authority. Thus, in the case of the Surgeon General's warning on cigarette packages, the data consists of the statement by the Surgeon General, the claim is the danger to your health (the qualifier being an implied probability), and the warrant is the assumed credibility of the Surgeon General.

When reasoning from analogies, the data are the details of the known half of the comparison, the claim is the extrapolation of the relevant details to that half of the comparison to which it is being compared, and the warrant is the assumption that the two cases are alike in all relevant respects. Thus, you might claim that year-round school would probably (qualifier) work in your district since it had worked well in a district in another state (data) which was similar in most respects (warrant) to yours (give details as support for data).

In addition to the foregoing patterns of reasoning from particular kinds of data, there are patterns of reasoning which emphasize certain relationships between data and claim. Of particular importance to persuasive communicators is *causal reasoning*. Sometimes the observation or data constitute a cause or effect from which we may reason to the corresponding effect or cause. In each case the warrant is the assumption of a causal link between the two. For instance, you may hear that the snow pack in the Rocky Mountains is double its normal depth (data) and conclude that there may be (qualifier) flooding in the Mountain West next spring (claim). The warrant is the assumption that the area can't handle that much run-off and the support for the warrant could be the records of past excessive snow packs that resulted in flooding.

A similar form of reasoning is *reasoning from sign*. A sign is not necessarily the cause or effect of something else but is associated with it consistently enough to make the relationship fairly predictable. In reasoning from sign the observation of the sign is the assertion of data, the claim is the prediction of the phenomena for which it is the sign and the warrant is the assumed connection between the two. The reservation would be the circumstances (if any) in which the relationship would not hold. Thus, you may see the crocuses blooming (data) and predict that the robins will soon be nesting (claim) since both occur in the spring (assumed warrant).

/ *Social construction of beliefs.*   Although beliefs are often developed through the rational process of observation and reasoning, one does not develop beliefs in isolation from other people. Your interaction with others has much to do with what you observe, how you observe it, and what conclusions you draw on the basis of your observations. The process of developing knowledge described above is something people do together. Rationality is social.

The cognitive system, which has beliefs as its core, arises out of interaction with others. Our meanings—and consequent interpretations—of events are worked out by communication. Ideas are rarely—if ever—born *de novo,* but arise in interaction with others. They are in turn modified as we sense others' reactions to our messages.

The social character of beliefs is important. The cognitive system is both the backdrop for and the target of communication. What we say, the character of our messages in communication with others, is affected directly by what we believe. In turn, that same interaction has the potential of changing the body of belief, the cognitive system itself. This is how the cognitive system grows and changes throughout life.

/ Attitudes

In the last section, we discussed the organization of beliefs. An important outcome of that organization is *attitudes.* As early as 1935 Gordon Allport claimed that the construct of attitude was the "most distinctive and indispensable concept in contemporary American social psychology."[8] Certainly it has remained to this day the most studied aspect of the cognitive system and until recently the study of attitude change was virtually synonymous with the study of persuasion.

What is an attitude? It has been defined in strikingly similar ways. Typical of many definitions are these:

> An attitude is defined as a relatively enduring predisposition to respond favorably or unfavorably toward an attitude object.[9]
> Generally we take the word *attitude* to mean a particular predisposition to respond in a given social situation.[10]

While its many definitions emphasize slightly different aspects of an attitude, most agree on several characteristics:

1. All definitions state or imply that attitudes are *implicit.* As components of a person's cognitive system, they cannot be observed directly, but must be inferred from what people do or say.

2. Most theorists agree that attitudes constitute *predispositions to respond.* That is, if a person holds the belief, "War is wrong," that person would be more disposed to speak against war or sign an anti-war petition than not. This relationship between attitudes and behavior is not perfect, however, and will be discussed in more detail later.

3. Attitudes predispose people to *respond in a preferential manner.* That is to say, attitudes have *vector,* or direction and magnitude. People are predisposed in a positive or negative direction and in varying degrees. Some writers[11] describe an *attitude* as a belief with a value. A person may hold attitudes strongly favoring capital punishment, mildly favoring the deployment of nuclear weapons, mildly disliking Gary Hart, and strongly opposing gun control.

4. Attitudes are *directed* at something. Many writers call this an *attitude object*. Petty and Cacioppo refine this to be a person, object, or issue.[12] Bostrom attempts to encompass all of these in a "social situation."[13] Thus a person may love his or her spouse, loathe beef liver, oppose air pollution, and avoid business meetings.

5. Most theorists claim or imply that attitudes are *relatively enduring*—that is, they are neither momentary nor immutable. Although attitudes tend to remain in the absence of intervening stimuli, they can diminish in intensity or be changed by a number of variables to be discussed later in this book.

6. Perhaps the most widely accepted characteristic of attitudes as well as beliefs is that they are *learned*. Although all humans have perhaps millions of beliefs and thousands of attitudes, no one belief or attitude is common to all members of the species. Rather attitudes and beliefs are acquired from our environment, and each person's portfolio varies from every other person's.

In our opinion, the best single definition of *attitude* has been advanced by Milton Rokeach: "*a relatively enduring organization of beliefs around an object or situation predisposing one to respond in some preferential manner.*"[14] This definition not only contains all of the characteristics of attitudes shared by other theorists but also stresses the interrelatedness of beliefs which go to make up an attitude.[15]

Let us return to the example of the MX missile. Depending on whether you are a rancher, a realtor, an environmentalist, or some combination of these, and which of the beliefs or clusters of beliefs outlined on page 47 are most salient to you, you might develop vastly different attitudes toward the race track method of deploying the MX. Not all of these beliefs can be held by any one person. Furthermore, a person may place any one of these beliefs above all of the others combined, as in the case of an extremely religious person who would oppose the MX location solely on the basis of the belief that "Religious values would be diluted" or a local merchant who would favor it only because he believed that the MX would "create a variety of new markets." Thus we see that the reality dimension of the cognitive system is a complex structure of interrelated beliefs, many of which are clustered or organized into attitudes toward objects or situations.

/ *The Goal Dimension*

The second main dimension of the cognitive system is the goal dimension. This dimension includes those aspects of beliefs and attitudes that are goal-directed and have to do with what an individual considers good or desirable. At their most fundamental level, goals function to maximize pleasure and minimize pain. We will discuss three elements of this dimension—values, needs, and motives.

/ Values

Although values have long been recognized by persuasion theorists, the concept was popularized and refined by Milton Rokeach in relatively recent times. Rokeach defines *value* as "a type of belief, centrally located within one's total belief system, about how one ought or ought not to behave, or about some end-state of existence worth or not worth attaining."[16]

/ Types of values.
Rokeach's definition implies two types of values. Values which have to do with how people "ought or ought not behave" are called *instrumental values*. These values are specific goals which guide a person's day-to-day behavior. They read like a litany of boy scout qualities: honesty, courage, cleanliness, responsibility, and so on.

Values which have to do with an "end-state of existence" are called *terminal values*. These values involve general goals toward which a person's life might be directed or characteristics of what one would consider a utopian life. Rokeach has identified such terminal values as freedom, equality, inner harmony, a world at peace, family security, and happiness.

/ Characteristics of values.
In addition to the characteristics which they share with beliefs and attitudes, values have some important characteristics of their own. First, because of their centrality in people's cognitive system, *values* are assumed to be more *resistant to change* than other beliefs or attitudes. It stands to reason that a life's goal such as salvation would be more stable than an attitude that you should avoid refined sugar or the belief that Australia is the world's largest island. But *values can change*. Rokeach's original research data from the late 1960s indicated that the number one and two terminal values of young adults were "a world at peace" and "family security." A decade later, informal surveys of our own and colleagues' classes placed "inner harmony" and "happiness" first and second, while "a world at peace" and "family security" had slipped to ninth and tenth. These shifts could represent a change in values or simply a change in their priority or strength in an individual's cognitive system.

As with other beliefs, *values* also *vary in their salience*. This probably accounts substantially for changes in priority. The foregoing shift from priority for "security" to "happiness" and "inner harmony" could be explained by the cessation of the Vietnam War and the emergence of what has been called the "me-generation" and the "decade of narcissism." With the removal of the threat of being drafted, the war issue became less salient.

Instrumental values can also change. Daniel Yankelovich has documented significant changes in values related to life-style in general and sexual behavior in particular during the sixties and seventies. Yankelovich also maintains that our system of beliefs, attitudes, and values became more complex during that period. He concludes, "The rules of social behavior have expanded, moving us from a society with relatively homogeneous definitions of family, sex roles, and working life toward an explosive pluralism on those and other fronts."[17]

/ The strength of our nationalistic value system was exhibited exuberantly at the 1984 Summer Olympics in Los Angeles.

As with other beliefs and attitudes, *values are organized in a complex system of interrelationships* which are not well understood. Rokeach has demonstrated that values can be placed in a hierarchical structure. That is, they can be ordered and clustered for any individual or group at a given point in time.

In addition to being organized in hierarchies of importance, *values* tend to *cluster into value systems.*[18] Values are usually acquired from our culture and in turn serve to define or distinguish a culture or subculture.

Middle American value system. American culture is one of the most heterogeneous on earth. Indeed, it is a complex mosaic of numerous distinct and valued subcultures contributing to the rich blend that is the whole. We will examine the concept of value systems by discussing those which are commonly found in one of these subcultures, the middle American culture. We will discuss the security, achievement, Puritan, progressive, and nationalistic value systems.

Most psychologists accept *security* or safety as a fundamental human goal. As a value system it would include beliefs like, "Every person is entitled to a humane standard of living" or "A strong defense establishment is the best protection of our way of life." Recall that two of Rokeach's top values, "a world at peace" and "family security," were part of the security value system. Insurance policies which protect us against the adverse effects of public liability, automobile accidents, catastrophic illness, and the destruction of our homes are mute evidence of the value placed on security. The vast billions in our state and national budgets are for entitlement and military programs which provide security for individuals and society. However, as fundamental as this security value system seems to be, even it can wax and wane in its salience and hence its importance. Generations of Americans who struggled for survival on the frontier or suffered through the Great Depression seemed virtually preoccupied with security. In contrast, recent generations seem to rank security lower on their hierarchy of value systems, presumably because they simply take it for granted.

A second middle American value system is *achievement*. Upward mobility is the primary goal of many Americans who strive to see that their children "have it better than we did." Every individual and organization wants to be number one. The achievement value system is buttressed by such individual values as competition, freedom from governmental restraint, and survival of the fittest. It has manifested itself in the seeking of status and material wealth as well as the exploitation of the environment and other people.

By contrast consider the traditional Japanese culture. In that system upward mobility and prestigious titles seem less important than doing quality work at whatever level of society one finds oneself. It is considered more honorable to be a superior dock-loader than a mediocre vice-president.

Still another American value system is represented by the Puritan work ethic. Basically an interrelationship of instrumental values, the *Puritan* value system emphasizes such instrumental goals as honesty, responsibility, punctuality, hard work, and cleanliness.

As we pointed out earlier, this value system may also be changing. The hippie movement of the sixties and the "me-generation" of the seventies have challenged many of the individual values of the Puritan value system. A book from that period, entitled *Celebrate the Temporary,* urges the reader to "stop and smell the roses" in order to reduce stress and its related physical and mental disorders.[19] But the fact that this relatively recent phenomenon is referred to as a *"counter*-culture" movement suggests that middle American culture is still deeply rooted in the Puritan value system.

Another value system characterizing middle American culture is the *progressive* value system, the system proposing that "every year things are getting better and better." As is the case of the achievement value system, the progressive system is rooted in our history and geography. Not only did our country seem to our ancestors blessed with unlimited natural wealth, but American inventiveness and enterprise had produced dramatic improvements in the standard of living for each succeeding generation.

In addition to the foregoing progressive value system, Rieke and Sillars also refer to an enlightenment value system which embraced beliefs in the scientific method, rationality, and the freedom to utilize these for our purposes. We would include this set of values as part of the progressive value system, since the underlying assumption seems to be that these values will ultimately lead to progress. Epitomized by Neil Armstrong's walk on the moon, it would seem as if American education, scientific investigation, and practical know-how could solve any problem, resulting in a progressively better society for every generation.

Still another American value system is the high regard we have for *nationalism*. Over the centuries Americans have believed that our country and its institutions were superior to those of other nations and cultures. Our capitalistic economy, our republican form of government, our Judeo-Christian religious tradition, our free public education system, our voluntary medical system, and our highly productive agricultural system have all combined to make the United States a world power.

Furthermore, few Americans are unmoved when the flag or National Anthem are featured at the Olympic Games or are encountered while traveling in a foreign country. This value system is most recently seen in what has been called the "New Patriotism" as exemplified by the various patriotic activities during the 1984 Summer Olympics.

An extraordinary example of the power of an appeal to middle American value systems is President Ronald Reagan. Many people attribute his political popularity to his charisma, delivery, or emotional appeals. We disagree. We think his popularity stems from his appealing to values instead of appealing to more specific beliefs and attitudes by addressing controversial issues. (Note Reagan's appeal to the foregoing value systems in the conclusion to his 1980 presidential debate with candidate John Anderson on page 73.)

Considerable research is still needed to enhance our understanding of values. However, values and their complex, hierarchical relationship to one another, as well as to other elements of the cognitive system, are a significant determinant of change and resistence to change not only in our cognitive system but in our behavior as well.

/ Needs

Psychologists have long believed that there are fundamental needs of human beings which influence their thinking and behavior. Early psychological studies focused on internal drives believed to be inherent in humans. Like other animals, people were believed to be driven by their needs for food, reproduction, self-preservation, and the like. As the field of social psychology developed, attention turned to more socially oriented influences such as the needs for social acceptance, recognition, and loving support. In an attempt to recognize and integrate both emphases, Abraham Maslow[20] posited a hierarchy of needs which included both physiological needs and social needs. Whether inherent or learned, these needs, according to Maslow, are crucial to a person's well-being, if not survival: physiological, safety, love or belongingness, self-esteem, self-actualization, and aesthetic.

/ Physiological needs.
Our most basic needs, claimed Maslow, are rooted in our physiology. Living organisms have the basic requirements of food, elimination of waste, reproduction, and, in the animal kingdom, movement. Physiological needs tend to influence our cognitions and behavior when we are deprived

/ **The need for belongingness powerfully influences our thinking and behavior.**

of their fulfillment. We can be moved to act when we feel constrained, hungry, thirsty, and so on.

/ *Safety.*   Like physiological needs, the need for safety is rooted in our survival instinct. Humans, like the lower animals, will go to great lengths to protect their young, build comfortable shelters for them, and fashion weapons for their defense. The need for safety seems to be activated when one's survival is threatened or when one is deprived of the feeling of safety. Cultures like the gentle Tasaday of Mindinao who have no natural enemies develop neither the implements nor the language of war. Conversely, cultures which exist in harsh environments develop more sturdy and enduring clothing and housing than do cultures in more benign surroundings. People become activists when their safety is threatened by crime, unemployment, the proliferation of nuclear weapons, or the careless disposal of hazardous wastes. In any case, the need for safety and security can profoundly influence human thinking and behavior.

/ *Love.*   A third basic need of human beings is for what Maslow called love or belongingness. Loneliness and rejection can be not only painful but downright fatal. Small children who do not receive regular stimulation and loving responses have been known to languish both physically and mentally and, in cases of extreme deprivation, even die. Teenagers obviously are driven by peer pressure, and adults who live as hermits are considered abnormal. Our need to be loved and to belong can even affect our perceptions. People have been known to alter what they say they see in order to conform to those around them.

/ *Self-esteem.* Still another social need which humans share is the need for self-esteem. We want to think well of ourselves. To ensure this, we spend considerable time and energy protecting our self-esteem or ego. One of the greatest gifts a parent can give a child is a healthy self-esteem, and yet in their attempt to correct trivial breeches of conduct, parents sometimes reduce or destroy the child's self-image and thereby cause far more serious problems than those they were trying to correct.

/ *Self-actualization.* The class of needs most closely associated with Maslow is self-actualization. Based on his studies of people who were high achievers, Maslow theorized that when people have satisfied their needs for physiological satisfaction, safety, love or belongingness, and self-esteem, they strive to develop their talents and to achieve the maximum of their potential. Rather than responding to any deprivation, they are motivated to go beyond normal expectations to higher and higher levels of achievement. Why else would people who seemingly have it made take on new and greater challenges? Why else would people who have achieved a successful and comfortable life turn to the service of the less fortunate?

We tend to notice more readily the need for self-actualization among the super achievers because they stand out so clearly. Teachers and counselors can also point out the over-achiever who is making the most of limited ability. For example, an increasing number of people are "running" marathons in wheelchairs. Consider also the remarkable achievement of the handicapped in the Special Olympics. Self-actualization is the need to do the best with what you have regardless of your innate ability.

/ *Aesthetic.* Maslow suggests that people who have satisfied the foregoing needs will display a need for aesthetic expression or enjoyment. Some people seem to have an inherent need to participate in artistic expression through music, art, literature, dance, or drama. Even Stone Age cultures left a heritage of paintings and carvings on the faces of cliffs and the walls of caves. While struggling just to survive, different cultures have produced objects of artistic expression which have survived for centuries.

Earlier we said that Maslow posited that the foregoing needs are organized in a generally hierarchical structure. Subsequent interpreters of Maslow, however, have tended to ignore the obvious and important exceptions to that generalization which Maslow himself readily acknowledged. We have all read of instances of exceptional heroism in which people risked their lives to save another, thus putting their need for love and belongingness or self-esteem ahead of their need for safety. In recent years it has not been uncommon for people such as André Sakarov or Sonia Johnson to go on hunger strikes to the point of death in order to demonstrate a belief or force a decision, thus placing their need for self-esteem or self-actualization above their physiological need for food. However, the fact that these instances receive widespread publicity is silent testimony to the generally hierarchical nature of the needs described above.

In addition to the foregoing qualification of Maslow's hierarchy of needs, we believe that people can operate at different levels of the hierarchy in different aspects of their lives.[21] For instance, you could be operating in a self-actualizing way at work or in social service and, at the same time, be at the love and belongingness or even safety level in your family. Conversely, you may be a self-actualizing spouse or parent and be struggling for safety at work or in some other major aspect of your life.

Although the general hierarchical nature of Maslow's system of needs requires such qualification, it remains a useful tool for understanding the goal-oriented dimension of a person's cognitive system. In sum, we consider that, whether hierarchical or not, inherited or learned, the foregoing needs constitute goal-oriented elements of the cognitive system which influence our thinking and behavior.

/ Motives

A final element in the goal dimension of people's cognitive system is motive. Early theorists defined *motive* as a socially acceptable way of satisfying a human need or needs. Thus, all people have a need for food, but some satisfy that need with a gourmet meal while others warm up a TV dinner. All people have a need to feel safe in their homes, but some will satisfy that need by purchasing a handgun while others will install a dead-bolt lock on their door, vote more taxes for police protection, or join a community security watch group.

Motives vary widely among cultures and subcultures. In some cultures beef in any form would be considered a delicacy, and yet we recently read that inmates in a state prison who were fed meatloaf for several meals were suing the state for inflicting "cruel and unusual punishment"!

Another way of looking at motives is advanced by Faules and Alexander.[22] They maintain that a motive is the way we talk about the satisfaction of our needs. Thus, a person might say, "I could sure go for a pizza right now!" as an expression of a physiological need for food, or "Slow down, your driving is making me nervous" as an expression of the need for safety. Whether we look at motives as socially acceptable ways of satisfying our needs or as the way we talk about that satisfaction, we are dealing with essentially the same phenomenon. In either case motives viewed as goals are very useful not only in explaining persuasive communication, but also in providing a more specific, observable object of study than do the more abstract concepts of need or drive.

/ The Arousal Dimension

/ Arousal and cognition

Clearly, human thought and action are affected by feeling or emotion. Early psychological literature treated emotion as an isolatable state. We do not believe it can be separated from other elements of the cognitive system, though it must be taken into account. We prefer to think of emotion as a dimension that crosses all aspects of the cognitive system. In brief, *emotion* is a relative state of arousal associated with information processing at a given time and in a given context. All elements of the cognitive system, whether in the reality, goal, or relationship dimension, will involve varying levels of arousal. The emotional association of a belief may change from moment to moment, depending upon how aroused we become when that belief comes into play in a given context.

Picture yourself on a typical day. You are sound asleep when the alarm goes off. Half-awake, you get your legs over the edge of the bed, struggle to your feet, and grope your way to the bathroom. After a shower you are more alert. Having consumed a cup of coffee and some breakfast you are ready to seize the day. Leaving for work, you are fantasizing pleasantly when you slip on the ice and fall. You shake with fear and anger. Although you calm down somewhat, you are irritable most of the morning. After lunch you get a little sleepy and complain about how stuffy the building seems. On a friend's advice, you have another caffeine fix. More alert now, you manage to survive the afternoon. That evening you attend an athletic event and become terribly excited as your team cinches a thrilling victory in the closing seconds of the game. You return home, but it is several hours before you can finally get to sleep.

Arousal is both general and specific.[23] One proceeds throughout the day with a general readiness to respond that is relatively undifferentiated. That general arousal level waxes and wanes as the events of the day force themselves upon us. Sometimes one feels generally energetic and charged; other times, one is lethargic, even dull. More interesting, perhaps, is when one's arousal level becomes attached to a particular event or situation perceived to be outside the self. In such situations we respond emotionally to specific stimuli such as a frightening encounter with another car on the way to work or a pleasant luncheon with a valued associate. Such arousals, attached to particular stimuli, are an integral part of the cognitive system.

Emotions both affect and are affected by other aspects of the cognitive system. Arousal not only makes certain conceptual associations more salient or intense in a particular situation, but can sometimes change the very character of the system itself. We have, for example, seen grief lead to profound realignment of values. On the other hand, cognitive organization also affects emotion in the sense that one's definition of *emotion* depends in large measure on conceptual associations. One's arousal in a situation is interpreted on the basis of relevant concepts; we conceptualize emotion just as we conceptualize any aspect of our experience.[24] Thus our feelings of arousal may be interpreted as fear, jealousy, love, or whatever. Different people do not always respond emotionally to the same stimuli because their conceptual tools for doing so vary. A child may not feel fear in a dangerous situation because he or she has not yet learned to conceptualize the situation as dangerous. Even among adults, dangerous situations spark rather different feelings—sometimes panic, sometimes adventure, sometimes bravery.

Contrary to the common notion that emotion is antithetical to reason, Janis maintains there is a cognitive dimension to fear. That is to say, an emotional response to a given situation includes a reasoned, evaluative process. In his analysis of fear arousal, Janis claims that the magnitude of a person's fear arousal "is roughly proportional to both the perceived probability of the dangerous event materializing and the anticipated magnitude of the damage."[25] In other words, we will experience more arousal from a threatening message if we think the results are likely and will hurt us a great deal.

The predominant meanings of one's social group or culture also greatly affect how emotions are defined, making feeling far more social than many believe. For example, death usually sparks fear in most Western cultures, but may elicit honor among the Shiite Moslems or the traditional Samuri. During the medieval period, an emotion called "accidie" was especially prevalent. *Accidie* was something akin to feelings of negligence, laziness, idleness, or sloth, which are not usually thought of as emotions today.[26] *Accidie* was prevalent because of the centrality of the concept of spiritual obligation and the sin of spiritual failure.

Think for a moment about the cognitive elements of two rather prevalent emotions today, envy and jealousy.[27] Although these emotions definitely involve arousal, they are not possible without certain moral conceptions. To be envious, you must make the concepts of ownership and acquisition salient. To be jealous, you must draw into play the added concept of comparative rights. The point is that these feelings are as much a matter of cognitive definition as they are physiological arousal. The Maori define emotions in an entirely different way. They have heart emotions (uneasy, grudging, gratified, excited), bowel emotions (eager, uncertain, disincluded), and stomach emotions (playful, cautious, quarrelsome).[28] If this conceptualization doesn't make much sense to you, it is because of the vast difference between the cognitive system of the average Maori and that of the typical North American.

/ *Characteristics of emotional concepts.*   Given the view that emotion is a product of cognition, what is the nature of emotional concepts? First, emotions are usually conceptualized as *impulsive.*[29] We do not normally think of emotional responses as planned or thoughtful. For that reason, many people experience emotions as arising quickly, but fading slowly.[30]

A second characteristic of emotions is that they are *influenced by external cues.* Emotional arousal is generally measured by such physiological indexes as heartbeat, sweaty palms, galvanic skin response, and the like. Although we experience emotional arousal as an internal feeling, however, it is related in some degree to what is going on around us.

Thirdly, people are motivated to *ward off painful* emotional responses and to *seek pleasurable* ones.[31] For instance, if you are living on an earthquake fault or a flood plain, you will attempt to avoid the discomfort of fear by ignoring suggestions of the threat or by rationalizing that the occurrence of an earthquake or flood is highly unlikely. If you can't escape the pain of the threat, you will probably escape the discomfort by moving. We know many people who avoid arguments with friends and intimates in order to avoid the discomfort of emotional arousal due to anger—sometimes to the detriment of the relationship. Remember, however, that what is considered painful or pleasurable is largely a matter of cognitive definition and that other values sometimes override this tendency.

Another factor related to emotion is *dominance*. Dominance is the degree to which a person perceives a freedom of choice or control in a given situation. Albert Mehrabian and his associates relate dominance to freedom of choice when they claim, "An individual's feeling of dominance in a situation is based on the extent to which he or she feels unrestricted or free to act in a variety of ways."[32] Mehrabian goes on to relate dominance inversely to such familiar concepts as privacy, territoriality, and crowding. Dominance can further be reduced by formal social situations (which constrain choice) and the presence of others of high status. It is interesting to speculate about a possible relationship between increase in depression in our modern society and a comparable increase in crowding, governmental controls, and a general feeling of a loss of control.

Finally, emotional responses can be *transferred* from one object to another. A small child who was once frightened by a large dog became intensely afraid of all dogs. Sometime later the child was at the beach, playing happily in the water, when a dog came by. For a considerable period thereafter the child was afraid to go near the water. She had transferred her fear of dogs to the water.

/ Emotion and persuasion

Most of the foregoing discussion has illustrated the relation of emotional arousal to an individual's behavior. What then is the relation of emotion to persuasion? The majority of formal studies of that question have been conducted on fear arousal. In his summary of that research Janis emphasizes the relationship between a person's residual level of arousal and the arousal attributable to the immediate situation or stimulus. Although intuitively we might infer that the more our emotions are aroused the more our attitude will change, McGuire describes a curvilinear relationship between fear arousal and compliance.[33] This interpretation would suggest that in most situations an *intermediate* emotional arousal will achieve greater change in attitudes and behavior than either no emotional arousal or extremely high emotional excitation.

Numerous research studies, however, have demonstrated that people respond to fear appeals in a variety of ways. (In other situations or other cultures, of course, different principles might apply.) Some studies, for example, have shown that the effects of fear arousal do not last very long. In order for such appeals to have long-term effects, they must be combined with the presentation of a rationale more completely integrated into the subject's cognitive system than a simple fear appeal can accomplish.[34]

Finally, some writers claim that emotion is nothing more than the degree or intensity of the vector of an attitude. We disagree. We think there is a significant, identifiable difference between calmly indicating a "strong" preference in favor of, say, adopting out the Grand Canyon burros and that extreme feeling we experience when highly aroused emotionally by a near accident in our automobile or by a stinging personal insult. However, the relationship between beliefs and attitudes on the one hand and emotional arousal on the other is complex and will require further study before it is very well understood.

/ The Relational Dimension

A fourth dimension of the cognitive system is made up of the relational bonds which exist among communicators. These relations can be viewed as beliefs and attitudes which people have toward one another and the self. However, because they constitute such an important part of the cognitive system and have been so extensively researched, we will treat them separately.

/ Attribution

Attribution is the process of developing beliefs about one's self and others.[35] Our attributions are characterizations of other people and of ourselves. When we believe that a person is industrious or lazy, happy or sad, bright or dull, or any of a variety of other characteristics, we attribute those qualities to them. We also make similar attributions to ourselves.

One of the most interesting aspects of attributions has to do with how we explain behavior. We have a strong tendency to try to explain the behavior we observe in ourselves and others. Typically, we attribute people's behavior to situational or dispositional factors. When we explain someone's behavior *situationally*, we believe that the behavior was caused by factors beyond the individual's control. *Dispositional* attribution explains behavior in terms of the individual's personal characteristics.

Suppose, for example, that your friend fails to show up for a date. Inevitably, you will try to figure out why. If you look to situational factors, you may decide that your friend was delayed by an accident or some unforeseen circumstance. If you look to dispositional factors, you may attribute your friend's absence to forgetfulness, laziness, insensitivity, or some other characteristic.

People often act like scientists when making attributions. They observe themselves and others over time in different situations and make inferences as to why behavior occurred. However, attribution is affected, at least in part, by other aspects of the cognitive system as well, such as prior beliefs, values, attitudes, and even arousal.

One's own self-interest often guides what may appear on the surface as "objective" attribution. For example, a persistent attribution error is a tendency to over-attribute behavior to disposition rather than to situation. Not only do people over-attribute to disposition in judging others, but they also over-attribute to situation when judging themselves.

Attribution is a fundamental element of the relationship cluster in the cognitive system because it lies at the heart of many—if not most—of our beliefs about ourselves, other people, and our relationships with others. The other elements of this cluster—trust, attraction, and similarity—all rely on the attribution process.

/ Bonds of trust

For centuries, students of human communication have searched for invariable dimensions or factors which serve to establish and maintain interpersonal bonds. Aristotle claimed that the single most important source of persuasive influence was *ethos,* or personal influence. He further claimed that the factors which contributed to that influence were the receivers' perception of good sense, good character, and good will. Subsequent rhetorical scholars have reconceptualized these factors as competence, integrity, and good will. During the decades of the fifties and sixties, ethos, or what experimenters called *source credibility,* was subjected to extensive experimentation. Taken together, almost all of these studies identified variables roughly analogous to the Aristotelian factors of competence and character. Although much less consistent, factors of dynamism and sociability are also mentioned.[36]

The factors of ethos or source credibility add up to *interpersonal trust.*[37] We trust communicators if we believe them to be competent, expert, or qualified, and we trust them if they appear to have character, integrity, or honesty.

Important as trust or ethos is, however, it is not derived from invariant factors. While competence and character are common contributors to ethos, in many cultures we find exceptions due to context, audience, and other aspects of the communication situation. For example, in a study of whether or not ethos is learned in basic speech communication courses, Jabusch, Alexander, and Faules found that while viewing the same videotaped speeches, teaching assistants' ratings were based upon "expertise" and "safety" while personnel directors' were based upon "safety" and "dynamism."[38]

The basis of interpersonal trust can vary not only with receivers but also with context. For example, Jabusch, Smith, and Wong studied pre-surgery patients' interviews with their anesthesiologists.[39] In an attempt to tap the arousal and reality dimensions of the patients' cognitive system, two open-ended questions were asked: "What were you *feeling* when talking to your doctor?" and "What were you *thinking* when talking to your doctor?" Numerous answers related to trust. Interestingly, all of the personal responses were based on competence, qualification, or expertise. None related to character, integrity, or honesty. Presumably, in some medical contexts, interpersonal trust is based almost entirely on the competence factor.

In sum, interpersonal trust is a critical element of a person's relational dimension of the cognitive system. Although trust is usually based on a combination of competence and character and to a lesser degree on dynamism and sociability, the source of trust and the factors which contribute to it are situational. That is, trust can vary with the context, participants, and other aspects of the communication situation.[40]

/ Attraction

Another element of the relational dimension which contributes to shared influence among people is the *attraction* people have for one another.[41] Attraction can be based on association, support, or personal qualities.

First, we tend to be attracted by other people by *association*. That is, interpersonal attraction can be based on past experiences, beliefs, or values which are associated with the other individual and, hence, are found to be rewarding. Imagine, for example, that you are at a reception where you know almost no one. Looking around, you spot a somewhat familiar face. Even though you hardly know the person, you are attracted to approach that person with whom you have an association, however slight.

We are also attracted to and influenced by people who *support* us. Throughout our lives we have friends, colleagues, and even admirers either who support us during difficult personal passages or who give impetus to our careers or other accomplishments. We tend not only to be more attracted to those people who support us but also to those we support, developing as a result relationships which culminate in mutual influence.

Finally, we tend to be attracted to people with certain *personal qualities*. At least initially we are more likely to establish interpersonal bonds with others we find *physically attractive*. Considerable evidence suggests that we are not only attracted to people we consider good looking, but we are more influenced by them as well. Recall that the personal qualities of *sociability* and *character* are related not only to interpersonal attraction but contribute to the trust bond as well.

/ Homophile

A third element of the relational dimension is the *similarity* or *dissimilarity* we share with other people. Contrary to the common cliché that "opposites attract," people tend to establish interpersonal bonds with those they perceive to be similar to themselves in significant ways.

First, people may perceive that they have had similar *life experiences*. How often have you established new relationships or at least wanted to find out more about new acquaintances when you discovered that they had lived in the same state as you had, traveled in the same area, studied the same major, had a common acquaintance, or shared the same profession or hobby? How often do salespersons or politicians stress the common experiences they have shared with their listeners in order to enhance their identification and, hence, their influence? Notice how people who have experienced major life crises such as a divorce, financial loss, natural disaster, or untimely death of a loved one seem to gravitate toward other people who have shared similar personal experiences.

/ **Maggie Kuhn, founder of the Gray Panthers, shares many of the salient experiences, beliefs, and needs of her elderly constituency.**

Further, we may perceive that we are similar or dissimilar to other persons in other major components of our respective cognitive systems. That is, we may share others' beliefs, attitudes, or values on the one hand or their needs, motives, or emotions on the other. We cannot share all of these with any individual, however, let alone a group of individuals. We tend to form the strongest interpersonal bonds with those groups and individuals which share our most *salient* experiences, beliefs, or needs. Since human values are by definition beliefs of exceptional importance to the individual, we consider them to be equally important factors upon which interpersonal bonds based on similarity are built.

Finally, *dissimilarity* plays a role in establishing interpersonal bonds. In his discussion of similarity and dissimilarity, Simons[42] introduces the concept of the *super-representative*. The super-representative is a person who is similar to a group or constituency in the experiences and components of the cognitive system discussed above. The super-representative is dissimilar, however, in that he or she transcends the group or constituency in important ways. The Reverend Martin Luther King, Jr., and more recently, the Reverend Jesse Jackson are classic examples of super-representatives who identified with the black experience while transcending their constituencies in their personal and leadership qualities.

A super-representative may be dissimilar from the group in such areas as competence, integrity, and communication skills. Just as surgery patients don't want "plain folks" operating on their brains, so most groups are influenced by leaders who, while sharing their values, demonstrate extraordinary competence in their intelligence, command of issues, experience, organizational ability, or dedication. Further, individuals and organizations typically expect superior character of their leaders. A minor infraction of moral conduct or the law by a common citizen may be forgotten or even overlooked, but a president might be forced to resign his office for the same infraction. Finally, the super-represent-ative usually transcends the group in communication skills. Not only do leaders convince followers to adopt new policies, but frequently an influential leader can articulate the beliefs, values, and feelings which other members of the constit-uency already possess but cannot communicate.

/ The Cognitive System and Behavior

Chapters 2 and 3 have dealt with the cognitive system and information process-ing. As we have seen, the cognitive system is a complex cluster of concepts related to one another in a network of associations. It is a system characterized by the reality, goal, arousal, and relationship dimensions.

One of the most difficult problems in the study of persuasion has been to establish the connection between elements of cognition and behavior. Research-ers, for example, have tried to develop models of attitude that would enable them to predict behavior. Although attitudes were defined as predispositions to act in preferred ways, experiments designed to illuminate that relationship produced conflicting results.

More recent studies have examined the subjects' attitudes toward an object in the context of their attitudes toward the situation in which it occurred. These have been more successful in predicting behavior.[43] Furthermore, behavior is more predictable from a specific attitude or intention (for example, "donating blood at the upcoming drive") than from a general attitude ("blood dona-tion").[44] The effort to predict behavior has been difficult largely, we believe, because of a misconception about human cognition. We do not think behavior can be easily predicted, precisely because individuals have the ability to choose rules of interpretation and action from a variety of contextual levels in the cog-nitive system.

Complicating this process is the fact that meanings are socially constructed action; thus, they are not strictly a matter of individual choice, but are partially determined by interaction with others. Because one is a member of a variety of social groups, the unique combination of interpretive schematas available to an individual can never be known precisely.

Consider the case of a business executive whose family had been pressur-ing for the purchase of a home computer. Initially, he was firmly against it. He believed the computer would be of no practical use to him, since he did not type well, had a secretary with a word processor at work, and believed it would be too time-consuming to use for balancing his checkbook. Further, he had a negative attitude toward expensive, complicated "toys" which break down easily. Finally, expensive computers violated his values of nonmaterialism and frugality. Surprisingly, this executive recently purchased a home computer. Further investigation of the conflicting elements of his cognitive system reveals why. First, he became interested in creative writing, which he knew he could not have his secretary type for him at work. Secondly, the company for which he worked offered to pay half the cost of home computers for executives in order to reduce clerical overhead. Finally, several colleagues purchased home computers and were singing their praises at business meetings, conferences, and cocktail parties. Considering the highly complicated nature of people's cognitive systems, along with the dynamic way the cognitive system develops and changes in interaction with the environment, it should not be surprising that behavior would be difficult to predict on the basis of the static measurement of an isolated belief, attitude, or value.

Suffice it to say, persuasion is an important part of the interaction which shapes the actions of an individual and has the potential to evoke change in the cognitive system. In the next chapter, we consider several of the processes by which that change may come about.

/ *Theory* / *Practice* / *Analysis*

Theory

1. A person's cognitive system is a complex relationship among the dimensions of reality, goals, arousal, and relationships.

2. The reality dimension is composed of millions of beliefs which are accepted data about the universe or simple propositions of "I believe . . .". Attitudes are clusters of beliefs organized around an object or situation.

3. Traditional argumentation theory provides insights into the formation and organization of beliefs and attitudes.

4. The goal dimension is composed of values, needs, and motives. Values are centrally held beliefs which are very resistant to change. Needs are related to physiological deprivation, safety, love or belongingness, self-esteem, self-actualization, and aesthetic expression. Motives are socially acceptable ways of fulfilling needs or ways of talking about needs.

5. Emotional arousal varies according to a person's general level of excitation or in response to the environment. It is experienced as pleasurable or painful, as well as varying in a feeling of dominance.

6. The relational dimension is based upon attributions people make about themselves and others. Shared trust, attraction, and homophile contribute to the relational dimension of the cognitive system.

Practice

1. Take Rokeach's list of American values and see how your classmates rank them. Compare the results according to subcultures such as religion, marital status, sex, and more.

2. Using the semantic differential scales of Berlo, Lemmert and Mertz, or McCroskey, assess the trust your classmates (or some segment of the broader community) have for local or national political figures.

3. Using either an Osgood or Likert scale, assess the attitudes of your classmates or some segment of the broader community regarding one or several local or national social issues such as a nuclear freeze, gun control, gay liberation, or pornography.

Analysis

1. Analyze your own cognitive system relevant to some issue. Is your basal state of arousal generally high or low? What are your priority values, salient beliefs and attitudes, and interpersonal relationships? If these came into conflict, which ones would prevail? How are your behaviors influenced by your cognitive system?

2. Select an interpersonal persuasion situation such as a family controversy or a disagreement at work. Using Maslow's hierarchy of needs/motives, try to assess the level on which various participants are operating. Is one motivated by a need for safety while another desires self-actualization? Does their being on different levels help or hinder their mutual understanding and influence? Are they aware of being on different levels? Does your awareness of the different levels give you added insight into the situation?

3. Repeat the analysis above using Rokeach's hierarchy of values.

4. Using published public opinion polls, trace how various subcultures within American society (political, religious, ethnic, and so on) have remained consistent or changed in their attitudes or values regarding historical or social issues (for example, abortion, censorship, nuclear power).

5. Consider what Senator Albert J. Beveridge said about America in 1898:

> It is a noble land that God has given us; a land that can feed and clothe the world; a land whose coastlines would inclose half the countries of Europe; a land set like a sentinel between the two imperial oceans of the globe, a greater England with a nobler destiny.
>
> It is a mighty people that He has planted on this soil; a people sprung from the most masterful blood of history; a people perpetually revitalized by the virile, man-producing working-folk of all the earth; a people imperial by virtue of their power, by right of their institutions, by authority of their Heaven-directed purposes—the propagandists and not the misers of liberty.[45]

Compare the values to which Beveridge appeals to those of then presidential candidate Ronald Reagan in the conclusion of his debate with candidate John Anderson.

> *Mr. Reagan:* Now as to my closing remarks, I have always believed that this land was placed here between the two great oceans by some divine plan. It was placed here to be found by a special kind of people—people who had a special love for freedom and who had the courage to uproot themselves and leave hearth and homeland and come to what in the beginning was the most undeveloped wilderness possible. We came from 100 different corners of the earth. We spoke a multitude of tongues—landed on this eastern shore and then went out over the mountains and the prairies and the deserts and the far Western mountains of the Pacific building cities and towns and farms and schools and churches.
>
> If wind, water or fire destroyed them, we built them again. And in so doing at the same time we built a new breed of human called an American—a proud, an independent and a most compassionate individual for the most part. Two hundred years ago Tom Paine, when the 13 tiny colonies were trying to become a nation, said we have it in our power to begin the world over again.
>
> Today we're confronted with the horrendous problems that we've discussed here tonight and some people in high positions of leadership tell us that the answer is to retreat, that the best is over, that we must cut back, that we must share in an ever-increasing scarcity, that we must—in the failure to be able to protect our national security as it is today—we must not be provocative to any possible adversary.
>
> Well, we the living Americans have gone through four wars, we've gone through a great Depression in our lifetime that literally was worldwide and almost brought us to our knees, but we came through all of those things and we achieved even new heights and new greatness.
>
> The living Americans today have fought harder, paid a higher price for freedom and done more to advance the dignity of man than any people who have ever lived on this earth. For 200 years we've lived in the future, believing that tomorrow would be better than today and today would be better than yesterday. I still believe that. I'm not running for the Presidency because I believe that I can solve the problems we've discussed tonight. I believe the people of this country can. And together we can begin the world over again. We can meet our destiny and that destiny can build a land here that will be for all mankind a shining city on a hill. I think we ought to get at it.[46]

Notes

[1]Milton Rokeach, *Beliefs, Attitudes, and Values: A Theory of Organization and Change* (San Francisco: Jossey-Bass, 1968), p. 113.

[2]Herbert Simons, *Persuasion: Understanding, Practice, and Analysis* (London: Addison-Wesley, 1976).

[3]It is interesting to note the similarity between these definitions and what traditional argumentation theorists have called "propositions of fact."

[4]Mary John Smith, *Persuasion and Human Action* (Belmont, CA: Wadsworth Publishing Co., 1982).

[5]These traditions of Western thought are discussed by W. Barnett Pearce, Vernon Cronen, and Linda Harris, "Methodological Considerations in Building Human Commu-

nication Theory," in *Human Communication Theory: Comparative Essays,* ed. Frank E. Dance (New York: Harper and Row, 1982), pp. 1–41.

[6]Stephen Toulmin, *The Uses of Argument* (New York: Cambridge University Press, 1964).

[7]Richard Rieke and Malcolm Sillars, *Argumentation and the Decision Making Process,* 2nd ed. (Glenview, IL: Scott, Foresman and Company, 1984).

[8]Gordon Allport, "Attitude," *Reading in Attitude Theory and Measurement,* ed. Martin Fishbein (New York: John Wiley and Sons, 1967), p. 3.

[9]Simons, *Persuasion: Understanding,* p. 80.

[10]Robert N. Bostrom, *Persuasion* (Englewood Cliffs, NJ: Prentice-Hall, Inc., 1983), p. 39.

[11]Simons, *Persuasion: Understanding,* pp. 82–83; Smith, *Persuasion and Human Action.*

[12]Richard E. Petty and John T. Cacioppo, *Attitudes and Persuasion: Classic and Contemporary Approaches* (Dubuque, IA: Wm. C. Brown Co., 1981), p. 7.

[13]Bostrom, *Persuasion.*

[14]Rokeach, *Beliefs,* p. 112.

[15]Note the close approximation between this definition of attitude and what traditional argumentation theorists have described as "propositions of policy."

[16]Rokeach, *Beliefs,* p. 124.

[17]Daniel Yankelovich, *New Rules Searching for Self-Fulfillment in a World Turned Upside-Down* (New York: Random House, 1981), p. 87.

[18]For a discussion of value systems, see Rieke and Sillars, *Argumentation,* pp. 124–31.

[19]Clyde Reid, *Celebrate the Temporary* (New York: Harper and Row, 1972).

[20]Abraham Maslow, *Motivation and Personality* (New York: Harper & Row, 1970).

[21]David M. Jabusch and Stephen W. Littlejohn, *Elements of Speech Communication* (Boston: Houghton-Mifflin, 1981), p. 104.

[22]Don F. Faules and Dennis Alexander, *Communication and Social Behavior* (Reading, MA: Addison-Wesley, 1978).

[23]Irving Janis, "Effects of Fear Arousal on Attitude Change," *The Process of Social Influence: Readings in Persuasion,* ed. Thomas D. Beisecker and D. W. Parson (Englewood Cliffs, NJ: Prentice-Hall, Inc., 1972), pp. 277–302.

[24]See J. R. Averill, "A Constructivist View of Emotion," *Theories of Emotion,* ed. Robert Poutchik and Henry Kellerman (New York: Academic Press, 1980); J. R. Averill, "On the Paucity of Positive Emotions," *Assessment and Modification of Emotional Behavior,* ed. Kirk R. Blankstein et al. (New York: Plenum Press, 1980).

[25]Janis, "Effects of Fear Arousal," p. 280.

[26]Rom Harre, *Personal Being* (Cambridge: Harvard University Press, 1984), p. 128.

[27]Harre, *Personal Being,* p. 124; see also John Sabini and Maury Silver, *Moralities of Everyday Life* (Oxford: Oxford University Press, 1982), pp. 15–34.

[28]Harre, *Personal Being,* p. 125.

[29]Averill, "Paucity."

[30]See Robert T. Oliver, *The Psychology of Persuasive Speech* (New York: David McKay Co., Inc., 1957), p. 253.

[31]Albert Mehrabian, *Basic Dimensions for a General Psychological Theory* (Cambridge, MA: Ocleschlager, Gunn, and Hain, Publishers, 1980), pp. 15–16.

[32]Mehrabian, *Basic Dimensions,* p. 18.

[33]William McGuire, "Personality and Susceptibility to Social Influence," *Handbook of Personality Theory and Research,* ed. G. F. Borgatta and W. W. Bamber (Skokie, IL: Rand McNally, 1970), pp. 1130–187; McGuire, "Persuasion Resistance and Attitude Change," *Handbook of Communication,* ed. I. Pool et al. (Skokie, IL: Rand McNally, 1973), pp. 216–52.

[34]Smith, *Persuasion and Human Action,* pp. 230–32.

[35]Attribution theory is summarized in *New Directions in Attribution Research,* ed. John K. Harvey, William J. Iekes, and Robert F. Kidd, vols. 1 and 2 (New York: John Wiley and Sons, 1976, 1978).

[36]Anderson identified clusters of scales he labeled "qualification" and "dynamism." Berlo, Lemmert, and Mertz identified variables of "safety," "qualification," "dynamism," and "sociability." McCrosky labeled his clusters of source variables "authoritativeness" and "character."

[37]Jabusch and Littlejohn, *Elements of Speech,* pp. 107–111.

[38]David M. Jabusch, Dennis Alexander, and Don Faules, "The Effects of Speech Training on Credibility as Perceived by Speech Critics and Personnel Directors," paper presented to Western Speech Association, Honolulu, November 1972.

[39]David M. Jabusch, Victoria Smith, and K. C. Wong, "Patient Image of the Anesthesiologist," paper presented to The American Society of Anesthesiologists, St. Louis, October 1980.

[40]See Jesse G. Delia, "Constructivist Analysis of the Concept of Credibility," *Quarterly Journal of Speech* 62 (December 1976): 361–75.

[41]Theories of interpersonal attraction are summarized in Stephen W. Littlejohn, *Theories of Human Communication* (Belmont, CA: Wadsworth Publishing, 1983), pp. 201–208.

[42]Simons, *Persuasion: Understanding,* pp. 161–62.

[43]See, for example, William J. McGuire, "The Concept of Attitudes and Their Relations to Behavior," *Perspectives on Attitude Assessment,* ed. H. W. Sineiko and L. A. Broedling (Champaign, IL: Pendleton, 1976).

[44]Martin Fishbein and I. Ajzen, *Beliefs, Attitudes, Intentions, and Behavior* (Reading, MA: Addison-Wesley, 1975).

[45]"The March of the Flag," *American Forum: Speeches on Historic Issues,* ed. Ernest J. Wrage and Barnett Baskerville (New York: Harper and Row, 1960), pp. 352–53.

[46]Ronald W. Reagan, Closing Statement, "Transcript of Campaign's First Presidential Debate, with Reagan vs. Anderson," *New York Times,* 22 September 1980, sec. 2: 6.

4 / Processes of Change

Sometime ago a professional colleague changed political parties. It was an interesting process to observe. He was raised in one of the major political parties by parents who remain staunch members. However, during his schooling he was exposed to some differing points of view in readings assigned by various teachers he respected. Candidates from his party seemed to be articulating values and positions on issues opposite from his own, while opposing candidates sounded more "right on" each year. He began noticing that professional colleagues whose judgment he respected were campaigning for candidates from the opposite party. Priding himself as being politically moderate and an independent thinker, he had always split his ballot—voting for those candidates he considered best qualified regardless of party. When he finally found himself voting for a significantly greater number of candidates from the opposing party, he quietly changed his party affiliation. Today he is a leader in the party opposing the one in which he was raised.

We discussed in Chapter 3 the various dimensions and components of the cognitive system. In Chapter 1 we defined *persuasion* in terms of change either within that cognitive system or in behavior or both. In this chapter we explore how such change occurs.

/ Cognition and Change

/ Changes in the cognitive system

Changes in the cognitive system occur constantly. As people perceive what is going on around them, they conceptualize the new information and integrate it into their cognitive systems, consequently changing the cognitive system to accommodate the new cognitions.

In the reality dimension, new concepts may complement or contradict existing concepts or beliefs, thus altering the existing concepts. New conditions may create new beliefs, which in turn combine with other beliefs and attitudes to alter the existing belief structure. New cognitions may contradict existing belief structures so seriously as to cause the entire cluster of related beliefs to collapse.

In the arousal dimension, perceptions may raise or lower the arousal level as well as activate latent beliefs and attitudes. New cognitions may also reinforce or weaken values within the cognitive system as well as satisfy needs or alter motives. Finally, new observations may reinforce, weaken, or alter in more radical ways people's perceptions of their relationships with other people.

/ Information and change

/ How information changes the system
Imagine that you are cooking up a pot of vegetable soup. You combine some broth, white onion, carrots, celery, and other ingredients. You taste the soup and decide it needs more onion. After adding more onion, you taste again—now the onion flavor overpowers the other ingredients. Each time you add another ingredient—an herb, a potato, some pasta—the complex taste combination changes again and again. According to *information integration theory,* an attitude is like this vegetable soup—it is made up of a complex mixture of beliefs about an object. Each time new information is added to the "pot" which is the cognitive system, the attitudes within that system change.

Martin Fishbein and his associates[1] have attempted to quantify the process whereby new persuasive information affects existing attitudes. They first assume that people assign two probabilities to new information or beliefs that are received and processed: value and weight. The *value* of the belief is the degree to which a person evaluates the new information positively or negatively. Thus, when an environmentalist hears that the deployment of the MX missile in existing missile silos will increase the population of Cheyenne, Wyoming, she may anticipate a degradation of the environment and evaluate that as a minus seven (-7) on a scale of ten. A Cheyenne businessperson, on the other hand, may anticipate increased sales and evaluate the same information a plus nine ($+9$).

The *weight* a person places on the new information or belief is the probability he or she assigns to the information being accurate or actually happening. The impact the new belief has on one's cognitive system is determined by multiplying the value times the weight of the information. Thus, if the environmentalist thought the probability of a population increase was a plus eight ($+8$), the total impact on her attitude toward MX would be minus fifty-six ($-7 \times +8$). If the businessperson was somewhat skeptical that the increase would occur and assigned it a plus two ($+2$), his attitude would be affected by a plus eighteen ($+9 \times +2$). This relationship is represented mathematically as:

$$\text{Belief} = \text{value} \times \text{weight}$$

or

$$B = v \times w$$

Few attitudes are composed of a single belief, however. The Cheyenne environmentalist or businessperson would also consider the likelihood of the Russian threat, the influence of the missiles' location on the lifestyle of their community, the cost of the program, and a variety of other beliefs related to MX. Information integration theory assumes that an attitude is the sum total of all of the relevant beliefs about a given attitude object. Thus, the mathematical formula for a single attitude would be:

$$A_0 = (v_1 w_1) + (v_2 w_2) + (v_3 w_3) + (v_{etc.} w_{etc.})$$

$$\text{Attitude} = \frac{\text{belief about}}{\text{environment}} + \frac{\text{belief about}}{\text{cost}} + \frac{\text{belief about}}{\text{population}} + \frac{\text{belief about}}{\text{new information}}$$

where $A_0 =$ the attitude toward object
$w =$ the weight of each belief
$v =$ the value of each belief

In reduced form the formula looks like this:

$$A_0 = \sum_{i}^{N} W_i \times V_i$$

As you can see, each new piece of information (belief) will change the total mix of the attitude just as the addition of any ingredient will change the flavor of your vegetable soup. Thus, attitudes can be changed in three essential ways. First, an attitude can be altered by changing the weight (believability) of any belief. For instance, suppose our Cheyenne businessperson received new information that caused him to think a population increase was very likely and the weight of his belief increased from $+2$ to $+9$. Then his belief would increase from $+18$ to $+81$ ($+9 \times +9$), thereby substantially affecting his attitude toward the MX missile.

An attitude can also be changed by changing the value of a belief. If the businessperson sold his business for health reasons and took up fishing, the value he assigned to a population increase might diminish or even become negative, thus significantly affecting his attitude.

Finally, attitude can be altered by the addition of new beliefs to the attitude structure. Suppose the environmentalist had lost her existing job and had heard the governor say that if the MX missiles were deployed in Cheyenne and the population increased, the state would need more employees in its environmental protection agency. The opportunity for a new job might have a profound effect on the environmentalist's attitude.

There is some controversy among information integration theorists as to whether the effect of new information on existing attitudes is additive or an average of the component beliefs. Furthermore, the approach can be criticized for oversimplifying the complexity of the cognitive system. That is to say, in practice it would be impractical to measure all of the components of one attitude, let alone all of a person's relevant, interrelated attitudes, in order to predict behavior. Furthermore, Fishbein's mathematical model makes no provision for components of the cognitive system other than attitudes and beliefs. Nonetheless, the information integration approach to change and the accompanying mathematical models are a significant improvement over less precise approaches.

/ How people use information. An interesting interpretation has been offered of the process whereby change in the cognitive system occurs as a result of integrating new information into the system. Although retaining the essential notion that attitude and behavior change is essentially a matter of information processing, Anthony Greenwald focuses attention away from messages and other variables in the communication situation and onto the receiver. Rather than viewing the receiver as a somewhat passive recipient and uncritical responder to persuasive messages, Greenwald's *cognitive response model* views the receiver as an active participant in the persuasion transaction. According to Greenwald, the most important generative force in the persuasion transaction is the process the receiver goes through of "rehearsing and learning cognitive responses to persuasion."[2] That is to say, the receiver generates his or her own arguments in response to persuasive situations, which in turn strengthens or weakens the existing position, or changes attitude or behavior altogether.

We have all had a discussion with a spouse, parent, child, friend, or colleague, only to realize later what we should have said. What wonderful arguments we can generate after the fact. We often regret that we think of them too late. Or is it too late? Perhaps it is too late to convince the other person, but not too late to change our own cognitive system either in the direction of our opponents' position or further away from it. Greenwald's cognitive response model explains not only the process of attitude and behavior change, but the weakening and strengthening of attitudes and the *boomerang* effect (to be discussed later) as well.

/ Direct and indirect impact of information. One explanation of attitude and behavior change which is particularly transactional and also compatible with the dimensions of the cognitive system proposed in Chapter 3 has been described by Petty and Cacioppo. In their Elaboration Likelihood Model (ELM),[3] they propose (as we do) that passive "listening" rarely occurs, that people are more or less actively involved not only in processing messages but also in generating on their own claims and data relevant to the topic.

This more- or less-active involvement by participants results in message processing, and therefore changes in cognitions and behavior via two distinct processes, according to Petty and Cacioppo. If receivers possess both the ability and motivation, messages will be processed through a *central route*. Receivers lacking either the ability or motivation will respond to messages via a *peripheral route*.

Message processing via the *central route* involves a basic comparison between incoming messages and existing cognitive structures, especially within what we have called the reality dimension. That is to say, issues are analyzed while data and claims are weighed against what is already "known" and believed. If these comparisons show that incoming information is complementary to the existing cognitive system (or when few contradictory comparisons result), then long-term attitude or behavior change is likely to occur. If, however, an incoming message stimulates the generation of negative arguments, not only will immediate changes in the cognitive system be unlikely, but resistance to subsequent persuasive appeals will be greater. In short, able and motivated participants will tend to process messages through a central route (what we have called the reality dimension), and the resulting change or resistance to change will be more enduring.

On the other hand, receivers who lack either the ability or motivation to process messages via the central (or reality) route will process incoming messages via a *peripheral route*. Message processing via the peripheral route places greater emphasis on such variables as the setting, mode of presentation, or attributions made about the source. (These variables parallel what we have described more broadly as the goal, arousal, and relational dimensions of the cognitive system.) In short, the peripheral route relies heavily on persuasive cues present in the immediate situation. Accordingly, Petty and Cacioppo predict that changes in the cognitive system and behavior achieved through this peripheral route will be less enduring or temporary than those achieved via the central route.

It is important to note the significance of involvement in this explanation of change. Thinking is hard work. Although ability is also important, it is the person who cares about the issue who will expend the effort necessary to critically evaluate the message and generate arguments which either support or refute it. The harder the person works at thinking, the greater will be the change or resistance to change and the longer it will endure.

/ Correlates of change

Over the past forty years, a great deal of research has been conducted on variables related to persuasion. Much of this research was done at Yale University during the 1950s.[4] Since then, many fine studies following the same tradition have been conducted at other locations. For the most part, these studies were done in controlled laboratory settings and used college students as subjects, which greatly limits the usefulness of the findings in creating generalizations. They were also based on a very transmissional model of communication which separated source, message, channel, and receiver variables. Thus, these findings do not fully reveal the transactional nature of the persuasion process.

However, several interesting and useful findings have emerged from this body of work. We do not believe that these findings are universal—in fact, they may apply only to some persuasion in certain situations. The results are, however, a starting place to identify some of the correlates of change. Our purpose in this section, then, is not to enumerate "facts" about persuasion but to identify potential variables related to persuasion.[5]

/ Source correlates. One of the most studied variables of persuasion is source *credibility* or *believability*. Source credibility, which is basically trust, consists of a variety of dimensions that seem to change from situation to situation, depending upon the interpretation rules of other communicators. Nevertheless, credibility, once established, is powerful in effecting attitude change. Although individuals' comprehension and recall of the content of a speech do not seem to be affected much by credibility, the degree to which they accept the message often is. On the other hand, many people seem to forget the source of a message over long periods of time, thereby minimizing credibility effects. At least in some situations, strong arguments seem to have a longer-lasting effect on persuasion than does source credibility alone.

Attractiveness also seems to affect persuasion. The basis of attraction is itself an interesting and complex question. We discuss some of the reasons why individuals are attracted to one another in Chapters 3 and 5. At this point it is important to know that attractiveness through similarity or because of physical attractiveness can boost one's persuasiveness.

/ Message correlates. Message variables are also important in persuasion. Some of the correlates established in research studies are:

1. Comprehension of message content paves the way for, but by no means guarantees, attitude change.

2. Some repetition of the message can increase attitude change, although too much repetition can reduce it.

3. Two-sided messages may have more effect than one-sided messages among individuals who disagree with you, but one-sided messages may have greater influence on individuals who are already on your side. For long-term effects, two-sided messages may be better.

4. Evidence can be important in a message, especially if the audience is unfamiliar with the topic or if the source does not initially have high credibility.

5. Moderate levels of an appeal to fear are more effective than low or high levels; the ultimate effect, however, may depend more upon what the receiver does with the information than with any intrinsic qualities of the appeal itself.

/ Channel correlates. Research on persuasion has focused on two elements of channel: distraction or noise and medium. Briefly, although one's comprehension may be disturbed by distractions, attitude change has actually been observed to increase in the face of channel noise. In general, studies support the idea that television, combining visual and auditory stimuli, is more persuasive than radio and that printed sources may be the least persuasive of all.

/ Receiver correlates: The persuasibility problem.   Finally, a number of receiver-oriented variables have also been studied, but with less clear results. For the most part, these studies have centered on correlates of persuasibility. Although the findings of these studies have not been clear, they have serious implications for how people interpret and act on information. We will discuss the physical and psychological persuasibility variables of sex, age, intelligence, self-esteem, extremism, and dogmatism and authoritarianism. These correlates of change represent general trends, and exceptional cases can readily be found which vary with the uniqueness of each persuasion transaction.

Age.   Of all the variables related to persuasibility, age seems to be the most straightforward. Studies have found age to be negatively related to persuasion. Whether "sadder but wiser" or "set in your ways," the older you become, generally the less susceptible you become to change. People and societies who shield their children from what they consider antisocial behavior and carefully educate them about the vicissitudes of life recognize the vulnerability of young people to persuasive appeals.

Ability factors.   Another way that people sometimes vary in their persuasibility is in ability factors such as intelligence, education level, and knowledge of subject. In general, these factors have a complicated relationship to change. That is, a person who is unintelligent or poorly educated or uninformed on a topic will not function well in the reception of messages and thus will be hindered in their persuasibility. Either they will not expose themselves to messages counter to their attitudes and behavior or, once exposed, they will not understand them as well as their brighter or better-informed counterparts. On the other hand, brighter or better-informed people should be more critical of counter-attitudinal messages and therefore resistant to change. However, those who are critical, due to their knowledge and intelligence, tend to expose themselves to a greater number of controversial messages, thereby making themselves more vulnerable to persuasive appeals.

This relationship between ability and persuasibility is further complicated when the complexity of the message is varied. Intelligent, well-informed listeners tend to respond better to well-reasoned and -supported messages, while less intelligent and informed listeners respond more readily to simpler messages. Numerous psychological studies, as well as "man on the street" media interviews, testify to the relatively low level of information and social awareness of the general populace, making the equally simplistic level of media advertisements and political campaigns appropriate for the general audience transaction.

A final ability factor was identified by Janis and Field[6] and qualified by Elms.[7] Janis and Field found that an ability to fantasize or imagine things that might happen to you in the future was positively related to attitude change. Elms maintains that the ability to fantasize empathetically, or to visualize oneself in another person's situation, makes a person more persuasible. This interesting phenomenon will be discussed in greater detail when we discuss role-taking.

Self-esteem. *Self-esteem* can be defined as the positive or negative self evaluation of one's personal characteristics. Early studies tended to find an inverse relationship between self-esteem and attitude change.[8] However, later studies revealed a curvilinear relationship between the two. That is, people with extremely low self-esteem tend to protect what little ego they have by blocking out counter-attitudinal messages, while people with very high self-esteem are so self-satisfied they see no need to change. People with moderate self-esteem, therefore, seem to be the most open to the effects of persuasive messages.

Aggressiveness/hostility. Aggressiveness or hostility can manifest itself as a somewhat general long-term phenomenon, or it can be induced temporarily through frustrating experiences. In either case it is often inversely related to change or persuasibility.[9] We all know that approaching the boss for a raise when he or she is having a bad day is not wise. On the other hand, if the message is particularly aggressive or hostile, advocating violent or punitive acts, hostile listeners are more likely to respond favorably than non-aggressive listeners.

Dogmatism and authoritarianism. Although authoritarianism and dogmatism are not synonymous, they share similar characteristics. Both tend to render a person generally more resistant to change. Although it would be a mistake to type a person as dogmatic in all realms of life, individuals sometimes interpret events in ways that can usefully be called dogmatic. Adorno and his associates have summarized such interpretations thusly:

1. *Conventionalism:* Rigid adherence to conventional, middle-class values.
2. *Authoritarian submission:* Submissive, uncritical attitude toward idealized moral authorities of the in-group.
3. *Authoritarian aggression:* Tendency to watch for and condemn, reject, and punish people who violate conventional values.
4. *Anti-introspection:* Opposition to the subjective, the imaginative, the tender-minded.
5. *Superstition:* The belief in mystical determinants of an individual's fate.
6. *Stereotype:* The tendency to think in rigid categories.
7. *Power and "toughness":* Preoccupation with the dominance-submission, strong-weak, leader-follower dimensions; identification with power figures; overemphasis upon conventionalized attributes of the ego; exaggerated assertion of strength and toughness.
8. *Destructiveness and cynicism:* Generalized hostility, vilification of the human.
9. *Projectivity:* The disposition to believe that wild and dangerous activities go on in the world; the projection outward of unconscious emotional impulses.
10. *Sex:* Exaggerated concern with sexual goings-on.[10]

Examination of the above conceptual system reveals some broader commonalities. In addition to a submissive attitude toward authority and dominance of those lower on the "pecking order," there seems to be a rigidity in thinking; a two-valued, "either-or" way of perceiving the world; an intolerance of people or ideas who are different; and an inability to express one's own impulses. Interestingly, although the foregoing tendencies make the individual generally more resistant to change, the same attributes can also make him or her more susceptible to persuasive appeals offered by the "right" authority.

Extremism.[11]   An *extremist* is typically a person whose attitudes fall on the far left or far right of a spectrum of views on a given topic. Extremists tend to interpret relevant events dogmatically. Besides being generally resistant to change, they have a "two-valued" orientation. That is, they perceive very little middle ground on an issue ("You're either for me or against me"). Although some individuals tend toward extremism on many issues, such is not always the case; extremism is best viewed on an issue-by-issue basis.

Sex.   Sex is one of the most studied and most confusing variables related to persuasibility.[12] Early studies found a strong positive relationship between sex and persuasibility. Women, at least in American society, seemed more persuasible than men. The rebirth of the women's liberation movement, however, prompted some probing questions. At the very least, it is argued, differences in persuasibility result from cultural expectations, not biological gender. Further, the sex variable could be confounded by other non-sex-related variables such as self-esteem. Finally, most of the early experimentation was conducted by men who used topics which would be more salient to men. Since it is commonly acknowledged that people are less susceptible to change on topics they care about, women might appear to be more persuasible on the basis of topic selection alone. It remains to be seen whether equal expectations and opportunities, enhanced self-esteem of females, more female experimenters, and topics which are more salient to females will eliminate or even reverse the generalization that men are less persuasible than women.

With a few exceptions, most personality variables have a curvilinear relationship to attitude and behavior change. William McGuire posits a perceptive explanation for this. He suggests a "compensatory assumption" which argues that personality characteristics such as self-esteem, intelligence, and knowledge or education have opposite and compensating effects during the reception and yielding phases of persuasive communication. On the one hand, high levels of these characteristics should make one resistant to change during the yielding phase. Conversely, extremely low levels of these variables would make a person ineffective during the reception phase, also resulting in low levels of change. Persons who have moderate self-esteem, intelligence, or knowledge would process more messages than those with extremely low levels of these characteristics. Yet, the moderates would not be as resistant to change as those with extremely high levels, leaving them the most susceptible to changes of attitude or behavior. In general, research has confirmed the curvilinear relationship between most personality variables and persuasibility.

/ Learning and Change

An important group of explanations of how people's cognitive systems change began from the assumption that attitude acquisition and change is a learning process.

/ Old paradigm

The oldest model of learning, and hence of persuasive communication, is a somewhat traditional linear model which posited a response (change) which could be connected either causally or correlationally to a stimulus, with the *organism* (or person) processing a message as the generative force for change. In model form, this process is the familiar S→O→R. The model was later refined by Doob[13] to allow for the response to be internal (attitude) and also for factors within the organism (attitudes, or what we have broadened to include the cognitive system) to themselves provide a stimulus for change. With the placing of symbols for internal response (R) and stimuli within the self (S) around the symbol for organism (O), Doob's model then looked like this:

$$S \rightarrow_R O_S \rightarrow R$$

Hovland and his colleagues at Yale further posited that as people dealt with messages in the learning process they went through a chain of learning responses. First, a person's attention must be directed to a persuasive message. Second, the person must comprehend the messages. Third, a person must believe or yield to the message (accept the message). Fourth, a person must remember or retain the message. Finally, the person must *act* in compliance with the message.

The Yale group focused their efforts almost exclusively on the yielding or accepting process which focused the study of persuasion on attitude change. Later, William McGuire[14] combined the five stages into a two-stage model which included reception (attention plus comprehension) and yielding (acceptance, retention, and action).

Viewed from this stimulus-response learning model, changes in the cognitive system can happen in essentially three ways: through exposure, association, and reinforcement. The first way one's cognitive system is changed by learning is through simple *exposure* to data, beliefs, or values. Research has demonstrated that often as people are exposed to a concept or even to an iso-

/ **One way changes in the cognitive system—and,
consequently, in behavior—occur is through
exposure to data, beliefs, or values.**

lated symbol, they come to like it. As children we are exposed by our parents to
concepts and values which eventually become our own and tend to remain our
own until we are exposed to other concepts and symbols.

In the display cases of the schools and *kibbutzim* of Israel one does not find
athletic trophies, but rather pictures of the young people who have died in the
recent wars with Arab countries. This continual honoring of the war dead may
create in the Israeli youth a cognitive system different than that of the teenagers
in other cultures.

A second way learning affects formation and change in the cognitive system
is by association. *Association* is the process of linking a perception or concept
with another perception or concept until ultimately one substitutes for another.
Thus, people may learn to associate certain tunes with related feelings, certain
word usage with education, or certain material possessions with socio-economic status. Although associations provide helpful shortcuts for processing
new perceptions, they can also lead to stereotyping and hasty conclusions.

Learning also affects the cognitive system through reinforcement. Reinforcement occurs when people find certain concepts or symbols satisfying or rewarding on the one hand, or unsatisfying or painful on the other. In general, if people find behaviors or concepts satisfying or rewarding, those behaviors tend to be repeated and the concepts strengthened within the cognitive system. If concepts or behaviors are not rewarding, they tend to be extinguished like a fire, or at least weakened.

/ New paradigm: Social learning

Both the foregoing learning approach in the Yale tradition and the information integration approach view the process of persuasion in a fairly deterministic way, with the receiver (or persuadee) a relatively passive agent. The social learning approach, developed by Albert Bandura,[15] looks at the receiver as a more active participant in the information-processing–persuasion process.

Bandura emphasizes the dynamic interactional nature of persuasion, while repudiating the transmissional, manipulative perspective, when he claims, "man is neither driven by inner forces nor buffeted helplessly by environmental influences."[16] This theory represents a major epistemological shift from emphasis on sources and messages to how an individual actively construes and interprets new information.

With its emphasis on internal interpretations rather than external stimuli, social learning emphasizes humans' ability to have insightful and foresightful behavior as well as their ability of self-regulation. Just as Rokeach views values as standards of conduct or life's goals, Bandura claims that people establish goals or standards for themselves. They then intentionally behave in such a way as to achieve those goals or live by those standards. The achievement of the goals or of living by such standards is perceived as rewarding, while failure to do so is perceived as unrewarding. Finally, people alter their behavior in order to better achieve the goals or standards, or perhaps alter the goals and standards in their cognitive system to make them more achievable or rewarding. Note how Olympic athletes, Amway salespersons, or high-achieving students set goals for themselves, many early in life. If either of us were to shoot a seventy-nine on a championship golf course, we would be rewarded to the point of elation and would head happily for the nineteenth hole. If Jack Nicklaus shot the same score, he would head for the practice tee.

According to the social learning approach, new information and behaviors can be acquired in three essential ways: through direct, personal *experience;* by imagining oneself in a given situation through *role-playing;* and by observing the behavior of others, or *modeling.* Once goals or standards of behavior in the form of values have been established, they not only become internal regulators of behavior, but are also significantly difficult to change.

Let us examine four practical models of self-persuasion based upon social learning—desensitization, behavior modification, role-playing, and modeling.[17] The first two models of change which follow from social learning do so as a result of people learning from direct experience. *Desensitization* results in changes in the cognitive system (usually arousal) on the basis of extended, incremental *exposure* to familiar objects, individuals, or situations. For example, a fear of heights may be desensitized by repeated exposure at gradually increased heights; similarly, anxiety or revulsion over firearms, explosives, or killing can be desensitized during an Army boot camp.

The greatest amount of research on desensitization has been conducted on fear in general and communication anxiety in particular. Paul compared desensitization with insight (or explanation), attention-placebo, and a control group in a public speaking context. The groups which received a placebo and an explanation of the stage-fright process as well as the desensitization condition reported less fear than the control group, while the desensitization group demonstrated significantly less actual arousal on physiological measures.[18]

Traditional public speaking teachers (as well as participants in toastmasters' clubs and Dale Carnegie courses) for years have combined desensitization with insight in order to overcome stage fright. They begin by explaining the process. Then students stand before the group for a series of progressively more difficult speaking experiences. First comes a simple self-introduction, then a short one-point speech. A speech or two to inform, perhaps with a visual aid for a "crutch," follows; finally, the more difficult and longer speeches to persuade are delivered. Except in cases of extreme anxiety, desensitization not only reduces anxiety in the public speaking situation, but many students report reduced communication anxiety and increased self-esteem in other situations as well.

A second social learning model of change derived from direct exposure is *behavior modification*. Contrary to the common misconception that behavior modification refers to anything that modifies behavior, this term refers to a very specific phenomenon. Earlier we said that social learning depends upon the individual's perceiving certain aspects of the environment as rewarding or punishing. Behavior modification is the process whereby one set of behaviors is substituted for another by altering (and ultimately internalizing) a new system of rewards and punishments. This is usually accomplished by creating some new, temporary rewards which can subsequently be withdrawn when the new behavior itself becomes rewarding. We once heard of a woman who, desiring to lose weight, put a twenty-pound chunk of pork fat in the refrigerator. Every week or so, after losing a few pounds, she would cut off a piece and throw it away. Hers was a very effective—and very visual—self-reinforcement system.

Although behavior modification has been used extensively on self-help programs, from quitting smoking to losing weight, perhaps its most extensive use has been with children. A teacher may offer children candy or money for reading so many pages of literature or for correctly solving so many math problems. It is assumed (or at least hoped) that in the process the children will not only learn the material or master the skill but internalize a self-reinforcing love of learning as well.

It may seem easy to substitute new rewards or punishments for the old ones, but discovering what is rewarding or punishing to people can be extremely difficult. A psychologist once advised mothers whose children exhibited behavioral problems to set an alarm clock to ring every half hour. When the alarm went off, they were to find their children and give them some love and attention. The psychologist wisely surmised that some parents pay attention to their children only when they are misbehaving and punish them. Presumably the children find the attention of their parents, even in the form of punishment, rewarding. Thus, after they are rewarded several times for playing quietly, the act of playing quietly becomes a self-rewarding experience. By making heretofore rewarding (though unwanted) behaviors unrewarding and by making new (and frequently contradictory) behaviors rewarding, strong systems of self-reinforcement can be created by the process of persuasive communication.

Role-playing, another social learning model of change, involves behaving "as if" you were in some situation. It is based on the ability of being able to fantasize or picture yourself in an imaginary situation.[19] A technique developed in the late 1940s and early 1950s by psychotherapists, called *psychodrama,* has been widely used by both therapists and educators to change the behavior of their patients and students.

Later, experimenters found that role-playing works best when the "as-if" situation most closely approximates the possible reality and is relevant to the role-player's personal well-being (that is, role-playing situations involving lung cancer, dental caries, and so on) or to self-established standards of behavior (values). It was further found that, given relevant situations, the more involved the role-player becomes, in the form of greater verbalization or imagination, the greater the change in the role-player. Finally, taken together, these studies indicate that role-playing results in more enduring, long-term change than does passive or less-involved listening.[20]

It is interesting how the research on role-playing correlates with much intuitive wisdom. When asked "How do I learn to love?" the philosopher-anthropologist Ashley Montague responded, "Act as if you are in love."[21] Further, most people role-play mentally in everyday life situations.

The social learning model of change for which Bandura is best known is *modeling.* Modeling takes place when a person observes the behavior of a valued other person, imitates that behavior, and finds the behavior more rewarding than punishing. This is how children learn most of their early behaviors, skills, beliefs, and values. How often have you seen a child who walked, talked, or exhibited some other mannerism peculiar to the child's parents? Notice how young gymnasts or ice-skaters perform with apparent ease movements which not so long ago were considered impossible or were the private domain of a few professionals.

Several factors affect the way people change through modeling. As the foregoing discussion suggests, modeling is affected by the degree to which a person finds the modeled behavior easy and rewarding. In addition, people tend to be influenced more by models with whom they can identify (for example, those with similar attitudes or of the same sex). Groups such as ethnic minorities or women are striving to establish role-models in all vocations in order to provide a point of identification for young people in those groups.

Other factors which enhance modeling are the status and competence of the models. Jabusch and Bohn and Jabusch found that superior models could raise the competence of students in public speaking and the use of visual aids.[22]

It is also important that the models behave consistently for maximum influence. Psychologists often urge parents and teachers to be consistent in their behavior in order not to confuse the children they influence. Finally, people tend to be more influenced by multiple models, especially if the individual models lack status. Observing repeated success by several people can enhance a person's modeling behavior.

In evaluating social learning, it is important to note the strong emphasis on the active involvement of the participants as they generate their own arguments and interpretations and internalize what are considered to be rewards, punishments, and standards of behavior. Further, the social learning approach encompasses not only attitude change but direct behavior change with a strong emphasis on those goals and standards Rokeach identified as values. Finally, a social learning explanation of change provides not only for people influencing other people without their consent or awareness, but also the voluntary and cooperative change seen so commonly in self-improvement programs.

/ Perception/Reception Theories

In the foregoing learning explanations of persuasion, the emphasis was on the *yielding* phase of the persuasive process. We now turn to explanations which emphasize the *reception* or perception phase. These explanations are much like information integration theory in that they focus on how people perceive new information and integrate it into their cognitive system. Perception theories are similar to social learning in that they focus on the active involvement of listeners in the process of perceiving and processing persuasive messages. We will discuss social judgment-involvement and attribution.

/ Social judgment-involvement theories

A social judgment explanation of change focuses on the judgment people make as they compare the position taken by other people on a spectrum of views on a topic to their own position on that issue. This judgment involves a person's perception of the new position, their assessment of their own position, and a comparison of the two.

The position on the spectrum of views with which an individual most closely associates is called the *anchor.* A person's anchor will determine to some degree how he or she perceives the position of other people. For instance, President Reagan is criticized by ultra-conservative groups as being too moderate or even liberal, while liberal groups or individuals consider him too conservative, and an ultra-liberal might see him as downright reactionary. Each group has a different anchor along the spectrum of views on political ideology, thus creating these widely divergent perceptions of the President.

A major contribution to the understanding of persuasion by social judgment research is that an attitude can best be represented by a range of more or less acceptable positions (or beliefs) on a spectrum rather than a single point or position. Sherif, Sherif, and Nebergall call these ranges of attitudes *latitudes* of acceptance, rejection, and noncommitment.[23]

The latitude of acceptance includes a person's anchor position as well as a spectrum of encompassing attitudes and beliefs which the person considers acceptable or can tolerate. Hence, while you may prefer that the company you keep not consume alcoholic beverages, you will accept their behavior so long as they don't consume so much that they become obnoxious (and even the term *obnoxious* represents a spectrum of behaviors which is different for different people).

The latitude of rejection is the range of beliefs, attitudes, and values which a person finds unacceptable under any circumstances. Thus a parent will reprimand one of his children for repeating an ethnic joke which had been told at school. Although some people might accept such a story in private and reject it in public, that parent found ethnic slurs unacceptable under any circumstances.

The latitude of noncommitment is the range of attitudes, beliefs, or values about which a person is undecided. Perhaps from ignorance or apathy, or because they have simply not made up their mind, some people may assume a position of noncommitment.

In diagram form, these attitudes would look like this for a moderate on a given issue:

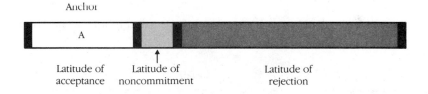

The importance of the social judgment explanation of change is the way it affects—even distorts—one's perception and cognitive system. As we pointed out earlier, your anchor can influence where you place incoming information on the spectrum. Furthermore, people tend to perceive finer distinctions among stimuli which are close to their anchor and much more gross distinctions farther from their anchor. A person who appreciates fine wine may discriminate not only the vintner and the grape, but also the year the wine was produced; to a casual imbiber, on the other hand, there are two kinds of wine, red and white.

The social judgment process affects not only our perceptions, but reorganizes our cognitive system as well. If a new piece of information is judged to fall within our latitude of acceptance, it is quickly assimilated into our belief structure. Furthermore, we usually judge it to be closer to our anchor than another observer might judge it to be.

If the new information is judged to fall within our latitude of rejection, it is not assimilated into our belief structure. Furthermore, we will perceive it to be further from our anchor than may actually be the case. This contrast phenomenon can lead to a reinforcement of one's original position, what theorists have called the *boomerang* effect.

Perhaps the major concept in the social judgment approach is that of ego-involvement. Ego-involvement is the degree to which we consider an issue close to the center of our being—how important it is to our self-image. There is an interesting relationship between one's ego-involvement with an issue and the latitudes of attitudes. With an increase in ego-involvement, the latitude of noncommitment decreases while the latitude of rejection increases and the latitude of acceptance remains basically the same. This increase in the latitude of rejection, of course, increases resistance to change and heightens the assimilation and contrast effect.

Thus, in diagram form, the latitude of a highly ego-involved extremist might look like this:

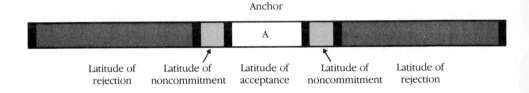

The latitude of a highly ego-involved moderate might look like this:

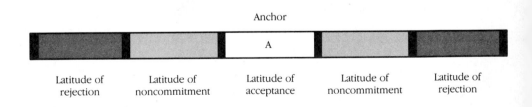

Taken together, the various assumptions of the social judgment explanation of change lead to a prediction of an inverted-U relationship between the discrepancy of the new information from the anchor and attitude change. (See Figure 4.1.) The closer the new information is to the anchor, the more easily it is assimilated but the less possibility there is for change. If, however, the new

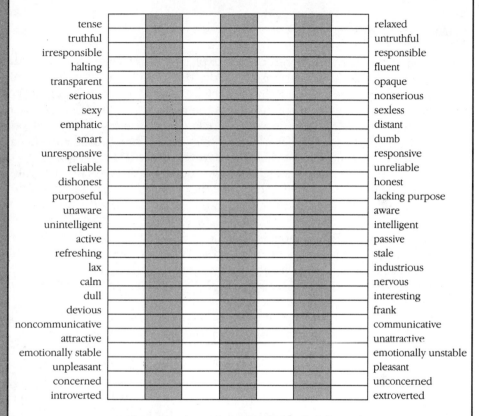

Communication Research and Training Laboratory

Employee Interview Rating   Form A

tense							relaxed
truthful							untruthful
irresponsible							responsible
halting							fluent
transparent							opaque
serious							nonserious
sexy							sexless
emphatic							distant
smart							dumb
unresponsive							responsive
reliable							unreliable
dishonest							honest
purposeful							lacking purpose
unaware							aware
unintelligent							intelligent
active							passive
refreshing							stale
lax							industrious
calm							nervous
dull							interesting
devious							frank
noncommunicative							communicative
attractive							unattractive
emotionally stable							emotionally unstable
unpleasant							pleasant
concerned							unconcerned
introverted							extroverted

As a final rating, how employable do you find the candidate? (Place an "X" in the most preferred spot.)

_____ I would definitely employ.

_____ I would probably employ, but I need more information.

_____ The data I have on the candidate seems insufficient for a decision.

_____ I doubt I would employ, but I am still open.

_____ I definitely would not employ.

/ FIGURE 4.1 Semantic Differential Scale

information is so far from the anchor that it is perceived to be within the latitude of rejection, it has either no effect on the cognitive system or perhaps creates a boomerang effect. The greatest change would occur either on the edge of the latitude of acceptance or within the latitude of noncommitment.

/ Attribution theories

Another class of perception-reception explanations of change have been termed *attribution theories.* As early as 1958, Fritz Heider and, later, Harold Kelly maintained that people behave as "naive social scientists" in an attempt to diagnose the behavior of other people as well as themselves.[24] On the basis of observed behavior, people attribute to other people (or themselves) certain intentions, motives, beliefs, or attitudes which serve to explain or rationalize the behavior.

These attributions can be either *situational* or *dispositional.* Situational attributions rationalize people's behavior on the basis of contextual "causes" somewhat beyond a person's power to control. For example, if a car with an out-of-state license cuts in front of you, you may say to yourself, "He couldn't be expected to know in advance he was in an 'exit only' lane."

Dispositional attributions explain people's behavior on the basis of internal, controllable predispositions to respond, or "reasons," such as beliefs, attitudes, or motives. Thus if a car with an in-state license and the name of a local dealership cuts in front of you, you may honk your horn and mutter to yourself, "Some people think they own the road!"

As we pointed out in Chapter 3, dispositional "reasons" which we attribute to other people can affect the interpersonal bonds, which in turn affect our mutual influence. Attributions of either favorable or unfavorable intent can influence the bonds of trust among people. Furthermore, attributions of beliefs and attitudes can affect people's perception of similarity or dissimilarity.

One of the most significant contributions of the attribution approach to an understanding of the persuasion process is in the area of self-attribution—that is, in the way people attribute to themselves certain beliefs, attitudes, emotions, or motives on the basis of what is going on around them and their response to the situation.

The model of self-attribution assumes, first, that a person is induced to act or behave in a particular way. Secondly, the person infers that his behavior is related to dispositional factors and changes elements in his or her cognitive system to reflect the behavior.

Changes in the cognitive system are affected by several factors:

1. The less a person is able to rationalize his or her behavior on the basis of situational factors, the more change will occur in the cognitive system. The less you can say "I had to do it; I had no choice," the more you must say, "Did I do that? I must believe it!"

2. If our actions produce desirable consequences, more change will occur in our cognitive system. This results from the common tendency to hold others accountable for their actions while blaming our own discrepant behavior on the situation. If the outcome is favorable, we are more likely to take the credit, but then our cognitive system will change to be compatible with the behavior.

3. The likelihood of changing the cognitive system increases with several behaviors in a variety of contexts. Both the repetition and the change in context makes it less possible to pass the behavior off as unusual or situational.

4. Changes in the cognitive system, based on dispositional self-attributions, are increased if contextual cues suggest that our behavior is consistent with our beliefs and if more time has elapsed between the behavior and the assessment of attitude change.

Three techniques of self-persuasion have been well-explained by attribution.[25] The first is what has been called the *"foot-in-the-door" phenomenon*. For example, suppose you agreed to help a friend or relative purchase an item you believed would be inexpensive. Later you find the cost is considerably greater than was represented to you. Finally, you find yourself paying the entire bill. If you had known the full extent of your commitment in the beginning, you probably would have said *no*. Self-attribution theory maintains that compliance with a small initial request results in a change in your cognitive system, which then leaves you open to subsequent escalating requests and commensurate changes in your cognitive system.

Salespersons frequently use a variation of the "foot-in-the-door" phenomenon called the "yes-response." They begin by getting the client to say "yes" to an issue of certain agreement. Gradually they move the client toward the desired conclusion by posing larger or slightly more controversial issues, while always eliciting a "yes" response to the question, "Doesn't that make sense to you?" When the final proposition or behavior is requested (that is, the sale), the client finds it difficult to say "no" because of each succeeding "yes," and the sale is made.

For the "foot-in-the-door" technique to work most successfully, each new escalating appeal must be great enough to effect some change or forward movement, while not being too great to inhibit or preclude acceptance by the other person. Furthermore, the "foot-in-the-door" technique seems to work best with people who are initially noncommitted or are slightly favorable to the source or the cause. As in all attribution techniques, results are greater if the new behavior cannot be rationalized by external inducements or other situational factors.

Proattitudinal advocacy is a second technique of self-persuasion which is well-explained by attribution. *Proattitudinal advocacy* is defined as advocating publicly any argument or attitude which falls within a person's attitude of acceptance, but which is discrepant from one's anchor. This public, slightly discrepant (though acceptable) behavior presumably serves to strengthen a person's attitude position, make action more likely, and make the person more resistant to change.

Several factors promote the effectiveness of proattitudinal advocacy. First, proattitudinal advocacy is more effective in self-persuasion when the advocate chooses freely to perform the act with a minimum of external rewards. As with the "foot-in-the-door" technique, the absence of external rewards or punishments precludes the possibility of the advocate claiming, "I had to say it."

Second, proattitudinal advocacy is more effective when the consequences of the advocacy are perceived to be desirable. Presumably our need to view ourselves as a good person interacts with our need for consistency.

Other factors which enhance the effectiveness of proattitudinal advocacy as a self-persuader have to do with the response of the audience. A person's advocacy will have increased effect on the advocate's cognitive system if the listener appears to favor the advocated position, indicates he or she believes the advocate is sincere, and if the advocacy is skillfully performed.

Much has been said about the impact of testimonials on audiences at worship services, sales-training meetings, or patriotic rallies. What attribution theory tells us is that testimonials, in whatever context, may have as much or more influence on the person *giving* the testimonial than on the other listeners.

A third model of self-influence which follows from attribution is a two-stage model of *emotional response*. In Chapter 3 we described *emotion* as a level of arousal in people in response to stimuli related to fear, anger, euphoria, and so on. We further maintained that emotion has both a cognitive and an affective dimension.

Building on a two-factor model of emotional arousal originated by James, Schlachter, and Singer[26] have advocated that, when people experience emotional arousal for which there is no clearly identifiable internal cause, they look for environmental cues—primarily the responses of other people—to explain and label the arousal. Thus, if we feel aroused for no obvious internal reason and we observe people around us looking sad, we label our emotional state as sadness.

In an impressive experiment, Schlachter and Singer induced physiological arousal in subjects with injections of the drug epinephrine. Some of the aroused subjects were informed of the effects of the drug while others were not. As predicted, those who were ignorant as to the cause of their arousal were more affected by the "emotional" behaviors of confederates of the experimenters than were the subjects who knew their arousal was due to the drug.[27]

In more recent studies of emotional responses, Maslach, Marshall, and Zimbardo have found that people can derive their attributions of emotion from past experience as well as from immediate environmental cues. The researchers also found that emotional self-attributions tend to be biased toward negative environmental cues, chiefly anxiety.[28]

The two-factor model of emotional self-attribution can explain a great deal about our emotional responses, especially such phenomena as mass hysteria, emotional responses to public speeches, and the like.

/ Tension-Reduction Theories

Another group of explanations of change in the cognitive system or behavior of people are the *tension-reduction* theories. Perhaps you have seen the punching bag clowns which are weighted at the base so that no matter how you hit or push them, they always bounce back to a state of equilibrium in an upright position. Tension-reduction theories posit that, like the clown, people endeavor to maintain a state of equilibrium within their cognitive system and between the elements of their cognitive system and their behavior.

More specifically, tension-reduction theories assume that (1) people behave in a basically rational manner, (2) psychological imbalance or disequilibrium produces tension within the individual, (3) this tension is unpleasant or uncomfortable, hence (4) people are motivated to reduce the tension. Tension can be reduced, of course, by altering relevant elements of the cognitive system or overt behavior which is not congruent with the cognitive system.

/ Drive-motive theory

In its earliest form, the drive-motive explanation of change stressed the effect of the tension produced by the deprivation of physiological needs (or drives) such as food, shelter, or sex on attitude and behavior change. Maslow extended this theoretical line of reasoning when he suggested that tension and subsequent changes in attitude and behavior resulted not only from deprivation of physiological needs but also from insufficient fulfillment of human needs for safety, love or belongingness, self-esteem, self-actualization, and aesthetic expression.

The drive-motive theory can be extended to include any tension resulting in a degression from optimum levels of arousal within the cognitive system discussed in Chapter 3. This would include not only physiological drives and Maslow's hierarchy of needs, but also departures from what a person perceives as a comfortable level of emotional arousal.

Different people can tolerate different levels of emotional arousal. Some people manage their lives so that they can stay "mellow." They avoid people and situations which create controversy or stress. They become uncomfortable when they have many problems to solve or numerous demands on their time and attention. The level of arousal they find comfortable is relatively low, and they will change their attitudes and behavior to stay at that level.

Other people thrive on arousal. They are constantly on the move, seeking out new thrills, taking chances, and reveling in activities. After a few days of vacation, they begin to miss the stimulation of the workplace. They change their cognitive system and behavior to restore their level of arousal to an optimum which is comfortable for them.

The discomfort felt when an individual moves from an optimum level of arousal can affect that individual in opposite ways at different times. You can have too *many* changes in your life—positive or negative. You may receive a promotion, move to a new home, and begin a new relationship. You may become so "hyped" that you need to sit in a hot tub or take sedatives. If the discomfort becomes too great, you may make some decisions to simplify your life.

At another time, you may suffer from inadequate arousal. You may find yourself stuck in an all-too-familiar environment with nothing to do but stare at the wall. You soon begin to seek out new company, organize a social group, start playing bridge, or begin a new hobby.

We know an elderly woman who lived in an apartment which opened on a dark courtyard, far away from the street. It was a nice, quiet place to live—too quiet. Her aches and pains were numerous and her attitude fairly negative. She didn't get out much. After moving to a small but bright home on a busy street, her attitude became more positive and her aches and pains seemed less troublesome. She could be seen happily puttering around the yard, watching neighboring children at play. She even seemed to enjoy the sounds of the street traffic. The isolated apartment simply had provided an insufficient amount of sensory stimuli and arousal for that individual's physical and psychological comfort.

In summary, the drive-motive approach explains changes in people's cognitive system and behavior as attempts to reduce uncomfortable tension resulting from an imbalance in their system of drives, needs, or level of arousal.

/ Cognitive consistency theories

Another group of tension-reduction approaches explain attitude and behavior change as resulting from the need for consistency among cognitive elements other than needs or arousal. Thus, one might strive to balance discrepancies among beliefs, attitudes, and goals; among these elements and behavior; and among these elements and the trust, similarity, and attraction shared with other people.

/ Balance theory.
The first theorist to use the balance approach, Fritz Heider,[29] attempted to explain attitude change on the basis of discrepancies between an individual's cognitions about a particular issue or object and other individuals. For example, if you do not smoke and are irritated by the smoking of others, your cognitive system will be in balance if a particular individual you care about does not smoke. On the other hand, if that person smokes, you will be inclined to bring balance to your cognitive system by either growing to dislike the person or learning to tolerate cigarette smoke. These two conditions can be represented by the following triangles:

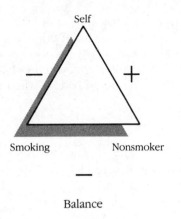

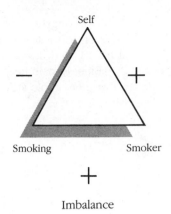

Several combinations of pluses and minuses are possible. In all, any odd number of minuses in any position on the triangle results in imbalance. Any even number of minuses, or no minus, will result in balance.

The example of smoking illustrates the major weakness in this simple balance approach—its "either-or" orientation. Rarely does imbalance occur on the basis of such simple discrepancies, and rarely would our attitudes or behaviors change in an all-or-nothing or completely positive or negative way.

A more useful notion is Theodore Newcomb's "strain toward symmetry."[30] According to Newcomb, more than one element of our cognitive system may change in varying degrees in order to restore balance or symmetry to the total cognitive system. Hence, to continue our example, we may grow to care somewhat less for our friend who smokes, grow to despise cigarette smoke somewhat less, and even learn to live with the reduced discrepancy.

Another balance approach to change has been proposed by Charles Osgood and Percy Tannenbaum[31] in what is called *congruity theory*. The congruity approach is designed to explain a variety of cases in which a concept (C) is linked with a source (S) by either negative or positive assertions. Listeners' evaluations of the source and the concept are quantified on a scale which ranges from strongly positive to strongly negative, with neutral or zero in the middle:

$$\text{bad} \quad -5 \quad -4 \quad -3 \quad -2 \quad -1 \quad 0 \quad +1 \quad +2 \quad +3 \quad +4 \quad +5 \quad \text{good}$$

Using again our example of a person we care about smoking cigarettes, a condition of imbalance would be represented by a strong preference for the person ($+5$) and a moderate dislike for cigarette smoke and the dangers it may pose for the person (-2). Osgood and Tannenbaum provide formulas for computing the degree to which our attitude toward the person would diminish and our attitude toward cigarette smoke might improve:

$$C \rightarrow \qquad\qquad\qquad \leftarrow S$$
$$\text{bad} \quad -5 \quad -4 \quad -3 \quad -2 \quad -1 \quad 0 \quad +1 \quad +2 \quad +3 \quad +4 \quad +5 \quad \text{good}$$

The congruity approach provides a method for analyzing not only the influence of opposites upon one another but their influence upon other relationships as well. For instance, if you dislike Fidel Castro (S) and he criticizes President Ronald Reagan (C), about whom you are lukewarm, you might adopt a more favorable attitude toward Reagan ("He can't be all bad if Castro hates him"):

$$\text{S} \qquad\qquad\qquad\qquad \text{C} \rightarrow$$
$$\text{bad} \quad -5 \quad -4 \quad -3 \quad -2 \quad -1 \quad 0 \quad +1 \quad +2 \quad +3 \quad +4 \quad +5 \text{ good}$$

Conversely, if someone you admire greatly, the Reverend Jerry Falwell (S), endorses Reagan (C), whom you like slightly, that endorsement should also enhance your feeling toward Reagan:

$$\qquad\qquad\qquad\qquad\qquad\qquad \text{C} \rightarrow \qquad \text{S}$$
$$\text{bad} \quad -5 \quad -4 \quad -3 \quad -2 \quad -1 \quad 0 \quad +1 \quad +2 \quad +3 \quad +4 \quad +5 \text{ good}$$

It is important to note that for negative statements, balance occurs at equal distances from zero, whereas for positive statements balance occurs with both S and C at the same point. For example, if former President Jimmy Carter endorsed Walter Mondale for the presidency and you liked both of them mildly, no change would be expected:

$$\qquad\qquad\qquad\qquad\qquad\qquad\qquad \text{CS}$$
$$\text{bad} \quad -5 \quad -4 \quad -3 \quad -2 \quad -1 \quad 0 \quad +1 \quad +2 \quad +3 \quad +4 \quad +5 \text{ good}$$

Similarly, if Vice-President George Bush, whom you disliked slightly, attacked Mondale, no change should occur:

$$\qquad\qquad\qquad \text{S} \qquad\qquad\qquad \text{C}$$
$$\text{bad} \quad -5 \quad -4 \quad -3 \quad -2 \quad -1 \quad 0 \quad +1 \quad +2 \quad +3 \quad +4 \quad +5 \text{ good}$$

Perhaps the major advantages of the congruity approach over previous balance theories are that it provides for a wider variety of situations, and especially that it provides for *degrees* of attitude change toward both disparate elements of a person's cognitive system as they "strain toward symmetry."

Despite these advantages, however, congruity theory has some shortcomings. Like previous approaches, congruity oversimplifies the change process by attempting to explain it on the basis of a person's attitude toward a source, a concept, or both. Surely there are more variables operating in the complex process than these three. Furthermore, it is frequently difficult to determine which element is the source and which the concept. In the foregoing examples, concepts look like sources—and indeed could be. These problems notwithstanding, Osgood and Tannenbaum's congruity theory, like Fishbein's information integration theory, has added increased sophistication in the conceptualization as well as the computation of attitude change from a balance perspective.

In addition, Osgood has made a major contribution to the measurement of attitude and attitude change. The semantic differential scales he developed have become one of the most widely used techniques for measuring attitudes in general and source credibility (interpersonal trust) in particular. Figure 4.2 gives a full set of semantic differential scales used in a study of source credibility.

/ Dissonance theory. Cognitive consistency approaches have viewed attitude and behavior change not only by looking at balance but also by stressing imbalance or dissonance. One of the most influential approaches stressing imbalance is Leon Festinger's theory of cognitive dissonance. Festinger claims that two elements of the cognitive system are unbalanced "if, considering these two alone, the obverse of one element would follow from the other"[32]—for instance, a person you despise performs an admirable act.

Like the theories of cognitive consistency which emphasize balance, dissonance theory assumes that people prefer balance in their cognitive system, find imbalance or dissonance uncomfortable, and seek ways to reduce the imbalance or dissonance. Further, the dissonance approach assumes that people avoid situations or new information that is likely to produce dissonance. Thus people are more likely to attend lectures, parties, or political rallies where they are likely to hear ideas with which they already agree.

An important aspect of dissonance theory is that it bears not only on discrepancies among attitudes toward the object, knowledge (beliefs), and interpersonal trust (attitudes toward other people), but also on discrepancies among these components of the cognitive system and *behavior.* A primary focus of dissonance theory is how the discrepancies develop following an important decision. Although Festinger includes highly probable beliefs (knowledge), he does

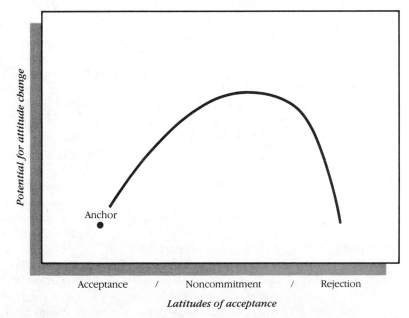

/ FIGURE 4.2 Relationship Between Discrepancy and Attitude Change

not mention highly ego-involving beliefs which we, with Rokeach, have called *values*.

The magnitude of the dissonance results from the salience of the discrepant elements and the number of elements of the cognitive system which are in a dissonant relationship. Dissonance, then, can result from a conflict between one attitude and another, as in the case of President Lincoln, who hated slavery and loved the Union even though the abolition of slavery threatened the Union. Dissonance can also result from a discrepancy between an attitude and a belief (whether "knowledge" or a value): "Although I believe cleanliness is next to godliness, I want my house to be 'lived in.'" Dissonance can result from a conflict between an attitude toward an issue and an attitude toward a person (interpersonal bond): "My best friend is voting for Proposition 13, which I oppose." Finally, dissonance can occur from a discrepancy between an element of our cognitive system (belief, attitude, or value) and our behavior: "Why do I do the thing I shouldn't do, and fail to do the thing I should do?"

Festinger suggests a person can deal with dissonance in several familiar ways. First, dissonance can be reduced by changing one or more elements in the cognitive system or by changing behavior. Having eaten a previously disliked food because you are famished, you conclude, "This food doesn't taste so bad after all." Or, finding yourself participating in a disliked activity (perhaps from peer pressure), you decide "I really don't want to be doing this," and you quit.

Second, a person can deal with dissonance by deciding the discrepant elements aren't as important as they were once thought to be. Thus, a person in an "odd couple" whose norms of cleanliness are highly discrepant from those of the partner might conclude, "My friend has so many fine qualities; cleanliness is really trivial."

Third, one who is facing dissonant cognitions might seek out information which is more consonant with the existing elements of the cognitive system. A person might seek new evidence that supports an existing attitude or seek confirmation from friends that a recent decision was a good one. One form of dissonance occurs after a person has made an important decision. This is referred to by those in business as "buyer's remorse." How often do you see people who have just purchased an automobile or have recently become engaged to be married pile up evidence of the wisdom of their purchase or seek the approval of friends and relatives of their choice of a spouse?

A fourth way of dealing with dissonance is to deny or distort the new information or attitude. When confronted with a damning accusation about a friend, a person might think "I know him too well. He would never do something like that." When confronted with a picture of earth rise, a person who believes the earth is flat might think, "It's trick photography."

One can also deal with dissonance by undermining the source. This can be accomplished either by discrediting the source ("Who would believe something *she* said?") or by attempting to convince the source that he or she is in error.

Finally, and of particular importance, a person can deal with dissonance by either ignoring it or living with it. Sooner or later everyone comes to the realization that life is not an uninterrupted series of consonant cognitions. Almost every person we know who does not smoke cigarettes has some friends and relatives who smoke, yet few have grown to like cigarette smoke or believe that it is good for your health or a trivial matter. Neither have they abandoned their friends or disowned their relatives. They simply live with the dissonance.

An interesting application of dissonance theory is the case of counter-attitudinal advocacy. Counter-attitudinal advocacy occurs when a person publicly argues a proposition which is in opposition to the advocate's cognitive system. Why would one do that? Sometimes he or she is under pressure from peers, parents, or a political party, or sometimes he or she is being coerced.

There are five factors that influence the extent to which counter-attitudinal advocacy results in changes in the cognitive system. As a general rule, these factors have to do with the degree to which a person can rationalize the discrepant behavior.

The first factor is *choice*. The less a person is coerced into performing the advocacy or the more choice he/she has to perform the act, the less the person will be able to excuse or rationalize the discrepancy and the more elements in the cognitive system will change in the direction of the advocacy.

The second factor is *justification* in the form of extraneous rewards. If a person is rewarded a great deal, say with money, he or she will be able to justify or rationalize the behavior without changing the attitude ("I did it for the money"). If the reward or payment is low, justification or rationalization will be difficult and the cognitive system will change more to come into alignment with the advocacy.

A third factor is *effort*. The more effort required, the less a person can rationalize the behavior and the more the cognitive system will change.

Fourth, if the *sponsor*—the person who induces the advocate to argue a position counter to his/her cognitive system—*is attractive,* the person who counter-advocates can rationalize, "I was charmed into it," and the cognitive system will not change as much as if the sponsor were not attractive.

Finally, counter-attitudinal advocacy is related to the perceived or anticipated *results of the advocacy.* If the person who is advocating something in which he or she does not believe anticipates an unfavorable outcome for the listener, the change in the advocate's cognitive system will be greater than if the anticipated outcome is favorable. Presumably, in the later case the advocate can rationalize, "I said something I didn't believe, but at least it helped someone." To summarize, if a person who is induced to advocate something he or she doesn't believe (1) perceives considerable choice, (2) expends great effort, (3) views the sponsor as unattractive, and (4) anticipates adverse effects on the receivers, the less reward or justification the counter-advocate receives, the less he/she can rationalize the discrepant behavior, and the more the cognitive system will change in favor of the counter-advocacy.

There is an interesting corollary to this generalization. What if the situation is somewhat less prejudicial to the advocate? For instance, what if the sponsor is attractive and the results are perceived as positive? Given a perception of choice, then the *more* reward or incentive that is provided, the greater the change in the cognitive system.

Although these results may seem contradictory at first, they are actually complementary in that they apply to somewhat different circumstances. Dissonance theory tends to explain the change in the cognitive system when an adverse situation precludes rationalization; incentive or greater reward explains the more favorable circumstance where rationalization of the discrepancy is possible.

/ Attitudes, beliefs, and values.[33]   One of the most recent and comprehensive explanations of change based upon congruity within the cognitive system has been advanced by Milton Rokeach.[34] His theory encompasses not only inconsistencies among beliefs, attitudes, and behavior, but discrepancies among values, needs, and various components of the relational dimension as well.

Rokeach conceives a well-organized system of beliefs, attitudes, and values much like that described in Chapter 3. This system not only guides behavior but, more importantly, supports the individual's self-regard.

Recall that *beliefs* are the numerous claims people make about themselves or the universe. Rokeach advances three hypotheses about the belief system. First, beliefs may vary in their degree of peripherality or centrality within the system. That is to say, the many less-important beliefs lie at the periphery of the system while fewer, highly-salient beliefs lie at the center of the system. Second, Rokeach claims, the more central the belief, the more resistant it will be to change. By definition, centrally-held beliefs are more well established and important to the individual's self-image. Third, posits Rokeach, more change in the total belief system will result from changes in the more centrally-held beliefs.

Recall also from Chapter 3 that Rokeach conceives of *attitudes* as clusters of beliefs organized around an object (or situation). Attitudes may predispose an individual to behave in a particular way toward that object or situation. In short, attitudes are seen as complex evaluations of situations or objects.

Unlike previous theorists, Rokeach elevates the concept of *value* to primary importance in the cognitive system. Recall that instrumental and terminal values are specific types of beliefs that are central in the system and act as guides or goals in life.

Perhaps the most important component in Rokeach's theory of change is the *self-concept.* The sum total of one's beliefs about the self compose the self-concept. Rokeach underlines its importance when he states, "The ultimate purpose of one's total belief system . . . is to maintain and enhance . . . the sentiment of self regard."[35] For Rokeach, a complex interrelationship of beliefs, attitudes, and values forms the components of the cognitive system, while its fundamental goal or purpose is the concept of self-regard.

As with other congruity theorists, Rokeach sees change in the cognitive system or behavior as resulting from pressure created by inconsistencies among components of the cognitive system or behavior. However, in discussing consistency, Rokeach goes far beyond other theorists by including more dimensions and components of the system (values and needs). Table 4.1 on page 106 represents ten areas in the cognitive system which interrelate and bear potential for inconsistency. Note how Rokeach's system not only explains inconsistencies posited by other theories, but suggests many other areas of potential imbalance. Note further how items B and C correspond to elements of what we have called the goal dimension of the cognitive system, items D and E correspond to elements of what we have called the reality dimension, and items F, G, H, and I correspond to elements of what we have called the relational dimension of the cognitive system. With the exception of the arousal dimension, Rokeach's system posits change in the cognitive system when any of the elements or dimensions are out of balance or inconsistent with one another or with behavior. Rokeach therefore sees consistency in the cognitive system as extremely complex.

Furthermore, Rokeach believes that the most important inconsistencies in a person's psychological system are those involving cognitions about the self. Only when inconsistencies involve the self-conception will there be significant, lasting change. The reason for this is that such contradictions increase self-dissatisfaction. Since maintenance of self-regard is the overall aim of the psychological system, it is natural that this should be so. Rokeach's theory of the attitude-belief-value system is complex and lengthy. We have only been able to sketch it here.

/ Factors of Resistance to Change

Heretofore we have been discussing explanations of change in individuals' cognitive systems and behavior. Now we will discuss ways of inducing resistance to change.[36] Fund-raisers may want people to continue to give to their cause. Politicians desire the unwavering support of their candidacy and career. Religious leaders want to avoid losing converts. Parents may desire that their children not use tobacco or alcohol or become sexually active. Indeed, resistance to change is an important goal of much persuasive communication.

/ Early approaches

Several explanations of change we have just discussed suggest insights into resistance to change. After all, change and resistance to change can be seen as opposite sides of the same coin.

First, if cognitive dissonance leads to changes in the cognitive system and behavior, then cognitive congruity or balance would create resistance to change. You know how difficult it is to persuade a very content person to change his routine or an individual behavior. It is a political axiom that an incumbent officeholder is difficult to defeat when the economy is strong, the country is at peace, and no scandals have occurred during the incumbency.

Organization of:

	A	B	C	D	E	F	G	H	I	J
A. Cognitions about self	Psychoanalysis				Cognitive-affective consistency	Rational therapy, Reality therapy, Emotional role playing	Nondirective therapy	Encounter groups, T-groups, Psychodrama		
B. Terminal value system										
C. Instrumental value system				Congruity theory, Belief congruence		Achievement motivation				
D. Attitude system					Syllogistic analysis of attitudes		Balance theory			
E. Attitude						Dissonance theory, Attribution theory	Communication and persuasion, Inoculation theory, Assimilation-Contrast theory			
F. Cognitions about own behavior									Modeling and observational learning	
G. Cognitions about significant others' attitudes										
H. Cognitions about significant others' values or needs										
I. Cognitions about significant others' behavior										
J. Cognitions about behavior of nonsocial objects										

Column key (same categories as the rows):
A. Cognitions about self
B. Terminal value system
C. Instrumental value system
D. Attitude system
E. Attitude
F. Cognitions about own behavior
G. Cognitions about significant others' attitudes
H. Cognitions about significant others' values or needs
I. Cognitions about significant others' behavior
J. Cognitions about behavior of nonsocial objects

▮**TABLE 4.1** Matrix of Contradictory Relations Possible Within the Total Belief System

/ **The public nature of the Mennonites' commitment to their beliefs enhances their resistance to change.**

Earlier we pointed out that people with moderate self-esteem are usually more susceptible to change than others. It follows that people with extremely high or low self-esteem might be more resistant to change.

Moderate levels of anxiety or other forms of emotional arousal were also identified earlier as factors that facilitate change. Accordingly, extremely low or high levels of arousal might be expected to induce resistance to change.

Finally, in the discussion of social judgment we found that ego-involvement and extremism made people less changeable than their less involved or moderate counterparts. In a sense this resistance is related to the commitment people have to the issue, goal, or relationship under question.

Resistance to change can be enhanced by developing commitment in several ways. Perhaps the most basic way of enhancing commitment and hence resistance to persuasive communication is the intensification of existing beliefs, attitudes, goals, or interpersonal bonds. In Chapter 3 we saw that various dimensions of the cognitive system tend to be hierarchical in nature and to vary in their salience. These dimensions can be intensified by making the given issues higher on the list of priorities within the system.

A more effective way of increasing commitment and thus resistance to change is by making one's position on an issue public. Earlier we saw how role-playing and testimonials enhanced change in a given direction. These two techniques, as well as other forms of public commitment, also enhance resistance to subsequent change in the opposite direction.

A third method of enhancing resistance is behavioral commitment. Following from dissonance theory, we are presumed to be more resistant to change if our behaviors coincide with the dimensions of our cognitive system. Thus, we become more committed and resistant if we become active in a political campaign, collect money for a charity, or accept a position of responsibility in an organization.

A final method of enhancing resistance through commitment is through external commitment. This occurs when a person is informed that other people believe he or she holds the belief, attitude, or value. Thus a campaign worker may be told, "Our candidate thinks you are one of the most committed supporters in this campaign" and then be more committed than ever. A child who is told by a teacher, "You are the best behaved child in your class" will be more resistant toward changing the praised behavior.

Whether it results from intensified elements of the cognitive system, public declarations, behavior, or external reinforcement, commitment is one of the most significant means of inducing resistance to change either within the individual or among others. It is also one of the most amenable to persuasive communication.

/ Later approaches

/ Inoculation.
In addition to approaches to resistance which follow as the obverse of strategies of change, there is a concept, suggested by William McGuire, that bears directly on resistance to change.[37] Using the analogy of medical inoculations which induce resistance to disease, McGuire posits that weak doses of arguments bearing on a cultural truism or primitive belief (one that has not been questioned) would induce the individual to generate antibodies, in the form of counterarguments, which would render him/her more resistant to subsequent attack and change. People would be particularly vulnerable on cultural truisms because, never having been challenged about these beliefs, they would be *unmotivated* to develop an argumentative defense and would be *unpracticed* in doing so.

McGuire also hypothesizes that certain variables in the way an inoculation was administered makes a difference. First, were the inoculating arguments supportive or refutational to the person's cognitive system? Supportive inoculation would constitute nonthreatening data and claims which bolstered the person's existing beliefs and attitudes. Refutational inoculation would be weak counterarguments which attacked the existing position. In addition, the refutational arguments could be either the same issue but on the opposite side as existing beliefs and attitudes, or they could be opposing arguments different from existing attitudes and beliefs but bearing on the same issue.

Thus, for the person who believes the MX missile should be deployed in existing silos (not a cultural truism) because of an assumed superiority of Russian missile systems, a supportive inoculation would be more reasons and evidence of a missile gap. Refutational arguments on the same issue would suggest that even though some people don't believe there is a gap, here is further evidence that there is. Refutational arguments different from existing attitudes would say that some people don't think there is a gap, but look at the economic advantages of deployment.

In general, McGuire and his associates found that:

1. Without any inoculation, subsequent attack significantly changed existing attitudes toward cultural truisms.

2. Pretreatment with refutational arguments on the same issue was significantly superior to pretreatment with supportive arguments and slightly superior to pretreatment with refutational arguments on a different issue in inducing resistance to change.

3. Supportive pretreatment can induce significant resistance to change if the person is threatened or warned of a subsequent attack.

A second major variable in the use of inoculation is the degree to which the inoculated person is active or passive in the generation of inoculating arguments. Will a person who actively generates his/her own inoculating arguments be more resistant to change than a person who is "given" those arguments? Who will be the more resistant over time? Results demonstrated:

1. A person who is inoculated with a warning and/or a refutational argument can generate his or her own inoculating arguments without help from an external source.

2. A person who actively generates refutational arguments different from existing beliefs or supportive arguments will become more resistant to change than one who passively receives those arguments.

3. A person who passively receives refutational arguments on the same issue will become more resistant than those who are left to generate those arguments on their own.

4. In general, people who passively receive inoculating treatments will experience more immediate resistance, while persons who actively generate their own inoculating arguments will experience greater long-term resistance to change.

People believing in cultural truisms who receive a warning that their position may be attacked, and who actively generate either supportive or refutational arguments to inoculate themselves against that attack generally will become significantly resistant to change, and that resistance to change will tend to last over time.

/ Linking.   A second approach to resistance to change has been called *anchoring*[38] or *linking*.[39] The basic concept of this approach is that several elements of the cognitive system which are related or dependent upon one another will be more difficult to change than any one of them alone. Just as it is easier to break a single piece of spaghetti than it is to break an entire package of spaghetti, so a complex interrelationship of beliefs, attitudes, and values, perhaps associated with strong interpersonal bonds, are more resistant to change than is an isolated belief.

Almost by definition, then, an attitude (which we have defined as a cluster of related beliefs) would be more resistant to change than would an isolated or subordinate belief. Similarly, an interpersonal bond which was supported by a variety of shared beliefs, values, or motives would be more resistant to change than one which was not built upon these similarities.

An important qualification exists to this generalization. If one key component of interrelated, linked, or anchored elements of the cognitive system is destroyed, all of the others become more vulnerable as well. Called the *multiplier effect,* this phenomenon is seen when a "true believer," either political or religious, swings to the opposite camp when any one of his or her cherished beliefs is destroyed.

/ *Theory* / *Practice* / *Analysis*

Theory

1. Change in the cognitive system can occur as a result of the way people integrate new information or beliefs into their cognitive systems. New information can introduce a new belief or change the value or weight of existing beliefs. New cognitions can change the system more if processed by the central (reality) route than by the peripheral (contextual) route. Change can be related to correlates of source, message, channel, and receiver.

2. Traditional learning is related to changes in attitude through exposure, association, and reinforcement. Social learning can influence behavior as well as the cognitive system by means of desensitization, behavior modification, role-playing, and modeling.

3. People's perception processes affect change. Attitudes constitute a range of possible claims. Attitude change and perception itself can be influenced by the way people perceive new information to correspond to their latitudes of acceptance, rejection, and noncommitment. Ego-involvement and extremism make people less changeable by reducing their latitudes of noncommitment.

4. People may attribute beliefs and attitudes to themselves and others on the basis of their own and others' behaviors. Self-attributions are evident in the phenomena of escalating expectations, proattitudinal advocacy, and responses to ambiguous emotional arousal.

5. Change can occur from a need to maintain balance or congruity among the various elements of the cognitive system and between the cognitive system and behavior. Imbalance or change can result from a deprivation of needs and inappropriate arousal, as well as from discrepancies among beliefs, attitudes, values, and relationships.

6. Resistance to change can result from cognitive congruity, high self-esteem, anxiety, ego-involvement, extremism, commitment, and linking. Inoculation with self-generated supportive or refutational arguments also creates resistance to change.

Practice

1. Pick a controversial issue to which you are either mildly committed or neutral. Research the issue from several different points of view. Write a paper describing how each new piece of information affected your own position on the issue.

2. Pick an undesirable behavior which you would like to change or a desirable behavior you would like to adopt. Using role-playing, modeling, or behavior-modification, design and implement a program for change. Write a report of your experience.

3. Select an emotion or feeling you would like to change (for example, communication anxiety, fear of dogs, revulsion of violence, or sexual arousal). Design a program of desensitization. Write a report of your experience.

Analysis

1. Select a friend or acquaintance (or yourself) who has recently made a big decision or change in his or her life (like our friend who bought the computer). Interview the person, carefully probing the arguments or influences which effected the change. Write a five-page analysis of the change process, relating the change to dimensions of the cognitive system in Chapter 3 or explanations of change discussed in this chapter.

2. Do the same as above with a recent decision or change in a group or community.

Notes

[1]Martin Fishbein and Icek Ajzen, *Belief, Attitude, Intention and Behavior* (Reading, MA: Addison-Wesley, 1975).

[2]Anthony Greenwald, "Cognitive Learning, Cognitive Response to Persuasion and Attitude Change," *Psychological Foundations of Attitude,* ed. Anthony G. Greenwald, Timothy Brock, and Thomas Ostrom (New York: Academic Press, 1968), p. 149.

[3]Richard Petty and J. T. Cacioppo, *Cognitive Responses in Persuasion: Classic and Contemporary Approaches* (Dubuque: W. C. Brown, 1981).

[4]See Carl I. Hovland, Irving L. Janis, and Harold H. Kelly, *Communication and Persuasion* (New Haven, CT: Yale University Press, 1953).

[5]This summary is based on that of Mary John Smith in *Persuasion and Human Action: A Review and Critique of Social Influence Theories* (Belmont, CA: Wadsworth Publishing Co., 1982), pp. 219–240.

⁶Irving L. Janis and Peter B. Field, "Sex Differences and Personality Factors Related to Persuasibility," in *Personality and Persuasibility,* ed. Carl I. Hovland and Irving L. Janis (New Haven: Yale University Press, 1959).

⁷Alan C. Elms, "Influence of Fantasy Ability on Attitude Change Through Role-Playing," *Journal of Personality and Social Psychology* 4 (1966): 36–43.

⁸See Janis and Field, "Sex Differences," pp. 55–68.

⁹See Irving L. Janis and Donald Rife, "Persuasibility and Emotional Disorder," in *Personality and Persuasibility,* ed. Carl I. Hovland and Irving L. Janis (New Haven: Yale University Press, 1959), pp. 121–40.

¹⁰See Theodore Adorno, Else Frenkel-Brunswick, D. J. Levison, and R. N. Sanford, *The Authoritarian Personality* (New York: Harper and Row, 1950), pp. 255–57.

¹¹For a brilliant and witty discussion of *extremism,* see Alan C. Elms, *Social Psychology and Social Relevance* (Boston: Little, Brown and Co., 1972), Chapter 3.

¹²For an extended discussion of sex and persuasibility, see Eleanor E. Maccoby and Carol N. Jacklin, *The Psychology of Sex Differences* (Palo Alto: Stanford University Press, 1974).

¹³Leonard Doob, "The Behavior of Attitudes," *Psychological Review* 54 (1947): 135–56.

¹⁴William McGuire, "Personality and Attitude Change: An Information Processing Theory," in *Psychological Foundations of Attitudes,* ed. Anthony G. Greenwald, Timothy C. Brock, and Thomas M. Ostrom (New York: Academic Press, 1968), pp. 171–96.

¹⁵Albert Bandura, *Social Learning Theory,* 2nd ed. (Englewood Cliffs, NJ: Prentice-Hall, 1977).

¹⁶Albert Bandura, *Social Learning Theory* (Morristown, NJ: General Learning Press, 1971), p. 2.

¹⁷For a more detailed discussion of these four models, see Smith, *Persuasion and Human Action,* pp. 199–205.

¹⁸Gordon Paul, *Insight Versus Desensitization in Psychotherapy* (Stanford, CA: Stanford University Press, 1966).

¹⁹Elms, *Social Psychology.*

²⁰See Alan C. Elms and Irving L. Janis, "Counter-Normal Attitudes Induced by Consonant Versus Dissonant Conditions of Role-Playing," *Journal of Experimental Research in Personality* 1 (1960): 50–60.

²¹Ashley Montague, Public Lecture, Salt Lake City.

²²See David M. Jabusch, "Effects of Filmed Speech Models in Beginning Speech Instruction," in Research Reports, *Central States Speech Journal* (Fall 1969): 219–21; and Emil Bohn and David M. Jabusch, "The Effect of Four Methods of Instruction on the Use of Visual Aids in Speeches," *The Western Journal of Speech Communication* 46 (Summer 1982): 253–65.

²³For a detailed discussion, see Carolyn Sherif, Muzafer Sherif, and Roger E. Nebergall, *Attitude and Attitude Change: The Social Judgment-Involvement Approach* (Philadelphia, PA: W. B. Saunders Company, 1963).

²⁴See Fritz Heider, *The Psychology of Interpersonal Relations* (New York: John Wiley, 1958); and Harold Kelly "The Process of Causal Attribution," *American Psychologist* 28 (1973): 107–28.

²⁵These techniques are adapted from Smith, *Persuasion and Human Actions,* pp. 149–59.

[26]Stanley Schlachter and Jerome Singer, "Cognitive, Social, and Physiological Determinants of Emotional State," *Psychological Review,* 69 (1962): 379–99.

[27]Schlachter and Singer, "Determinants."

[28]See Christina Maslach, "Negative Emotional Biasing of Unexplained Arousal," *Journal of Personality and Social Psychology* 37 (1979): 953–69; and Gary D. Marshall and Philip G. Zimbardo, "Affective Consequences of Inadequately Explained Physiological Arousal," *Journal of Personality and Social Psychology* 37 (1979): 970–88.

[29]For a discussion of early balance theories, see Robert B. Zajonc, "The Concept of Balance, Congruity, and Dissonance," *Public Opinion Quarterly* 24 (1960): 280–96.

[30]Theodore M. Newcomb, "An Approach to the Study of Communicative Acts," *Psychological Review* 60 (1953): 393–404.

[31]C. E. Osgood and P. H. Tannenbaum, "The Principle of Congruity in the Prediction of Attitude Change," *Psychological Review* 62 (1955): 42–55.

[32]Leon Festinger, *A Theory of Cognitive Dissonance* (Evanston, IL: Row, Peterson, 1957), p. 13.

[33]This section is adapted from Stephen W. Littlejohn, *Theories of Human Communication,* 2nd ed. (Belmont, CA: Wadsworth Publishing Co., 1983), pp. 151–56.

[34]Rokeach presents his theory in *Beliefs, Attitudes, and Values: A Theory of Organization and Change* (San Francisco: Jossey-Bass, 1968), and in *The Nature of Human Values* (New York: Free Press, 1973).

[35]Rokeach, *Human Values,* p. 216.

[36]For further discussion of resistance to change, see Gerald R. Miller and Michael Burgoon, *New Techniques of Persuasion* (New York: Harper and Row, 1973).

[37]William J. McGuire, "Inducing Resistance to Persuasion: Some Contemporary Approaches," *The Process of Social Influence: Readings in Persuasion,* ed. Thomas D. Beisecker and D. W. Parson (Englewood Cliffs, NJ: Prentice-Hall, Inc., 1972), pp. 197–218.

[38]Miller and Burgoon, *New Techniques,* pp. 18–44.

[39]See David M. Jabusch and Stephen Littlejohn, *Elements of Speech Communication* (Boston: Houghton-Mifflin, 1981), pp. 112–13.

Part 2

The Interpersonal Arena

5/ Persuasion in Relationships

She was seventeen. She had no particular reason to think they wouldn't trust her, but she had never before asked to spend a weekend away from home without adult supervision. Janelle was smart enough to know that asking her parents' permission to go to the mountains for the weekend with three girl friends was more important than just getting something she wanted. It was a test of the relationship between her and her parents, a first step in establishing a sense of adult trust. She knew that if they said *yes,* her relationship with the family would have reached a new stage. A negative answer, on the other hand, would have more than minor implications for her sense of maturity and self-esteem.

Janelle's mother and father were not the type of parents who made snap judgments about important matters involving their children. For that reason, she did not expect an immediate *yes* or *no,* but was prepared for a lengthy discussion. When Janelle's mother first heard her request, she did not seem surprised or unduly concerned; neither did she accede. She asked for details and expressed her concern for the safety of Janelle and her friends. Her father was the first to point out that young adults need opportunities to develop independence and that the cabin was, after all, only two hours away. Her mother was more hesitant. After a little more discussion, talks with the other girls' parents, and about a day's thought, they agreed to Janelle's request.

Much of what we have taught traditionally about persuasion addresses the public arena. This emphasis on public persuasion probably arises from the common image that public speaking and media are "aimed" at "audiences." A moment's reflection, however, should reveal that most persuasion occurs not from the public platform, but in interpersonal relations.

Interpersonal communication is all around us. We are influenced in subtle and obvious ways in our daily relationships at home, at work, and in social situations. In this chapter we discuss persuasion as it occurs in everyday conversations.

/ Interpersonal Communication and Persuasion

Persuasion is enormously important in our daily interactions with others. Although we often communicate without having persuasion as a conscious objective, we frequently attempt consciously to influence other people. We also use interpersonal communication as a way to be influenced and changed.

Let us emphasize from the beginning that an interpersonal exchange is never an isolated event. Not only does it occur in a complex social and cultural context, but it is also part of a relationship that affects what communicators say and do. Whether one's contact with another person is brief and fleeting or lasts a lifetime, communication is always understood in terms of the relationship. Let us now look at the nature of relationships and the role of persuasion in them.[1]

/ The interpersonal relationship

/ Expectations in relationships. You probably most often think of *relationships* as enduring love partnerships. Although loving is a kind of relationship, we are using the term much more broadly. A *relationship* is any link between two or more persons who have expectations for one another. Therefore, a marriage that has lasted fifty years is indeed a relationship, but so is a conversation lasting only minutes at a cocktail party. What do these two relationships have in common? Both are governed by mutual expectations. The expectations in the golden marriage are far more numerous, subtle, and complex than are those of the party guests, but even the briefest encounter is guided by expectations. Essentially all interpersonal communication is involved in a relationship of some kind and should be viewed in terms of its relational demands and consequences.

Communication is the device by which people define their relationships. In other words, communication enables us to understand others' expectations and to help others understand ours. Not only does our communication affect relational expectations, but expectations surely affect in turn what we say and do. Communication in a relationship is characterized by this constant give-and-take between establishing and responding to expectations.

/ Relationship rules. In Chapter 2, we discussed the ways in which communicators use rules to interpret and act. We can think of expectations as rules, which are negotiated through communication in subtle and often subconscious ways. We are often guided by *external rules,* which are commonly held expectations about how to behave in a particular situation. Such rules come from a lifetime's expectations of what is "normal" or "acceptable." Through external rules we know how to say *hello* or *goodbye,* what subjects are acceptable or not acceptable at a particular moment, and how to be comfortable in new situations. We rely on external rules to guide our behavior when we do not know what others really expect. Such rules are important in conversations with people we

/ **Relationships between friends are guided by both external and internal rules.**

do not know very well, and they are almost always relied upon at the beginning of a relationship.

The study of external rules is interesting because such expectations tell us a great deal about a culture and about how a society defines its values. Such rules are not trivial, for without them one would have no idea of how to be human; nor are they arbitrary, for they emerge from interaction itself. In other words, external rules are the result of communication from person to person, group to group, and generation to generation. External rules change, as you will no doubt observe in talking with and observing your own parents and/or children, and such rules vary from group to group. Think twice about the difference between how you act at dinner with your parents and at a pizza parlor with your friends, and you will see that this is true.

We use the word *external* here because such rules are pretty much in place before the beginning of a new relationship. Although external rules are extremely important in new or brief relationships, they become much less important in enduring ones. Instead, people in an ongoing relationship rely much more on their *internal rules,* which emerge in interaction between the partners in that relationship. These are the expectations that each person comes to have for self and for the other person. Such rules may remain like the external rules used initially, but in most cases they will take on their own flavor and essence. In some cases internal rules for handling a situation are considerably different from corresponding external rules. Obviously, there is great potential for internal rules to change, although they can also become very stable over time. In fact, unchanging but unwanted rule patterns constitute a common problem in long-term relationships. Think of the development of rules as a negotiation process in which people establish, reinforce, and change their relationships through communication.

As an example of how internal rules develop, consider the hypothetical case of Roy and Connie. Roy and Connie were introduced by a mutual friend in the University Student Center in their sophomore year. They went on their first date that very evening, which marked the beginning of a continuing relationship. Their first date was pretty standard, being governed largely by typical college dating rules. Roy asked Connie to meet him later that evening for coffee at the University Center, she accepted, and the ensuing interaction followed the typical pattern easily predicted by external rules. Even before the end of their first date, however, they had learned enough about each other to begin developing a few internal rules. For instance, when walking into the dorm, Connie rushed to grab the door first, telling Roy nonverbally that she did not want him to take the customary male role of opening the door for her. Although this made Roy a little uncomfortable at first, he learned to adjust to this pattern of behavior.

One of the important functions of persuasion in interpersonal communication is to establish, maintain, or change rules. By inducing change in one or both of the partners, persuasive messages can set up new rule patterns or change old ones. Often in response to anticipated unwanted change in a relationship, our persuasion is aimed at reinforcing or maintaining existing rule patterns.

For example, several months after Roy and Connie started dating seriously, Roy considered transferring to another university for a year on the National Student Exchange program. Although he assured Connie that his move was strictly for his personal development and did not mean that he loved her less, she was threatened by the incredible independence that his plan implied. After having established patterns of interaction that involved their being together almost all the time, Roy's plan was the first step in making a major change in the relationship. This subject dominated their conversations for about a month. There is no question that Connie aimed to change Roy's mind, and in the end he decided not to transfer. Their often emotional exchanges on the subject definitely served to establish rules that increased the dependence level in their relationship.

Recall from our discussion in Chapter 2 what rules are. Communication rules, like game rules, guide people's interpretations and actions in a given context. Of course, people can choose whether or not to follow a rule, but there will be consequences for not doing so if the rule is well established in the relationship. Rules are contextual, meaning that they apply only in certain situations. For example, Roy's decision not to transfer to another university established a strong rule that under most conditions, neither he nor Connie could say that he/she wanted to do something alone. Although this rule was never actually stated between them, it could have been written as follows: "I am not allowed to suggest that I do something by myself."

/ Goals of interpersonal persuasion

/ Relationship goals.

Interpersonal persuasion involves one or more goals. The first possible goal of persuasion is to maintain or change the relationship itself. We have already seen that persuasion which leads to profound change almost always alters the rules of a relationship. Some persuasion is actually aimed at accomplishing such rule changes. (We have also seen that persuasion may maintain or reinforce a particular rule pattern.) On the other hand, not all interpersonal persuasion is intended to make such fundamental changes, and just because partners in a relationship are induced to comply in one way or another does not necessarily mean that the rule structure of the relationship itself will change.

/ Instrumental goals.

The second possible goal of persuasion in interpersonal settings is to achieve instrumental objectives. These are cognitive changes that do not have a direct bearing on the relationship itself. A simple example should suffice. Tom and Bill learned to play racquetball together in college. It not only opened a new interest for them, but also helped to structure their relationship and time together. Over a period of about five years, Tom became an excellent player and Bill kept up enough to provide sufficient competition for Tom, but Bill never grew to love the game as Tom had. One day on their way to the court, Bill realized that he just had to start doing something else for a while. He did not bring the subject up just then, but gave it considerable thought that evening. He knew how important the semiweekly games had become to their relationship, and he did not want to drift away from Tom. The answer, he thought, was to suggest a new activity. Bill brought up his desire to broaden his physical activity, and Tom quickly agreed to jog with Bill once a week, reducing racquetball to a single session per week. Although this persuasion might have had relational consequences, in this case it did not, nor was it intended to change any fundamental rule patterns in the relationship.

/ Self-identity goals.

The third possible goal of interpersonal persuasion is to change or maintain one's self-identity. This goal is often primary, and in many cases it is an important secondary goal of persuasion. In its broadest sense, self-identity may be involved in all persuasion. When you engage another person in potential change, you are always operating from the perspective of how you see yourself. People tend to want others to conform to their view of things. In the case of Bill and Tom, for example, Bill's sense of self-identity with Tom and his own desire to remain physically active bolstered his desire to maintain some kind of shared sport with Tom. In persuading Tom to jog instead of play racquetball, he not only accomplished an instrumental objective, but also maintained an important element of his own self-identity.

Sometimes people become unhappy with some aspect of the self. We believe that interpersonal persuasion is one of the key ways in which people attempt to resolve conflicts in the self or to open the self to personal development and change. Keep in mind that persuasion is not simply affecting others;

rather, in the spirit of transaction, people seek out opportunities to "be persuaded," or to have others affect them. We rely on those with whom we have relationships to help us change.

Robert was interviewing for jobs in his senior year. After talking with representatives from several companies, he realized that he was unable to tell interviewers honestly what he was looking for in a position. No matter what company he was considering, he always led the interviewer to believe that that organization was top priority for him. This problem came to a head when he received an offer to sell fire alarms door-to-door. He had to decline the job, even though in the interview, he pretended that he would rather sell fire alarms than anything. Robert never directly stated his increasing discontent about this problem to his parents, although he always kept them informed about each interview and what had happened. When he had to call the fire alarm company to turn down the job offer, Robert's mother could tell that he was just not handling things right. She talked to him directly about the problem, laying out some alternative ways to deal with job interviews. She told him that he had to learn to be assertive and that honesty in a job interview would build more credibility in the long run. This persuasive attempt was easy because Robert was crying out for guidance. He used his mother's persuasion as an opportunity to learn and resolve a conflict in himself.

It would be a mistake to assume that persuasive communication aims at one and only one of the above goals. Most persuasion in interpersonal settings involves a mixture of these goals. Robert's discussion with his mother about job interviews achieved primarily an instrumental goal from her standpoint, but it accomplished a self-identity goal for him. Actually, this communication may also have affected his mother's sense of her own competence, which is a self-identity goal, and although it had no serious consequences in the relationship, the transaction no doubt affected the relationship a little bit by reinforcing existing rule patterns.

/ The Process of Interpersonal Persuasion

We have learned that persuasion is an important element in the maintenance and change of relationships. We also have learned that it fulfills a number of functions in the interpersonal arena. More important than this basic understanding, however, is a knowledge of how persuasion comes about.

Keep in mind that persuasion is social influence. It is the process by which messages create personal change. How does such change occur?

/ Sources of personal influence

There is no question that people influence others. In the previous chapter, we discussed the process of change in persuasion, including learning, perception, and tension-reduction. All of these factors operate in each contextual arena, including the interpersonal.

Here we discuss sources of personal influence especially pertinent in the interpersonal arena—power, control, and trust. These sources should not be considered as separate from the general factors of change, but as manifestations of them.

/ *Power in interpersonal relationships.*   Personal influence is built on power. We are not referring to physical or material power here, but to an array of resources used in personal influence.

Power and control are not really the same things, although they are mutually dependent to a large extent. Power is access to resources that may be used to influence another person in a relationship. Naturally, most of these resources in the interpersonal arena are psycho-social. Control, on the other hand, is the actual pattern of dominance and submission in a relationship.[2] When one makes use of power, control is visible. Control requires power, but power by itself does not necessarily mean that control will be exerted. Control is discussed in the next section.

What kind of resources for power are available in interpersonal relationships? Some of these resources may be material or physical. If one partner has a great deal more money than the other, causing the poorer member to be dependent, then money itself is a source of power. If one person is stronger and/or more willing to use physical force than is the other, violence becomes a resource for power. However, these sources of power are really not very relevant to persuasion, because their use rarely coincides with the exercise of choice. Use of such sources of power usually constitutes force or coercion, which is not the subject of this book (see Chapter 1). The fact is that anybody could exert negative power to the point of forcing someone to comply, but people generally are unwilling to use all the negative resources available because of respect for the rights of the other person. (Recall our discussion in Chapter 1 of choice and ethics.) Most of us are restrained in use of power by ethical considerations, although individual ethical limits vary.

Rarely does one individual in a relationship have all the power and therefore all the control. Power and control are usually distributed, although the distribution may not be equal. Who gets the power, and who subsequently exerts control, is itself often the object of persuasion. Let us look more closely at the emergence of power in relationships.

From a transactional perspective, power is a product of interpersonal perception. In other words, a person's power is what another person perceives it to be. Characteristics such as status and position may bring about the perception of power, but perceiving power is more complicated than simple attribution.

There are many such resources of power, which can be grouped into three types.[3] The first kind of resource giving rise to power is *control of outcomes* or consequences of behavior. In other words, the ability to control what someone gets from complying is a form of power. For example, supervisors may control pay raises, parents control children's privileges, and friends can give or withhold attention. Controlling outcomes can lead to coercion, especially where a threat or promise is applied. Strict coercion of this type would not be considered persuasion.

The second category of resources involves valuing the powerful person or one's relationship with that person. Such power is referred to as *relational identification*. In a relationship in which the communicators have rescue rules, for example, the perpetual "victim" may actually be controlling the behavior of the "rescuer" by capitalizing on that person's desire to be perceived as "loving." Another example of the use of relational identification as a source of power is the threat of withdrawal or silence. Relational identification is an important source of power, which is why the person least committed to a relationship may have more power than the person who most wants the relationship to endure.

A good example of the power of relational identification is in new romantic relationships. In predominant Western culture at least, the "falling-in-love" phase of a relationship is often accompanied by strong fears of losing the other person, making jealousy during the period an especially prevalent emotion. Lovers are often quite compliant because of the fear of rejection. A partner willing to take the risk of asserting a particular action or position may find persuasion easy because of the power of relational identification.

The third kind of resource involves the ability to *identify values* or obligations that the other person should meet. This kind of power arises from the ability to define the values and obligations that can control the relationship. One person may be able to point out to others that they are not behaving consistently with a value or obligation within the relationship. The example of the reciprocity norm illustrates this kind of power very well.

When Bob and Sally got married, Bob's father Herm was eager to help. He gave Bob and Sally a lot of good used furniture and "loaned" them quite a bit of money to pay the necessary costs of getting an apartment. Bob and Sally were naturally appreciative and often did small chores and ran errands for Herm in return. As they got on with their careers and had a child, however, they became increasingly busy and preoccupied. Herm's arthritis was getting worse and he needed more help around his small house, but he found Bob and Sally less and less willing to provide it. He certainly was not begrudging because he remembered all too well how busy he used to be when his family was young and he was "up and coming" in his firm. At the same time, however, he really needed help and thought that Bob could do more. A gentle reminder of the ways in which he had helped the young couple after they got married was all it took. Embarrassed, Bob and Sally decided to spend two hours every Saturday morning at his Dad's helping with odds and ends. The couple had quickly accepted his definition of a relational obligation based on reciprocity.

This discussion may seem to imply that the attribution of power is always clear. Actually, power in relationships is not always clearly established, and people often struggle to define it. We do not intend to discuss power struggles here, except to note that people often use persuasion in order to work out who possesses the power at a particular time, on a particular issue, or within a particular situation. Power struggles will often involve messages that define what expectations or outcomes are to be sought, what qualities intrinsic to the relationship are legitimate to guide behavior, and what the values and obligations of the persons are. These three bases of power—control of outcomes, relational identification, and values identification—are very important in interpersonal persuasion, and we shall return to them later in our discussion of the process of compliance seeking.

/ *Control in interpersonal relationships.* As we have said, power and control, although related, are not the same thing. Power is the perception that one or both members of the relationship have access to resources that can influence. The actual influence pattern as it is played out through communication is control.[4] When we talk about *power,* we are referring to the resources that a person possesses to influence others, but whether these resources are actually used to control is a different matter. *Control* refers to the messages used in communication and the kinds of responses the messages receive. As we will see, people choose when and how to exert control, a question central to persuasion.

This last statement is especially important from a transactional point of view because it captures the relational quality of interpersonal persuasion. Persuasion in interpersonal settings is largely a matter of give and take, talking and responding. Control patterns are therefore defined by interactional sequences by initiating and responding to messages. (Recall, however, that persuasion, by definition, involves the perception of choice so that in places where individuals believed that they were forced to comply, some other form of influence is operating.)

There are three kinds of control messages in communication. *One-up messages* are statements that attempt to exert control over the relational rules of the moment. Such messages make suggestions or demands, provide direction, or attempt to influence in some other way. *One-down messages,* on the other hand, characterize submission. They are messages that accept the control of the other. Many statements neither exert control nor accept it. Such messages are called simply *one-across.*

Conversations are obviously peppered with one-up, one-down, and one-across messages. A useful exercise which illustrates the transactional nature of communication and the way in which influence constantly shifts back and forth is to listen carefully and objectively to a conversation between two people. Note the ways in which each person attempts to direct the course of the interaction but then, moments later, accepts the partner's directions. You will find that influence and control are distributed between the partners in the relationship.

The distribution of control in a relationship varies from couple to couple, from situation to situation, and from moment to moment. Some relationships are marked by equal shifting of control back and forth. Other relationships are marked by unequal distribution of control, in which the control is more often taken by one partner than the other. You can tell what the control pattern in a relationship is only by observing the interaction for a long time and in different situations.

When you listen to a conversation from the control point of view, listen not to whether particular messages are one-up, one-down, or one-across, but to how such messages are greeted by the other person. Researchers interested in relational control always study sets of at least two contiguous messages. A message is always examined in the context of what message follows. These message sets are called *interacts*.

There are three kinds of interacts: complementary, symmetrical, and transitional. A *complementary interact* consists of a message (one-up or one-down) followed by its opposite: one-up/one-down or one-down/one-up. Here the attempt to control or be controlled is "agreed to" by the other. The second kind of interact is *symmetrical,* in which case the message is met by the same kind of message: one-up/one-up or one-down/one-down. Here one's attempt to control or be controlled is not accepted by the other. Such interacts are potentially problematic because they may mean that the couple is not yet clear on the direction of the influence. *Transition interacts* involve a one-across message in some way. They are not clearly meaningful and are probably just a transition to some other state.

What is really important, of course, is not the type of interaction present at any particular moment, but the overall pattern of such interacts through time. What you say at any given moment rarely has significance. What matters is the character of the relationship, the distribution of control, and the implications of the control pattern for the rules of the relationship.

A *complementary relationship,* then, is one in which, at any given time, one partner is apt to take control and the other is submissive. Attempts to persuade are met by compliance. A *symmetrical relationship* is one in which there is either struggle for control or inaction owing to no control responsibility. These classifications are temporal: they are characteristic of particular time periods in the life of a relationship. Consider a relationship you are having with another person right now. If you think very seriously about it, you will soon realize that during any period—a minute, a day, a year—a predominant pattern can be discerned. You can quickly see that the question of relational dominance is more complex than was implied earlier. Figure 5.1 illustrates this more complex view. This figure shows that in some relationships the pattern is *complementary and stable*. In other words, the one-up position is taken by the same partner most of the time. Other complementary relationships are *flexible;* that is, the control moves back and forth as appropriate. At any given moment, one person seems to take control, but that individual does not control the direction of the interaction all the time, and the other partner frequently takes over.

Consider the example of roommates Sarah and Jewitt. Soon after they moved in together, their relationship was one of competitive symmetry: both were attempting to exert control.

Sarah: I would like my friend Marla to come with us to the show tonight, okay? [one-up]

Jewitt: Does she really have to come! [one-up]

Sarah: Why not? The more the merrier. [one-up]

Type of Relationship

	Complementary	Symmetrical
Flexible	Control flows back and forth appropriately.	Pattern changes from struggle for control to unwillingness to assert control.
Rigid	One partner consistently takes one-up position, the other one-down.	Couple consistently struggles or gropes for control.

Control Pattern (row label)

/ **FIGURE 5.1** Relational Control Patterns

Jewitt: I just don't like Marla very well. [one-up]
Sarah: Then stay home. [one-up]

After they had worked out their internal relational rules a little better, Jewitt and Sarah enter a period in which Jewitt was dominant in a rather complementary way. The relationship could be characterized as complementary-rigid. The following exchange illustrates a pattern that could often have been observed in their conversations during the first year or so after taking the apartment.

Jewitt: Let's meet at the Commons about five o'clock for dinner. [one-up]
Sarah: Okay. [one-down] By the way, what show are we going to see Saturday night? [one-down]
Jewitt: *Butch Cassidy.* [one-up]
Sarah: Great. [one-down]

Flexibly complementary relationships are healthiest, in our opinion, because they allow both partners an equal power and voice in establishing relational rules. The direction of influence in persuasion will tend to move back and forth in an adaptive and flexible way. Flexible complementarity is characteristic of relationships in which the partners share power; they are assertive, yet will-

/ **Players of chess choose when and how to exert control; so do people involved in interpersonal persuasion.**

ing to listen; they influence, yet are open to being influenced. Eventually Sarah and Jewitt developed such a pattern. The pattern remained complementary, but was much more flexible than before. Observe a typical conversation during this period:

Sarah:	Hey, guess what. My Friday lab was cancelled. I sure would like to get away this weekend. Wanna go somewhere? [one-up]
Jewitt:	Wow. That sound's great. [one-down]
Sarah:	Yeah. Well, I was thinking of going down to the city. You know, I could show you some of the old spots, and. . . . [one-up]
Jewitt:	I dunno, Sarah. The city makes me nervous. How about that backpacking idea we talked about before. [one-up]
Sarah:	We could consider it, I suppose. [one-down]
Jewitt:	Come on. Let's do it. You'd love French Pete's Trail. [one-up]
Sarah:	But when would I get to take you to the city? [one-across]
Jewitt:	Next time, I promise. [one-down]
Sarah:	Okay, we'll go to French Pete's. [one-down]

/ *Trust in interpersonal relationships.*   We do not want to leave the impression that interpersonal persuasion is strictly a matter of power and control. In Chapter 3 we saw the importance of the trust bond. That bond is especially important in the interpersonal arena.[5] Trust involves relying on another person when one has something to risk. If the other person fails to follow through, a loss will be experienced. Trust means faith that the other person will act in ways that will keep the loss from occurring. If you are relying on a climbing partner to secure ropes at the top of a cliff, you are literally risking your life on this trust.

In communication, what is at risk is far less tangible, but can also be important. We risk our self-esteem, the stability of relationships, interpersonal understanding, and other similar relational values when we communicate with others.

Trust means that a person communicates what is meant and felt genuinely, that one's actions and statements are congruent with one's meanings and feelings. It also involves communicating with the best interest of self and others at heart. In short, it is a spirit of communication in the sense of ethical responsibility, as we define it in the first chapter.

Trust is important in persuasion because when we put ourselves on the line by changing attitudes, beliefs, values, and actions, we almost always put something at risk. When trust is lacking, one is less likely to go along with the messages of the individual whose trustworthiness is at question. If you lack trust, you question whether complying with the other person is really in your best interest.

Power, control, and trust, like all elements of persuasion, are embedded in the cognitive system. Let us now examine the role of cognition in the interpersonal arena of persuasion.

/ Compliance-seeking messages

The subject of compliance-seeking in interpersonal relationships is one of the most heavily researched topics of communication.[6] We know from this research that there is no end to the number of tactics people can use in gaining compliance from others. (Less researched, unfortunately, are the ways people seek the assistance of others in their own change.) It would be fruitless to present a long list of "methods" of persuasion at this point. What is more important is to establish a basis for understanding how and why people make certain message choices. In other words, why do you say what you do when you seek compliance from another person?

/ Strategic dimensions   Earlier in this chapter, we discussed the problem of power. Recall that there are three general kinds of power in relationships—control of consequences, relational identification, and value and obligation identification. Most compliance tactics are related to these because people develop persuasive messages on the basis of where they think they have power.

Message strategies are also connected to particular kinds of pressures to act. In other words, your tactics in a persuasion transaction are based on your belief that they will create some kind of pressure for the other person to respond as intended. We refer to this pressure as a force. Recall from the last chapter that individuals change their cognitive system by the activation of a variety of change processes involving learning, perception, and tension reduction. *Strategic force* is the pressure arising from communicators' intentions to bring one or more of these processes into play.

Actually, any statement or series of statements intended to influence may make use of several of these forces. Each force thus corresponds to a strategic dimension of the compliance-gaining message. Although compliance-gaining strategies set up forces of influence, there are usually counterforces influencing the person not to comply. This is why persuasion is always a matter of transaction.

One cannot tell an individual's compliance-gaining strategy from just listening to the message. You will not necessarily detect on the surface what kind of force a communicator is really using. A single message might involve any number of strategic dimensions, which would only be apparent if you knew the individuals' own perceptions of the kind of power in the relationship, their perceptions of one another, and the rule structure of the relationship.

Any strategy may have a variety of dimensions, several forces, and hence more than one basis of power. There are many useful ways to present the dimensions of compliance-gaining. For purposes of clarity, we will narrow down the strategic dimensions to eight. We think these explain most of the factors that operate in one form or another in compliance-seeking message strategies, at least in our society. Keep in mind that these are dimensions; they are not separate tactics or strategies.

Table 5.1 lists the strategic dimensions of compliance-gaining communication. Next to each dimension is the corresponding force believed to result from the dimension. Notice that the strategic dimensions are organized according to the basis of power employed. This classification is important because it reminds us that most elements of strategy are in fact related to one's perceived basis for power in the situation.

The first power base is *control of expectations and consequences*. This source of power involves the perceived ability to apply rewards and punishments in the future. The strategic dimension arising from this source of power is *sanctioning*. Here the individual states directly or indirectly that one's compliance will lead to certain desired rewards or that noncompliance will be punished in some way.

The type of force leading to influence in this case is reinforcement. *Reinforcement* is an action following a behavior that increases or decreases the likelihood of the behavior being repeated. Typically, rewarded behavior is repeated

TABLE 5.1
Strategic Dimensions of Compliance-Gaining

Power Base	Strategic Dimension	Force
Expectations/Consequences	Sanctioning	Reinforcement
Relational Identification	Authority	Credibility
	Relational Bond	Commitment
Values and Obligations	Exchange	Reciprocation
	Social Expectations	Social Facilitation
	Personal Identity	Self Maintenance and Enhancement
None	Personal Belief	Logic
	Open	(Self Defined)

and punished behavior is not, although this division is overly simple. Promises, threats, inducements, allurements, and warnings often embody the sanctioning dimension of influence. Power through reinforcement is the basis of coercion. Persuasion, too, can be based on this form of power, so long as the control of consequences is shared between the participants.

Recall from the last chapter that people have the tendency to reinforce their own behavior. We set up our own rewards and punishments. If you wanted to change some aspect of your life and felt unable to provide your own reinforcers, you would probably respond well to the sanctioning of another person.

The second base of power is *relational identification*. Here the individual makes use of a value or quality of the relationship itself as a basis for influence. We have already discussed several elements of persuasion in Chapter 4 that relate to this basis of power. These include trust, competence, similarity, and attraction. In addition to these, and often as a result of them, commitment to the relationship often creates a power bond. Strategies that make use of relational commitment appeal to the individuals' sense of commitment to the relationship itself. Messages that involve altruism, cooperation, devotion, loyalty, and the like may also involve the relational bond dimension.

The third kind of power is the *appeal to values or obligations*. Here power arises out of a person's ability to identify a value of the other person and to link the desired behavior to that value, or to define an act as an obligation. Exchange, social expectations, and personal identity are strategic dimensions frequently tied to this source of power.

Exchange involves tactics and strategies that include reciprocity in some way. In other words, the listener is induced to follow through on some exchange with the speaker. Promises, debts, and guilt are examples of particular appeals that might fall under this category. The *social expectation* dimension makes use of social norms and external rules. The force behind this dimension is social facilitation or the need of the person to associate and be included. Messages that included statements of group obligation, sense of membership, social acceptability, and conformity may involve this dimension. The third strategic dimension in this category is *personal identity*. This dimension relies on self-maintenance and self-enhancement as a basis for influence. Here the appeal is to the individual's self-identity, self-esteem, or need to promote the self. Flattery, esteem, and self-feeling appeals may involve the personal identity dimension.

The last category on Table 5.1 embraces those dimensions that are not connected to the personal power of the speaker. Two are significant. *Personal belief* is aimed at the individual's own belief system and argues logically within that realm. This would include messages that do not involve some of the other kinds of forces listed above. In each case the individual comes to a logical conclusion about the subject at hand based on consistency with his or her own beliefs.

Sometimes in persuasive transactions people make no appeals at all, or at least there is no intent to do so. A request is made and one partner is left to his or her own devices to establish whether there is sufficient force in any aspect of the relationship to comply. The basic difference between this strategic dimension and the others is that it involves no sense of force by the initiator. The opportunity for compliance is made available without prejudice, and the other person is moved or not moved on the basis of whatever forces are most salient at the time.

It would not be practical to illustrate all of these strategic dimensions of message choice. For the most part they are self-explanatory. However, to give an idea of how the dimensions operate, consider the case of Paul and Ray. Paul knew he was gay by the time he was a senior in high school, and he struggled with this sexual identity throughout his freshman and sophomore years in college. By his sophomore year, he had become a regular member of a gay support group and with its help became content with his sexual orientation. He had also by that time developed a regular relationship with Ray. Although their closest friends knew they were homosexual, Paul and Ray had not really come out publicly. During the summer between their junior and senior years, however, Ray began to put more and more pressure on Paul to come out. Ray wanted them to live together and be more open about their relationship, but Paul's reluctance stood in their way.

"You know things aren't going to change for you," Ray asserted on one occasion. "Why not go all the way? Summer is a good time to make the move, and by fall, we can just be ourselves without all this fuss."

Paul balked, but Ray would not let up. "I really want to come out," Ray said. "I care about you and want to come out together. We'll just go to the group and say, 'We're doing it; gonna start by talking to our parents this weekend.' You know that'll go over really well with the group. Plus you will be a model for some of the other guys who are still dragging their feet."

The couple did talk to the group about it. With a lot of support from some of the older men, Paul decided to visit his mother and father, which marked perhaps the most difficult step in his coming out.

The strategic dimensions of persuasion are not readily apparent from analyzing the message itself, but knowing something about this situation allows us to ascertain the sources of power used by Ray in his appeal to Paul. First, power by controlling consequences, although not a highly salient part of the persuasion, may have nevertheless had an impact because of the implicit threat that Ray would come out one way or another, with Paul or without him. Paul may have felt this pressure and have bent in part to indirect sanctioning. More direct, however, were the strategic dimensions of relational commitment, exchange, social expectations, and personal identity. Ray's personal involvement with Paul created a strong bond that affected the persuasion in a very direct way. His willingness to make coming out a joint venture illustrates the dimension of exchange. The support group really wanted Paul and Ray to go public, so that social expectation also created pressure for change, and Ray smartly made use of it in his appeal. Finally, Ray pointed out to Paul that his personal identity was wrapped up in a decision as to whether or not to come out, the dimension of the message that may have been the strongest of all.

/ Strategic dimensions and processes of change. The dimensions outlined here are ways in which communicators attempt to bring about various pro-

cesses of change. As discussed in Chapter 4, these mechanisms can be grouped into three broad categories—learning, perception, and tension reduction. The strategies detailed here do not bear any one-to-one relationship with these change processes, but can relate to all of them in one way or another. Table 5.2 illustrates the relationship of strategies of cognitive change. The cells in the table mention some of the ways in which the strategic dimensions may bring about learning, perception, and tension reduction. The statements in Table 5.2 are illustrative only, however. Strategic dimensions can trigger the three kinds of change in numerous ways, and how an individual will respond to persuasive messages depends upon his or her social construction of reality, including the interpretation and action rules in force.

TABLE 5.2

Strategic Dimensions and Factors of Change

Strategic Dimensions	Factors of Change		
	Learning	*Perception*	*Tension-Reduction*
Sanctioning	Sets up positive and negative reinforcers	Modifies ego-involvement	Creates approach-avoidance situations, depending upon one's place in the need hierarchy
Authority	Provides "expert" guidance for individuals to structure their own learning	May affect perceptual anchor or attribution	Creates tension between perception of person and attitude toward object
Relational Bond	Builds a basis for modeling	Increases salience of attribution process	
Exchange	Provides a reason for a person to put self in a learning situation	Affects self-attribution	Provides a "solution" to tension in the form of reciprocation
Social Expectations	Provide a reason for a person to put self in a learning situation	Create setting for pro-attitudinal advocacy	Provide way to meet certain "social needs"
Personal Identity	Promotes role playing	Affects ego-involvement	Facilitates change in situations in which self-identity depends on consistency
Personal Belief	Provides a reason for a person to put self in a learning situation	Basis for foot-in-the-door technique	Traditional logic is based on consistency

/ Elements of compliance situations.   The above discussion describes compliance-gaining strategies, but it does not provide much of a sense of why people choose the strategies employed in their messages. Message choice can be effective or ineffective. Some people are usually effective in appealing to other people; others are often ineffective. Most people, however, vary from day to day and from situation to situation in the success of their message choices.

Several factors are important in message choice. We will consider (1) perceived objectives of compliance, (2) benefits of compliance, (3) locus of control, (4) self-justification, (5) involvement of the communicators, (6) the availability of sanction, and (7) relational consequences. Again, the objective of this discussion is to provide not a recipe for how to persuade, but a basis for understanding message choice.

The first element of compliance-gaining situations in interpersonal relationships is the participants' *perceived objectives for compliance*. Are the objectives of this transaction primarily instrumental, interpersonal, identity maintenance, or a combination? (We discussed these objectives earlier in this chapter.) The point is that what one wishes to accomplish within the relationship is an important consideration in message choice. Further, the degree to which these objectives are shared by the partners makes an important difference in the strategy employed.

The objective of Ray and Paul's discussion was certainly instrumental; they wanted to get a task done—to decide when and how to come out. At the same time, their self-identities were an important consideration, and they were well aware that the outcome would have relational consequences as well. Ray's self-identity in this situation was probably a strong factor in his decision to tell Paul that he wanted to come out, which helped Paul understand why something had to change.

The second factor of importance in deciding how to seek compliance is the *perceived benefits of compliance*. Communicators in a relationship should think about the benefits for both parties. What disadvantages might also come about if compliance is achieved? For example, if Ray had taken an unyielding position on the issue by giving an ultimatum or by threatening a negative sanction, he would have run the risk of Paul's complying grudgingly or not at all, which could have harmed the relationship itself. He understood Paul's discomfort and the potential negative consequences of compliance and therefore chose a strategy that would both achieve his objective and help to make Paul feel good about it.

The third situational element of persuasion in interpersonal settings involves the attribution process, as discussed in Chapter 3. *Perceived locus of control* is an especially important situational variable of attribution. Locus of control is one's perception of whether behavior is controlled from within or without. In some situations we attribute our behavior to situational factors that are beyond our control. In these situations, the locus of control is perceived to be outside of ourselves. Often, however, we believe that we have the power to control what happens to us. Under this condition, the locus of control is internal. If the other person feels that situational factors are especially strong, one will probably appeal on the grounds of external pressures or force, or attempt to help the other person regain some power to overcome situational pressures. If the other person feels he or she has control over the situation, one's persuasive messages will probably appeal to that sense of choice. Persuasion can, for instance, help the other person visualize taking control of some aspect of the cognitive system. When this happens, the changing person mentally role-plays being different, and change results.

Ray undoubtedly understood Paul's sense of internal control in deciding to come out. Therefore, Ray knew that he had to appeal to Paul's sense of values by having him identify with other members of the group.

The next situational factor that enters into message choice is *self-justification*. This involves the perceived rights of the participants to attempt persuasion. In other words, one feels the need to justify compliance seeking. Status often enters into the decision of whether to try persuasion. Often persons with lower status in a relationship are not considered to have the "right" to seek compliance. Relational rules certainly enter into self-justification. Rules will prescribe when and what kind of compliance seeking is permissible in the relationship.

A challenging situation is that in which you are compelled to seek the compliance of another person, knowing that person would consider your persuasion inappropriate. Such a situation might involve two persuasive objectives: gaining compliance and changing the rule prohibiting persuasion itself.

Such was the case in the relationship between Myra and her sister Jenny. Myra, just a year older than her sister, was Jenny's idol. Throughout their childhood, Myra had always taken the role of Jenny's protector, basking in her younger sister's admiration and loyalty. At school, they were inseparable, and family and friends were constantly amazed at how close they were in all of their activities. Myra and Jenny attended the same high school and the same college. A very strong rule in their relationship was to do things together and to keep no secrets.

Myra and Jenny had both dated regularly in high school and college and were quick to tell one another about their dates. Neither, however, developed any serious relationships, and they certainly never let their boyfriends interfere with their relationship with one another. In fact, Myra often wondered if she was not letting Jenny prevent her from getting serious with a man.

Soon after graduating from college, Myra took a job as an entry-level accountant. There she met and began dating a coworker. The couple soon became quite serious and within a few months became engaged. A problem developed when the couple decided to move out of the area after they got married. Jenny's first reaction was to "share" in this plan by suggesting that she could move to Myra's new town, "so we can stay close." That suggestion did not set well with Myra, and she decided to face the issue head-on.

Myra knew this would be no easy task. It involved not only convincing Jenny not to move, but also changing the rule structure of the relationship so as to allow that possibility. She decided to deal with the inseparability rule itself. In so doing, she was seeking two forms of compliance on Jenny's part—to agree to a change in the rule structure of the relationship and to allow her to move away with her fiancé.

"Jenny, we really have to talk about my move. I'm never going to be farther than a phone's reach away from you, but we just can't continue to stick together like two pieces of a dress. Eventually we have to have some independence from one another, and I think now is the best time to do it. Fred is never going to replace you, but I need him in a special way. And you need to be freer to get close to other people too."

Jenny's first reaction was to feel hurt. She predictably thought that Myra was trying to brush her off. After they talked it over for several hours, however, Jenny realized that Myra was right. She even felt a little guilty to have reacted so defensively. This transaction was significant because it marked an important passage in Myra and Jenny's relationship. Soon Jenny herself began enjoying her independence, and although the sisters remain close after several years, they each have their own lives in distant cities.

Let us look again at what Myra said to Jenny. Myra had to deal with two objectives—changing the rules of the relationship to permit her to bring the subject up and getting Jenny not to move to the same town. She relied almost completely on relational commitment strategies. Because of their implicit trust, the persuasion was effective. If that level of trust had not existed, Jenny would have had genuine cause to attribute malice to Myra's suggestion that they live apart. In other words, Myra was relying on her years of credibility as big sister to help her out in this difficult situation.

The fifth factor in the compliance situation that will guide communicators in choice of message strategies is the *perceived involvement of the communicators*. This element is the degree to which each communicator is involved cognitively in the problem. To what extent will each be able to attend to its complexity? Perceived involvement is important because it partially controls the degree of attentiveness of the communicators and the amount of information and motivation they may require. In a recent *New Yorker* cartoon, a wife says, "I told him I've decided to leave him, but he doesn't seem able to take it in." In a case in which both partners are heavily involved in the compliance situation, messages can be based on assumptions of knowledge and concern on the part of the other. If one partner is not very involved, the compliance-seeker will have to supply more information and press harder for attention and response.

One of the basic rules of most relational persuasion is to provide just enough information to achieve agreement, but no more. Just how much do you say in seeking agreement from another person? You know that you have to choose your message tactics from an infinite set of possible statements. Your problem is to determine how much of what you could possibly say should actually be said. We have discussed several factors that enter into that decision, not least of which is the degree of involvement and attention the other person already has in the issue.

The next situational factor is the *perceived availability of sanctions*. Here the communicators assess whether they have any power by virtue of being able to control consequences. Parents usually have a great deal of control over the consequences of their children's behavior. Therefore, sanctioning is a frequent dimension of parental compliance-gaining. Although children have fewer options for sanctioning adult behavior, they are not powerless in this regard, as any parent will testify. For example, many a small child lets the parent clearly know that a certain behavior will lead to an embarrassing temper tantrum in public. Interesting research on the ways in which children seek the compliance of adults shows that with age and maturity, children tend to increase in their ability and willingness to use relational and value dimensions of message strategies, relying less on simple-minded threats and promises.[7] They seem to come to understand their limited ability to invoke sanctions and therefore rely on other kinds of message strategies. This is not to imply that people abandon the use of sanctioning; most adults use it often, but other sources of force also become options in persuasion situations.

The final situational element affecting message choice is the *perceived relational consequences* of the message choice. This factor involves the individual's assessment of the nature and stage of the relationship, the value of the relationship, the importance of the relationship to one's personal esteem, and the internal rule structure for the use of compliance-gaining. Obviously, the answers to these questions determine in a major way what kinds of messages will be used in seeking compliance. That certainly was the case in our examples of Ray and Paul and of Myra and Jenny.

It should be clear from this discussion of compliance-gaining that interpersonal persuasion is complex and involves many factors. Compliance-gaining communication is a fact of social life. Our relationships are built on a base of consensus and compliance, give and take, offering and asking. Much of the time compliance is not a problem; it is accepted and negotiated as part of daily life. Often, however, consensus is not easily achieved because of conflict. Persuasion and conflict are inextricably intertwined. Let us now turn our attention to the role of persuasion in conflict.

/ Persuasion and conflict

What is conflict? We all know conflict intuitively when we see it. Defining *conflict* is somewhat more difficult. Unlike the situations we discussed above, conflict involves struggle for control. In conflict, one's compliance-gaining attempts are met not only by resistance, but by counterattempts to persuade. In short, conflict is a situation in which individuals' goals are perceived to be incompatible and/or power seems scarce enough to require a struggle to achieve it.[8]

/ Types of conflict.
Reduced to its simplest terms, conflict can be of two types.[9] *Distributive conflict* is one in which the potential outcomes are fixed. In other words, the parties literally compete for particular payoffs that will be either won or lost. In the end, then, the payoffs will be "distributed" between the parties, and the one who gets the most is perceived to "win." We are reminded in this

context of the old rule of life: "Who dies with the most toys wins." Certain sporting events, such as boxing and football, in which there is a clear winner and loser are perfect examples of distributive conflicts.

Integrative conflicts are those in which the outcomes can be molded such that both parties benefit in some way. Of course, the outcome for each may not be what was originally desired; otherwise, there would be no conflict. In integrative conflict, however, the parties perceive some chance for "integration" of their separate interests. Notice that the type of conflict is a matter of perception; what is important is the kind of conflict perceived by the parties to be facing them. This qualification is important because it means that the type of conflict can change: what was perceived as an integrative conflict can become distributive, and what is perceived originally as a distributive conflict can change to an integrative one. This condition is important for persuasion, and we shall return to it in Chapter 8.

/ *A note on avoiding conflict.*   There is a genuine temptation in human relations to avoid conflicts. Conflict is rarely pleasant, and, as the foregoing discussion clearly demonstrates, working out conflict takes time and effort. However, conflict is a natural part of life, and avoiding it not only forgoes growth opportunities but also creates additional problems in the future.

Certain message strategies can signal that important conflict is being avoided. These include silence, denial, changing the topic, abstractness, inappropriate joking, postponing, inappropriate teasing, and others.

Conflict can be managed productively by defining conflict situations as problems of integration rather than distribution and by aiming one's persuasion toward the development of solutions that will benefit all parties involved. Such an approach greatly broadens the bases of power that can be used to influence other people, making more dimensions of compliance gaining available. We cannot promise that the problem-solving attitude will always succeed, but it certainly has a better chance of success than the win-lose trap.

Conflict is a crucial topic relevant to persuasion. Although we depart temporarily from that subject at this point, it will be taken up separately as it relates to groups and organizations in Chapter 6, negotiation in Chapter 7, and social movements in Chapter 11.

/ *Theory* / *Practice* / *Analysis*

Theory

1. Interpersonal persuasion occurs in the context of a relationship, which is a link between two or more people who have expectations for each other's behavior. The nature of the relationship is determined by its rules.

2. Rules are used to guide persuasion in relationships.

3. The goals of persuasion are (a) to maintain or change the relationship, (b) to accomplish instrumental objectives, and (c) to change or maintain one's self-identity.

4. The functions of persuasion are (a) conflict management and (b) the dissemination of ideas in society.

5. The sources of personal influence are (a) power, (b) control, and (c) trust.

6. The dimensions of compliance-gaining message strategies are (a) sanctioning, (b) authority, (c) relational bond, (d) exchange, (e) social expectations, (f) personal identity, and (g) personal belief.

7. The elements of compliance situations are (a) objectives of compliance, (b) benefits of compliance, (c) locus of control, (d) self-justification, (e) communicator involvement, (f) the availability of sanctions, and (g) relational consequences.

8. The nature of persuasion in conflicts depends upon whether the conflicts are perceived to be distributive or integrative.

Practice

1. Think about an important relationship in your life that involves persuasion from time to time. Make a list of the sources of your power in this relationship. What was or is an issue in the relationship which you have discussed or might discuss in the near future? Devise a compliance-gaining message for each source of power listed. What dimensions of compliance gaining are embodied in your message statements? Now write a composite message combining several or all of the dimensions of compliance identified above. (Remember that this is only an exercise; what you would actually say would depend upon a number of situational variables not included in this exercise.)

2. Pair up with another person. Discuss some conflicts in which you have recently been involved. Choose one conflict for a role-playing exercise. Explain enough about this conflict with your partner so that he or she can take the role of the other person. Define the conflict as distributive. Take a few minutes to role-play the conflict from this perspective. Now define the conflict as integrative. Role-play again. Discuss the differences between the message strategies employed under the two conditions. Now repeat the exercise using one of your partner's conflicts.

Analysis

1. Consider a relationship with someone close to you. If necessary, take a few days to observe your interaction with this person. Tape-record some conversations between the two of you if possible. Now carefully analyze some of the rules guiding the relationship. Distinguish between interpretive rules and action rules. Go over the rules you think are operating and indicate how these might enter into your choice of compliance-gaining strategies. Now indicate what compliance gaining dimensions are apparent in your strategies and what sources of power seem to be operating in the relationship.

2. Attend a meeting of a committee or body discussing an important and controversial issue. Listen for how the conflict is defined. Note the message tactics used in the persuasion of individuals in the group. Is the problem defined in distributive or integrative terms? To what extent do you think that the persuasive messages are affected by the group's definition of the conflict?

Notes

[1]This discussion of relationships is taken largely from the research and theory in relational communication and rules theory. One of the seminal works in relational communication is Paul Watzlawick, Janet Beavin, and Don Jackson, *Pragmatics of Human Communication: A Study of Interactional Patterns, Pathologies, and Paradoxes* (New York: Norton, 1967). See also Susan B. Shimanoff, *Communication Rules: Theory and Research* (Beverly Hills: Sage Publications, 1980) and W. Barnett Pearce and Vernon Cronen, *Communication, Action, and Meaning* (New York: Praeger, 1980).

[2]This distinction is taken from L. Edna Rogers-Millar and Frank E. Millar, "Domineeringness and Dominance: A Transactional View," *Human Communication Research,* 5 (1979): 238–46.

[3]This discussion of power is based primarily on Lawrence R. Wheeless, Robert Barraclough, and Robert Stewart, "Compliance-Gaining and Power in Persuasion in *Communication Yearbook 7,* ed. Robert N. Bostrom (Beverly Hills: Sage Publications, 1983), pp. 105–145.

[4]Several fine sources are available on the subject of control in relationships. Among the best known work in this area is that of Rogers and Millar. For a summary of the theory behind their work, see Frank E. Millar and L. Edna Rogers, "A Relational Approach to Interpersonal Communication," in *Explorations in Interpersonal Communication,* ed. Gerald Miller (Beverly Hills: Sage, 1976),pp. 87–103. See also L. Edna Rogers-Millar and Frank E. Millar, "Domineeringness and Dominance: A Transactional View," *Human Communication Research* 5 (1979): 238–46.

[5]For a more complete discussion of trust, see David M. Jabusch and Stephen W. Littlejohn, *Elements of Speech Communication* (Boston: Houghton Mifflin, 1981), pp. 103–111, 139. See also Kim Giffin and Robert Patton, "Personal Trust in Human Interaction," in *Basic Readings in Interpersonal Communication,* ed. Kim Giffin and Robert Patton (New York: Harper and Row, 1971), pp. 375–91.

[6]For an excellent synopsis of this literature, see Wheeless, Barraclough, and Stewart, "Compliance-Gaining." This discussion of dimensions of compliance-gaining relies heavily on that source. See also Michael J. Cody, Mary Lou Moelfel, and William J. Jordan, "Dimensions of Compliance-Gaining Situations," *Human Communication Research* 9 (1983): 99–133; Richard L. Wiseman and William Schenck-Hamlin, "A Multidimensional Scaling Validation of an Inductively-Derived Set of Compliance-Gaining Strategies," *Communication Monographs* 48 (1981): 251–70; and William J. Schenck-

Hamlin, Richard L. Wiseman, and G.N. Georgacarakos, "A Model of Properties of Compliance-Gaining Strategies," *Communication Quarterly* 30 (1982): 92–99.

7Jesse G. Delia, Susan L. Kline, and Brant R. Burleson, "The Development of Persuasive Communication Strategies in Kindergartners through Twelfth-Graders," *Communication Monographs* 46 (1979): 241–56.

8This definition is adapted from Joyce Hocker Frost and William W. Wilmot, *Interpersonal Conflict* (Dubuque, IA: W.C. Brown, 1978), p. 9.

9For discussions of these types of conflict, see Alan L. Sillars, "The Sequential and Distributional Structure of Conflict Interactions as a Function of Attributions Concerning the Locus of Responsibility and Stability of Conflicts," in *Communication Yearbook 4,* ed. Dan Nimmo (New Brunswick, NJ: Transaction Books, 1980), pp. 217–35; and Linda L. Putnam and Tricia S. Jones, "Reciprocity in Negotiations: An Analysis of Bargaining Interaction," *Communication Monographs* 49 (1982): *171–91.*

6 / Persuasion in Organizations

Consider the case of the Melville Environmental Center (MEC), a community-based educational organization. Melville is a city of about 30,000 in central California. It is located just a short distance from several other medium-sized cities and about 150 miles from the San Francisco Bay area. Because none of the other nearby cities have similar organizations, the MEC serves a rather broad geographical area and sponsors programs in most of the communities in its service area. It is funded by grants, donations, municipal contracts, and patron fees.

Among its many activities, the organization sponsors educational programs for the schools, recycling centers, walk-in exhibits, media presentations (including a regular weekly television series on a local station), and conferences. MEC is currently assisting the nearby city of Newton to develop a major grant proposal for the funding of a model municipal solar utility demonstration project. The MEC has twenty-five paid employees and several volunteers.

The organization was founded in 1975 by Allison Russell, then a recent graduate from the University of California. Allison had majored in environmental studies and minored in business administration. She and two classmates started the neophyte organization on a shoestring; her own clever entrepreneurship quickly expanded the operation. The two classmates left for better paying jobs in 1977, but the organization continued to develop into a solid community service group. Allison remains the executive director; four of her associates are the other key employees: Benjamin Chin is the associate director, Lauren Kendall the office manager and secretary, Rich Blumenthal director of school relations, and Alan Herrera an intern from Cal State. All are stationed in the central office in Melville although, with the exception of Lauren, they work out of the office much of the time.

Although fictional, the case of the Melville Environmental Center can help us understand persuasion on a number of levels, including both persuasion aimed at groups and individuals outside the organization, and persuasion among those affiliated with the company. We will return to look at this case again later in the chapter as we encounter important concepts relevant to persuasion in groups and organizations.

In the last chapter we discussed persuasion in interpersonal settings, emphasizing relational communication. Here we change the focus of our lens a bit to look at persuasion in one of the most common settings for interpersonal communication, the organizational network. Specifically, this chapter deals with persuasion in work groups and organizations. All of the principles and concepts discussed in the last chapter apply to persuasion in this setting, but additional considerations must be taken up in our study of persuasion in organizations and groups.

/ The Nature of the Organizational Arena

Human beings are by nature organizational creatures. We do not exist as independent entities, nor are we just points in an undifferentiated mass of humanity. The real human condition lies somewhere between these two extremes. In every culture, people find identity in groups and other social structures. Naturally occurring social groups, such as families and friendship cliques, are largely governed by the principles discussed in the last chapter, but there is another kind of group that looms into importance. This is the work group, which exists because people join together in cooperation to accomplish tasks. In turn, work groups link together in larger networks, or organizations, which constitute the essence of the world of work. Much of our daily communication, including persuasion, occurs in and through task groups and organizations. We communicate to make shoes, to serve health needs, to teach, to catch fish, to play ball, and to accomplish innumerable other work tasks.

/ Characteristics of groups and organizations

There are many kinds of groups. For purposes of discussion, we have divided these into naturally occurring social groups and task groups. The latter type of group and its larger complement, the organization, are the subject of this chapter. Thus one of the distinguishing characteristics of groups and organizations most important to this discussion is their task nature. By *task,* we simply mean that these groups exist to accomplish something other than their own maintenance, that they aim to achieve certain goals beyond social bonding among the members themselves. (Of course, social cohesion in such groups is also very important, as we shall see throughout this chapter.)

An important characteristic of the organizational setting is its formality. All social structures have form, brought about by repeated patterns of interaction among the members of the group. In the organizational setting, however, the formality of the group takes on special importance. The formal structure of the group and organization have great impact on the nature of the communication

/ A zoning board is definable as an organization because it exists to accomplish a specific task.

which occurs there. How an organization such as the Boy Scouts of America is structured determines in large measure what its members talk about and how that talk is accomplished.

What gives form to the group and organization? Several elements of structure will be considered in this chapter, including the interactional patterns among members, norms, roles, and rules. For now, let us discuss rules as a manifestation of formality. As we saw in the last chapter, rules are expected patterns of interaction, or guidelines for how to interpret and how to act. Most organizations have rather clear rules. As a member of an organization, you would probably have a definite sense of how to interpret the actions and statements of those with whom you work as well as how to respond. Many of the rules go unstated, but they are clear nonetheless. In organizations we know who can initiate interaction, who can be approached, who can propose a delay, what topics can or cannot by discussed, who can interrupt or be interrupted, who can terminate interaction, and how long interaction should last. Many other interactional rules pervade the daily life of organization members. Again, organizations and groups differ in the clarity and rigidity of their rules. Organizations that have more flexible or ambiguous rule structures are less formal; those that have more rigid rule structures display high formality. That difference is evident between, say, a self-formed youth club and the Cook County Public Assistance Department.

/ The linking function of communication

The fundamental structure of any group or organization arises from communication. Communication, it has been said, is a process of organizing.[1] In other words, all elements of form, including norms, roles, and rules, arise because of communication transactions. An organization is not the physical plant, the equipment, the product, or even the people. Without communication and persuasion, the organization simply would not exist.

/ *Organizational structure.* Organizations are created by communication links among the people in the organization. The organizing process begins by interaction among two individuals, the *dyad*. Dyads are linked into groups, and groups are joined to form organizations. The link itself is always a communication transaction. Figure 6.1 illustrates.[2]

Actually, the structure of the organization is established by patterns of interaction. This structure of communication links is called a *network*. If there were no pattern of repeated links, communication contacts would be random, and there would be no structure, no organization. On the other hand, the structure brought about by the links among individuals is fluid, never occurring in exactly the same way. This quality of fluidity in organizational communication is what makes organizations behave like organisms: they are alive, always in motion, always changing; yet, they have a discernable structure as well.

We must complicate this view of organizational structure with another qual-

/ **FIGURE 6.1** An Organizational Network

ification. Not only are organizations constantly in flux, but they also have several simultaneous structures or networks, depending upon the function of the communication. For example, the organization may have an authority-task network, a social network, a grapevine network, and perhaps several others.

/ *Communication and the reduction of uncertainty.* Although communication has many functions in organizations, the overriding reason for communicating in the group or organization is to reduce uncertainty.[3] To accomplish a goal, the group must eliminate alternatives—competing interpretations, behaviors, values, problems, solutions. This is not to say that all uncertainty is removed; some ambiguity is necessary to maintain creativity and flexibility in dealing with problems. But the field must be narrowed, and communication is the way that people achieve consensus or agreement on what to eliminate and what to include in accomplishing the task. Another way to describe this process of narrowing is that through interaction important concepts in the reality dimension of cognition come to be shared.

When particular roles are established for individuals and rules of interaction emerge, we become more certain about what others mean in their statements and about how we are supposed to act. Organizational structure or form, as described above, is nothing more than the achievement of clarity through the elimination of alternatives. If you are a carpenter working on a building project, you are probably clear about what to do at work. You know when to arrive, how to find out what to do in a given day, and how to do it. If the situation is still uncertain, you will attempt to clarify by asking coworkers or the boss.

Consensus, of course, is not something that just jumps into existence when people organize. It is achieved over time, imperfectly, largely as a consequence of people's influence over one another. That people influence the behavior of others makes organization possible. There are a variety of forms of influence; persuasion is one of the most prevalent. This is why persuasion, as a dimension of communication, is so important in groups and organizations. In this chapter we will see how persuasion functions in reducing uncertainty.

We pointed out above that the structure of an organization is determined by the communication links among the individuals in the organization. As illustration, let us look again at the example of the Melville Environmental Center, outlined on the first pages of this chapter. Consider three sets of links, or structures, of the MEC. The first structure consists of the formal lines of authority on the organization chart. Although the MEC relies quite heavily on participative decision making, the lines of authority are known and followed as necessary. These lines form one of the structures of MEC. On the other hand, if you look at the actual work relationship in terms of frequency of contact, you will see another structure. Because of friendship and social ties among the members of MEC, a third structure is also apparent. Figure 6.2 illustrates these three network structures in the MEC.

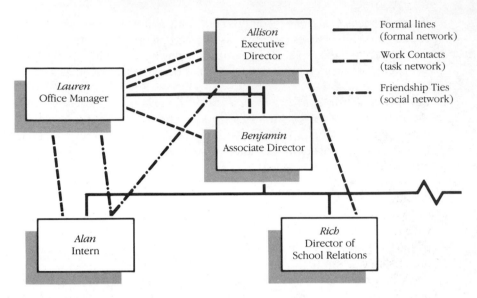

/ FIGURE 6.2 An Illustrative Network

/ The culture of an organization

When you think about it, organizations are really cultures because they are comprised of people with shared meanings and behaviors.[4] In other words, through communication, the members of the organization create their own realities. Normally we do not consciously think about the cultural elements of organizations in which we work. However, a moment's reflection reveals that in an organization we are constantly giving "performances" or acting in ways that reveal and reinforce the reality in which we believe we are working. Communication is the vehicle of organizational performance; it is the way in which people create the organizational culture.

Consider for a moment the types of performances in which people engage. Some are rituals: they are performed repeatedly in just about the same way in order to reinforce our meanings for the world around us. Going to the coffee machine at 10:00 every morning, eating lunch with the same group at the same time in the same place each Wednesday, having retirement dinners, having an 8:30 conference with the secretary every morning—all of these are rituals.

Another manifestation of an organization's culture is the use of language. Members of the organization use language to transform their activities into meaningful cultural realities. A dean at one of our universities once coined a phrase to describe backward thinking people: "bare-handed fish-grabbers in a world of seiners and netters." Everybody who heard that cracked up. The expression caught on. For years, the term "fish-grabber" was a common expression among certain groups at the university and was used even by people who did not know its origin and really couldn't explain why the expression referred to "a person who resists what we want to accomplish."

There are, of course, many other examples of cultural performances in organizations, such as social courtesies, pleasantries, joking, political moves, and others. The important thing to remember is that the interpretation and action rules of the members of the organization are reflected in communication performances. Persuasion in organizations must make use of these cultural realities. Throughout this chapter, we will discuss the many ways in which individuals rely on the cultural milieu of their associates in organizational persuasion.

/ Elements of Organizational Persuasion

We have already seen that control in organizations is an outcome of reducing uncertainty. By their very nature organizations and groups require interpersonal influence and, hence, persuasion. In fact, organizations and groups functioning without persuasion are inconceivable.

/ Elements of power in organizational persuasion

We discussed power at some length in the last chapter. This basis of persuasion is no less important in the organizational setting. You may recall from Chapter 5 that power involves access to resources that can influence.

Power is extremely important in organizational influence. The allocation of roles and authority in an organization grants a clearer distribution of power than is usually the case outside organizations. Supervisors, merely by their legitimate authority, have certain power subordinates do not have. Individuals with access to certain information in the organization have a kind of power. Power also arises from having access to certain individuals in the communication network by being a member of a large number of groups.

How power is used is terribly important.[5] Rich Blumenthal, the Director of School Relations of the Melville Environmental Center, tells of an incident in a large corporation for which he formerly worked. The direction of that company had become economically unprofitable. Many decision makers at various levels in the organization recognized the problem and moved to establish diversification and change. The executive vice-president, who had been with the company for twenty-six years and was generally perceived as quite effective, felt personally threatened by the new ideas. Instead of critically and constructively examining the suggestions with an eye to improving them, he used his power to obstruct their implementation. He argued blindly and vigorously against all the proposals and successfully persuaded his immediate staff that the company should not expand into new areas. He drafted recommendations to the president and board of directors, which led to a continuation of old products and services.

Rich now considers himself lucky to have gotten out of the company before it filed for bankruptcy. He often contrasts this negative situation to MEC, where, due to Allison's strong influence, the organization has grown, changed, and thrived.

To say that persuasion results from a power base, though true and important, really tells little. In this section we outline some of the important ways in which the power of persuasion is used by individuals to control aspects of the communication process. Specifically, we refer to three categories—structure, message, and communicator.[6]

/ Structural elements of organizational persuasion

You already know that one of the primary characteristics of organizations is structure, defined by the pattern of communication among members. The nature of the network itself, its structure or form, plays an important role in organizational persuasion. To the extent that individuals can control structure, persuasion itself can be affected, although organizational structure is not easily controlled.

/ *Hierarchiality.* A structural element especially relevant in large organizations is hierarchiality. This element refers to the "height" of the organization chart, or the number of managerial levels in the organization. The more levels, the greater the chance for distortion in upward and downward communication. At the same, time, however, individuals in "tall" organizations have more opportunities for direct contact with their subordinates and superiors, and thus more individual attention. In the "flat" organization the span of supervision is greatly increased, and the manager is unable to remain very accessible to any one subordinate.

What are the implications of hierarchiality for persuasion? In taller organizations individuals probably are able to effect more change through persuasion within the work group itself. Work groups are smaller, and with the opportunity for more individual attention, workers have a greater chance to communicate persuasively with subordinates, superiors, and peers. They also have greater opportunity to establish trust bonds, which are one of the most potent sources of persuasion. This increased persuasive effectiveness within the work group in a tall organization comes with a trade-off, however. Such work groups tend to be isolated within the formal organizational chart in tall organizations. Consequently, the opportunity for influence outside the work group is made difficult by the great number of links upward or downward. Keep in mind that these generalizations do not take into consideration other network structures operating in the organization, which may mitigate the effects of hierarchiality.

/ *Flow control.* The amount of control individuals have in opening or closing channels of communication from moment to moment is itself an interesting and important structural variable. Referred to as *flow control,* this aspect of structure involves the degree to which individuals can regulate the dissemination of information. The key question for the persuader here is, "Can I establish who will receive this message and when?" This element involves channeling one's own messages as well as deciding what messages from others one wants to receive. Timing is very important in organizational persuasion, and one's power to influence is increased by the ability to decide when and to whom to release a message.

Small and informal organizations often exhibit low flow control. Because of the size and relative openness of such organizations, individuals are not free to "sit on" a message very long or to control who hears it. In 1982, certain members of the Newton City Council seriously considered closing its recycling center, which was operated by the MEC. Rich Blumenthal heard this information through the grapevine in one of the schools at which he was then working. Rich knew that the threatened closure was strictly a political move, and had nothing to do with the center's effectiveness. Rich thought that Benjamin Chin could intervene informally and privately with the council members involved. Given Benjamin's reputation with these particular council members, Rich was certain that Ben wold persuade them not to push for closure. On the other hand, Rich was equally certain that if everybody at MEC knew about the closure, the organization would have to "go public" with their objection and probably lose the recycling center. Rich knew that Ben would be reluctant, though he was certain he could talk Ben into taking action by approaching him quietly and directly. The problem was that MEC does not operate this way, and Rich's approach to Ben would erode the openness of communication that Allison had worked so hard to sustain. Needless to say, Rich was in a dilemma. In the end, he decided not to talk with Ben privately, but to mention the news openly in a staff meeting instead. As it turned out, those who wanted to discontinue the center were outvoted at the regular council meeting anyway.

/ Connectedness.   The way in which networks link people together is vital in organizational persuasion. Connectedness is the degree to which individuals are linked together through communication. When connectedness is high, there are a great number of links in comparison to the number of people in the organization; when it is low, the link-to-population ratio is lower and people are therefore more isolated. Connectedness is directly correlated with influence possibilities for two reasons. First, connectedness naturally brings about redundancy in information; with increased links, individuals are more apt to hear the same information several times. Redundancy can reinforce particular points of view and increase the chance that persuasive messages will be effective. Second, in highly connected networks any person's point of view is more apt to be known, increasing that individual's potential influence.

There is, however, a counterforce in highly connected organizations that may mitigate attempts to influence. Connectedness can lead to strong consensus and homogeneity in the organization. If attitudes and values are similar among most members, a different point of view may fall on deaf ears. The sheer weight of opinion may be against attempts to change.

So far we have applied the connectedness variable only to the organization as a whole. It can just as easily be applied to particular groups within the network. Some groups are more connected to the organization than others and probably have more influence in the organization, especially if their members have consensus on particular points of view. The philosophy and style of top management in an organization, or of the supervisor of a work group, greatly affects structural connectedness in the organization or group.

/ *Integrativeness.*   A cousin concept to connectedness is integrativeness. It is applied to particular people in the network and tells us the extent to which any person is connected to the organization as a whole. Even networks with low overall connectedness have some individuals who are well integrated into the network. (When the connectedness of the network is high, more individual members will be integrated.) Highly integrated individuals have many communication contact with others throughout the organization. People who are not very integrated are more isolated. Highly integrated individuals are said to be central, while isolated persons are peripheral. (In the following section we will discuss the various kinds of communication roles that people assume by virtue of their centrality, further clarifying the importance of individual contacts in organizational persuasion.)

There are two kinds of integration. A person may be integrated because he or she knows people who know other people. Such individuals have influence because of indirect connections to many others. The second kind of integration occurs because the individual is personally and directly linked with many others without the help of intermediaries. People who have a large number of direct contacts with others are highly accessible.

The Melville Environmental Center, in part because of Allison's style and in part because of its small size, is an example of accessibility. Everybody at MEC knows everybody else, and, if necessary, a member can speak directly with any other member. In larger organizations, of course, complete accessibility is impossible and may not even be desirable. In very large organizations, accessibility is a condition of the work group or suborganization rather than of the entire organization.

Accessibility affects persuasion by determining potential audiences. The amount of influence a person can exert depends in part on the contacts permitted. Certain highly accessible individuals naturally will have more influence than those who are restricted in the number of people with whom they have contact.

/ *Communication load.*   Another structural variable in organizational persuasion is communication load. *Load* refers to the amount of information individuals are required to process. Overload can inhibit organizational persuasion for a variety of reasons. When individuals have too much information to handle effectively, they may respond by ignoring or filtering out some of the information, by responding in programmed or unthoughtful ways, or by escaping through avoiding communication. Any of these responses can inhibit persuasion because they prevent people from considering what others are saying. Under certain conditions, however, overload can also promote persuasion. Some individuals are more persuasible under stress. Often in overload situations people accept what others are saying less critically because they do not have the energy or time to assess carefully what they read or hear.

On the other hand, underload, or inadequate levels of information, leads to boredom and lack of stimulation. Depending upon an individual's optimum level of arousal, a persuasive message can be more or less effective when the receiver is underloaded. If the listener finds stimulation in involvement, he or she may take the time to "go after" the message critically, resulting in a resistance to change. If the underloaded listener finds stimulation merely in trying something new, the persuasive message might be quite effective.

/ Message elements of organizational persuasion

We have seen that structural elements of persuasion in the organizational setting are usually out of the immediate and direct control of communicators. Message elements, on the other hand, are directly controllable by those who create and consume them. Here we discuss both the transmission and the form of messages.

/ Distribution of information.
The distribution of information involves both structural and message elements. It is a structural concern because choices about who gets a message are somewhat limited by the various structural elements outlined above. On the other hand, one makes active decisions within the realm of choice about potential audiences. The choice of who gets a message not only affects who is potentially affected by the proposal, but also determines in large measure how, when, and to whom the message will be further disseminated.

The choice of message recipient is a tactical decision. If you wish to influence a single individual with whom you have personal contact, you will undoubtedly decide to communicate directly only with that person, but if you wish to influence the group as a whole or parts of the organization with which you do not have direct contact, you will need to route your ideas through others who link you to the appropriate other parties. That is why liaisons have such influence in organizations, as we will explore later in the chapter.

Coalitions are a natural part of organizational life. Coalitions are groups of individuals linked together in the network who share a common point of view and have the potential, as a group, to influence other parts of the organization. One objective of many persuaders in the organizational network is to solicit the cooperation of others by establishing a coalition. Other individuals may have different bases of power, different audience contacts, and perhaps greater influence within the organization itself. There is also some truth to the common belief that strength exists in numbers. Coalitions are a good example of the transactional nature of organizational persuasion. Individuals often come together in coalitions because they all seek a certain objective; transactions about the problem giving rise to the objective actually create the bond that make the coalition.

It should be clear by now that although the structure of the network cannot always be controlled, a smart communicator can learn to use that structure to further his or her persuasive aim. The dissemination of influence in an organization can work to the benefit of both "sender" and "receiver." Individuals in search of direction can use the network to their advantage by using those channels in which ideas and innovation are most apt to come.

/ *Frequency and volume.* The frequency and volume of messages comprise another message element. *Frequency* refers to the rate at which messages are received, and *volume* refers to the total number of messages within a given time period. Although there are obvious exceptions, high volume and/or frequency has the potential of influencing receivers. Mere exposure to repeated information can have effects. Further, message repetition increases the chance that others will receive and think about the contents of a message.

/ *Message form.* Organizational and group cultures establish expectations about how messages should be put together, including what they should look like or sound like, what they should include, and how they should be organized; they have, if you will, *organizational syntax.* People expect to have messages framed in certain ways, and deviations from those patterns can lead to confusion, irritation, or downright rejection.

To get a sense of organizational syntax, take a look at the forms typically used in an organization. They certainly disclose a great deal about organizational expectations. Many legislative bodies, for instance, require proposals to be stated as "resolutions," in which reasons are stated as "whereas" clauses and proposals stated as "be it resolved" clauses. In these kinds of organizations, formal proposals will not even be considered if this format is not employed. Individuals therefore become quite effective at being persuasive within the framework of "whereas" and "be it resolved." Although this is an extreme case of organizational expectations in terms of message arrangement, all organizations have subtle—and sometimes not-so-subtle—expectations about oral and written messages.

There are, of course, many relevant message variables in persuasion, which are discussed at various places in this book. All are as relevant to persuasion in organizations as they are to any other setting. The important thing to remember is that messages within an organization must be framed in ways that fit the demands, structure, style, and expectations of the organizational culture. Messages also have to be consistent with the role of the individual and be cast in a way that has the best chance of being seen or heard, given the constraints of the network.

/ Communicator elements of organizational persuasion

Although the three types of elements of persuasion affect each other to a large degree, communicator elements are perhaps most important in organizational persuasion, just as they are in most other settings. Who the communicator is, what the communicator wants, the trust and credibility the communicator has engendered, and the skill with which the communicator approaches the task are highly important in whether or not persuasion will work.

In Chapter 1 we referred to communicator qualities in the aggregate as *competence*. You may wish to turn back to that chapter at this point and review what constitutes competent communication. In a nutshell, it consists of understanding, sensitivity, skill, and ethical responsibility.

Persuasion occurs most frequently when the individuals involved in the persuasion transaction have a sense of identity or sharing. The identity bond, which was discussed at some length in the last chapter, is also important in the organizational network. We are referring to more than a communication link. The communicators need to feel that they share meanings and feelings, that they are part of a group that plays an equally important part in their lives, that they have some common experiences—in short, that they can relate to one another. The commonly held belief that people who are similar communicate well with one another is usually accurate. In developing ideas and implementing change or innovation, persuaders are well advised to keep this principle in mind.

/ Persuasion and the Role Structure

One of the most important processes in organizations is the establishment of roles. Roles are expectations for how an individual should behave.[7] In this section we discuss the relationship between roles and persuasion.

/ Persuasion and the establishment of roles

Roles, like all other elements of organizations, are a product of communication. Specifically, roles involve individualized rules for behavior. Roles do not come with people; they are created for people through communication and are therefore an outcome of the organizing process.

Roles arise through an interplay between individual's behavior and other's expectations.[8] Expectations and behaviors build upon one another until relative consensus is achieved regarding how one should act; this process results in a role. Any individual in the organization will have several roles. Some of these are work-related, defining what tasks are assigned. Other roles are less formal in that they govern activities that may not be obvious. Formal task-related roles are often defined by job descriptions and are a matter of record; informal roles are rarely defined in the organization's manuals and policies. How an individual conducts his or her "organizational life" depends in part on the constellation of formal and informal roles assigned.

When Linda Macy first arrived at the Weber Elementary School in 1977, she had a fairly good idea of what a school secretary does, but little sense of the specific responsibilities of this particular office. The principal and assistant principal trained Linda in a half-day orientation session her first day, which gave her a better idea of her formal role, but she actually had to perform the duties for a while to get a sense of what that role entailed. Linda spends most of her time in the office and is almost always available. She is usually the first person people meet when they come into the office. She is also intimately aware of the administrators' schedules and work loads. Within just a few weeks of her arrival, Linda took the informal role of "gatekeeper" to the administration. In other words, she receives messages and information from teachers and other employees and passes them on to the principal and vice-principal. She decides when to give the messages and often holds information for brief periods when she knows that her superiors are particularly busy. The administrators, though they are not consciously aware of Linda's role in this regard, appreciate the way in which she helps them pace their work. Figure 6.3 illustrates this role communication episode.

Although Linda was hired strictly as a secretary and office manager for the school, she now does some clerical work for the PTA president as well. This role began when Joan Miller, a PTA president several years ago asked her to do some work for the association. She talked to Linda persuasively about her needs, pointing out the advantages of having her become more familiar with PTA. Linda was reluctant at first to take on additional responsibilities, but decided to try just a few jobs. She found that she could incorporate these into her work load without too much difficulty. By the end of that year, Linda was so involved with PTA work that it seemed natural, and the new president just assumed she would help. This example demonstrates how role emergence is sometimes a product of persuasion.

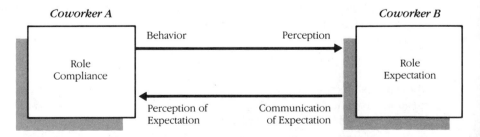

/ **FIGURE 6.3a** Role Communication Expectation

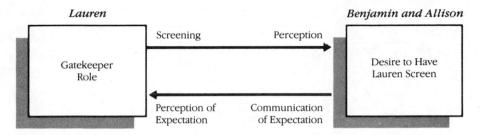

Lauren

Benjamin and Allison

Gatekeeper
Role

Screening   Perception

Desire to Have
Lauren Screen

Perception of   Communication
Expectation   of Expectation

/ FIGURE 6.3b Role Communication Illustrated

We already know from material presented earlier in the chapter that roles restrict what a person can and will do. Roles therefore affect one's communication and persuasion. Persuasion is both facilitated and limited by one's role. For example, because of her position at the school, Linda Miller does not take an active formal role in shaping school policies, but her informal influence is substantial. At meetings, she takes notes and distributes information, serving as recording secretary. She normally does not speak to the group about issues on the agenda since that is not considered part of her role. In the office, however, because of the respect everybody has for her and her breadth of access to information, she is often consulted. In fact, members of the organization, including both the principal and vice-principal, often ask Linda her opinion, and she is not shy about asserting a point of view when she feels compelled to do so. Her role as office manager and gatekeeper gives her certain kinds of power that permits her some informal influence not shared by all of the employees.

/ Network roles and persuasion

/ Centrality and peripherality.   You will recall that a network consists of groups linked together by communication channels. Individuals take different communication roles in the network, depending upon their place in it. Other things being equal, individuals who are more connected and central in the network will be more influential. *Centrality* is the degree to which an individual is linked with others in the organization; *peripherality* is the relative isolation of an individual. Central individuals are more integrated; peripheral individuals less. Centrality-peripherality is therefore a variable related to individual influence in groups and organizations. One's place on this continuum can be determined by a number of factors, including task role, physical space barriers, place in the hierarchy, personality and communication style, status, expertise, and others.[9]

Figure 6.4 illustrates three groups with different centrality configurations. In group A, one individual links everybody else. That individual is central, while the others are peripheral. Clearly, there is a high probability that the central

(a) *(b)* *(c)*

/ FIGURE 6.4 Centrality-Peripherality

individual will take leadership roles and will have a good deal of persuasive power in the group. In group B, members are more equal in centrality, resulting in moderate "shared centrality," but one member is still more central than the others and may therefore have more influence. In group C, the shared centrality is high: no member has more connections than any of the others.

Placement in the network is only one of many factors affecting persuasion in groups and organizations, but it is important nonetheless because it partially determines the network roles an individual may take.[10]

/ *The liaison role, gatekeeping, and opinion leadership.* An important network communication role is that of *liaison*. The liaison role is one of connecting two or more groups within the organization. Because of their connections among groups, liaisons facilitate passage of information from one group to another. Consequently, liaisons tend to be quite influential. They are gregarious, tend to hold higher positions with more power, have many contacts, usually have more experience on the job than most other workers, and have a sense of the importance of their role.

Gatekeeping is one of several communication roles arising from one's place in the network. Gatekeepers control the flow of messages. Recall in our example how Linda Miller became a gatekeeper because of her placement as a highly central individual in the network at the elementary school. Gatekeepers typically have quite a bit of influence because they have access to much information and can manage the timing of communication.

Another role related to centrality is *opinion leadership*. Opinion leaders directly influence the opinions of other people and function to spread ideas and innovations in the organization. They use their contacts with others for purposes of dissemination and are usually very persuasive. Organizational persuasion commonly occurs not by direct appeal from "management," but by spread of influence via opinion leaders through the network.

Theoretically, gatekeeping, opinion leadership, and liaison roles are separate, but in practice they are often correlated. Individuals in highly central positions may take any combination of these roles. When they control the flow of information, they are behaving as gatekeepers; when they attempt to influence others' opinions directly, they are acting as opinion leaders; and when they facilitate the exchange of information, they are fulfilling the liaison role. Often such individuals will enact all three roles simultaneously. The point here is that centrality leads to informal roles of great persuasive potential.

/ Authority, leadership, and persuasion

/ Authority in organizations.
One of the outcomes of organizing is consensus on who has the right to exert power to do certain things. This right is known as *authority*. All formal roles carry some form of authority; that is, they legitimize a person's use of certain kinds of power. Authority that comes with a person's position or formal role is therefore known as *legitimate authority*.[11] Everybody agrees that, by holding a position, the occupant has certain kinds of authority. Legitimate authority, however, does not mean that everybody will necessarily be influenced by the exercise of power. We may agree that an individual has the right to exert power, but not be influenced by the person's exercise of that power. When it comes right down to it, we may comply with authority because we have to, but that doesn't mean we will change in any fundamental way.

Another kind of authority evident in organizations is *attributed authority*. Here members agree that an individual has the right to exercise power toward certain ends because of trust in that individual and the feeling that the person has earned the right. Unlike legitimate authority, attributed authority is granted to the person, not the position. It is especially important in persuasion because it stems from credibility and leads to highly potent influence. When an individual with attributed authority exerts power, genuine influence may well result. We have already discussed many of the factors that may lead to this kind of authority; briefly, they are perceived competence, integrity, and trust.

It often happens that individuals with legitimate authority also have attributed authority. Such a case would be a supervisor whose subordinates readily and happily comply. Unfortunately, it also happens that some individuals with legitimate authority do not really have much influence because those with whom they work do not attribute authority to them. Such individuals are usually not very effective in fulfilling their formal roles. Organizations often operate under the burden of a "fiction of superior authority," which means that superiors who are granted legitimate authority may not actually be able to exercise the power that is their "right." Again, one's organizational effectiveness is much more a matter of communication competence and performance than status of position.[12]

/ Leadership and persuasion.
Like other forms of influence, leadership too arises more out of what a person actually does and how a person communicates and influences others than it does from "assigned" duties per se. Traditionally, leadership is correlated with individuals' positions; we believe, however, that real leadership emerges out of the functions that an individual assumes as part

of both formal and informal roles.[13] Let us turn now to the relationship between leadership and persuasion.

Like all of the other elements discussed in this chapter, leadership is a product of communication. Leadership results from an individual's recognizing a need and effectively garnering the cooperation of others to address that need. Leadership therefore is not a personal trait or condition, but a group of functions that are fulfilled by various members from time to time. Whenever a person acts to elicit cooperation to solve a problem, that person is assuming a leadership function. Within organizations and groups, some people assume leadership more frequently than do others, and certain individuals are even expected to do so. Just because an individual does not have a leadership role, however, does not mean that he or she must stand mute in the face of an obvious need that no one else is addressing.

When an individual seeks the cooperation of others to address a need, persuasion almost always operates. Leadership is therefore a direct function of persuasion. Persuasion in leadership occurred, for example, when George Santos, the county librarian, realized that the Sage County Courthouse had no information about the library. He saw great opportunities for distributing library information there, ranging from a display room to a brochure rack. He brought up the idea at a staff meeting, pointing out the advantage of soliciting the County Administrator's cooperation in publicizing the activities of the library. The other members of the staff agreed and, after a brief discussion, decided to develop a proposal for the board of supervisors. Eventually a kiosk was erected in the entry way of the courthouse. The task of disseminating information about the library was accomplished as a direct result of George's original concern and his leadership, which was manifest in the form of persuasion.

George's actions in this case is an example of task leadership. Actually, there are two kinds of leadership in groups and organizations. *Task leadership* is activity that assists the group or organization in accomplishing its goals. *Socio-emotional* leadership involves actions that elicit cooperation in furthering group maintenance or dealing with interpersonal problems within the group or organization.[14] Both are important, and they are related to one another. The group cannot effectively deal with its tasks without simultaneously dealing with the

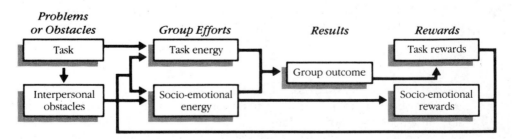

/ FIGURE 6.5 Task and Socio-emotional Leadership

human needs and interpersonal problems of those engaged in the task. Further, tasks are accomplished more effectively when individuals in the group pool their ideas and energy through cooperation. Figure 6.5 illustrates the relationship between these two kinds of leadership.[15]

Persuasion that exerts task leadership directly addresses job objectives. Task leadership involves proposing solutions, analyzing problems, and offering values, goals, or criteria of evaluation. It may also involve attempts to influence the process by which decisions are reached or to energize the group toward a goal. Much of the give-and-take of ordinary talk in organizations, especially at meetings. is directed toward task persuasion. The substance of the argumentation accompanying task persuasion is what guides the organization.

Socio-emotional persuasion is a bit more difficult to identify. It involves persuasion that assists individuals to readjust their orientations toward the ideas of others. It may be designed to help people feel better about themselves and their ideas and work. Persuasion that relies on feedback and response to the ideas of others may fulfill both task and socio-emotional functions because it motivates others toward particular task accomplishments while building identity and harmony in the group.

It should be clear by now that persuasion is an important tool in the establishment of authority and leadership in organizations. Individuals in search of guidance and change will seek out people of authority to provide direction. On the other side, individuals assert their own authority through persuasion, and one's authority is built by others' perceptions of the extent to which that persuasion is successful and ethical. Leadership too is a product of persuasion. Without attempts to influence, task and socio-emotional functions would not be fulfilled, and leadership would not occur.

/ Persuasion in superior-subordinate communication

Hierarchy is usually a condition of organizational life. In most organizations some individuals have authority over others. This explicit superior-subordinate relationship affects organizational persuasion in important ways.[16] The superior has access to sources of power that the subordinate does not have. Subordinates have the need to protect themselves from personal harm that may result from the exercise of power higher up the line.

Ego defense seems to be especially important when communicating with a superior. In other words, one's own sense of self-worth, not to mention others' perception of one's worth, requires nurturing and protection. Because of the power difference, subordinates will communicate with superiors in ways designed to enhance their own control of the situation. Consequently, subordinates tend to distort upward information to ingratiate the superior, especially when the news is negative. Subordinates tend to screen upward information so that the superior gets just the information the subordinate wants to convey, stressing what they think the superior wants to hear. Positive information tends to be communicated upward; negative information tends to be withheld. Because superiors usually have decision-making power over subordinates, upward persuasion is important to the subordinates sense of control. At the same time, however, upward persuasion is problematic because the subordinate may well face an especially careful and critical receiver.

The answer to this problem, of course, is trust. When superiors can engender trust and come to possess attributed authority, subordinates will find a fuller range of persuasive options available to them. The *Pelz effect* is the tendency of subordinates to be more open and satisfied with superiors who are perceived to have high upward influence.[17] In other words, the supervisor who is seen as effective in persuading higher-ups to go along with ideas generated at the lower level will elicit more honesty and openness from subordinates. This effect is enhanced when the supervisor is also supportive with subordinates.

The way in which a superior responds to subordinate persuasion is very important in establishing future openness to upward communication. Superiors may agree or disagree with subordinates' proposals, but the manner of response, with its implications for the relationship, makes all the difference. Agreement or disagreement that reflects respect for the subordinate tends to build confidence and openness. Messages that imply negative evaluation of the person will harm future openness on the part of the subordinate. Even agreement can be damaging if it is stated in negative relational terms. Consider the following examples:

> "I love it, George. Good job as usual." [agreement with positive relational tone]

> "Well . . . I guess this will have to do." [agreement with negative relational tone]

> "I'm really sorry, George, because I know you put a lot of time in on this. I wish I could accept it, but it just won't fit. Let's get together tomorrow to talk about what else we might do." [disagreement with positive relational tone]

> "Don't bother me with another one of your silly ideas." [disagreement with negative relational tone]

Any response by a superior with negative relational implications may close doors to upward communication in the future.

So far we have concentrated on upward persuasion. What about downward persuasion? We have already discussed the ways in which authority and power can be used to influence, and superiors often have such resources available to influence. The problem is that superiors have to consider carefully how to exert downward influence because of its implications for future communication within the work group. Indeed, a superior may be able to exert power in such a way as to elicit compliance, but that compliance will exist only on the surface and lead to damaging relations in the future if deeper motivation is not sought at the same time. Brute application of sanctions and coercion can quickly close off future upward communication with the potential of greatly restricting the superior's own ability to accomplish the task in the future.

All of this means that persuasion remains the most valuable tool for downward influence. Persuasion based on argument implies that the superior trusts the subordinate to be able to weigh evidence and reasoning and make decisions; it also means that the superior grants the subordinate some decision-making authority, which communicators take as supportiveness and confirmation.

/ Persuasion and Group Influence

Social science research long ago established the validity of the common belief that groups influence the beliefs, values, and behaviors of their members. Much persuasion, especially in groups and organizations, involves the effects of group influence. This is especially true in cases where the majority of a group tries to talk the minority into going along with the predominate viewpoint of the group. In this section we address the role of group influence in persuasion.

/ Cohesiveness and group norms

In the previous section we defined *roles* as expectations for how particular individuals should behave; as such, roles establish a person's responsibilities. *Norms,* on the other hand, are expectations for how all members should behave. Roles distinguish the responsibilities of one member from another, while norms characterize the group as a whole. Both roles and norms are outcomes of group rules. Rules that govern the behavior of a person as an individual define that person's role; rules that govern the behavior of all tell what the norms are. In this section we concentrate on norms and their effects, accenting the ways in which they are implicated in persuasion.

The basis for group influence is affiliation. Groups enable us to achieve goals we could not meet alone. In turn, groups affect how we think, feel, and act. In other words, we use groups to our benefit, but they leave their mark on us as group members. Such influence is apparent in all kinds of groups. Here we are concentrating on work or task groups, which are no less important in our lives than families, friendship groups, educational groups, or any other.

We do not want to leave the impression that one's cognitive system is completely a product of the group. Groups involve give and take: we both affect and are affected by those with whom we associate in a group. Consider also that any person is a member of several groups, each affecting that individual's sense of reality, arousal, goals, and relationships. It is therefore unlikely that any one group will shape entirely what a person becomes.

Of course, some groups are more influential than others. The key to group influence seems to be *cohesiveness,* or group feeling.[18] Cohesiveness is the degree to which members of a group identify with one another, the extent to which there is a spirit of camaraderie within the group. The interpersonal bonding mentioned in the last section is especially strong in highly cohesive groups, meaning that such groups will have relatively greater influence on the individual. Persuasion among the members of the group is apt to be especially effective because of this "we-feeling." In fact, one of the real dangers in highly cohesive

/ **The strength of the group feeling in the Guardian Angels organization increases the group's influence on individual members.**

groups is that persuasion is "too easy," that people want to keep the group together so much that they suppress their critical faculties and accept whatever other members, especially strong leaders, prescribe.[19] In short, cohesiveness is a sign of shared dimensions of the cognitive system.

/ Conformity and persuasion

/ Levels of conformity.
The kind of influence exerted in groups varies, depending upon a variety of personal and situational factors. Here we discuss three types of influence that differ in terms of personal commitment—compliance, identification, and internalization.[20] *Compliance* is outward conformity without inward commitment. It involves public actions and statements that are consistent with the norms of the group. *Identification,* like compliance, is basically public conformity, but it is accompanied by emotional feelings of identification or attachment to the group. *Internalization* is personal and private acceptance of the belief, an integration of the norm into one's personal repertoire of rules. In short, compliance is going along; identification is going along and feeling good about it; internalization is going along out of a more fundamental change in one or more elements in the cognitive system.

Compliance may be the first stage in the development of real change or commitment to an idea or action. On the other hand, it may be temporary, a sign of lack of cohesiveness in the group, or the prelude to an individual's leaving the group. If not followed by identification or internalization, compliance will probably be short-lived. Persuasion in groups rarely involves compliance alone; the ultimate goal is usually internalization.

Consider the case of the new office at the Colby Medical Center as an example. Bob Burgess, the office manager for the laboratory, was stuck in a terrible little office for his first two years at the center. He put up with it for a year, but in his second year, after gaining some security and comfort in the organization, he began to feel constrained by the space in which he had to work. By the end of the second year he was ready to push hard for a change.

The answer was simple, but costly. A wall could be removed between two small offices, a new window cut, and built-in cabinets constructed. Although not necessary, fresh paint, carpeting, and attractive appointments would add to his satisfaction. The problem was that the entire remodeling job would cost about $15,000, a high figure for an organization with complex fiscal obligations.

Bob first mentioned the idea in a staff meeting. His analysis of the situation was persuasive. Almost everybody initially thought it was a good idea. There was no question that most of the individuals who worked in and around the office favored putting the money into remodeling, but the necessary commitment was not yet cemented. Let's look at the feelings of three people, all of whom said they were in favor of the change, but who had different levels of commitment.

Jo Minty, the bookkeeper, had to share Bob's little office. She was committed to the idea from the beginning. Because of her personal work situation and lack of knowledge about the budgetary constraints of the organization, her commitment was easily internalized. Of course, Jo had little influence and would not even have tried to put much pressure on the higher-ups, but she did give Bob a lot of moral support.

Stephanie Billings, the pathologist and head of the office, was not convinced that the remodeling should be a priority. She questioned whether the money could be used more effectively to upgrade the equipment in the lab. Her initial reaction was one of compliance. She said she would go along if the directors all agreed, suppressing her private doubts. Morey Findlay was in the middle. In principle, he shared Stephanie's doubts, but he believed the team-feeling of the directors was more important, and he did not want to alienate Bob. Morey exhibited conformity by identification. On the surface, then, all four individuals were conforming to the predominant opinion that the remodeling should be done, but not all were privately committed. The project was stalled by Stephanie and Morey for several months until Bob seriously considered taking a position at Cal Rubber. As he explained to Stephanie, "The pay is about the same, but the working conditions are really great." Bob decided to stay at the center, and the remodeling was started almost immediately. His original persuasion was effective in garnering support, but the actual job was not done immediately because the real decision-makers were not truly committed. In fact if Bob had not received another job offer, the remodeling might never have been done. After the remodeling was finished, everybody loved it, including Stephanie Billings. Her compliance quickly changed to internalization, as did Morey Findlay's.

It is clear that group cohesion is very important in determining a group's influence. We also know that individuals within the group vary in their susceptibility to influence. Individuals who are more submissive and have lower self-esteem seem to be more easily influenced by group norms than do more confident individuals. Perhaps that is one reason why Jo, the bookkeeper, went along so quickly with the apparent group consensus on the remodeling project. Stephanie, the head of the lab, who had every reason to be confident and dominant in the organization, was perhaps least persuaded initially.

Notice that two factors seem to play against each other in group influence. These are group characteristics and individual tendencies. As a rule, when you feel comfortable in a group and you are less certain of your own beliefs, groups norms will have a powerful effect. On the other hand, when you are less confident in the group and are more reliant on your own predispositions, you are less likely to be influenced. This generalization does not necessarily govern how you would respond to all persuasion in the group, but it is important in establishing the degree to which group norms enter into the effectiveness of that persuasion.

/ *Critical thinking in group action.* The above discussion applies most directly to situations in which group norms are being established or in which established norms enter into group influence. Much persuasion in groups, however, is not of this type. Often the members of a group are not of one mind on an issue. Many group decisions are hammered out in long sessions of discussion and debate. In fact, quick acceptance of an idea that reflects a group norm may be a red flag that the group is not being critical enough in weighing points of view and proposed solutions. True, persuasion does involve group influence, but such influence need not—indeed, should not—dominate the influence that occurs in the group. This is especially true in task groups, where the primary goal is effective problem solving or decision making. (In groups where the primary goal is social maintenance and bonding, group influence effects may be more desirable.)

In task groups, in most Western cultures, the best decisions are made in a spirit of careful examination. Effective groups weigh evidence, listen carefully to arguments, and approach problems analytically and creatively. The best way to overcome the negative effects of group conformity is through constructive argumentation. This means that individuals try ideas by framing them as persuasively as possible, knowing that they will be tested by the critical acumen of others. Ideas, when accepted, will be appealing not because of compliance norms, but because they overcome objections and are perceived to lead to positive results. When ideas are accepted in this way, after thorough examination and discussion, they are more apt to be genuinely internalized by those who accept them.

The manner in which issues are argued in a group is very important in shaping the outcome of the group's communication. Blind, dogmatic argument without creative and constructive dialogue can actually decrease a group's effectiveness. It can lead to a disintegration of cohesiveness and cooperation. The best persuasion in groups is based on mutual respect and a desire to succeed as a group without going so far as to "sell out" to group norms. In short, the successful persuader tries to pitch to an optimal level of cohesiveness on the one end and criticality on the other.

How one responds to the arguments of others seems to be important to the outcome of argumentation. Negative reactions can spawn polarization and subsequent inaction, while positive reactions can promote constructive problem solving. Positive reactions do not necessarily mean agreement, but they do reflect mutual respect and a desire to reach a constructive solution. Table 6.1 lists a number of corresponding positive and negative reactions to arguments.[21]

In general, the responses in the first column, which are positive and produce careful decision making, are designed to reflect on, amplify, or put a previous argument in context. Such statements may also legitimize and acknowledge the relevance of previous statements, or they may confirm the

TABLE 6.1

Types of Reactions to Arguments

Positive Reactions	Negative Reactions
1) Respond with a paraphrasing of the previously stated argument	1) Respond with an argument which is the opposite of the one previously forwarded
2) Respond with a new argument, but one that generally argues for the same position	2) Respond with a new argument which takes a position that is generally opposite that of the one previously stated
3) Respond with a statement which enhances the source credibility of the previous speaker	3) Respond with a statement designed to denigrate the source credibility of the previous speaker
4) Respond with a statement which implies that the facts were correctly interpreted by the previous speaker	4) Respond with a statement which implies that the facts given by the previous speaker are wrong
5) Respond with a statement which implies that the conclusion reached by the previous speaker is plausible	5) Respond with a statement which implies that the conclusion reached by the previous speaker is wrong
6) Respond with a statement which implies that the line of reasoning forwarded by the previous speaker is important and should be pursued	6) Respond with a statement which argues that the topic issued by the previous speaker is unimportant and should be changed
7) Respond with a statement which implies that the previous speaker's argument is consistent with what has been argued previously	7) Respond with a statement which implies that the previous argument is inconsistent with what has been argued earlier on in the discussion
8) Respond with a statement which implies that the previous speaker's argument is relevant to the discussion	8) Respond with an argument which states that the previous speaker's argument is irrelevant to the discussion
9) Respond with a simple affirmation of the previous speaker's position	9) Respond with a simple negation of the previous speaker's position

importance of the other individuals in the group. Statements in the second column, which are negative and polarizing, generally contradict, invalidate, or fail to recognize the positive contribution of one's opponent.

/ Persuasion and Motivation in Organizations

Motivation is usually defined as cognitions that move an individual toward a goal. Motivation and persuasion are closely related because the aim of much persuasion is to motivate: persuasive transactions can create motivation, and motivated individuals sometimes seek out persuasive transactions for guidance.[22]

/ Evaluation and motivation

In groups and organizations people constantly provide feedback to one another about performance. Evaluation is a built-in element of organizational life. In this section we concentrate on evaluation and its effect on locus of control.

/ **The evaluator.** Generally speaking, self-evaluation is more effective than evaluations from other people. People often like to be self-controlled, to determine for themselves how they have done and what to do next. Internal motivation, as opposed to external motivation, is usually considered more desirable, but much of what we learn about our performances comes from others. It is important to consider, therefore, that the closer the communicator to the individual, the more apt the evaluation will be taken as reflective of internal control and the more effective it will be. Feedback from a workmate will probably be more effective than that from someone outside the work group. The weakest feedback of all comes from distant sources like "the company."

This principle lends weight to the notion that personal contact is important in persuasion. In organizations and groups, individuals often have the kind of personal contact that can be effective in motivation, but contact alone is not enough. The shared trust of the communicator has a great impact on how the feedback will be received, as we have seen repeatedly throughout this text. The major components of trust are integrity and competence. Evaluation from individuals who are trusted is usually potent.

Notice that credibility is not necessarily a matter of status. Because status is correlated with power, evaluation from a high status source can be perceived as a power play or an attempt to manipulate, reducing one's sense of internal control. We may indeed respond to people with high status, but internalization is not likely to follow such compliance.

/ **The evaluation message.** One of the ways to analyze evaluation is to look at the feedback message itself. What is said in response to another individual, the actual verbal and nonverbal components of the feedback, are obviously important. The giving of evaluative feedback is governed by rules. Especially important is the degree to which the individuals share rules as to who has the right—

or, in some cases, the obligation—to evaluate and how that evaluation should occur.

After Stephanie and Morey decided to order the office remodeling at the medical lab, Jo, the bookkeeper, said, "Oh, that's great. I know Bob is really happy." This kind of response seemed very appropriate from Jo, who had the least amount of authority of the entire staff. The feedback was accepted happily by the supervisors and probably increased their sense of internal control, the feeling that they had made the decision to remodel from internal motivation. On the other hand, imagine how they would have felt had Jo violated rules of status and hierarchy by saying, "I'm glad you guys finally came through on this remodeling." The point is that when interactional rules are violated in giving evaluation, the other person is more apt to consider one's message to be an attempt to manipulate from the outside.

Evaluation can provide either *knowledge of results* or *knowledge of performance.* Results are outcomes or end products. When we get knowledge of results, we know how we did, what our "score" was, so to speak. Knowledge of the results of a game would tell us who won. Performance, on the other hand, deals more with process. Knowledge of performance in a game tells much more than who won; it includes information about how the winning or losing came about. Feedback that conveys information about performance may reduce a person's sense of self-control; feedback that concentrates on results leaves process questions up to the actor.

Jo's response was strictly a results-oriented message: she described her happiness about the outcome. Bob's response, however, was more performance-oriented: "At last! I wondered if you would ever get around to the remodeling." His statement expresses relief, but it also provides an evaluation of the performance, namely, that it took Stephanie too long to act.

When telling someone our reaction to a performance, we often forget that the other person is probably making private judgments of his or her own behavior. Feedback that departs greatly from a person's own judgment is apt to be perceived as illegitimate or unfair. Even positive feedback may be perceived as manipulative if it is a great deal more favorable than the person's own sense of how well he or she did. This is an important principle to remember in persuasion. Too much enthusiasm about what a person has done may actually inhibit that individual's motivation because of its inconsistency with the person's own perception. Negative feedback that is realistic and consistent with the actor's own judgment may be quite effective in motivation because it reinforces the other person's sense of the adequacy of his or her own internal evaluation.

The more specific the feedback, the more it helps a person understand the outcome of performance. "I sure like working with you" is less motivating than "I really appreciate the way you organize the office." Further, the referent of the feedback is crucial. If feedback centers on the person, it is apt to be taken as external control and reduce motivation: "Alan, you're a great guy. . . . Now about that report I mentioned. . . ." On the other hand, feedback that focuses on the task or the behavior may have a greater potential for motivating the receiver: "Alan, your report was well written."

/ The importance of goal setting

We began this section by noting that motivation is an inducement to achieve goals. Who sets one's goals is very important in determining motivation to achieve them. Intuitively, we know that people will probably be more motivated to achieve self-established goals than goals set by others. We also know that internal motivation, arising out of a sense of self-determination, is more powerful than external motivation, or the feeling that one has to follow through because of pressure from outside.

For these reasons, interpersonal persuasion in organizations and other settings will be more effective if it involves genuine transaction, with shared responsibility for the establishment of goals. The way in which group or institutional goals are established is the most important factor in the motivation of workers to work toward the goals. A scheme which imagines that one group will set up goals and "persuade" others to go along is unrealistic. Indeed, management often sets up goals and, in a sense, forces labor to go along, or goals are hammered out in negotiation through the application of sanctions and counter-sanctions. These types of influence, however, do not usually result in internalized motivation.

/ Theory / Practice / Analysis

Theory

1. Organizing is a process accomplished through communication in which uncertainty is reduced and consensus achieved on goals and rules. The outcome of the organizing process is the organization's culture.

2. Organizations are characterized by structure in which individuals are linked in a network through communication. Persuasion is an important element in the communication system.

3. Organizational persuasion often involves the exercise of power and is affected by organizational structure, messages, and communicator characteristics.

4. Persuasion is also affected by norms and group influence. Such influence may bring about uncommitted behavioral compliance or deeper changes in attitude and value.

5. Roles, which are a product of communication and persuasion, in turn affect the outcome of persuasion transaction. Of special importance are network roles, which define, in part, the character of a person's persuasion in the organization.

6. Authority is one of the central elements of roles. The most influential authority arises from trust and competence.

7. Leadership, the establishment of cooperation to meet organizational and group needs, is largely a product of persuasion.

8. Persuasion between superiors and subordinates is an important element of organizational communication, its quality largely affecting many other aspects of persuasion throughout the organization.

9. Persuasion, and the accompanying critical examination of ideas, is a central factor in successful organizational decision making.

10. Persuasion in organizations often involves motivation. The nature of the motivation is critical to the outcome of the persuasion transaction. Motivation is largely affected by the way in which individuals respond and provide feedback to one another.

Practice

1. Form a laboratory organization. Join with several other members of your class or other interested individuals and start an organization from scratch. Begin by talking about what the organization could do. Discuss the nature and structure of your organization. Then begin working toward your goals. Occasionally "freeze" your work to discuss the nature of the persuasion that has emerged in the process of organizing. This activity can be done on a small scale in the classroom or as a term assignment. Competing organizations can be set up to solve business problems or compete in a simulated market. Such a laboratory experience could involve two organizations that design model homes and build them with paper and other materials; later their creations could be judged by a panel of "consumers."

2. Establish a study group for the term. At the end of the term discuss the communication dynamics of the group. A paper analyzing the persuasion occurring in the group makes an excellent term project report.

3. At your place of work, or in another group or organization of which you are a member, decide upon something that you believe needs to be changed. Choose something about the group or organization which you think you have the power to do something about. This objective may require the cooperation of others. Using the principles of this chapter, design a persuasion strategy and seek to accomplish your objective.

4. Almost all colleges and universities have opportunities for students to become involved in student affairs and general university business. (Many university committees, for example, have regular student members.) Make a concerted effort to become involved in your college's decision-making system. Use the principles of this chapter to guide your activity as an organizational persuader. Be sure to take some time to reflect on what is happening, and relate these experiences to the theories presented in this chapter.

Analysis

1. Attend a meeting of a committee as an objective observer and analyze the persuasion you witness. After taking notes on your observations and hypothesized interpretations, interview several members of the group to get their impressions of what was going on. Find out about the roles of the various members and their perceptions of the group's norms. Now return to your notes and revise your interpretations based on the additional information collected. Write a paper addressing several of the points of this chapter as you observed them in this committee.

2. As a variant of the above activity, become a regular visitor of a committee or other group over a period of several weeks, attending all of the meetings during this period. Observe the apparent roles of members, the ways in which the group influences its members, the persuasive elements of the speeches given during committee meetings, the management of conflict, and other interesting persuasion dynamics. Write a report of your observations.

3. Become a participating observer in an organization. This is especially valuable as part of an internship. Take time every day or every few days to record your observations of persuasion occurring in the group or organization.

4. Read the following case and then answer the questions that follow it.

The Appraisal

John was not at all comfortable as he walked into Mr. Callaway's office. Mr. Callaway joined the company about a year ago, and John had never seemed to be able to relate well to him. "I wonder what it is this time," he thought to himself.

"Good morning, Mr. Callaway," John said, looking at his boss across the four-foot-wide desk.

"Sit down, John."

John sat on the stiff little chair across from Callaway's desk. He wanted to light a cigarette, but decided not to. Callaway continued to read the papers on his desks. He hadn't yet looked up.

"John, I'll get right to the point. Your department is just not performing as well as it should."

"Well, I thought we were doing pretty well. . . . "

"Now, I have the production record here, and your department is well below average in output."

"Do you have the quality assurance record also, Mr. Callaway?"

"So I was wondering what we're going to do about this situation."

John sat for a moment thinking. Mr. Callaway got up, sharpened his pencil, and returned to the desk.

"You know, John, I do value your service to the company," he indicated as he thumbed through a report on his desk. "But I just don't understand how your outfit could fall so far behind."

"In all due respect, Sir, I really don't think. . . . "

"Besides, I worry about the image that you are projecting to the other department heads," Mr. Callaway interrupted.

John felt his stomach turn. He dropped his gaze to the floor. He honestly believed that his department was doing an excellent job, given recent problems in obtaining materials, a batch of new personnel, and a new product line. He also knew that his quality performance was the best of all of the departments under Mr. Callaway. Right now he was very angry and frankly scared.

Gazing at his shoes, he did not see Callaway look up at him. Callaway set the paperwork aside.

"Let's look at the new product line, John. It's been in production for six months now, but you're only putting out about twelve a month, on the average."

"Uh, do you have a copy of our original prospectus, Mr. Callaway?"

"Uh, yeah, it's here somewhere."

"The prospectus called for only ten units a month during the first year," John said, looking back up.

Callaway thumbed through the new product prospectus. "Where? Where does it say that? . . . Oh, yes, I see it. Well, I guess you're right about that, but you ought to be capable of a lot more than that. I never agreed with that figure anyway. Besides, your productivity on all the other lines is also low."

"Well, in all due respect, sir. . . ."

"Take women's sandals, for instance," Mr. Callaway said. He took off his glasses and wiped them.

"Yes, what about women's sandals?" John glanced about the room. A trickle of sweat ran down his cheek.

"And how about girls' shoes?"

"You know, we've had very few returns on girls' shoes in the past several months," John replied.

Mr. Callway swung around in his chair and looked out the window. "I'd like to set up a performance review for your department."

"Well," John hesitated, "I guess I would like to see you do that for every department then."

"But the other departments don't have a problem."

"But I don't think we have a problem either. . . ."

"Look, John, let's not quibble about this. I just think it would be a good idea to increase your output a bit, that's all."

John looked up. "Have you noticed that Wanda's department has been having a lot of problems with quality control? Maybe she needs a performance review too."

"Well, Wanda's okay. I mean . . . well, maybe I should check out the record on that."

"Will the performance review take into account our new personnel and the latest restrictions that have been placed on us?"

Callaway got up and stood over John. "Yes, I suppose so. . . . But I think we are getting off the track here. The point is we need a performance review."

"Let's set one up for everybody," John repeated.

"That's all I need with everything else that's going on here—five performance reviews at once. Well, I guess I'll think about it, but that doesn't mean that I'm happy about your production. Understand?"

John nodded silently. Mr. Callaway sat back down and picked up his pencil. John paused a moment waiting for a cue, then quietly turned and walked out.

Mr. Callaway picked up the phone. "Hello, Betty, can I speak to Ms. Kully? Thanks. Hello, Ms. Kully, I just wanted to tell you that I've been working on the little problem we spoke about the other day. Yes, I know my production is down, and I'm doing my best to deal with it.... I've tried to do my best, Ms. Kully; I'm sure you'll see a big improvement next reporting period.... Yes I know the consequences for my job if our output is not up by then, but I *am* working on it.... Okay, I'll keep you informed."

Questions

a. Who is persuading whom in this case? Discuss the case from a transactional perspective.

b. In what ways is the persuasion in this case affected by the structure of the organization?

c. Do you detect any information load problems?

d. Discuss leadership as it affects persuasion in this case.

e. Discuss the role of feedback as a form of motivation in this case.

Notes

[1]Bonnie M. Johnson, *Communication: The Process of Organizing* (Boston: Allyn and Bacon, 1977).

[2]Adapted from Richard V. Farace, Peter R. Monge, and Hamish Russell, *Communicating and Organizing* (Reading, MA: Addison-Wesley, 1977), p. 192.

[3]This point of view is most notably espoused by Carl Weick in *The Social Psychology of Organizing* (Reading, MA: Addison-Wesley, 1969).

[4]The cultural approach to the study of organizations is summarized by Michael E. Pacanowsky in "Organizational Communication as Cultural Performance," *Communication Monographs* 50 (1983), 126–47; see also *Communication and Organizations: An Interpretive Approach,* ed. Linda L. Putnam and Michael E. Pacanowsky (Beverly Hills: Sage, 1983).

[5]For a summary of research findings on power, see Marvin E. Shaw, *Group Dynamics: The Psychology of Small Group Behavior* (New York: McGraw-Hill, 1981), pp. 293–304.

[6]Richard V. Farace, James A. Taylor, and John P. Stewart, "Criteria for Evaluation of Organizational Communication Effectiveness," in *Communication Yearbook 2,* ed. Brent D. Ruben (New Brunswick: Transaction Books, 1978), pp. 271–92.

[7]For a summary of research on roles, see Shaw, *Group Dynamics,* p. 270.

[8]This view of roles is well explained by Daniel Katz and Robert Kahn, *The Social Psychology of Organizations* (New York: John Wiley, 1966), p. 182.

[9]Shaw, *Group Dynamics,* p. 150.

[10]Network roles are discussed in greater detail by Everett M. Rogers and Rekha Agarwala-Rogers in *Communication in Organizations* (New York: The Free Press, 1976), pp. 132–39.

[11]The concept of legitimate authority was first developed by Max Weber in *The Theory of Social and Economic Organizations,* trans. A. M. Henderson and Talcott Parsons (New York: Oxford University Press, 1947).

[12]The idea of a "fiction of superior authority" was first developed by Chester Barnard, *The Functions of the Executive* (Cambridge: Harvard University Press, 1938).

[13]The functional approach to persuasion is discussed in more detail by David M. Jabusch and Stephen W. Littlejohn, *Elements of Speech Communication* (Boston: Houghton Mifflin, 1981), p. 188.

[14]The task-interpersonal distinction is most notably developed by Robert F. Bales, *Personality and Interpersonal Behavior* (New York: Holt, Rinehart, and Winston, 1970).

[15]Adapted from Barry Collins and Harold Guetzkow, *A Social Psychology of Group Processes for Decision Making* (New York: Wiley, 1964), p. 81.

[16]The dynamics of this relationship are explained by Patricia H. Bradley, "Power, Status, and Upward Communication in Small Decision-Making Groups," *Communication Monographs* 45 (1978): 33–43; see also Frederic M. Jablin, "Message-Response and 'Openness' in Superior-Subordinate Communication," *Communication Yearbook 2,* ed. Brent D. Ruben (New Brunswick: Transaction Books, 1978), pp. 293–309; Samuel C. Riccillo and Sarah Trenholm, "Predicting Managers' Choice of Influence Mode: The Effects of Interpersonal Trust and Worker Attributions on Managerial Tactics in a Simulated Organizational Setting," *Western Journal of Speech Communication* 47 (1983): 323–39; and Paul D. Krivonos, "Distortion of Subordinate to Superior Communication in Organizational Settings," *Central States Speech Journal* 33 (1982): 345–52.

[17]See Frederic M. Jablin, "Superior's Upward Influence, Satisfaction, and Openness in Superior-Subordinate Communication: A Reexamination of the 'Pelz Effect,' " *Human Communication Research* 6 (1980): 211–19.

[18]For more detailed discussions in conformity, see Shaw, *Group Dynamics,* p. 280; Jabusch and Littlejohn, *Elements,* pp. 191–93; and Lawrence Rosenfeld, *Human Interaction in the Small Group Setting* (Columbus, OH: Merrill, 1973), pp. 67–75.

[19]This idea is developed by Irving Janis in *Victims of Groupthink: A Psychological Study of Foreign Decisions and Fiascos* (Boston: Houghton Mifflin, 1967).

[20]Herbert C. Kelman, "Compliance, Identification, and Internalization: Three Processes of Attitude Change," *Journal of Conflict Resolution* 2 (1958): 51–60.

[21]From Steven M. Alderton and Lawrence R. Frey, "Effects of Reactions to Arguments on Group Outcome: The Case of Group Polarization," *Central States Speech Journal* 34 (1983): 88–95.

[22]This analysis is taken largely from Louis P. Cusella, "The Effects of Feedback on Intrinsic Motivation: A Propositional Extension of Cognitive Evaluation Theory from an Organizational Communication Perspective," in *Communication Yearbook 4,* ed. Dan Nimmo (New Brunswick: Transaction Books, 1980), pp. 367–87.

7 / Persuasion in Negotiation

The shocking photograph was plastered across newspapers and magazines throughout the world: a desperate pilot looking out the window of his Boeing 727 with a terrorist's gun to his head. TWA Flight 847 from Athens to Rome had been hijacked by Shiite terrorists, with some forty passengers and crew remaining on board.

The government of the United States was paralyzed. Unable to strike back or to retrieve its citizens, only one recourse remained. Diplomats scrambled to arrange whatever negotiations were possible. American negotiators could not talk directly with the hijackers and had to rely on a network of connections with Algeria, Lebanon, Israel, and Syria. Throughout the month of June 1985, the world watched as, inch by inch, a trade was hammered out: the hostages for some 700 Shiites held prisoner in Israel. The hostages were home by the Fourth of July.

This frightening case dramatically illustrates the importance of negotiation in resolving conflict. Negotiation in its many forms is one of the most important and common communication events in our society. Indeed, almost every culture uses some form of negotiation.

/ Conflict and Negotiation

/ Negotiation and decision making

Negotiation, or bargaining, is a method for managing conflict. As such, it is one of the several ways in which social groups make decisions. Groups and societies typically make decisions in three ways in conflict situations.[1] *Coalition decision making* involves numerical power as determined in voting. In coalition decision

/ **In some areas of New England, the town meeting, a form of coalition decision making, is still the principal organ of government.**

making, issues are framed as proposals in which one group wins and the others lose. Various forms of collective choice have been developed to arrive at coalition outcomes, including, for example, direct voting, parliamentary law, representative government, public initiatives, town meetings, and so forth. Coalition allows for discussion and debate, but in the end always involves some kind of numerical counting in which a winner is declared.

Judication is a hierarchical form in which an authority makes the decision. The authority may be a judge, a jury, an executive, government leader, church head, or any of a number of other individuals who are responsible for choosing. Again, argument may be allowed, as in a court or conference room, but in the end, a judgment is rendered which settles the conflict, at least for the moment. A significant element of judication is that the judge is able to create his or her own solution, which may or may not align with the proposals of the disputing parties.

Negotiation is a decision-making form in which parties, usually two, make proposals and counterproposals in an effort to reach a common solution to a set of contentions. The parties initially have opposing objectives, and the aim is to work out an agreement that enables them to live with or resolve their differences. The distinguishing characteristic of negotiation is that it aims to achieve a joint solution rather than an authoritative or numerical decision. In the case of coalition and judication, persuasion occurs before a final decision is reached in an effort to affect that decision. In negotiation, persuasion is part and parcel of the decision itself.

Negotiation is not necessarily superior to the other decision-making forms. In fact, it is often inappropriate, ineffective, or impossible. Negotiation seems to work best in situations where a limited number of individuals or groups, usually only two, are involved in a power struggle to win concessions from the other. Parties should be committed to seeking a joint agreement and be relatively equal in power. Where an absolute impasse is reached, judication is usually required, but up to that point negotiation may be the most effective avenue available to settle the conflict. Judication and coalition usually have firmly established rules which all parties agree to follow. In many conflict situations, however, there is no consensus of how differences are to be settled, or even of the form a settlement might take. In such situations negotiation is the preferred method of working out the rules.

This is not to say that negotiation itself is rule-free. In fact, like any communication event, negotiation must proceed by rules, though the rules internal to the bargaining itself often have to be worked out initially before substantive negotiation can begin.

/ Negotiation as social construction

As a rule-generating system, negotiation is an important way in which groups construct their social worlds. What develops as the framework for action is often the outcome of negotiation. For example, in organizations individuals have expectations about their rights, roles, and responsibilities. They come to know what the job entails, what the organization accomplishes, and how the organization figures into their lives. The organization and their involvement in it become real. Meanings for the actions within the organization are important, but they are not immutable structures of their own apart from human interaction. They are social constructions, often the direct result of formal and informal negotiations within the organization, for negotiation not only enables groups to work out solutions, but gives them the means to accomplish those solutions as well.

How does negotiation work?[2] Traditionally, negotiation has been viewed as a process of simple compromise. The disputing parties are believed to give in little by little until they meet on a compromise somewhere in the middle. This view of negotiation has been called the *incremental convergence model*. In other words, the solution is reached by a process of convergence from extreme positions to a common, shared agreement. Although this model is appealing— and it certainly operates in simple bargaining situations—it is probably not a fair representation of the most significant negotiations. A better model is called for.

The formula/detail model of bargaining presents a more realistic picture of the process. Here bargainers construct a framework of rules, a common set of meanings, with which to understand and act. The incremental convergence model assumes that the negotiators already know the form an agreement will take and merely bargain specific details of that agreement. Usually, however, the nature and force of an agreement, the form an agreement will take, the process by which agreement will be reached, and a host of other formula concerns are worked out in the process. This kind of negotiation boils down to a two-fold process in which a "formula" for an agreement is created and specific "details" worked out. This is not to say that compromise is unimportant, but it occurs in a broad context of establishing a coordinated framework of rules.

Consider the analogy of the game. Negotiation is a kind of game in itself, but it is also a process for establishing other games to be played in the future. The incremental convergence model assumes that the players are just bargaining for positions on the game board. Instead, however, most negotiation involves (1) developing the rules of the negotiation game, (2) establishing the rules of the agreement game, and (3) bargaining for positions once those rules are established.

If you play contract bridge, you know that the players first go through a bidding process in which the "power" of certain suits is established. This process is akin to incremental convergence: the players make bids in turn until a final "contract" is established. However, in the game of bridge, the rules of play and the nature of the contract are already spelled out before the game begins. In much real-life negotiation, that is not the case.

Because negotiation is a rule-generating process, it is an important means by which our rules for interpreting and acting in social groups are worked out. It is, in short, one of the many ways in which people construct their realities socially.

Because it is a process of social construction, negotiation involves persuasion. In the incremental convergence model, bargainers just take turns making concessions, but in the formula/detail model, they spend much of their time trying to influence one another's views of what a contract means, why it is or is not necessary, the process by which it should be achieved, and how it should operate. In short, elements of the reality, goal, or relational dimensions of participants' cognitive systems may be changed in the process.

/ The Negotiation Process

/ Levels of influence in negotiation

The title of this section implies that negotiation is a single process. In one manner of speaking it is, because there is a process between the negotiators themselves. Most negotiation, however, is not that simple. Rarely do bargainers represent only themselves; almost always the outcomes of negotiation affect a larger system or organization. When negotiators are formal representatives of those groups, the process is known as *collective bargaining.*

The parties in collective bargaining have three concerns.[3] First, they must establish their own objectives. Second, they must deal directly with the opposition. Finally, they must take into account and sometimes influence that broader organization or system within which the negotiations are occurring. Each of these processes involves persuasion. The "in-group" is subject to persuasion to establish its own position, which changes as a result of the negotiation. In-group persuasion, therefore, is ongoing throughout the negotiation period. Then, there is the persuasion between the conflicting parties in the negotiation sessions. Finally, the groups are subject to influence by the larger system and may in turn decide to exert influence on that system.

In 1985 one of the world's largest airlines experienced a pilots' strike. Pilots for United Airlines walked out over a salary structure issue after an impasse in collective bargaining. The pilots wanted a single salary structure for all pilots, while the management was pushing for a tiered structure in which new pilots would be paid on a lower schedule than experienced pilots. Both labor and management in this situation had to discuss, debate, and establish their own positions on this issue apart from their negotiations with each other. The pilots' union also had to debate and make internal in-group decisions as to whether and when to strike, and management was forced to deal internally with how it would respond to the strike. One of the keys to success in this strike was the cooperation of the flight attendants, who walked out in sympathy with the pilots. Here we see an example of influence within the union bringing about an action that would influence the opposition, and an example of the pilots affecting the larger system (other employees) to make changes that would extend the pressure against management.

The multiple arenas of persuasion affecting negotiation can create problems. A negotiator is faced with three sets of forces or influences that may not always be consistent. *In-group forces* are those pushing for particular positions within the group represented. *Out-group forces* are those pushing for change in the opposition. *System forces* are those directed to and arising from the larger organization or social system. Success or failure is thus measured three ways— in terms of in-group objectives, out-group objectives, and system objectives. In collective bargaining, then, a completely successful outcome is one that satisfies all three. One can succeed in achieving an agreement with the opposition, but fail to "sell" that agreement to one's own group. Or an agreement may be satisfactory to the two conflicting parties, but create undue stress or difficulty in the larger community. Remember the SALT II agreement resulting from years of hard negotiation between the Soviet Union and the United States in the 1970s. The negotiators were satisfied with the agreement, but it was never ratified in the U.S. Senate.

/ The rule structure of negotiation

Like any communication, negotiation is governed by rules. In Chapter 2 we discussed the ways in which the cognitive system makes use of interpretation and action rules to understand and respond to events. We use interpretation rules to assign meaning to events, and subsequently respond in accordance with action rules. Negotiators are in a peculiar interpretation/action situation. They are required to analyze the actions of the opponent critically and make their own moves carefully in an attempt to get the best possible outcome for themselves and those they represent.

/ *Rules and logical force.* In Chapter 2, we pointed out that rules arise in response to certain logical forces emanating from various salient contextual associations. Logical forces are the reasons or justifications for one's actions. They form the rationale by which one's actions are viewed as "logical." One may frame an interpretation or action in terms of ultimate visions of truth, cultural practice, relational expectations, episodic patterns, and other concerns. Some logical forces are *causal* in that the individual feels more or less compelled to act in certain ways based on prior events or expectations. Other forces are *practical* in that they arise from the communicator's aims or goals. Like all communicators, negotiators are guided in their interpretations and actions by these same sorts of forces, resulting from the interaction between their cognitive systems and the environment.

Figure 7.1 illustrates the rule structure of a negotiator. This figure shows a negotiator (in boldface) and the opponent (in lightface). For simplicity, the figure features the rule structure of a single negotiator. In reality, however, negotiation is a complex transaction in which two or more negotiators are interpreting and acting with one another. A negotiator's actions are guided by four sets of forces. It is important to note that the causal and practical forces are not the acts themselves, but logical forces that give rise to the rules used to guide

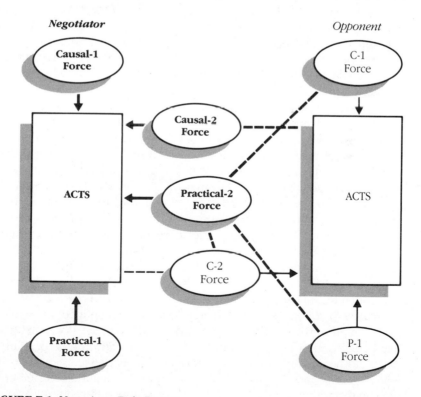

/ FIGURE 7.1 Negotiator Rule Forces

acts. A given act may be guided by any combination of forces. For example, a concession as an act of the negotiator may be motivated by a variety of rules: a sense of ethics, perhaps, or reciprocity, or strategic planning. Most importantly, the concession may have been guided by rules arising from a combination of some, or perhaps all, of these forces. Consequently, within the mind of an individual negotiator, various rule forces are linked to one another, and it would be a mistake to think of logical forces as independent.

The first set of forces in Figure 7.1, termed *causal-1,* arises out of a cognitive response to the situation. By *situation* here we mean any event or condition that lies outside the negotiation itself, including strong moral commitments of the negotiator, cultural practices, relationships with members of the in-group or others, situational exigencies, and a host of other variables. Whenever a negotiator feels compelled by such conditions to act in a certain way, causal-1 forces are at work.

For example, many cultures promote deference to elders, in which one is obligated to follow the advice of older people. If two individuals were trying to work out a conflict and went to an elder for advice, they would be strongly influenced to follow that advice. The advice of the elder would be a causal-1 force. Another example is the use of peer group consensus and democratic decision making in many Western cultures. Negotiators are usually obliged to state the case of the party exactly as prescribed by the vote of the group represented. No matter how much the negotiator may agree or disagree with that case, the initial bargaining position is treated as if it were prescribed. Under such circumstances the negotiator might freely admit to the opponent, "I'm sorry; my hands are tied." This same dynamic might be even more characteristic of a negotiator representing a powerful dictator. In either case, causal-1 forces are at work.

The second sort of causal forces, labelled *causal-2,* arises from the actions of the opponent, and are internal to the negotiation itself. Often negotiators feel compelled to respond to the opponent in a certain way, as though the opponent "caused" them to do so. Such might be the case, for instance, when the negotiator felt pressured into a particular move. Causal-2 forces would also operate when a negotiator felt that a certain action was unavoidable because of social propriety or by the internal rules of the relationship with the opponent (see Chapter 5). Certain social amenities may be required at various points in the negotiation, or one may feel compelled to reciprocate a concession. Anytime the negotiator senses that there are no other acceptable options in response to the opponent, causal-2 forces are at work. Here the negotiator might report back to the in-group, "I'm sorry; the other side left me no choice."

Both kinds of causal forces have one thing in common: *They seem not to be controlled by the negotiator.* The actions appear compelled and without alternative. In other words, actions based on causal forces are not seen by the negotiator as chosen or designed, but as necessary in a given state of affairs. Causal forces do not identify objective causation, but perceived causation. In other words, such forces are entirely individual to the negotiator's personal set of meanings; another negotiator might respond quite differently to the same set of circumstances.

The second set of forces that enter into the negotiation rule structure is termed *practical.* These are pressures arising from the negotiator's desire to affect the negotiation process or outcome in some way. These forces are of two sorts. *Practical-1* forces relate to actions aimed at achieving an explicit or implicit outcome objective. The objective may be internal or external to the negotiation. It may be an act designed to achieve one of the main goals of the negotiation, or it may arise from some other intent, such as solidifying the negotiator's relationship with members of his own party. Initial bargaining positions, for example, are almost always the product of forces designed to gain advantage. Much of the debate in negotiation sessions is directed by the speakers' practical-1 forces.

Practical-2 forces relate to tactics designed to influence the opponent's acts. They are almost always linked to practical-1 forces since they are an indirect way of achieving outcome objectives. Practical-2 forces lead a negotiator to try to influence the opponent's logical forces in some way. Much persuasion in negotiation is motivated by practical-2 forces, as explained in the next section.

/ Influencing Logical Forces. Persuasion in negotiation is a process of influencing the opponent's logical forces in order to affect actions. For example, the negotiator tries to influence the opponent's causal-1 forces by changing the adversary's interpretation of or response to the situation. A management negotiator, for instance, may try to persuade labor representatives that membership support for the position advocated is not as great as they think it is.

Sometimes the negotiator attempts to influence the opponent's interpretation of or response to his or her own outcome aims, affecting the opponent's practical-1 forces. For example, a tenant may persuade a landlord that the rent increase proposed is not necessary or that it conflicts with a cherished value like altruism.

Finally, negotiators frequently influence the opponent's interpretation of or response to the negotiator's power or image (causal-2). A faculty union once tried to gain members by pushing its ability to get the most experienced negotiators in collective bargaining. Their point was that these negotiators would command more respect in bargaining sessions than other negotiators could.

Negotiation is a game of judgment, and the logical forces affecting interpretation and action will vary from one negotiator to another. Likewise, the salience of rule forces may differ at various points in the negotiation. At some moments, certain causal forces may be especially strong, while very different forces might come into play at other points.

/ The world of the negotiator

We have seen how the negotiator acts on the basis of rules of interpretation and action. The negotiator constructs a world of realities and proceeds to play the game of negotiation on the basis of those rules. What are some of the most important elements of the negotiation reality? We could never cover all the contingencies here, but negotiation positions usually contain at least four parts.

/ The Conflict.   All negotiation begins with some sense of conflict. The parties perceive that disagreements of some form prevent consensus in their relationship. The perceived nature of the conflict consists of ideas about issues and intensity.[4] *Issues,* or areas of disagreement, form the essence of the conflict. When they begin to talk, negotiators have some idea of what those issues are, but rarely do the actual issues that emerge in the bargaining sessions match these preconceptions exactly.

A second element in the negotiator's image of the conflict is *intensity.* Negotiations range widely in the degree of conflict not only on the issues, but also in terms of the personal relationship between the negotiators. Often negotiators brace themselves for very sharp differences on the issues; other times they anticipate only mild disagreements. In our various administrative positions, we have frequently gone to a meeting expecting mild differences of opinion, only to be bowled over by vociferous objection to our proposals.

Needless to say, images of the conflict will change almost constantly during negotiations. The communicators involved must be able and willing to adapt to differing levels of conflict and new issues throughout the process.

/ Justice.   Another part of the negotiator's constructed reality is a theory of justice. This involves an idea of how the disputed resources should be distributed.[5] In other words, a theory of justice is a set of criteria of fairness. Typically in our society, negotiators adopt one of three such theories. The first is the theory of *equality.* In it, *justice* is defined as an equal split of resources. This position is one most often adopted by weaker bargainers. The second theory is that of *equity,* which bases fairness on a division proportionate to original size or power. Larger contingents should get more, according to the theory of equity, and smaller ones less. Groups should be rewarded in proportion to their contributions. Typically, larger or more powerful parties prefer this theory. Finally, the *social welfare* theory seeks a settlement that benefits the external system, or the greater community. The particular gains of any party are less important than is the benefit of the largest portion of society as a whole. This theory is often adopted by such outside parties as mediators, judges, legislators, and bureaucrats, but also by individual negotiators who value the greater community.

/ Utilities.   The third component of the bargainer's world is frequently called utilities.[6] This term refers to the limits negotiators place on the outcome. What do they want ideally, what do they realistically think they can get, and what is the least they are willing to settle for? This element of the negotiator's world is very important in establishing bargaining positions and concessions. If Jonathan is trying to strike a deal to buy Joan's car, he has a low price he would like to pay, a higher price he thinks he will probably end up paying, and an even higher price beyond which he will not bargain. Joan, on the other hand, has a high price she would like to get, a lower price she thinks she probably can get, and a price below which any offer would be unacceptable. These are Jonathan and Joan's

/ **The parties involved in plea bargaining must have a clear sense of utilities—what they want ideally, what their realistic expectations are, and what they will settle for.**

respective utilities. If the negotiation is successful, a final price between their bargaining limits will be reached.

When we travelled in some Mediterranean countries, we were told that we should bargain in the shops. On several occasions we tried to do so without success. Sometimes, shopkeepers would even grab items away from us, as if insulted, and ask us to leave. We now understand that we badly misestimated the shop keepers' utilities by making an offer too far below their lowest bargaining level. In other words, we did not play the game correctly, and the merchants therefore refused to play at all.

/ *Procedures.* Procedures are naturally important in any negotiation. Part of the negotiator's world consists of ideas about how the negotiation process itself should proceed.[7] Often these notions come from previous experience, published procedures, or ideas about how conflict should be handled. If the opposing groups or individuals have very different ideas about how to negotiate, agreement on substantive issues will be difficult to achieve. That is why the rules are often among the first items to be negotiated. In the negotiation to end the Vietnam War, for example, discussions of actual issues were postponed for weeks while the disputants haggled over the shape of the negotiating table.

In summary, negotiators enter the process of negotiation with a particular view of reality. Except in the most mundane bargaining situations, that view consists of a complex set of interpretations, images, and beliefs. Although we cannot spell out all of a negotiator's reality, images of the conflict, theories of justice, utilities, and procedures are usually salient. Negotiators have the tricky task of meshing their realities, not to the point of making them identical, but to the point of enabling themselves to coordinate their rules so that they can achieve an outcome agreeable to both. That is a process of change in which the realities may undergo significant alteration. Some parts of the reality, like images of the conflict, may change easily and often. Other aspects, like criteria or fairness, may never change.

/ Persuasion and Negotiation

/ The coordination problem

The progress of a negotiation depends in many ways on the rule structures of the participants, how they interpret and act. Negotiation, like all communication transactions, becomes a task of coordination, in which at least two rule systems and perhaps several cognitive systems must mesh. The individual negotiators bring their own logics of action to the transaction, and if coherent communication is to be achieved, a new interpersonal system of rules must emerge (see Chapter 2).

The most important implication of this discussion of rule structures is that negotiators should seek to understand and adapt to the rule forces and cognitive systems of the opponent. Good negotiators do not follow a standard pattern of bargaining; they must interpret and reinterpret, act and react, depending upon the moves of the opponent based on his own sensibilities and outcome aims. There is no set recipe for doing this. The key is flexibility and the ability to think like your opponent so that you can anticipate his or her interpretations and actions and play your own moves. To the extent that both negotiators are able to anticipate and plan, coordination will be achieved more quickly and, potentially, the dispute will be resolved more readily.

Coordination in negotiation is a two-part process. It involves interpreting the opponent's reality and adapting to and influencing that reality.[8] Although this process is not different from what happens in any communication event, the two elements—interpreting and acting—are typically more conscious than would be the case in less formalized interactions.

/ Interpretation in negotiation

The first element of communication in negotiation is making inferences about the opponent's rules, which are the bases of the adversary's actions.[9] This involves interpreting the opponent's view of the conflict (including issues and intensity), rules of justice, utilities, and procedural concerns. The inferences are very important because they will guide the negotiator in making adjustments.

Negotiators assess the opponent's system of rules in two ways: by carefully observing the opponent's moves, and by direct verbal communication. Bargainers can reveal a great deal by their demands, offers, and concessions, just as chess players reveal strategy by the moves they make on the board. For example, the initial bargaining position tells the opponent something about what issues are deemed important, and the rigidity of that position may say something about the intensity of conflict. A common tactic in bargaining is to make a test offer to observe the opponent's response. Such offers essentially check the flexibility and commitment of the other party.

Of course, negotiators are aware that their own moves may reveal their positions to the opponent, and they may therefore attempt to disguise their interpretations, at least for a time. On the other hand, bluffing and deceiving can be extremely harmful to a negotiator's credibility in the long run. For this reason, ultimatums should be used sparingly and taken seriously, since they may signal one's ultimate bargaining limit. A further concession beyond the commitment level will probably be costly and should therefore be undertaken cautiously.

In deciding how to respond to a demand, one is usually faced with the dilemma of whether to take a tough or an easy stand. This *bargainer's dilemma,* or *concession dilemma,* stems from the question of whether to signal flexibility or commitment.[10] The so-called "easy" stand may tell the opponent that you are friendly, flexible, and willing to seek an acceptable solution. On the other hand, it might also say that you are not very committed and will make concessions easily. The "tough" stand, on the other hand, signals resolve but may also build resistance in the opponent.

Information about the opponent's utilities is especially important. On the face, such information would seem to be an advantage. However, in some situations, possessing information also seems to increase one's willingness to make concessions, whereas uninformed bargainers may be afraid to concede. In such situations, giving information about one's utilities may increase the opponent's advantage in the bargaining situation.[11] As a general rule of thumb, shared openness and responsibility are ideal, but not always possible (see the discussion of ethical responsibility in Chapter 1). In bargaining, if both parties are not equally willing to share information, unilateral revelation of utilities can hamper and even prevent a fair and agreeable settlement. The more realistic and typical course is gradual and progressive revelation of utilities through moves and countermoves.

The second way in which negotiators interpret the reality of the opponent is through direct communication. Negotiations are not just moves and countermoves as in a game of checkers. Instead, they consist of a great deal of discussion and argumentation relevant to those moves and countermoves. Negotiators make a case for their position, telling the opposition why they think it is fair and right. They also argue against the opponent's position, telling why they are unable to accept it. This kind of exchange can reveal a fair amount about the parties' images of conflict, including their definitions of both the issues and intensity. A negotiator can usually tell the degree of personal animosity held by the opponent by the intensity of language used, and issues are revealed by the amount of time and energy devoted to the various points of contention. Likewise, negotiators' talk says much about their theories of justice and their expectations for procedure. What is usually not revealed in the interchange is the bargainers' utilities, which usually have to be inferred from their actual bargaining positions, demands, offers, and counter offers.

/ Acting in negotiation

The second element of negotiation involves acting in ways that may affect the process and outcome of the negotiation. That influence may take three forms— affecting procedure, affecting the opponent's aims, and affecting the opponent's actions.

Different negotiators make use of different tactics of change, but on the whole, negotiation as a process periodically will make use of all of the processes of influence discussed in this book.[12] In Chapter Four, we discussed the ways in which cognitive change can occur, including learning, tension reduction, and perception. Negotiators attempt to tap into these processes. Of special importance in negotiation are threats, promises, warnings, and mendations.

Promises and *threats,* of course, involve invoking positive and negative sanctions against the opponent. *Warnings* tell of bad consequences from the environment that will result if the opponent makes the wrong move, and *mendations* encourage the opponent to act in certain ways because they will be rewarded by the environment. For example, a parent may threaten a teenager, "If you don't start taking better care of your teeth, I'll make you pay your own dentist bills," or promise, "If you get good grades, we'll go to Disneyland this summer." Just as effective, however, might be the warning, "If you don't take good care of your teeth, they'll rot out of your head!" or the mendation, "I'm pretty sure you'll get into Cal the year after next if you keep your grades up."

Threats and promises are especially prevalent in negotiations because negotiation by definition is basically a power game. Conflict itself arises out of and makes use of power. Since power involves control of resources, it is perfectly understandable that those resources will be used to pressure the opponent.

The question of effectiveness of threats and promises, although important, cannot be answered in the abstract. Whether a particular threat or promise will work depends in part upon the power of the opponent, the opponent's rule system, and his or her reality and goals. Most important perhaps are the ability and willingness of the bargainer to follow through with the promise or threat, and the degree to which the opponent perceives the pressure to be justified based on the criteria of fairness and the structure of an agreement sought.

Because negotiation is a power-laden process rife with threats and warnings, the potential for escalation, especially on the arousal dimension, is great. Escalation to the point of impasse, outburst, actual sanctions, or even violence is always to be avoided if possible. One method of reducing escalating conflict has been called "gradual reduction in tension," or GRIT.[13] This method involves the use of promises to reverse conflict escalation. Wishing to avoid the negative consequences of escalation, one of the negotiators offers the opposition an unconditional reward, in hopes of having the offer reciprocated. This method can be effective if the negotiators both abide by a norm of reciprocity as part of their view of the process. It may not work very well if the power is unequally distributed between the parties. For instance, if one party is less committed to a settlement, that group can withhold cooperation, and the other group can do little about it. If it works, the offer of reward is followed by a promise by the other party, and a series of good-faith moves may then be made.

We once observed a landlord-tenant dispute in mediation. The tenant was irate over a rent increase, and the two were trying to negotiate an agreement with the help of a mediator. The conflict escalated until the landlord offered to repair the kitchen floor, which had been a source of irritation to the tenant. At that point, the tenant offered to help pay for the repair, and the intensity of the debate subsided almost at once.

GRIT is an example of a move that actually changes the rules by which the negotiators are acting. In the face of a goodwill move, the opposition may have to shift from a tough stand to a softer one.

Another common tactic employed in negotiation is to change the perceived value of the contested resources. This can be done in two ways. One involves building up the value of a resource to make it seem more desirable to the opponent. That maneuver has the potential of creating demand. In bargaining salary, for example, a professional group may try to convince the management that the employees provide a service hard to obtain in any other way. The air traffic controllers tried that tactic, but failed when the President proved them wrong by firing them. The converse tactic is to withdraw motivation by suggesting that the contested resource is less valuable than previously supposed. We know of a management negotiator in collective bargaining with clerical workers who actually said, "We won't budge on salary because secretaries can be bought for a dime a dozen." That prejudicial and sexist comment outraged the labor negotiators and prolonged negotiations far beyond what might have otherwise been the case.

Another method commonly used in negotiation is to suggest renegotiation of the agenda. Often negotiators become stuck on a set of issues that seem unresolvable. Sometimes it is helpful to narrow or widen the range of issues being discussed. Narrowing the range of issues allows the parties to concentrate on certain more difficult issues and to ignore others, at least for a time. Widening the range of issues may enable the negotiators to see new areas of agreement and get respite from the conflict over more difficult ones. In the Strategic Arms Limitations Talks, for example, the negotiators may leave discussions of intercontinental ballistic missiles to discuss intermediate range weapons or submarines.

TABLE 7.1

Sample Negotiation Rules

Cueing Rules: Attacking	*Responding Rules: Attacking*
CR1. Discrediting, weakening, or in other ways attacking an opponent's position obligates the opponent to respond or defend himself, or risk conceding the point being attacked.	RR1. When the opponent relinquishes control of the negotiation through a defending or regressing cue, the negotiator has a right to change the topic or in other ways control the direction of the interaction. Exercising this right obligates the opponent to continue the expressed direction or risk appearing weak in retreat.
CR2. Threatening an opponent or his position obligates the opponent to respond or acknowledge the threat or risk antagonizing the user of the threat. Threats are to be viewed as serious unless otherwise stated because threats are generally used as a last resort.	RR2. Either negotiator has the right to initiate the negotiation when no prior initiation rights have been negotiated. Exercising this right obligates the other also to begin the bargaining process or risk appearing uncooperative.
CR3. Proposing an offer to an opponent obligates the opponent at least to consider the offer because offers tend to structure bargaining parameters. If the offer is ignored, it will be interpreted as a rejection. When an offer is repeated, it tends to act as a commitment indicating a firm expected outcome.	

Cueing Rules: Defending	*Responding Rules: Defending*
CR4. Successfully rejecting an attack by devaluing the opponent's products or denying the accuracy of some information sustains the user's position but does not necessarily demand a response from the opponent unless it is combined with an attack.	RR3. When the opponent cues with an attack, the negotiator is obligated to reject or in some way challenge the attack. Failure to challenge can be viewed as support for the attacking points. Rejecting an opponent's position is the most common means of defending against attacks.
CR5. Providing information supporting the negotiator's own point of view bolsters the user's position but does not necessarily constrain or in other ways control the next utterance unless the information is heard as an attack.	RR4. When the opponent cues with an attack that is difficult for the negotiator to reject without appearing uncooperative, the negotiator is still obligated to reject or in some way challenge the attack. Failure to challenge would also be viewed as support for the attacking point. However, the negotiator can reject the attack cooperatively by supporting the opponent's point as a set up for a refutation (e.g., "Yes, I agree, but..."). This conditional support prior to rejection generally communicates cooperativeness, creating a more favorable climate for the user's position.

/ Communication tactics

There are, of course, many possible tactics available to influence the negotiation system. Table 7.1 lists sample negotiation tactics that have been examined in research.[14] You may want to pursue this set of tactics to get a sense of some of

TABLE 7.1 *(continued)*

Cueing Rules: Regressing	*Responding Rules: Regressing*
CR6. Making cueing utterances that are unclear or unrelated to the negotiation are generally viewed as demonstrating lack of confidence or inadequate information, thereby compromising the speaker's information power. Regressions do not constrain a next utterance and may result in relinquishing control of the interaction. CR7. Perhaps the most severe cueing regression that can be made is a concession (an offer less than an immediately prior offer) because concessions are viewed as a clear indication that the speaker has decreased his expected outcomes. This is particularly the case when a concession is made in the face of an attack because such a concession admits weakness.	RR5. When the negotiator gives unqualified agreement, assistance, acceptance or approval to any cue the opponent presents, the negotiator acknowledges the legitimacy of the cue. Such support clearly communicates that the negotiator's expected outcomes have been reduced. RR6. When the opponent cues with an attack (or other statement requiring a specific response), the negotiator is obligated to address the substance of the attack. Failure to address the cue by changing the topic, or in other ways ignoring it, can be viewed as tacitly conceding or supporting the point being attacked. This disconfirmation reduces expected outcomes. RR7. Given the competitive nature of the interaction the negotiator is expected to provide a "competent" response to the opponent, i.e., one that provides a recognizable and orderly strategic position. Failure to present a strategic utterance as a response can be interpreted as some evidence that the user's focal-point is unfirm or inexact.

the ways in which negotiators maneuver through the bargaining game. The list is not complete, but it does provide an interesting set of illustrative moves.

The structure outlined in Table 7.1 uses a two-fold classification system. *Cueing messages* provide a stimulus and essentially initiate change. *Responding messages* react to the cues of the opponent. This scheme also classifies acts in terms of attacking, defending, or regressing (giving-in).

We could fill an entire book on strategies for bargaining, but a proliferated list of practices is less important than is the attitude discussed earlier of learning to ascertain the reality, goals, and relationships of the opponent, taking those into account, and, hence, thinking like the opponent. Because each negotiator's cognitive system differs, we are reluctant to prescribe any particular set of practices in the abstract.

In most situations, constructive negotiating strategies involve compromising, exploring alternative solutions, seeking a mutually-beneficial solution, rewarding the other person, seeking areas of agreement, and expressing trust. On the other hand, actions based on insults, threats, use of guilt, defensiveness, hostility, anger, criticism, intimidation, and name-calling often prove counterproductive to an effective negotiation outcome and, hence, are usually used as a last resort, if at all.

/ Third-Party Negotiation

It should be evident by this point that negotiation is a difficult process. Often intervention by an outside party is necessary to assist in bargaining, to help resolve an impasse, or to prevent the natural destructive consequences of failed negotiation.[15]

Numerous kinds of individuals and organizations involve themselves in dispute intervention, including human relations commissions, religious groups, governmental agencies, psychologists, lawyers, civil rights groups, and marriage counsellors, among others. Although there are various kinds of intervention, *mediation* is especially interesting, and because of its function as intermediary between conflicting parties, it will be highlighted here.

Mediation is a process by which two conflicting parties seek the assistance of an impartial agent in reaching agreement. Unlike an arbitrator, a mediator does not make an outward judgment as to which side should win or how the contested resources should be divided. Rather, mediators structure the communication situation in such a way that the parties themselves are better able to reach an agreement.

/ The triad of influence in mediation

Mediation is fundamentally different from unmediated bargaining because of the introduction of a third party into the dispute.[16] A new set of negotiation rules must be developed to accommodate the mediator. Sometimes these rules are set by the mediator, but other times they are worked out as mediation proceeds. In

/ **The Camp David accord between Egypt and Israel was negotiated with the help of a third party mediator.**

mediation, too, another set of persuasive influences are at work. Not only do the parties engage in persuasion with one another, but they also have to be induced to play a particular mediation game. In a mediation session we observed, agreement could not be reached because one of the parties was never able to accept the role of the mediator. He wanted the mediator to make a judgment as to which side should win and directed all of his communication at "persuading" the mediator that his case was the soundest.

The mediator is an active participant in the process of negotiation and can thereby exert considerable pressure on either party or on the process. Messages are relayed between the disputants by the mediator, who makes active decisions about when and how to reveal information or whether to relay information at all.

In addition, the mediator affects the realities of the disputants in important ways. Mediators may try to modify the parties' meanings for a concession, help change their levels of aspiration, provide opportunities for saving face, and introduce new rules relevant to such concerns as fairness.[17] Because they seek to reorient the disputants' relationship toward one another, mediators may change the negotiation game entirely. In fact, some would say that if mediation is effective, it *must* change those rules and relationships. We were once involved in a mediation of a family dispute, primarily between two parents and their teenage son. When the family tried to solve the problems on their own, the old system prevailed; but the mediator added a new element to the system so that the agreement took on different meanings for the family members. They no longer viewed a potential agreement as an outcome of their own flawed system, but as an "official" contract sanctioned by an outside agency.

The mediator can also be used strategically by the disputants.[18] Disputants sometimes try to influence the mediator to have sympathy with their side so that subtle pressure will be brought to bear on the opponent. Although smart mediators actively resist such pressure, we personally have observed mediators being duped into supporting one side or another. Mediators can also be used as scapegoats by negotiators who sense a "loss" and need to save face with the group they represent. Even if the mediator cannot really be blamed for a bad outcome, the negotiator can always claim that even the mediator, try as he or she did, could not work out a better solution, leaving the negotiator blameless.

Because mediators are active participants in the negotiation, they cannot legitimately be considered neutral, even though mediators sometimes think of themselves in such terms. They have commitments to the mediation process, to a certain model of rational decision-making, and to particular theories of justice, and they influence the process and the outcome in important ways. We can accurately describe some mediators as disinterested, in that they may not take sides, but they are never neutral.

/ Roles of the mediator

The general role of the mediator is to provide some kind of constructive structure wherein disputes can be settled. There is, however, no single way in which to accomplish this goal. Good mediators are flexible enough to adapt to the situation in which they find themselves. Even within a single session, the mediator may change roles several times, depending upon the functions that need to be fulfilled at the moment. The various roles of the mediator can be listed in order of relative involvement: passive mediator, coordinator, enunciator, prompter, leader and arbitrator.[19]

/ *Passive Role.* The passive mediator role is one of mere presence. By being in the room when the parties argue, the mediator can influence the parties to be more constructive and to moderate their style. Individuals tend to speak in more socially acceptable terms in the presence of an outsider. Just as you would be reluctant to have it out with another member of your family when Aunt Tillie comes to visit; negotiators are less apt to insult and degrade each other when the mediator is present. Likewise, having to explain one's case to an outsider often elicits clearer and more complete statements.

/ *Coordinator.* More often than not, the mediator will assume the role of coordinator. Here the mediator keeps order and prescribes procedural rules. This role can be especially important in initial stages of the mediation in proving the mediator to be competent and in engendering the trust of the parties. We remember vividly a moment in a rather complex mediation between several college roommates when the mediator lost control, became confused, and stumbled through one of the sessions. That particular mediation may have been unsuccessful in part because the mediator was perceived as an ineffective coordinator. As coordinator, the mediator may also influence the agenda and the parties' interaction in important ways. The mediator may determine how long individuals talk, when to terminate debate, when to let the other side speak, and what comments are in or out of order.

/ *Enunciator and Prompter.* The mediator as enunciator clarifies the rules of negotiation as well as previous commitments, expectations of outside parties, and issues. The enunciator role allows the mediator to exert considerable influence by making queries and summary statements for clarification. In several mediations we have observed, for instance, mediators begin each private session summarizing the position of the party present as the mediators understand it.

The role of prompter is a stronger version of enunciator. As prompter, the mediator actually makes tentative suggestions about issues and provisions of the agreement. The mediator may interpret one of the parties to the other. The primary difference is that the enunciator role sticks to formalities, while the prompter role deals with the substance of the negotiation. In a mediation between two parties in an assault case, for instance, the mediators wisely suggested wording of a provision that would relieve the accused of a sense of personal guilt. This wording turned out to be acceptable to both sides and was instrumental in achieving an agreement.

/ Leader and Arbitrator. The leader role is one of making direct statements of opinion. It serves to move the negotiations from a position of impasse in which the parties themselves seem unable to think of creative solutions or to re-evaluate their positions. Leaders are sometimes necessary during stalemates.

Arbitrators actually make decisions or judgments. Traditionally, mediation has been distinguished from arbitration on this very point. Arbitrators are hired to make a judgment; mediators are paid to facilitate the process by which the disputants themselves can generate an agreement. Therefore, the arbitrator role is very uncommon in mediation, but may be necessary from time to time.

/ Facilitating resolution

Actually, the task of the mediator is like that of the negotiators themselves. Remember that negotiators have two challenges—to interpret the reality of the opponent and to communicate in ways that move toward resolution. Mediators are also faced with these challenges.[20] In order to accomplish these functions, the mediator too has a set of interpretation and action rules which should be adaptive to the situation encountered. Ultimately, if effective, mediation will bring about the most productive coordination possible between the disputants.

Table 7.2 lists a variety of skills or techniques mediators use in achieving this function.[21] Once again, we cannot prescribe any single method, since the chief skill of a mediator must be to adapt method to situation through incisive interpretation and adaptive action. Therefore the skills listed in Table 7.2 should be considered as a selection of tools from which the mediator can draw.

/ A mediation model

Although a competent mediator will adapt the procedure to the dispute and the situation, it would perhaps be helpful to describe one popular model.[22] We have observed this model in use on several occasions and have seen it both succeed

TABLE 7.2

Mediation Skills

Refereeing the Interaction	*Planning and Preparing for the Future*
Terminating repetitive discussions	Teaching mediation techniques
Providing equal air time	*Initiating Agendas*
Being nonevaluative	Placing less controversial issues first
Clarifying parties' views by restatement	Identifying issues under dispute
Encouraging Interpersonal Feedback	Introducing superordinate goals
Asking for exchange of perceptions	*Diagnosing Conflict*
Using role reversal	Identifying pitfalls of aggressor-defender
Inducing a Problem-Solving Orientation	conflict
Using humor	Using problem-solving methods
Seeking common goals	*Presenting Options*
Creating deadlines	Formulating options

and fail. Most importantly, however, no model should be adopted rigidly. The model presented here has the virtue of including several important objectives in a sensible order. It is an excellent beginning point for the study of the mediation process. Note also that this model makes use of a team of two mediators.

/ *Opening Remarks.* As in the case of most communication events, the opening session has as its primary function the building of identification among participants. In negotiation this requires building trust between the contesting parties and the mediator, but also, insofar as possible, between the parties themselves. Mediators also try to focus the parties' attention on the goals of the negotiation (that is, to build a settlement) and to outline the process whereby that settlement will be achieved.

/ *First Full Session.* The primary function of the first session with all disputing parties present is to develop an overview of the nature of the dispute by identifying the key contested issues. This usually involves allowing the parties to confront each other in a safe way and to ventilate their grievances. The mediator must demonstrate respectful listening and attempt to facilitate nondestructive communication between the parties.

/ *Mediators' Caucus.* Whether there is one mediator or several, they usually take time following the first full session to evaluate the session and plan for later sessions. With more than one mediator this can involve comparing perceptions and notes about the first session. The caucus may be necessary to release tension, keep up one another's morale, and in other ways begin to develop a sense of working as a team. Finally, planning for subsequent sessions is usually necessary.

/ *First Private Session.* In cases where mediators meet with the disputing parties separately, the first private session is designed to help the party clarify his or her own thinking and begin to identify that party's terms for settlement and/or willingness to meet the other party's terms. Additional trust is built and confidentiality is assured in this session. The mediator allows the disputant to expand on his or her views and give a more personal and confidential view of the dispute. The mediator may be able to help the party see the other side's perspective and to reinforce any positive outcomes of the first full session.

/ *Mediators' Caucus.* Following each session the mediators meet together to pursue the objectives cited above for the first caucus. Individual mediators may want time to analyze the situation and plan subsequent sessions.

/ *Second Private Session.* The first private session with the second disputing party is similar to that of the previous private session. Although the mediator has the advantage of additional information in this session, the second disputant has been waiting (and wondering) for some time and so additional care may be necessary in building trust and easing tension. Essentially the same objectives are pursued as in the first private session. Appropriate information from the first private session may be transmitted.

/ Mediators' Caucus. Following the second private session, mediators may caucus in order to determine to what degree agreement is emerging. In addition to exercising the functions of previous caucuses, mediators begin to define potential areas of agreement and, if possible, begin to draft the terms of a final agreement.

/ Additional Sessions. From this point on, additional full sessions or private sessions with either or both parties are conducted as necessary. In addition to transmitting information, mediators will attempt to develop ideas for solution by looking for ideas from one party that solve a problem for the other party. It may be necessary for the mediator to build the will to settle as well as the confidence that a settlement is possible.

/ Additional Mediators' Caucuses. Each additional session may be followed by a mediators' caucus as necessary. In addition to the objectives and functions listed for previous caucuses, later caucuses will work on the fine-tuning of the eventual agreement. During a prolonged negotiation, reducing tension and keeping up morale may become increasingly important during these caucuses.

/ Final Session. If the mediation effort is successful, ultimately there will be a final session for signing or otherwise ratifying the agreement. All parties must understand and agree to all the terms. It may be necessary to fine-tune the wording at this point. The mediator usually finds it desirable to transfer the responsibility for resolving the dispute to the parties and congratulate them for their hard work.

/ Final Caucus. The mediators will usually meet to evaluate the process and formalize notes for further reference. They may also want to celebrate a successful resolution of the dispute.

/ Theory / Practice / Analysis

Theory

1. Negotiation is an important kind of decision making in conflict situations.

2. Most complex negotiations involve bargaining formulae and detail.

3. Several persuasive forces are present in negotiation, including in-group forces, out-group forces, and system forces.

4. Negotiation is governed by causal and practical rules.

5. Negotiators have concepts of the conflict, theories of justice, utilities, and procedures.

6. Persuasion in negotiation is a coordination problem consisting of interpreting and acting.

7. Mediation is a form of intervention in which a third-party assists in resolution of the conflict.

Practice

1. College and university towns often have mediation services. Visit a mediation organization near you and interview the staff about their operations. If they make use of volunteer mediators, consider joining.

2. Make a list of five of your most prized possessions. Consider each one separately. What would you do if someone wanted to buy or trade for that item? What would be your ideal payoff? What would be the least you would take for the item? What other considerations would enter into your negotiations on trading that item?

Now think of five of the most important nonmaterial possessions in your life. This might be a close relative, a child, a life-style, the geographical area in which you live, or some other equally important facet of life. Don't abandon this exercise because you think it is unrealistic: some of the most important negotiations in one's life—divorce agreements, offers by one's company to move to another part of the country, a job offer with higher salary but a substantially different life-style—deal with just such things. Imagine yourself bargaining for these items. What persuasive forces would affect you? What actions might you take?

Now formalize your ideas on the latter exercise by writing a role-playing exercise. Get a partner and acquaint him or her with the problem. Assign your partner a role in a mock negotiation. For example, imagine your partner is your spouse and you are negotiating a child-support and child-custody agreement; imagine that your partner is the owner of your rented house and you are negotiating a deal for a better home; or create some other equally difficult bargaining situation.

Conduct the role play. Take your time and go through several sessions if necessary. After you have completed this exercise, approach your instructor about arranging to video-tape a second role-play so that you can see yourself and analyze the negotiation afterwards.

Analyze your role-plays in terms of the interpretations and actions undertaken by yourself and the other player. Consider the causal and practical forces that guided your choice of negotiation rules. What theories of justice were you using? What were your utilities? To what extent did you bargain on procedure, and what procedure did you end up using for the negotiations?

Analysis

1. Interview a professional negotiator. Before the interview, carefully construct an interview guide based on the concepts of this chapter. Try to discover the extent to which and the ways in which the concepts discussed here are used by the negotiator.

2. Follow your student newspaper closely. Look for events in which two groups on your campus are involved in a conflict and are attempting to settle it. Get as much information about the conflict as possible from the newspaper. In addition, arrange interviews with several key individuals in the conflict and gather more information in that way. Attend to the ways in which negotiation is involved in settling the conflict. After the dispute is resolved (assuming that it is resolved), interview the key disputants again, getting as much information as possible about the negotiation process. Write a paper reporting your findings in terms of the concepts spelled out in this chapter and other relevant concepts.

Notes

[1] I. William Zartman, "Negotiation as a Joint Decision-Making Process," in *The Negotiation Process: Theories and Applications,* ed. I. William Zartman (Beverly Hills: Sage, 1978), pp. 67–86.

[2] See Zartman, "Negotiation," pp. 76–77.

[3] This analysis is adapted from Ian E. Morley and Geoffrey M. Stephenson, *The Social Psychology of Bargaining* (London: George Allen and Unwin, 1977), pp. 28–29.

[4] Adapted in part from William A. Donohue, Mary E. Diez, and Deborah Weider-Hatfield, "Skills for Successful Bargainers: A Valence Theory of Competent Mediation," in *Competence in Communication: A Multidisciplinary Approach,* ed. Robert N. Bostrom (Beverly Hills: Sage Publications, 1984), pp. 226–28.

[5] James T. Tedeschi and Paul Rosenfeld, "Communication in Bargaining and Negotiation," in *Persuasion: New Directions in Theory and Research,* ed. Michael E. Roloff and Gerald R. Miller (Beverly Hills: Sage Publications, 1980), pp. 229–30.

[6] Tedeschi and Rosenfeld, "Communication," pp. 227–28.

[7] Adapted from Donahue et al., "Skills."

[8] Adapted from Donahue et al., "Skills," p. 229.

[9] This section adapted from Tedeschi and Rosenfeld, "Communication," pp. 230–33.

[10] See Tedeschi and Rosenfeld, "Communication," p. 232; and Morley and Stephenson, "Social Psychology," pp. 40–41.

[11] This is the so-called "Schelling hypothesis." See T. C. Schelling, *The Strategy of Conflict* (New York: Oxford University Press, 1960); see also Donald L. Harnett and L. L. Cummings, *Bargaining Behavior: An International Study* (Houston: TX: Dame Publications, 1980).

[12] For an excellent summary of methods of influence used in negotiations, see Tedeschi and Rosenfeld, "Communication."

[13] C. D. Osgood, *An Alternative to War and Surrender* (Urbana: University of Illinois Press, 1960); see also Tedeschi and Rosenfeld, "Communication," p. 239.

[14]William A. Donohue, "Development of a Model of Rule Use in Negotiation Interaction," *Communication Monographs* 48 (1981): 106–120.

[15]Third-party intervention is discussed in some detail in James Laue and Gerald Cormick, "The Ethics of Intervention in Community Disputes," in *The Ethics of Social Intervention,* ed. Gordon Bermant, Herbert C. Kelman, and Donald P. Warwick (Washington, D. C.: Halsted Press), pp. 205–32.

[16]The triadic relationship in mediation is discussed by P. H. Gulliver, *Disputes and Negotiations* (New York: Academic Press, 1979), pp. 209–12.

[17]J. T. Tedeschi and S. Kindskold, *Socially Psychology: Interdependence, Interaction, and Influence* (New York: John Wiley, 1976), p. 389.

[18]P. H. Gulliver, *Disputes and Negotiations* (New York: Academic Press, 1979), pp. 218–19.

[19]Gulliver, *Disputes,* pp. 220–27.

[20]See Donahue et al., "Skills."

[21]Composite list compiled by Donahue et al., "Skills," pp. 223–24.

[22]This model is used at the University of Massachusetts Mediation Project. The table is from Albie Davis and Suzanne Goulet Orenstein, "Mediation Objectives: Step by Step," unpublished handouts.

Part 3

The Public Arena

8 / Persuasion in the Public Arena

If you were to visit the Korean village of Oryu Li, you would arrive by the paved highway. You would see over a hundred homes crowded together just on the other side of the railroad track, below the foothills. The television antennae perched atop the tile roofs would undoubtedly attract your attention, and as you traveled along the small stream toward the town, you might notice, when you got close enough, the small concrete bridge crossing it. As you entered the village, you would soon see the strikingly new white church, rice mill, and belt factory. As you walked to the other side of the town, you would discover the chestnut tree nursery a little beyond.

That was not the scene encountered by the team of communication researchers who arrived in Oryu Li by dirt road in 1973. All of the huts had thatched roofs; there was no television, no factory, no bridge. The farmers forded the stream on stepping stones to get to their fields each day, and there was no direct vehicular passage from the village to the rice fields across the stream. The people were poor in 1973, and they had little of what we in this country consider basic services. But Oryu Li was no ordinary village, even then.[1]

Oryu Li came to be known as the "miracle village." It was the subject of the twenty-seven-part television series, "Pearl of the Soil," and is now famous in Korea and throughout the world as a model of social change. How did this change come about? Everett Rogers and his colleagues studied the process of change as it occurred through communication in Oryu Li. They found that the real story of the village is not one of roofs, television sets, bridges, factories, and paved roads. It is a saga of people who cared about their village and their lives and acted to create change through persuasion. It is a story about the "Mothers' Club" which, over a fifteen-year period, worked for village development, economic sufficiency, and, most of all, family planning. This village is exemplary, but it is not unique. The changes that occurred there are part of a general movement throughout the Republic of Korea: what we see in Oryu Li is being duplicated, although perhaps not as dramatically, in hundreds of villages throughout the country.

In this chapter we examine some of the ways in which persuasion creates change in society. Here we are interested in a larger arena than that covered in the previous section of the book; we paint a picture in broad brush strokes of persuasive communication as it affects large numbers of people and social institutions. This we call the *public arena*.

Public persuasion is a process of convergence, in which interpretations and actions in various communities come together. In this chapter, we discuss this convergence process and the ways in which it is accomplished through the creation, reinforcement, and transformation of public realities. In subsequent chapters we will discuss in more detail the roles of media, public speaking, social movements, and campaigns.

/ Moments of Public Persuasion

The public arena of persuasion is characterized by the extensiveness of its scope and the variety of its forms. Although public persuasion sometimes involves unorganized and scattered attempts at persuasion, it is most often based on planned and coordinated communication.

Public persuasion can be designed to achieve a variety of ends. What do you see when you observe instances of public persuasion? First, on the surface level, you see television and radio programs, films, speeches, books, newspapers and magazine articles, advertisements, and more. On a deeper level, however, each act of public persuasion is a moment in a broader fabric of societal change or resistance to change.[2] Some public persuasion involves *revolutionary moments,* in which advocates push for change. Some are *campaigning moments,* in which specific organizational objectives are sought. Some are *organizational moments* and involve attempts to achieve order and structure among people with common interests. Finally, there are *value-affirming moments,* which bolster public reality.

These moments occur in different types of persuasion. Below we discuss their occurrence in three broad types of public persuasion—special interest persuasion, social movement persuasion, and social control persuasion.

/ Moments in special interest persuasion

Special interest persuasion involves the use of societal channels to achieve the particular objectives of an organization. Such persuasion is expected in a society such as ours; it is neither revolutionary nor extraordinary. This form of persuasion is identified by its rather distinct and focused objectives. Three of the most obvious examples of special interest persuasion are political, commercial, and religious. *Political persuasion,* of course, involves the attempt to build support for a candidate or initiative. *Commercial persuasion* involves product and

/ **Pope John Paul II's persuasive influence is felt in both religious and political arenas.**

service advertising, and *religious persuasion* aims to maintain support or win converts for particular religious beliefs. (We will discuss special interest persuasion in some detail in the chapters on media persuasion and campaigns.)

Special interest persuasion may involve a variety of persuasive moments, although by its very nature it is rarely revolutionary. Advertising, for example, is often an important element in campaigns. Political communication may involve organizing, and it almost always affirms public values in one form or another. Religious persuasion consists of campaigning moments, organizing moments, and especially value-affirming moments.

A Billy Graham crusade, an example of special interest persuasion, involves organizing moments during which local organizations are established and procedures are set up for planning, staging, and following up on the crusade itself. The crusade also involves campaigning moments in which the events of the crusade are advertised, local audiences are sought, and national publicity released. Finally, the events of the crusade exemplify value-affirming moments, in which Christians celebrate their collective beliefs and values.

/ Moments in social movements

Social movements are mass attempts to change establishment practices and values. A movement involves large numbers of people and numerous organizations attempting to achieve some fundamental changes in the fabric of society, or to resist such change. Examples are the Civil Rights Movement, the Women's Movement, the anti-war movement of the sixties, the present-day anti-nuclear weapons movement, the New Right, and many others. Movements are important in a society such as ours, and we therefore discuss them in greater detail in a later chapter.

Most public discourse produced by social movements is revolutionary in that it calls for substantial change in public awareness, values, or practices. Movement persuasion, however, also includes other moments, necessary for achieving specific objectives, organizing, and building internal commitment by affirming the values of participants. The anti-nuclear weapons movement, for example, involves many revolutionary moments in which direct rhetorical pressure is applied to establishment power to change its arms policies. The movement also includes moments in which groups are organized, events are publicized, and members' collective values are affirmed.

One of the most stunning moments in the anti-nuclear weapons movement occurred in August of 1985, when thousands of people descended on Washington, D. C., and literally wrapped a huge "ribbon" made up of hundreds of handcrafted segments around the Pentagon. Although that single event involved all four of the elements discussed above, it was primarily a value-affirming moment in the life of the movement.

/ Moments in social control

The third kind of persuasion typically found in the public arena is that of social control. Social control persuasion involves the attempts of governments and other establishment institutions to maintain support for existing conditions or to achieve establishment goals. Such persuasion may involve special interests embedded in the three types listed above, but it may also include much more. Press conferences, governmental reports and documents, reports from commissions and agencies, church communications and decrees, and many other forms are used to achieve the goals of social control.

Social control, while almost never revolutionary, is typified by the other three moments. Campaigns for new practices under old policies are common in public persuasion. Much organizing persuasion accomplished the goal of social control, and some of the most revered moments in public life are turned over to affirmation of values.

President Reagan's return from the 1985 Geneva summit exemplifies social control persuasion. A carefully orchestrated event designed to further the administration's goals, Reagan's speech to Congress upon his return was a moment of collective value affirmation.

/ Convergence in the Public Arena

The goal of all public persuasion is convergence. In other words, persuasion involves an attempt to have people come together, to share understanding, agreement, and action.[3] In Chapter 2 we wrote that communication is a process of interpretation and action. People interpret situations and act upon those interpretations by applying rules. Convergence occurs when various groups in society begin to share rules and interpret and act in similar ways.

/ Social conflict and convergence

Clearly, social conflict is marked by persuasion. Because of the numerous voices in modern society—some pushing control, others calling for change—conflict is inevitable. Often such conflict involves direct confrontation, of which terrorism is an extreme example. The force and coercion embodied in these forms of social conflict are not themselves examples of persuasion; but many other moments in the evolution of conflict are. We discuss conflict at various points in this book. Negotiation and mediation, for example, are forms of conflict management found most typically in the personal arena, although negotiation can also be a form of conflict resolution in the public arena as well. Especially important in creating, sustaining, and resolving conflict in the public arena are clashes between social control and social movement forces, and conflict finds its way into special interest persuasion when different interests clash. Political persuasion is perhaps the most common example of this form of conflict. It is important to remember in this context that social conflict and persuasion are two sides of the same coin.

Initially, public persuasion is a response to perceived divergence in interpretation and action. In other words, two or more groups differ in their understandings and beliefs of some aspect of common life. Persuasion in the public arena consists of action designed to bring these understandings and beliefs into line. If convergence results, mutual agreement, understanding, and sometimes joint action result.

We are, of course, describing the ideal goal of public persuasion; convergence may not result from public persuasion, in part because of the many counterforces within a society. In some cases, divergence may actually occur. In this section we will discuss the public persuasion process and the ways in which convergence can be achieved. Specifically, we present the role of the media, the network, and personal advocacy; then we discuss a significant sign of convergence known as the rhetorical vision.

/ The convergence process

How does planned change occur in a society? A good deal of research and theoretical attention has been devoted to this question. Basically, it demonstrates that public influence is a result of the media and personal advocacy operating together. The media may provide some initial impetus and information, but influence itself almost always requires people to talk to one another about that information and their opinions of it.

Originally, communication scholars thought that the process of social change was fairly simple. The media would deliver an idea or point of view to certain individuals called *opinion leaders*. These influential people would then spread the word among their friends, who would follow suit. Computers now make it possible to analyze the pathways of influence in much more detail, demonstrating that, while opinion leaders are still important, influence does not happen in just two steps. Rather, influence is a process of many steps, as people interact with one another in rather complex *networks.*[4]

Think of an important change that has recently occurred in your life. It might be the acquisition of an important new possession, the adoption of a new practice, or possibly a new attitude or altered value. If you think about how you came to make this change, you will probably discover that it involved discussion with others in face-to-face situations. You may have watched advertisements in the media, seen a television program that provided information, or followed relevant reports in the newspaper; but, eventually, if you are like most of us, you talked to more than one person about the idea. After the change occurred, you probably talked to others, spreading the idea even further. This kind of communication is what we mean by the interpersonal network.

The innovations adopted in Oryu Li were a direct consequence of the communication network there. In fact, Oryu Li was small enough for researchers to draw an actual diagram of the network: it illustrates how individual women in the village talked with certain other women about birth control, leading to the eventual adoption of contraception by every single one of them. The study of Oryu Li also shows how one woman, Mrs. Cheung, kept the network together and was responsible for spreading much information and influence. Mrs. Cheung made a point to read and watch the media for information on a variety of subjects. For example, she read about another community's success with a belt factory, and then decided to try to get one started in Oryu Li. The factory, thus, was an outcome of the original idea from the media, followed by discussion in the interpersonal network. Let's take a closer look at each of the components—the media and the network—in the convergence process.

/ *The Media.* The communications media are extremely important in a society such as ours. Except for an occasional retreat to the wilderness, you cannot escape the media; but, then, people do not often try to escape. In fact, they actively use media for a variety of purposes, which we will discuss in Chapter 10.

Media are involved in public persuasion in two ways. First, they provide important information, which is used by certain individuals to make decisions; these individuals later talk with others about their decisions. Second, media actually provide a stimulus for the personal conversation that may eventually lead to change.

Consider some of the ways in which people use television to support their personal communication.[5] Television can be a means of *setting the discussion agenda.* What we choose to talk about is often influenced by what we have seen on television. Second, television can be useful in *providing information* later used in conversations. Third, television provides copious *illustrative material* that later finds its way into our personal conversations. Television also provides a vehicle for *social criticism,* since we often share our judgments of various television programs *stimulate fantasy,* which is often shared interpersonally with others. (Because this special fantasy function is intriguing and important, we discuss it in more detail below.) We return to the uses of television and other media in Chapter 10.

/ ***The Network.*** Recall from Chapter 6 that the network is an organization of sorts. It is a communication structure consisting of links between people. We are all members of a number of networks, not just one. Remember also that we do not communicate with equal frequency with everybody we know. The unevenness of communication gives the network structure. If you want information, you will go to certain other individuals to get that information. If you are considering adopting a new practice or are toying with a new idea, you will discuss it, not with just anyone, but with certain others you trust, someone you believe may have relevant information, or someone who is close to you relationally or physically.

The story of the New Christian Right is largely one of networks. The success of the Moral Majority, for example, was largely due to the personal network of fundamentalist ministers throughout the organization. The Moral Majority itself was begun when a few men from business got together to establish a new political organization; they contacted Jerry Falwell and recruited him to be its leader and organizer. They later built a respectably large support group of individuals who act as opinion leaders in the organization. The various organizations of the New Christian Right use a variety of tools in their persuasion, not least of which is the media, but interpersonal channels remain an extremely important instrument in their work.

/ Personal advocacy

The lesson from research on convergence in the public arena is that, although the media are vitally important, convergence is unlikely without individual human contact. In other words, convergence is a product of people talking with other people. Personal advocacy is of two types. First, much influence occurs by advocates in the network, people with whom individuals have relationships and who exert influence in social groups. Such individuals are essentially *private advocates.* Although their influence is exerted in private situations, they are still an important part of public persuasion because they spread the word through the network and thereby accomplish public objectives. Second, influence also occurs by individuals making appeals publicly in speeches, books, editorials, and other forums. This we call *public advocacy.*

The literature in communication refers to the private advocate as an opinion leader. Opinion leaders are individuals who are quick to pick up ideas from the media and pass them on to others. As network leaders, they are especially important in the public arena. In traditional societies such as Oryu Li, people like Mrs. Cheung may lead opinions on a variety of subjects; but in more complex societies such as our own, opinion leaders tend to be specialized. You turn to different people for leadership on different subjects like style, politics, religion, technology, or education. You may have different opinion leaders at work, at your place of worship, at school, and at home. The influence channels may be different on matters relevant to each social group to which you belong.

What distinguishes opinion leaders? In general—and there are probably plenty of exceptions to this—opinion leaders tend to have greater exposure to the mass media, they tend to be more gregarious than others, they may have higher social status than many others within the social group, and they are typically more innovative.[6]

Although private opinion leadership is crucial to the dissemination of ideas, advocates often go public with their views. Essayists, book authors, columnists, speakers, and others present messages intended for audiences beyond the individual group. Such persuasion may take place through print media, electronic media, or in live speeches.

Public advocates have special obstacles to overcome: they must understand the ways in which their own interpretations mesh with or depart from that of the audiences they address; they must consider how to frame arguments and what kind of supporting material to employ; they must think about organizing and delivering their messages; and they are perhaps more concerned with conscious use of language than are private advocates. Because of its importance and unique place in the public arena, we devote the entire next chapter to public advocacy.

/ *The cognitive dimensions of convergence*

We have described *convergence* as a coming together or sharing of cognition. Recall from Chapter 3 that the cognitive system has four dimensions—reality, goal, arousal, and relationship. Let us look again at these dimensions in terms of the public arena.

The *reality dimension* involves interpretations of what is considered real. It is the system of beliefs and attitudes held by the individual. Much public persuasion aims to change beliefs and attitudes. The anti-nuclear arms movement tries to change the belief that more weapons will deter nuclear war, the American Cancer Society tries to change attitudes about smoking, and advertisers try to show how their products will meet viewers' needs and wants. Because it lies at the heart of the cognitive system and is so vitally important to public persuasion, the reality dimension is discussed in greater detail later in the chapter.

The *arousal dimension* involves emotion. Almost all public persuasion attempts to affect arousal in one way or another. Mothers Against Drunk Driving (MADD) aims to have the public share their anger about the tragedy of drunk driving accidents, while Michelob wants beer drinkers to feel good about drinking with friends. Environmentalists capitalize on Humphrey, the lost whale in the Sacramento River, to build public pathos for an endangered species, while commercial fishing organizations in the Northwest spread their anger at being barred by governmental regulation from making a living.

The *goal dimension* involves values, needs, and motives. The Christian Broadcast Network is filled with programs designed to reinforce traditional values and make inroads against more liberal and humanistic values. Advertising is heavily laden by values and attempts directly to influence one's sense of need and motive. Virtually all public persuasion is based on some sense of shared value.

Finally, the *relationship dimension* involves perceptions of and actions toward self and others in relationships. It involves trust, attraction, similarity, and attribution. Much public persuasion is designed to establish more favorable relationships between advocates and audiences. Speeches try to build trust, and editorials impugn or defend the behavior of certain officials.

/ Rhetorical visions

As individuals and groups converge, they come to hold certain common visions of what is real and good. Common visions are apparent in shared stories reflecting what communicators believe. These shared stories are known as *fantasies*. We certainly do not mean by this term that the stories are necessarily fictional.

/ **Protestors of nuclear armaments reiterate the themes that make up the rhetorical vision of nuclear weapons and nuclear war.**

Rather, group fantasies are representations of what group members believe to be real. They are mechanisms by which individuals share their interpretations of events.[7] Next time you have a prolonged conversation with another individual, listen for the stories each of you tell and think about the ways in which these stories are visions of reality.

A complete story or complex account of an event or situation is called a *rhetorical vision*. It represents the shared image of events as they were, are, or will be. For example, in a study of the rhetorical vision of nuclear war, we found that people have a strong shared vision of what a nuclear war would be like, even though they have never experienced it.[8] This vision comes in part from public depictions like those seen in films, but it also comes from talking with others.

The rhetorical vision is a product of interaction. People develop their stories as they talk to others, and these stories are elaborated, changed, and become somewhat solidified as they are passed from person to person, again and again. Rhetorical visions are therefore "chained out" as more and more people become involved in them. Those stories are rarely told in their entirety at any given moment, but parts of the vision are revealed in the form of *fantasy themes*. Themes are elements of the total vision that appear repeatedly in the conversations of a group. Convergence occurs as more and more themes come to be shared. You may notice, for example, that in anti-nuclear weapons groups, people may restate the same themes of nuclear arsenals, proliferation of weapons, mutually assured destruction, dangers of nuclear war, blast effects and fallout, ecological disaster, and many others. As a group, these themes constitute the rhetorical vision of nuclear weapons and nuclear war. Once a fantasy theme becomes well known in a group, individuals will refer to it with an abbreviated code that everyone in the group understands. That is why people in a group may laugh at an inside joke, while outsiders do not understand what is being said. Such abbreviated references to fantasy themes are called *fantasy types*.

Although fantasy themes are spread by word of mouth, they are reinforced by public advocates as well. Almost all forms of public advocacy make use of fantasy themes. Political speeches, advertising, sermons, campaign literature, and other forms include fantasy themes that may capture the attention and conviction of audience members. The movie *The Day After,* which was aired on national television in November of 1983, for example, seemed to resonate deeply with the rhetorical vision of nuclear war that has chained out in society at large, making it one of the most viewed and discussed television programs of all time.[9]

A rhetorical vision, in other terms, reflects shared elements in the cognitive systems of communicators. Let us turn briefly to the ways in which public persuasion involves these dimensions.

Persuasion and Public Reality

Communication is a process of constructing reality. In this section we will discuss the ways in which public persuasion affects interpretation influencing the creation, reinforcement, and transformation of reality.[10]

/ The creation of public reality

As explained in Chapter 2, interpretation is a product of the social construction of reality. By this we mean that people develop notions of reality through communication. How does public persuasion enter into this process? Persuasion in the public arena is primarily a means of establishing a sense of community and developing commitment to that community.

/ Community.

Public persuasion aims to establish a sense of community within an audience. Two important elements of community which are often created by public discourse are (1) ideology and (2) time and place. *Ideology* is a system of fundamental beliefs as to what is real and good and assumptions about how people come to have knowledge. In other words, ideology is one's basic assumptions about human experience. One's ideology lies at the heart of the cognitive system, affecting beliefs in the reality dimension, interpretation of emotions in the arousal dimension, values in the goal dimension, and assumptions about the nature of human relationships.

The Puritan ethic is an example of an ideology. It values traditional roles, hard work, and responsibility. Although no strictly "Puritan" community exists any more, many groups still abide in large measure by this world view. They are confident in their knowledge of the reality of these values because of divine revelation. The Puritan ethic, however, is by no means the only or even predominant ideology of our society. Other groups hold quite different ideas about what is real and good.

Marxist ideology, for example, points out that industrialism, which is based in large measures on Puritan assumptions, is merely a social construction designed to distribute power to an elite class. What is real for Marxist groups is class division, exploitation, and power assymetry. Therefore resistance, disruption of traditional values, and revolution are valued among Marxist groups. Unlike Puritans, Marxists have no faith in divine revelation, but base their beliefs on the incisive critique of leading thinkers. The Puritan ethic and Marxist thinking are obvious ideologies and illustrate ideological difference very well; but there are numerous other ideologies that guide communities, and these may differ in subtle but important ways.

Community also depends upon a sense of shared *time and place*. Nationalism, for example, is easily promulgated in public discourse by reference to time and place. Loyalties to schools, sports teams, families, commercial establishments, products, and clubs are all based, at least in part, on the sense of sharing a place and a time. Public discourse often attempts to create such a sense.

Consider, for example, some recent advertisements from a popular magazine. An automobile: "Destined to become another American classic; the 1986 Seville. The perfect combination of luxury and technology." A perfume: "The Extraordinary American: Giorgio of Beverly Hills." A men's store: "Park Avenue just didn't seem like Park Avenue without Sulka. But now, Sulka is back on Park. . . . a 90-year tradition of uncompromising standards in both product and service."

Public persuasion, then, serves in part to create ideology, time, and place, which together provide a sense of community. The community may be professional (as the American Medical Association), religious (as Roman Catholics), cause-oriented (as Pro-Life), political (as supporters of Ronald Reagan), and innumerable other possible groups. The fantasy themes of a group are rife with ideology, time, and place.

As an example of how public discourse aims to create community, consider a brief excerpt from a 1985 speech by Senator Edward Kennedy on apartheid:

> The people in every American city who care about this issue are proving by their protests that the 1980s need not be a decade of disinterest, a time of lonely hopes and narrow horizons. They're demonstrating as so many have in South Africa, that individuals are still ready to respond when they are challenged, to stand up not only for themselves, but for others; not only for their interests, but for their ideals.

The elements of time and place are easy to see in this passage. Perhaps less obvious are ideological elements, but they are there: Kennedy assumes that changes are made by human intervention, that expression through demonstration is appropriate, that racial class is bad, and that human concerns transcend national boundaries. Listeners who are sympathetic to this ideology and who have identification with this time and place may be led to recognize a community of concerned activists.

/ Commitment.   Public persuasion aims to establish not only a sense of community, but also commitment to that community. Such commitment is established in three ways. First, communicators attempt to have audience members *understand their personal place in the community.* Commitment means more than recognizing the existence of a community; it requires knowing how one's own beliefs fit into the broader framework of that community. For example, many feminists have a Marxist orientation. They recognize their own beliefs about gender and power, and have come to see how those concerns are also part of a larger Marxist ideology. Other feminists may well recognize the Marxist community, but do not see their own feminist concerns as consistent with that ideology.

Second, communicators try to elicit *agreement on issues* relevant to the community. For example, the New Right has assumed great power in American politics in the mid-1980s. Many people who have identified with that community of conservatives have not supported all of the policies of the Reagan administration. Tax reform is an issue on which even staunch Republicans have disagreed, and the administration has maintained a steady campaign among followers to elicit agreement on its favored tax reform measure.

Finally, public persuasion aims to engender a sense of *faithfulness* in the community. One learns to see one's place in the community, to use its ideology to make decisions on issues, and to be loyal to the community. Faithfulness means deferring to the collective wisdom of the ideology in times of doubt. In Congress it is assumed that senators and representatives will follow the party unless they have extraordinary personal or political reasons for voting independently.

/ The reinforcement of public reality

Much public persuasion is aimed not at winning new adherents, but at bolstering existing members of the community of believers. Reinforcement of the reality of the community is accomplished in four general ways.

Doctrinaire strategies involve preaching dogma to those who already believe. Sermons and political speeches at $100-a-plate dinners are examples. *Participatory strategies* involve members of the community in organizational activities and rhetorical practices. Consciousness-raising groups, campaign recruitment, and solicitation of funds are examples. *Isolationist strategies* attempt to wall off the group from outside influence. Parochial schools and restrictions on reading and other activities are examples. Since physical isolation is usually impossible, isolationist persuasion often takes the form of dissuading members from exposing themselves to outside views. Finally, reality is

/ Most Soviet citizens receive their news only through *Pravda*, the official newspaper of the Communist party. Such control over communication resources reinforces the public reality by isolating the Soviet people from outside influences.

often reinforced by *confrontational strategies,* in which opposing groups are named, labelled as wrong, and refuted.

Rhetoric designed to bolster reality is basically a kind of social control, as briefly defined above. Let us examine more closely the social control function.[11] Social control consists of efforts by organizations to prevent, suppress, or control changes. As systems, established communities and groups tend to maintain themselves and fight change from outside. Generally, four broad forms of social control can be observed. These include control over communication resources, persuasion opposing change agents, creation of symbolic structures, and repressive techniques.

/ *Control of Resources.*   Communication resources are the arteries of any society. The language itself has deep roots into cultural traditions and reinforces traditional values. The Women's Movement devoted a great deal of energy to linguistic issues such as the title "Mrs." and the female descriptor "girl." In addition, the establishment also tends to control the media, which means, in large measure, control over access to media and control over information. Even when representatives of opposing views are given access to communication resources, they frequently represent only mild opposition that the establishment can tolerate. An example is Booker T. Washington's accommodation to "separate but equal" doctrine toward blacks.

We are not necessarily referring to deliberate and repressive control here. Rather, we are referring to the normal state of affairs as having inherent bias and limitation. That bias, because it is part of the status quo, is often in opposition to the ideology of social movements. For example, the New Christian Right, which will be discussed as a case in Chapter 11, has accused the media in this country as having a secular humanist bias. The very nature of media in a free society creates a bias in favor of diversity, balance, and tolerance, all humanistic values. In addition, the philosophy and practices of media in a society are controlled by those who own and manage them, and they are part of the establishment in most cases. This is why movements in our country make such heavy use of news coverage as a means of persuasion and communication. They may not themselves be able to broadcast to the public at large, but they can create events that attract the attention of the news media.

/ *Counterpersuasion.*   Often social control takes the form of direct counterpersuasion. Such persuasion attempts directly to counteract those who are trying to change the group's definition of reality. Partisan political campaigns illustrate this kind of control very well. Not only does one party try to win votes, but it also reinforces its own values in an attempt to maintain its own order of things.

The creationism movement in our country is an example of bolstering by counterpersuasion. The advocates of creationism base their beliefs on biblical accounts of the origin of the world and of life. That belief system is reinforced in part by attacking the research and theories of scientific evolution.

/ Symbolic Structures.   Social control can also involve various symbolic gestures toward both adherents and opponents. Such gestures include promises, token rewards, studies and hearings, and the like. In these cases, various establishment organizations are making gestures toward the disenchanted in order to make them feel that the establishment is working on their behalf or, in some cases, is punishing miscreants. Often believers revel in the symbolism of the community, and symbolic structures almost always have the effect of reinforcing the ideology of the community.

Two very different examples of symbolic structures will suffice. The first is the grand jury, a group of citizens chosen on an annual basis to investigate public offices and functions. Although grand juries can have an important substantive impact on governmental operations, their symbolic value is also great. As a symbol, the existence of the grand jury tells the public that citizens can have an impact on governmental and judicial functions. As a part of the establishment, the grand jury functions in a way that is not threatening to the existing order of things.

The second example is the parade permit. Cities and towns require large public demonstrations that will block traffic to have a permit. Giving a permit gives official "permission" to any kind of parade or gathering, bringing it into the existing order and sanctioning the rights of individuals to gather in public places for celebration or demonstration.

/ Repressive Techniques.   Finally, social control can involve direct repression. Sometimes that involves brute power, as in dispersing a public demonstration. Most of the time, however, repression is less intense. It may, for example, consist of controlling entry or exit to important places and then refusing to admit representatives of a group, effectively preventing them from stating their demands. Direct repression is often coercive and as such may not really constitute persuasion. On the other hand, although repression may not function as persuasion for those directly repressed, it also has symbolic value, which may act persuasively on other observing groups, including those sympathetic to the establishment. The act of excommunication by a religious organization is coercive toward the person excommunicated, but also sends a powerful persuasive message to other members.

/ The transformation of reality

The third way in which public persuasion operates to affect cognition is by transforming or changing a group's definition of reality. That means changing the definition of community or shifting commitment from one community to another. Much public persuasion between 1965 and 1972 was directed at the issue of the Vietnam War. In essence, two huge communities came into conflict during that period—the establishment order which promoted the ideology of a free people struggling to stop the spread of communism in the Third World, and the community of peace advocates which promoted an anti-imperialistic ideology of self-determination and non-involvement. The rhetoric of the former community was designed primarily to reinforce the establishment reality; that of the latter was designed to transform it. Transformational persuasion is accomplished in a variety of ways. We will consider four general strategies in turn.

/ Elevating. Elevating involves raising otherwise mundane events to the level of a value. Here the objective is to have people look at their experience in new ways—to see it as more than simple action, as the expression of ideology. For example, in a very effective Republican television commercial during the 1984 Presidential campaign, "Morning in America," various scenes of people preparing for an ordinary day were made to reflect deep American values and a sense of patriotism.

/ Reducing. Reducing strategies accomplish the same thing as elevating strategies, but go about it in the opposite way. Instead of elevating, the speaker begins with desirable values and points out how these are manifest in ordinary things. In a startling and controversial pro-life film, *The Silent Scream,* a doctor asserts that life starts at conception and that abortion is murder. He then proceeds to "prove" his case by showing sonagram photographs of an actual abortion in which the movements of the fetus are taken as evidence that his assertions are correct.

/ Associating. Elevating and reducing strategies move from one level of abstraction to another. Associating strategies, on the other hand, link one value with another at the same level of abstraction. Audiences are led to believe that adoption of a particular belief is tantamount to adoption of another. The Reagan administration, for example, links events in Central America to international Marxism and the Soviet Union. Public persuasion by representatives of the administration says that supporting the Sandinista government in Nicaragua or the rebels in El Salvador is the same as supporting Soviet expansionism. On the other hand, aid to the Contras in Nicaragua and support of the government in El Salvador means fighting for freedom. One of the chief strategies of the opposition to this policy, therefore, is to argue against that assumed association.

/ Refuting. Refutational strategies are defensive and attack the assertions of the opposition in an attempt to win adherents from those not yet committed to one's position. One of the most effective political speeches in American history was given by Richard Nixon in the 1952 vice-presidential campaign. Nixon had been accused of garnering $18,000 from campaign funds for personal use. His speech made use of all of the strategies discussed here, but most directly exemplifies the refutational approach. He clearly and directly denied the allegation and refuted the claims of the opposition point by point.

This chapter has introduced the subject of persuasion in the public arena. In the following chapters, we consider the subjects touched upon here in greater detail. In Chapter 9, public advocacy is discussed; Chapter 10 deals with persuasion and media; and Chapter 11 concludes with a discussion of social movements and campaigns.

/ *Theory* / *Practice* / *Analysis*

Theory

1. The types of public persuasion are special interest persuasion, social movements, and social control. Moments of persuasion are revolutionary, campaigning, organizational, and value-affirming.

2. Public persuasion is a process of convergence, in which media provide information that is disseminated throughout networks by personal advocates. An important product of convergence is a shared rhetorical vision.

3. Convergence is a process of coming to share cognitive dimensions of reality, goals, arousal, and relationships.

4. Convergence, or shared public reality, consists of a sense of community and commitment to the community. Persuasion aims to create, reinforce, or transform public reality.

Practice

1. For a period of about a week, take the role of opinion leader on some subject of interest to you. Attend to information from the media on that subject and make a concerted effort to "talk it up" to people you know. At the end of the exercise, make a list of all the people you spoke to about the information. This list constitutes a portion of a network. Is this a standard network to which you belong? In what ways has this network operated in the past? How successful was your attempt to establish convergence? How comfortable were you in the role of opinion leader?

2. Repeat the above exercise with another issue. Before discussing the issue with others, make a conscious attempt to construct messages that establish, reinforce, or transform some sense of community and/or commitment to a community. What strategies were used? Now go back to the original information you got from the media and figure out how that information attempted to establish, reinforce, or transform a sense of community and/or commitment to the community. To what extent did your strategies as a personal advocate resemble or differ from those of the media you used?

Analysis

1. Tape-record a lengthy conversation among a group of friends with whom you are comfortable. (Try to tape a naturally occurring conversation rather than a simulated one.) Carefully review the tape for fantasy themes. What rhetorical visions seem apparent in these themes? Were any fantasy types used? Divide the fantasy themes into those you think are private in the group and those that are shared with other groups in society. Find examples of the fantasy themes in the second group in various public persuasion messages like movies, books, magazines, and television programs.

2. Based on your survey of news articles and broadcasts, choose a clash between movement and social control forces. Study the public discourse of the various groups involved in the clash. Classify the messages according to revolutionary, campaigning, organizational, and value-affirming moments. (Some messages may involve more than one.) Isolate the reality, goal, arousal, and relationship dimensions apparent in these statements. In what ways do they attempt to create, reinforce, or transform a sense of community and commitment to the community? Attend to the specific strategies being used to accomplish these goals. (This exercise makes an excellent term project.)

Notes

[1]For details about this case, see Everett M. Rogers and D. Lawrence Kincaid, *Communication Networks* (New York: Free Press, 1981), pp. 1–30.

[2]Adapted from Roderick P. Hart, "The Functions of Human Communication in the Maintenance of Public Values," in *Handbook of Rhetorical and Communication Theory,* ed. Carroll C. Arnold and John W. Bowers (Boston: Allyn and Bacon, 1984), pp. 749–91.

[3]The idea of convergence comes from Rogers and Kincaid, *Networks,* pp. 31–78; Ernest G. Bormann, *The Force of Fantasy: Restoring the American Dream* (Carbondale, IL: Southern Illinois University Press, 1985), pp. 1–25; and Ernest G. Bormann, *Communication Theory* (New York: Holt, Rinehart and Winston, 1980), pp. 188–91.

[4]Communication networks are discussed in Rogers and Kincaid, *Networks,* pp. 220–324.

[5]For details on this subject, see James Lull, "The Social Uses of Television," *Human Communication Research* 6 (1980): 196–209.

[6]Opinion leadership is discussed by Everett M. Rogers and F. Floyd Shoemaker, *Communication of Innovations: A Cross-cultural Approach* (New York: Free Press, 1971), pp. 218–19.

[7]Bormann, *Force.* See also Ernest G. Bormann, "Fantasy and Rhetorical Vision: The Rhetorical Criticism of Social Reality," *Quarterly Journal of Speech* 58 (1972): 396–407; and Ernest G. Bormann, "Fantasy and Rhetorical Vision: Ten Years Later," *Quarterly Journal of Speech* 68 (1982): 288–305.

[8]Karen A. Foss and Stephen W. Littlejohn, "*The Day After:* Rhetorical Vision in an Ironic Frame," *Critical Studies in Mass Communication,* 3 (1986).

[9]Foss and Littlejohn, *Day.*

[10]This analysis adapted from Hart, "Public Values."

[11]This analysis is adapted from Herbert W. Simons, Elizabeth W. Mechling, and Howard N. Schreier, "The Functions of Human Communication in Mobilizing for Action from the Bottom Up: The Rhetoric of Social Movements," in *Handbook of Rhetorical and Communication Theory,* ed. Carroll C. Arnold and John W. Bowers (Boston: Allyn and Bacon, 1984), pp. 792–868.

9 / Public Advocacy

In 1949, the U.S.S.R. first successfully tested an atomic weapon, thereby breaking the United States' nuclear monopoly which had existed since the detonation of the first atomic bomb in New Mexico in 1945. For nearly thirty years thereafter the two countries developed increasingly more powerful and sophisticated nuclear weapons and deployed them in subterranean silos, on aircraft, and in submarines. Negotiations designed to control the nuclear arms race were attempted. As a result of these negotiations, nuclear testing in the atmosphere was prohibited and the development of defensive weapons was controlled, thus leaving massive retaliation as the major deterrent against aggression from either side.

In the 1970s, the U.S. Air Force conceived of a missile which not only had greater power and accuracy, but also carried several nuclear warheads. They named it MX. A major question regarding MX within the defense establishment was where and by what basing mode should it be deployed. Suggestions ranged from mobile shallow water submarines to existing silos which had housed Minuteman missiles. In the late 1970s Frances Farley, a nationally obscure member of the Utah state legislature, became aware of plans to deploy the missile at the Utah-Nevada border on a subterranean race-track system which would have taken hundreds of square miles of rangeland and cost several billions of dollars to accomplish. In a series of speeches and television appearances, Senator Farley forced the U.S. Air Force to answer her challenges, and the race-track proposal was finally withdrawn. This controversy prompted a great deal of public advocacy.

Although a variety of mechanisms of persuasion operate in the public arena, personal advocacy remains a powerful force for change. Public advocates are individuals who, because of commitment, opportunity, skill, and/or access, make personal statements to an audience. Public advocacy can range from a local expert talking at a meeting of the Lion's Club to the President addressing the nation on television. Public advocacy may occur in media such as television, radio, books, and newspapers, or it may occur in live speaking situations. Although the principles discussed in this chapter apply to all kinds of public advocates, our model is that of the public speaker. When Frances Farley spoke out against the MX missile in Utah, she exemplified this kind of persuasion in the public arena.

Like all forms of persuasion, public advocacy is a process of using rules to interpret and act. This chapter is therefore divided into two sections: the first deals with challenges of interpretation facing the public advocate, and the second deals with the actions of the public advocate.

Interpretation in Public Advocacy

Faced with the challenge of advocating a point of view in public, speakers and writers naturally go through a process of interpretation. The advocate makes sense out of the situation encountered, coming to an understanding of the people, places, events, and issues involved. Let us discuss how each of these is involved in the advocate's interpretation.

The participants

In Chapters 2 and 3 we examined ways in which communicators process information. Specifically, we discussed four dimensions of the cognitive system— reality, arousal, goal, and relationship. These dimensions of information processing apply in public advocacy as they do in any setting in which persuasion occurs. An important part of the interpretation undertaken by an advocate is the understanding of one's own reality, arousal, goals, and relationships as well as those of the audience.

The Reality Dimension.   As defined in Chapter 3, the reality dimension is the basic set of concepts and beliefs that form one's definition of reality. You stand up in public to advocate a point of view because you believe your definition of reality differs in an important way from that of your audience. That initial sense of difference motivates public advocacy. When Frances Farley discovered the plan of the U.S. Air Force, she took action to make a change in the opinion of the public to whom the Air Force had to appeal.

Speech teachers have referred to this process of interpretation as *audience analysis.* It leads advocates to understand the ways in which their own beliefs, attitudes, and values depart from or conform to that of a community of listeners. Advocates base this interpretation on a variety of factors. First, because persuasion is a transactional process, advocates are listeners as well as speakers. They become consciously aware of the persuasive forces around them and thereby come to understand what people believe, want, and feel. Sometimes this "listening" is in the form of public opinion polls, but more often it is informal and comes from having one's ear to the ground.

/ Advocates of a position employ audience analysis in order to understand the ways in which their own beliefs, values, and attitudes depart from or conform to those held by members of the audience.

In addition, advocates base their interpretation of others on inferences made from characteristics of the groups that constitute a potential audience. Such inferences are based on observations of categories like vocation, religion, and geographical location.

Vocation is often a powerful predictor of individuals' belief and value systems. Since most adults spend half of their waking hours at work, it stands to reason that their occupation will profoundly influence how they process information and the rules by which they will interpret and act. For example, business people will generally have fairly predictable opinions about free enterprise, and individuals in the helping professions will be concerned about social issues. Many college professors are notoriously liberal, and military personnel favor a strong defense.

Religion is another predictor of belief, especially on moral issues. Opinion polls often divide their results according to religion. Quakers, for example, have traditionally been strongly for human rights and against violence of any kind. Fundamentalists usually support prayer in the schools, and Catholic opposition to abortion and birth control is well known.

Geographical location is another category on which advocates make interpretations of audience beliefs.[1] Frances Farley was likely to have support for her opposition to the race-track plan in an area where the population values its environment and where that environment is threatened. Geography is important in part because issues affect various locations differently, as the MX missile example cleary illustrates. Politicians are acutely aware of the effect of geography and consider it carefully in framing their public arguments.

Information based on vocation, religion, and geography may help an advocate understand the images people carry in their heads. Individuals as well as groups have stories or pictures of themselves that affect how they observe, think, or behave. Groups as well as individuals may imagine themselves as leaders or followers, active or passive, urban or rural, successful or unsuccessful.

/ *The Arousal Dimension.* Generally people are not motivated to publicly make a persuasive appeal unless the issues are important to them. That means their arousal level must go beyond simple concern. Public advocates also tend to speak on issues that have aroused considerable feeling in audiences as well. Remember from Chapter 3 that one's interpretations of events are affected by his or her emotions, and, inversely, one's emotions are understood in terms of the belief system. Good public advocates are aware of this connection between the dimensions of cognition and make use of it in their appeals.

It is no accident, for example, that Representative Claude Pepper has been such an influential and popular congressman. An elderly statesman from Florida, he has been an outspoken advocate of legislation for the older population in the United States. His credibility on these issues is great because of his own personal involvement and level of feeling, and for this reason he also appeals strongly to his own constituency, which is one of the oldest in the country. Certainly, Representative Pepper and those he represents have a particular reality not shared by younger members of society. That reality is undeniably tied to a level of arousal and depth of feeling stemming from living through the problems and prospects of old age in America.

/ *The Goal Dimension.* The goal dimension, which is most affected by values, needs, and motives, drives our actions. It provides a set of action rules that are used in deciding how to act in various situations. An important part of any advocate's interpretation of the situation consists of understanding the values, needs, and motives of one's supporters, opponents, and the audience at large. It also means having to deal with one's own persuasive objectives.

The advocate determines which aspects of the listeners' cognitive systems or behaviors he or she wishes to have altered, intensified, realigned, or bolstered. Several kinds of public advocacy goals are common: (1) establishing, changing, or intensifying belief; (2) altering the advocate's relationship with the audience; (3) intensifying audience arousal; (4) affecting behavior; and (5) inducing resistance to change. Each of these is discussed briefly below.

The goal that has received the most research attention is altering the reality dimension of the cognitive system. This involves *establishing, changing, or intensifying beliefs and attitudes.* Speakers often attempt to establish a belief among individuals who are initially uncommitted on an issue. Such uncommitment may stem from a lack of knowledge or lack of awareness of the issue. It could also be due to a lack of a sense of the importance of the issue. The case of the MX missile is a good example. One of Farley's major goals was to establish awareness of the issue and create opposition among people who had previously known little about it.

Often advocates want to facilitate change in the cognitive system from belief to disbelief, positive to negative attitude, or vice versa. When viewed as a spectrum of possibilities, the establishment, change, or intensification of the elements of the cognitive system become somewhat gross approximations of an infinite number of small changes that individuals undergo. Indeed, dramatic shifts of opinion, feeling, or attitude are somewhat rare. More often, persuasion occurs through a series of smaller, incremental changes.

The second kind of goal of persuasive discourse is *changing the relationship dimension*. Politicians, for example, center much of their advocacy on establishing a positive relationship with the public. The entire function of public relations, as another example, is to develop favorable attitudes toward an organization.

Another major goal of public advocacy is *intensification of arousal*. Although this goal is usually combined with one of the other major goals, it is sometimes an end in itself. "Inspirational" speakers at such events as conventions and training meetings are used to build emotional feelings around a product, organization, service, or profession.

Also, persuasion is often aimed directly at *changing behavior.* This may include the adoption of new behavior, the cessation of a behavior, or even increasing or intensifying a behavior. A speaker, for example, may try to get an audience to cut back on smoking or stop smoking altogether. Persuasion may relate to buying a product, voting for a candidate, becoming involved in a movement, or innumerable other actions.

Finally, public advocates often attempt to *induce resistance to change* in cognition or behavior. Knowing that young people are particularly vulnerable to peer pressure, antismoking campaigns are often aimed at getting teenagers not to take up smoking. The processes by which "inoculation" against change happens are outlined in Chapter Four.

/ The Relationship Dimension.　The final dimension of communicators' cognitive system is the relationship dimension—beliefs and feelings about oneself and others, and the bond between self and others. Earlier we discussed the relationship dimension in terms of the trust bond, similarity, attribution, and attraction.

Perhaps the most important aspect of the relationship dimension in public advocacy is the trust bond. Trust is largely a function of listeners' perception of a persuader's competence and integrity. Trust exists when individuals believe that an advocate has their best interest at heart. Actually, trust is closely associated with each of the other factors of the relationship dimension.

We tend to trust advocates who are like ourselves. The Utah audience felt a kinship with their local representative, and Farley was therefore able to accomplish a level of trust that someone from outside the area might not have engendered. Those we trust are also individuals to whom we are more likely to be attracted, and we are less likely to attribute ill motives to individuals we trust.

Why, for example, was Dr. Helen Caldicott such an effective advocate in the nuclear peace movement earlier in this decade? Dr. Caldicott left a successful career in Australia to speak out against nuclear weapons. In the perception of the audiences to whom she spoke, she had nothing personal to gain from this dramatic act. In her personal appearances, she projected a deep commitment, not only out of sincere belief, but out of emotional feeling as well. Audiences trusted Helen Caldicott; they were attracted to this dynamic personality; and they attributed her actions to high motives.

/ The social situation

In addition to interpreting the communicators, public advocates are also faced with the problem of understanding the context in which the event will occur. Advocates usually analyze both the physical setting and the social context.

/ Physical Setting. An important component of the context within which persuasion occurs is the physical setting. Think how differently the same information about sexual behavior would be interpreted if encountered in a hospital conference room, church, health classroom, or veteran's hall. Most political candidates select the site for announcing their candidacy with great care, depending upon what issues, goals, or personal relationships they wish to establish or reinforce. Public persuasive events can be scheduled for large auditoriums, classrooms, libraries, lounges, or even cafeterias, depending upon the atmosphere desired.

/ Social Climate. The social climate of public advocacy is also important, and the advocate's interpretation depends in part upon perceptions of what is going on in the group addressed or in the society at large. Here we discuss the importance of current events, traditions, and conventions.

Current events can have a profound effect on the transaction. Consider the impact of a well-publicized execution on an appeal to abolish capital punishment. Think of the impact of the TV movie *The Day After* on a discussion of the deployment of the MX missile.

A second element in the social climate is the *tradition* shared by the participants. Most groups have shared traditions which they honor, and even if the group itself does not, it undoubtedly is part of a larger community that does. Traditions can take the form of events such as festivals, parades, rodeos, art and crafts displays, theater productions and the like. Each of these traditions is firmly rooted in the culture or subculture within which it occurs and, hence, suggests cultural values which may significantly affect persuasive transactions.

In addition to traditional events there will be *conventions* or cultural norms or expectations which are typically observed. In some sections of the country public meetings are opened and closed with prayer, while in other sections any reference to religion or reference to the wrong religion would be offensive. Politicans often desire to be introduced by particular local leaders or at least have them seated nearby on the podium. Acknowledgment or at least recognition of locally valued traditions can serve to accentuate relational, issue, and goal dimensions of the cognitive systems of participants in public persuasive events.

/ The issues

The final aspect of an advocate's analysis is interpreting the issues. An *issue* is a question of disagreement. It is a point on which there is debate or controversy. Issues emerge from conflicting propositions or claims in public discourse.

A *proposition* is a declarative sentence which states the general position of a persuasive message. If the basic issue were, "Should the MX missile be deployed in existing missile silos?" a corresponding proposition would be, "The MX missile should be deployed in existing missile silos." Let's look at the way issues are discovered from propositions.

/ Discovering Issues.　Not only does a proposition state a position on an issue, but most propositions can be analyzed or broken down into subordinate issues or claims. An advocate can begin the analysis by brainstorming questions which might bear on the proposition. Using the MX example, for instance, one might ask:

1. Will it be too costly?
2. Will it serve as a deterrent to foreign aggressors?
3. Does sufficient deterrence now exist?
4. Is the silo-basing mode the most effective mode?
5. What will be the environmental impact of the MX?
6. What will be the effect on surrounding communities?

The foregoing questions represent only a few of dozens of issues that might be raised. Indeed, when we brainstorm significant social issues in our classes, students usually pose from forty to sixty issues without great difficulty. The brainstorming approach to identifying issues is an inductive method.

A second way of determining potential issues is deductive. If the advocate is very familiar with the topic, it is possible to proceed directly from the general proposition to progressively specific issues or claims. Stock issues are useful for this purpose. A *stock issue* is an issue that recurs over and over again on a particular subject or in similar persuasive situations. Let us look at stock issues for three kinds of propositions.

/ **Propositions of Policy.**   A proposition of policy is a declaration which states or implies a course of action and contains the word *should*. Along with our general proposition on the deployment of the MX missile, the following would be propositions of policy:

1. People should get more exercise.

2. People should give to their favorite charity.

3. People should vote for Frances Farley.

Stock issues related to propositions of policy tend to focus on five policy questions:

1. Is there a *need* for a change from the status quo?

2. Is a *workable plan* available?

3. Will the plan *meet the need*?

4. Is the proposed plan the *best plan* available?

5. Will the *advantages* of the plan outweigh the disadvantages?

The *need* question centers on a problem or dissatisfaction. For example, if you value human life, reports of starving people in Africa present a need for action.

The *practicality* issue has to do with the workability of the plan. In many instances experts know what they would like to do to solve a problem, but the technology or organizational machinery for doing so simply does not exist. For example, plentiful energy can be produced from heavy hydrogen found in sea water, but at this writing the plan won't work because more energy goes into the process than can be gained from it.

The *plan-meets-need* issue is not a workability question. Given a workable plan, will the plan solve the problem? Numerous government agencies can testify to the claim that not all proposed solutions eliminate the problem. You have probably heard possible solutions criticized as "throwing money" at the problem.

The *best plan* issue is always a consideration. Even if there is a workable plan for solving a serious problem, people will still argue about whether a better plan could be found. The deployment of the MX missile in existing silos was presented as a superior alternative to the race-track basing mode. Shallow water submarines have been suggested as a mode superior to the silos.

The *comparative advantages* issue is one that frequently becomes crucial in persuasive transactions. Almost any proposal will have both positive and negative repercussions, quite apart from the main issue under consideration. With MX, national defense is the main issue, but comparative advantages issues like positive and negative effects on the environment, the economy, and the population may well decide the fate of the proposal.

/ Propositions of Fact. A proposition of fact is a declarative statement which sounds like a fact and contains some conjugation of the verb *to be*. Such propositions are usually simple statements of belief. The following are propositions of fact:

1. The defendant is guilty.
2. Many people in Africa are suffering severe hunger.
3. The deployment of the MX missile in existing silos will increase the population of surrounding areas.

Stock issues relevant to propositions of fact are difficult to find, since they tend to be more bound to the topic or specific situation than are stock issues relevant to propositions of policy. In the legal context, for example, the issues involved in the proposition, "The defendant is guilty," depends upon the specifications of the crime. If all of the characteristics of the crime are not met, the defendant is not guilty of that particular crime. In most states first degree murder is characterized not only by (1) the death of the victim (2) caused by the defendant, but (3) premeditation or intent of the perpetrator of the crime must also be proven. If premeditation cannot be proven, the charge may be reduced to second-degree murder or some other lesser crime.

You may have noticed that each of the stock issues in the proposition of policy itself suggests a proposition of fact. For instance, "There is a need to deploy the MX" and "Deployment of the MX missile in existing silos is a practical plan" are both propositions of fact.

Need-oriented propositions themselves have recurring and significant subordinate issues. The first is *harm*. Who or what is the problem hurting? Harm itself has subordinate issues of fact. What is the magnitude of the harm? What is the likelihood of its occurring? For example, opposition to further production of nuclear weapons results largely from people's fear of the destruction of life as we know it and a perceived increase in the likelihood of that happening.

When analyzing problem-oriented needs, persuaders frequently look at the causes or effects of the problem. The scope and historical development of the problem are also analyzed.

The factual propositions of practicality and workability usually have subordinate issues of cost, organization, existing technology, and even public acceptance. Note, for example, how many "needs" could be met if people only had the money.

/ Propositions of Value. Propositions of value call for a judgment that cannot be verified objectively. Examples are:

1. Frances Farley is a superior candidate.
2. Irish Spring soap smells manly.
3. The MX missile is a peacekeeper.

There are probably no real stock issues of value propositions, but issues depend on the nature of the value judgments made in the proposition. For example, suppose you were on the selection committee for the NCAA basketball tournament. In determining the "success" of a particular team, two criteria seem important: its win-loss record and the relative strength of its opponents. Certainly you would not select a team with a losing record even if that team had played only teams ranked in the top twenty. On the other hand, if the win-loss record were the only criterion, a junior-college team with a five-year undefeated string would have to get the vote. Surely, both criteria must be taken into consideration.

Although the foregoing issues are useful in analyzing types of propositions, there are also recurring issues which grow out of particular situations. The various possibilities of different situations are too numerous to discuss here; we will illustrate the idea with a few instances.

Imagine a political leader trying to convince his or her followers to declare war. What issues would need to be addressed? Can the nation win? Has it expended every alternative through negotiation? Does it have a choice, or has the war already begun? Is the cause just? Will allies provide support? These issues were addressed by Patrick Henry, Woodrow Wilson, and Franklin Roosevelt at the outbreak of the Revolutionary War, World War I and World War II, respectively. They were issues that were determined by the situation.

Imagine that as a spokesperson for a group of citizens that has suffered from discrimination, you are attempting to persuade the power structure to acknowledge the human rights of your group. What issues would you address? Is discrimination hurting your group? Does the discrimination violate governmental and religious principles? What level of government should have jurisdiction over the insuring of the rights? Will denying other people their human rights undermine your own? These issues were addressed by Abraham Lincoln, Susan B. Anthony, Martin Luther King, Jr., and many others as they discussed such issues as slavery, women's suffrage, and civil rights.

/ *The Advocate's Proposition.* The analysis of the proposition and situation produces potential issues, but how do these relate to the goals of the advocate? If, for instance, the audience already believes that the deployment of the MX missile is necessary to meet a perceived threat from the U.S.S.R. and that deploying it in existing silos is the best basing mode available, then the advocate would be able to concentrate on the comparative advantages of deployment in terms of population increase, environmental issues, and the like. On the other hand, if most of the audience was convinced that the U.S. already had more than enough missiles to deter Soviet aggression, then the advocate might decide to concentrate on the need issue and defer other issues until later. The central focus of the advocate would then be, "There is (or is not) a need for the deployment of the MX missile in existing silos in order to deter foreign aggression."

Furthermore, with some audiences, what is apparently a relatively minor point may turn out to be the deciding issue. For a pacificist religious organization, the central value that "Weapons are immoral" might outweigh all other arguments. For an audience of local residents, the impact (positive or negative) on the local life-style may be the deciding issue. For people who live near the silos, being made the "bull's eye" of Russian ICBMs may outweigh all other considerations.

Thus, the advocate's position can vary significantly in specificity and in focus, depending on the audience and situation. Consider the following examples:

1. The MX missile should [should not] be deployed in existing silos. [policy proposition for a general audience]

2. The deployment of the MX missile in existing silos would have great advantages [disadvantages] for our community. [factual proposition for a local audience who already believes in MX]

3. Deployment of MX in existing silos is [is not] the best basing mode. [value proposition for an audience who believes it is needed and practical but who would like to see it put somewhere else]

4. Deployment of MX would have [not have] advantages for ranchers. [factual proposition for nearby ranchers who worry about their water, range lands, or life-style]

So far in this chapter, we have discussed the interpretive processes involved in public advocacy. Specifically, we have examined interpretation of participants' realities, the social situation, and issues. We now turn our attention to ways in which the advocate responds to this analysis.

/ Action in Public Advocacy

Communication is a two-fold process. It involves interpretation and action: the advocate makes sense out of the situation encountered and responds to or acts on that situation in some way. We have just seen how advocates interpret the situation. Let us now turn to forms of action inherent in public advocacy.

Public advocacy presents a coordination problem to the communicator. In Chapter 2, we noted that all communication must involve coordination between the realities and actions of the participants. In other words, one's actions have to mesh with those of others in the group. Public advocacy is no different in this regard. Advocates do not just "behave"; rather, they carefully consider ways to make their public statements fit the expectations of the audience. The attempt is not always successful. One of the marks of successful public advocacy is a feeling on the part of both the advocate and the audience that what each has done is appropriately organized into a logical system. That happens when audience expectations relevant to the dimensions of cognition are taken into consideration. Such expectations constitute a system of rules of acceptance.

/ *Rules of acceptance*

Part of the social reality of a group or culture are rules by which the group evaluates the acceptability of an assertion or proposition. So far we have talked as if the advocate's audience has a single, consistent set of such rules. In situations where the audience is small and homogeneous, that may be the case. Much public advocacy, however, involves a large and heterogeneous audience or even several audiences at once. In such situations, the advocate may have to coordinate with a variety of systems. The problem is compounded by the fact that any single person, as a consequence of belonging to a variety of groups and having a complex cognitive system, may go back and forth among a number of rule systems and seem quite inconsistent from moment to moment in what is taken as acceptable.

Since audiences vary in how they evaluate acceptability, no single set of strategies guarantees success. Instead, success is an outcome of the coordination between a particular advocate or group of advocates and a particular audience or audiences. Four groups of rules are important in public advocacy (and in private advocacy, too). These are rules of validity or believability, rules of personal relevance, rules of involvement, and rules of confidence.

/ *Rules of Validity.*

Rules of validity are used by people to evaluate the degree to which a proposition is *believable*. Such rules are intricately tied to the belief system and are therefore largely embedded in the reality dimension of cognition. Some groups, for example, place great faith in "scientific" evidence and evaluate "truth" on the basis of whether the proposition conforms to norms of scientific proof. Other groups believe messages that are couched in terms of their stories of reality. Other groups may make belief a question of authority. Although it would be impossible for us to list all the rules used by various audiences to test believability, we will provide some examples later in the chapter.

We recall years ago talking with a colleague who was concerned about the disruption of the ozone layer of the atmosphere caused by aerosol cans. That information seemed ludicrous at the time. Since it was so inconsistent with our image of hair spray, deodorant, and air freshener, we could hardly refrain from laughing. The proposition, in short, was just not believable in terms of the rules we used for such purposes. Not long thereafter, however, reports of scientific studies on the problem began to emerge, and because of our faith in that kind of evidence, we changed our belief on the subject.

/ *Rules of Relevance.*

Acceptability is only partially a question of believability. In addition, people evaluate the degree to which an assertion is personally relevant. Relevance is largely a matter of being persuaded that a proposition is *needed or valuable*. Rules for deciding personal relevance are deeply embedded in one's sense of need and value and as such is part of the goal dimension of cognition. When one sees a proposition as personally relevant, he or she is more apt to be motivated to learn about and take action on the problem.

/ Rules of Involvement. Rules of involvement affect *emotional arousal.* They tell us what should capture our emotions and how we should feel about issues. Such rules have much in common with rules of personal relevance, because the latter almost always involves the former. But involvement rules guide us a step beyond to affect the character of our feeling about the issue.

Although we came to believe the hypothesis that the use of aerosal cans threatened the earth's ozone layer, that issue was never very salient for us. We suspect that we never were convinced of its personal relevance and therefore remained relatively unaroused on the issue.

/ Rules of Confidence. Confidence rules relate to the audience member's sense of relationship with the advocate and with the sources used as support by the advocate. Such rules primarily define whether a source is *trustworthy.* As such, they are embedded mainly in the relationship dimension. Some groups trust only those who are part of the group, and are suspicious of any outsider. Other people look for signs of expertise. Some want corroboration by other trusted sources. Still others rely on evidence of the advocate's knowing the stories of the group.

Part of our initial skepticism about the ozone problem resulted from our lack of confidence in the colleague who first mentioned it to us. We had considered him to be a bizarre person and were frankly not surprised to hear him advocate a "silly" point of view. The real surprise came later when we found out that his statement was not so silly after all.

When we reconsider this example of aerosol cans and the atmosphere we are struck by how the rules by which we accept or fail to accept a position are intertwined. The categories of rules listed above are not discrete; rather, they are dimensions of evaluation emerging from the cognitive system. It would be a mistake to consider believability, personal relevance, involvement, and confidence as separate elements. They affect and were affected by one another and should be viewed together as a whole system. It should be obvious, too, that acceptability is not an either-or proposition: people do not accept or fail to accept. Instead, they accept in different ways and to different degrees, depending upon their evaluation of the message. In the case of the aerosol-can hypothesis, we accepted the validity of the premise, but we never made it a personally involving problem.

Our discussion of rules of acceptance may seem to imply that an advocate merely adapts his or her message to the rules of acceptability of the audience and that is that. Public advocacy is never so simple. Coordination is a problem of meshing one's own reality with that of others. The advocate also has rules of acceptability, and cannot grab just any set of standards to adapt to an audience. Instead, coordination involves a coming together in ways that make the statement acceptable to both speaker and listener. This coming together is not always easy to accomplish and, in fact, may sometimes be impossible.

/ Stages of action in public advocacy

Public advocacy involves four stages of action, including (1) developing ideas, (2) organizing the statement, (3) making linguistic decisions, and (4) delivering the message. These stages do not always occur strictly in order.

Public advocacy proceeds in an almost infinite variety of ways. We therefore cannot present a complete or composite picture of the process. The following discussion is merely a series of snapshots of various strategies used to coordinate with certain rule systems prevalent in our society.

/ Developing Ideas.

The stage of developing ideas involves selecting materials and creating arguments. Although many methods of developing ideas for public advocacy can be observed, the task is always to create and frame ideas in a way that meets the acceptability rules of the audience and speaker. This is why the advocate's interpretation of the participants and the situation is so important. He or she must understand what those rules are.

Selecting materials. Materials cannot be guided by formula. Let us look at some of the factors that an advocate might consider in selecting materials. Surely, audience *rules of validity* should be taken into consideration. There are a great number of validity rules; three which are used frequently in our society are consistency, representativeness, and comparison.

Consistency is a common rule of validity. People using this rule question data in terms of whether it is consistent with what they already think they know about a subject. They also look for consistency within the data presented. In his famous "Checkers" speech, Richard Nixon defended himself against allegations that he had taken money from his 1952 vice-presidential campaign fund for personal use. He employed a variety of materials to support his claim of innocence, including personal testimony, a personal report of his assets, and a Price Water house audit. Given the gravity of the accusation and the political consequences of an inadequate defense, Nixon took special care to meet the consistency rule in all of his data.

Another rule frequently used by members of an audience is *representativeness,* or the degree to which the material presented is considered typical. This rule is often employed when an audience is presented with examples and statistics. The overriding question is how typical the statistics and examples are. Is the doctor who is overcharging Medicaid typical of all doctors? Is the exorbitant cost of a spare part for a military vehicle the exception or the rule? Is the sample upon which a public opinion poll is based representative of the voting population?

Two subordinate questions may add to one's estimation of representativeness. First, are there sufficient numbers of examples, or are the statistics based on a sufficiently large sample to provide a reasonable change of being representative? We all know that it is possible to find a few examples to "prove" almost anything; however, if our intention is not to prove something but rather to arrive at the most useful or dependable inference or conclusion possible, we will be concerned with the number of examples or the size of our sample.

A third rule often used in weighing validity involves *comparison*. Here one comes to believe in something when it is made to look like something else more familiar. The two phenomena compared need not be identical or even alike in most respects, but they must be comparable on each of the variables which bear on the issue at hand.

Advocates also select material that conforms to *rules of personal relevance*. Although such rules are extremely situational, some common rules of relevance can be observed. For example, *specific and personal* materials are frequently effective in eliciting acceptance. Vague statistics, hypothetical examples, and generalized references may or may not be verifiable or accurately interpreted. They frequently will not be seen as relevant by listeners. With most audiences, general claims such as "Scientists have proven" are not effective.

Along the same line, in our time-conscious culture, *recent evidence* is usually seen as more relevant than old evidence. This tendency to believe recent data and ignore insights from earlier times is common in our culture because of the pervasive belief that "progress" is achieved by "advances" in knowledge. An historian we know calls his problem "present-ism." It results in an inability to see the world as other people at other times have seen it. Not all groups, however, are so enamored with recent developments. Many revere history and tradition in such a way that historical material is especially compelling to them. The kinds of material used to "sell" the MX missile to the Veterans of Foreign Wars would be quite different in this regard from those used with an audience of physics majors at M.I.T.

The third consideration in selecting material is *rules of involvement*. Here the advocate asks what criteria will be used by the audience to establish an emotional response. Such materials will probably have to be seen as personally relevant according to such rules as those discussed in the above paragraph. In addition, material that is consistent with the audience's *images and fantasies* are more apt to elicit feelings of involvement.

Leo Buscaglia tours the country talking to audiences about love. Buscaglia is known as a very emotional speaker who elicits extreme feeling and involvement from his audiences. He does this in part by his own emotionality while speaking; but much of his success stems from the fact that he seems to understand the audience so well. He has a repertoire of stories that resonate with the audience's images of life and love.

The final set of rules used in determining acceptability of materials involve *rules of confidence*. Advocates often choose materials for their power in eliciting the audience's trust. That may mean, for example, using *personal materials* that tell the audience something about the speaker. Former detective and disguise artist Baretta, on whose life the television series was based, now tours the country talking to school children about drugs. His speech, which is extremely

/ **Leo Buscaglia elicits feelings of involvement from his audience not only by exhibiting his own emotionality while speaking, but also by selecting materials consistent with his audience's images and fantasies.**

graphic and emotional, is especially effective because he tells personal stories about himself, his family, and those with whom he worked. Among children, he is perceived as very trustworthy because of this personal involvement. Not all audiences demand or even want this level of personal involvement on the part of the advocate. Some people perceive such self-disclosure as "corny"; others fear it is manipulative.

Advocates, of course, rely on a variety of materials to engender trust. A common type of evidence is the *testimony of authorities.* Different groups will define *authoritativeness* differently. Let us look briefly at a set of rules used by many to test authorities. First, one might ask, "How qualified is the source? Has the source had the necessary training and experience in the relevant area?" Such rules of authoritativeness are especially common in our education-oriented society. Sometimes judgments about expertise are very discriminating. For example, Dr. Edward Teller, a pioneer in the development of nuclear weapons, is frequently quoted as favoring the deployment of new nuclear weapons systems, yet he describes himself as basically a "technician" and may not know as much about the socio-cultural, political, or economic questions as do authorities who have specialized in those areas.

A second question some ask about authoritative data is, "Was the source close enough to the event to be a reliable observer?" Confronted with two advocates with equal qualifications, you may want to place greater credence on the source who was more closely involved with the issue or event. An eye surgeon, for example, recently testified on a radio talk show that he did not believe in radial keratotomy, the operation to cure nearsightedness. However, when pressed, he admitted that he specialized solely on the retina and had never performed an operation on any other part of the eye. In arguments between two scientists or foreign affairs experts, one has actually been more closely involved with the issue under consideration. An otherwise unqualified eyewitness to a crime would certainly be a more dependable source on some aspects of the crime than a renowned criminologist who was not present. Once again, however, not all individuals use the "proximity" rule to judge sources. Other rules might include the character of the witness, the language used by the authority, or a host of other criteria.

A final question used by some individuals to determine authority involves the potential bias of the witness. If selective perception distorts our observations, how much more will bias distort our conclusions? What does the observer or authority have to benefit or protect? As the "father" of the hydrogen bomb, might not Teller be biased in favor of nuclear weaponry?

Creating arguments. Besides selecting materials, the advocate who is developing ideas is involved in creating arguments. An *argument* is an assertion or proposition supported by reasons and evidence. An important qualification is necessary at this point. While many groups in our society demand arguments to establish acceptance, other groups do not. In fact, in some subcultures, the whole notion of logical argument is ludicrous. Instead, other forms of demonstration are required in order for acceptance to be granted. The following discussion therefore is relevant in many, but not all, advocacy situations.

Chapter 3 discussed the ways in which reasons and evidence are used to establish belief in the reality dimension of the cognitive system. Eliciting acceptance by an audience often conforms to the modes of argument discussed there. Arguments, for example, can be built inductively, from specific evidence to generalization. They can be constructed deductively, from general premises to specific applications. Or they can be developed in parallel fashion, moving from assertion to assertion by showing the logical link among the various claims. People go through a reasoning process to establish, bolster, or change their beliefs, and public advocates are often influential in providing the building blocks for doing so.

We do not dwell on arguments in this chapter because of our relatively lengthy discussion of them in Chapter 3. It is important to remember, however, that creating arguments, like selecting materials, is a coordination problem and must take the reality of the audience into consideration. If, for example, the audience has a number of specific beliefs, the advocate might demonstrate ways in which those beliefs can be chained together into a higher order value or attitude, using the *elevating strategy* discussed in the last chapter. A student in a speech class recently used this approach when trying to change the class's attitude toward older people. He made use of specific experiences that most of the members of the audience had with the elderly and showed how these all added up to a positive image.

If an audience has a general principle or value, the advocate can lead the group to see how more specific beliefs are necessary to bolster the value, using a *reduction* strategy. Another student speaker, for instance, took general audience concern for the environment and the love of natural beauty and used it to affect their options of a local mining project.

Associating is also a way to create an argument. Here the advocate would begin with audience beliefs or feelings and relate these in parallel fashion with other beliefs or feelings relevant to the advocate's proposition. One of the best student speeches we have heard recently promoted running as a form of exercise. Instead of listing the many advantages of running, she talked about the exhilaration and excitement of running, using almost a narrative form. She also played the theme music from *Rocky* in the background, and the total effect was very motivating.

An issue that sometimes has to be considered in creating arguments is whether to present one or both sides of an issue. Research has found that one-sided messages work better with audiences that are favorably disposed to the persuader's position at the outset, while two-sided messages may have a greater effect on initially antagonistic audiences. Furthermore, audiences which receive two-sided messages may be more resistant to later attempts at counter-persuasion than audiences who receive only one side of the issue.[2]

/ *Organizing the Statement.* The second stage in public advocacy is organization of the message. Organization involves grouping ideas and establishing an order in which those ideas will be presented. Again, as with developing ideas, there is no best way to organize a statement. Organization is successful or not depending upon the extent to which it meshes with audience rules for acceptance. This section addresses a variety of forms of organization relevant to various acceptance rules. The advocate considers what elements of acceptance are most important and tries to come up with a pattern that makes sense within that constraint.

When rules of validity seem most important. When validity seems to be the major objective of the message, certain kinds of organizational patterns will probably be most effective, depending upon the rules used by the audience. The *topical pattern,* which groups ideas according to topical similarity, builds a sense of consistency and rationality to one's arguments. With some propositions, especially those of fact or value, the main ideas may support the central idea but have no particular relationship to one another. In the case of the value proposition that "Deployment of the missile MX in existing silos is the best basing mode," questions of cost, vulnerability, or danger to populations are all important, but do not necessarily depend on one another. Here a topical organization plan makes sense.

When one uses a topical organization pattern, the question arises as to what order to use in placing the groups of arguments. Two tendencies are relevant to this decision. The first is the *primacy effect,* in which the first set of arguments would have the greatest effect. The second is the *recency effect,* in which the last set of arguments would have the greatest effect. Research has found very few instances of arguments in the middle having the greatest impact. There has been quite a bit of research on the primacy-recency question, but results are not altogether consistent, suggesting that audience predispositions are probably most important in determining what kind of effect to expect.[3]

Sometimes a connection can be made between argument clusters. In such cases, that connection might be pointed out by the manner in which the arguments are organized. Although all planned patterns of organization are "rational," rationality is accented in patterns that rely on the connection among arguments and are therefore referred to as *rational patterns*. In a rational approach, some arguments simply follow from one another reasonably, and listeners may not be able to comprehend, let alone care about, one argument until the groundwork is laid with other arguments. An example of a pattern that uses a rational approach is the *need-remedy pattern,* in which the speaker first argues that there is a need for a change, then presents a plan for handling the problem. A variant of this pattern is the reflective-thinking sequence of John Dewey: (1) What brought this problem to our attention? (2) What is the nature of the problem, including its scope, causes, and effects? (3) What are the possible solutions? (4) What is the best solution? (5) What action will be required to implement this solution?[4] Notice how well this pattern coordinates with audiences that hold a utilitarian or instrumental reality. Such audiences think in terms of problems, solutions, and actions, and the Dewey sequence feeds right into that method of ordering the world.

When rules of arousal and relevance are important. How would an advocate handle a situation in which the audience already believed the proposition, but was unable to see a personal connection? Again, depending upon the rule system in use by the audience, a variety of strategies might be employed. One such pattern is called the *motivated sequence:* In the beginning of the speech, the advocate calls *attention* to the problem. Then he or she builds a sense of *need,* followed by a solution that provides *satisfaction*. Next, the desired alternative is *visualized* for the audience, and in the end they are told what they can do about it in a kind of *action* step.[5] This pattern is not altogether different from the above two plans, but it emphasizes the personal relevance of the problem and solution to the listener.

When arousal and relevance seem to be an issue, coordination can sometimes be achieved by *narrative patterns* that are nothing more than telling a story chronologically. The most sacred and influential communication among primitive peoples is narrative, and much informal and private communication in our own society is organized the same way. Public advocacy can also use the narrative as an organizational model. Such speeches tell a story or stories which have embedded in them the ideas being advocated.[6] Fred Rogers of Mr. Rogers' Neighborhood uses the narrative to appeal to children about all kinds of issues. Adults too can respond to stories, as revealed by the popularity of television docudramas. One of the most powerful means of persuasion used in Alcoholics Anonymous is the personal testimony, in which an alcoholic stands up to tell his or her "story" at an A. A. meeting. Here the rule structure almost demands this form of organization.

/ *Making Linguistic Decisions.*   In addition to analyzing the persuasive situation and proposition, setting goals, and preparing the message, the persuader considers the language to use to share meanings with the listener. Here we discuss a general overview of language and then consider such specific variables as self-references, intensity, metaphors, and rhetorical questions.

Overview of language.   The meaning shared by participants in a persuasive event does not reside only in the words spoken. Shared meaning is also affected by the cognitive systems of the people involved, their relationships (especially trust), their perceived intentions, the context or scene within which the persuasion occurs, and the medium through which the message is conveyed.[7]

The shared meaning which is created by the word or combination of words is called *denotative meaning*. Denotation is a meaning on which virtually all speakers of a language would agree. It is basically a dictionary definition. *Connotative meaning,* on the other hand, is the personal associations one has with a word. Connotations may be shared with others, but they are much more situational than are denotations. Thus, people at a rally of war veterans on the steps of the Capitol would share a particular connotation for *patriotism* spoken by the President. A quite different connotation of the word might be shared if spoken by a nuclear freeze protestor who is being hauled off to jail for having blocked the delivery of a new ICBM. Some might consider the latter as the highest or most profound form of patriotism, while people with different interpretations might consider it treason. Remember that meaning resides not only in words but also in people, contexts, intent, and media. We turn next to some of the language characteristics that relate to public advocacy.

Self-references.   An important message variable in public persuasive transactions is the use of references to personal involvement with the topic. Research has strongly supported the use of self-references and references to prestige sources that support one's own view.[8] Such use of language is thought to appeal to both validity and confidence rules in many audiences. In some groups explicit references seem to be more effective than implied references. It stands to reason that many audiences will be more affected by the claims of advocates they know have personal involvement with the subject.

Intensity.   Intensity seems to be the language variable most closely associated with persuasion. Research has uncovered some interesting findings on language intensity in persuasion.[9] At least in some persuasive situations, intense language reinforces a proposition for audiences that already agree with the advocate's point of view, while it may inhibit the effect of propositions not already believed. Sometimes language intensity interacts with the credibility of the advocate. Some groups apparently like to hear advocates they admire speak in intense language, while noncredible sources are made even less believable when they use intense language. When an advocate expresses a point of view different from that held by the audience and does so intensely, the audience may judge the speaker as not very believable. In addition, highly aroused listeners will sometimes be less inclined to agree with an intense advocate than they will a calm one. Finally, research has found that in some situations, men's persuasiveness is enhanced by intense language, while women's persuasiveness is reduced by speaking intensely.

Obscene language constitutes a rather special case of language intensity. Does the use of obscenity help or hurt the public persuader? Again, that depends, but research shows that in some groups obscenity reduces both attitude change and source credibility.[10] Other studies have found that obscenity (especially sexual and scatological references) makes a speaker appear more dynamic, but may lessen audience's judgment of the speaker's competence and character.[11]

Unfortunately, this research was limited to certain kinds of audiences and particular situations, so it gives us only a limited view of language. As with all variables, the effect of intensity depends upon consumer rules of acceptance in the situation in which the advocacy occurs.

Opinionated language. Similar to the variable of intensity is that of opinionated language. Opinionated language tends to be dogmatic and unqualified. A non-opinionated statement might be, "In most circumstances, I tend to feel that MX would be relatively invulnerable to attack." An opinionated statement would be, "MX is absolutely invulnerable, no doubt about it."

Research tends to support the generalization that opinionated language produces greater credibility and attitude change, although that conclusion depends upon the rules of acceptance in force. For example, in some groups, opinionated language works better with a highly credible source and with a message that is consistent with the listeners' point of view, while less opinionated language may be more effective with less credible sources or with messages that oppose the audience's opinion.[12]

Metaphors. One stylistic device frequently recommended for public advocacy is the metaphor. A *metaphor* is an unstated comparison, like Churchill's "An iron curtain has descended."

Researchers have verified that, in some situations, messages containing brief metaphors are more persuasive than messages without metaphors.[13] Further, some evidence suggests that an extended metaphor can often enhance source credibility.[14] In sum, metaphors can enhance speaker-listener identification, thus appealing to rules of confidence.

Rhetorical questions. Another stylistic device that is frequently used by public persuaders is the rhetorical question. A *rhetorical question* is a highly transactional device since it requires no overt response, but assumes the listener will supply the answer from within. Patrick Henry, for example, never expected the audience to answer his question: "they say that we are weak, but when will we be stronger?" Yet, he knew that the answer would be apparent to his listeners.

Research has generally supported the use of rhetorical questions in persuasion. Claims stated as rhetorical questions were found to be more effective than those stated directly in the summation of defense attorney's arguments.[15] Other researchers, however, discovered an important qualification, concluding, "The use of rhetoricals enhanced elaboration of the arguments when the issue was of low personal relevance, but it disrupted elaboration when the issue was of high personal relevance."[16] It would seem that rhetorical questions aid persuasion by appealing to rules of involvement and arousal, while running the risk of distracting audiences that are already involved in the transaction.

We conclude our discussion of the use of language in public advocacy by repeating an important caution. While the foregoing generalizations may hold in some situations, we suspect that the very transactional and subjective nature of language makes it more situational than research has heretofore suggested. For example, there are probably situations in which obscenity is appropriate and situations in which self-references would be taken as bragging. Language in persuasion depends more on the expectations of participants than on universal effects.[17]

/ Delivering the Message.   A final consideration in public persuasion is delivery. Rhetorical theorists have long discussed such elements of delivery as posture, gestures, bodily activity, facial expression, eye contact, and voice.[18]

In actual practice, however, these isolated elements tend to combine to produce patterned behavior. Just as language varies with its intensity, immediacy, and variety, so delivery varies with its intensity, variety, emphasis, clarity, and appropriateness. Thus a speaker might increase the volume and pitch of the voice, get a stern facial expression, and use an emphatic gesture to achieve emphasis for a particular argument.

Delivery and confidence.   Most of the information we have about the relationship between delivery and persuasion is derived from studies on nonverbal communication and attitude change. These studies have resulted in a number of findings. In general, good delivery seems to increase believability.[19] What is good delivery, of course, depends upon the expectations of the audience in the situation. In large measure, good delivery seems to relate to audience rules of confidence. Audiences get a sense of authority, confidence, and poise from such cues as vocal tone, fluency, rate, volume, eye contact, facial expression, gestures, and other cues. Some studies even show that physical attractiveness enhances persuasiveness. When the advocate projects a positive relationship with the audience through delivery, in the form of affiliation, liking, or approval, attitude change may increase.

These research findings are hardly surprising. Intuitive wisdom has long supported the idea that nonverbal cues effect our relationships with others, and the relationship between advocate and audience should be no exception.[20] Of

/ **A good delivery, which involves such cues as vocal tone, eye contact, facial expression, and gestures, can increase the believability of a persuasive message.**

particular importance in most western groups is eye contact. Speakers are counselled to watch their audience, not only for feedback but to maintain contact and, hence, enhance attraction and liking. However, this admonition is far from universal. Many groups take eye contact not as a sign of friendliness, but of dominance, aggression, or intrusion. This difference makes the point we have been stressing throughout the chapter—that different audience groups have different rules of acceptance. In the case of eye contact, typical western cultural groups use eye contact as a way to judge their confidence in a speaker, but other groups may respond in the opposite way.

    Delivery and involvement.   Delivery also relates strongly to involvement and arousal.[21] Nonverbal delivery variables seem particularly important in influencing people on the arousal dimension of the cognitive system. Put another way, we share emotions and feelings predominantly through nonverbal cues, and those come across in delivery.

/ *Theory* / *Practice* / *Analysis*

Theory

1. Public advocacy is a process of interpretation and action.

2. Interpretation involves understanding the realities, goals, and feelings of advocate and audience; the relationship between self and audience; the social situation; and the issues.

3. Action is based on rules of acceptance, including rules of validity, involvement, relevance, and confidence.

4. Public advocacy is accomplished by developing ideas, organizing the message, making linguistic decisions, and delivering the message.

Practice

1. Pick a typical group to which you have access that could be the target of a persuasive speech. Analyze the audience according to demographic variables. Following your armchair analysis, survey the audience with a questionnaire on the specific issues related to your chosen topic. Compare your analysis to the results of the questionnaire. How well did your educated guesses compare to the more accurate assessment of the audience's cognitive system? How effectively were you able to interpret the audience's reality, arousal, goals, and relationships?

2. Now interpret the social situation in which the persuasive speech might be given. What current events and other factors would influence the predispositions of the audience?

3. Conduct an issue analysis of your chosen topic. List propositions of fact, policy, and value and some corresponding issues.

4. Develop a persuasive speech for the chosen audience. Carefully consider materials, arguments, organization, and language. Deliver the speech.

Analysis

1. Find two speeches on similar topics by the same speaker with two different audiences and settings. How do the two speeches vary? What different strategies did the speaker use to create identification with the two different audiences? The greater the difference between the two audiences or situations, the more interesting this analysis will be.

2. Find two speeches on similar topics to the same or similar audiences delivered by different speakers. Explain the similarities and differences in terms of the concepts of interpretation and action from this chapter.

Notes

[1]A popular and overgeneralized, but interesting, exposition of geographical differences is Joel Garreau, *Nine Nations of North America* (Boston: Houghton-Mifflin, 1981).

[2]See, for example, Carl Hovland, Irving Janis, and J. J. Kelly, *Communication and Persuasion* (New Haven: Yale University Press, 1953).

[3]See, for example, N. Miller and D. Campbell, "Recency and Primacy in Persuasion as a Function of the Timing of Speeches and Measurements," *Journal of Abnormal and Social Psychology* 59 (1959): 1–9.

[4]John Dewey, *How We Think* (Boston: Heath, 1933).

⁵Douglas Ehninger, Bruce E. Gronbeck, Ray E. McKerrow, and Alan H. Monroe, *Principles and Types of Speech Communication,* 10th ed. (Glenview, IL: Scott, Foresman and Co., 1986), pp. 153–55.

⁶The nature and significance of narrative is discussed by Walter R. Fisher, "Narration as a Human Communication Paradigm: The Case of Public Moral Argument," *Communication Monographs* 51 (1984): 1–22.

⁷For further discussion see David Jabusch, *Public Speaking: A Transactional Approach* (Boston: Allyn and Bacon, 1985), pp. 96–102.

⁸See, for example, Terry H. Ostermeier, "Effects of Type and Frequency of Reference Upon Perceived Source Credibility and Attitude Change," *Speech Monographs* 34 (1967): 137–44.

⁹J. Bradac, J. Bowers, and J. Courtright, "Three Language Variables in Communication Research: Intensity, Immediacy, and Diversity," *Human Communication Research* 7 (1979): 257–69.

¹⁰Bradac et al., "Three Language Variables."

¹¹For more detailed discussion, see Velma J. (Wenzlaff) Lashbrook, "Source Credibility: A Summary of Experimental Research," paper presented at Speech Communication Association Convention, San Francisco, December 1971.

¹²Lashbrook, "Source Credibility."

¹³See, for example, J. Bowers and M. Osborn, "Attitudinal Effects of Selected Types of Concluding Metaphors in Persuasive Speeches," *Speech Monographs* 34 (1966): 147–55.

¹⁴See, for example, N. Reinich, "Figurative Language and Source Credibility: A Preliminary Investigation and Reconceptualization," *Human Communication Research* 1 (1974): 75–80.

¹⁵See, for example, D. Zillman, "Rhetorical Elicitation of Agreement in Persuasion," *Journal of Personality and Social Psychology* 21 (1972): 159–65.

¹⁶Richard Petty and John Cocioppo, *Attitudes and Persuasion: Classic and Contemporary Approaches* (Dubuque, IA: Wm. C. Brown, 1981), p. 247.

¹⁷Bradac et al., "Three Language Variables," p. 266.

¹⁸For a more detailed discussion of these elements, see David Jabusch and Stephen Littlejohn, *Elements of Speech Communication* (Boston: Houghton Mifflin, 1981), pp. 277–80.

¹⁹For a more detailed discussion see Judee K. Burgoon and Thomas Saine, *The Unspoken Dialogue: An Introduction to Nonverbal Communication* (Boston: Houghton Mifflin, 1978), pp. 273–301.

²⁰For a more detailed discussion see Burgoon and Saine, *Unspoken Dialogue,* pp. 172–93.

²¹For a more detailed discussion see Burgoon and Saine, *Unspoken Dialogue,* Chapter 8.

10 / Mass Media and Persuasion

It is autumn and the campaign for President of the United States is heating up. As you browse through the morning newspaper, you see a story about the upcoming visit of one of the candidates to your city. On your way to work you see a billboard display supporting the same candidate. As the time of the visit approaches, notices are given on the evening television news and advertisements begin to appear in the newspaper.

The day of the visit you miss a major policy speech delivered by the candidate, but on your way home from work you see an airplane trailer supporting the candidate. Later, you see a rebroadcast of the speech on a late-night television show. A report of the speech appears in the newspaper the next day along with an editorial endorsing the candidate.

For days after the visit, feature articles about the candidate and family appear in the newspaper, along with advertisements supporting the candidate and the party. Pictures in the paper feature the presidential candidate with other candidates for local offices.

In this chapter, we deal with persuasion as it occurs in and through the various media of communication. This kind of communication is usually referred to as mass communication. Although this label captures the broad scope of media communication, it is something of a misnomer because, as we have already seen, genuine mass communication involves a combination of media and interpersonal channels. We therefore prefer to use the label *media communication* when we are referring to this form.

Communication through mass media has three major characteristics that distinguish it from interpersonal communication. First, the *audience is large,* usually more than would be found in one place at one time. Second, the *source of communication is* not typically an individual, but *an institution or organization.* Third, the *message is mediated* by some mechanism other than the human body: it involves electronic or mechanical operations to transfer the message to a new "medium."[1]

The mass media of communication have achieved unquestionable importance. Not only are the media ever-present in our lives, but they have an important influence on how we use our time. Media get a great deal of information out to large numbers of people relatively rapidly. The *information base* for making decisions, then, is much larger and more immediate than it would have been a hundred or more years ago.[2] The real advent of media communication occurred with the invention of the printing press in the fifteenth century. With that innovation came a huge leap in the capability of human beings to communicate beyond their immediate place and time. The creation of electronic communication in the twentieth century has led to an even greater information revolution.

/ The Media Transaction

In considering the effects of mass media, it is easy to slip into a linear way of thinking. Too often we see the media as injecting information and influence into society in a transmissional fashion. That is an erroneous view. This "hypodermic needle" or "bullet" theory of mass communication has long been put to rest.[3] Instead, we know that media communication, like all other forms of communication, is a transaction.

/ The role of the media

Let us examine more closely the role of the media in this transaction. The media create information for the public. Much of that information is intended to influence the consumer: advertising, political messages, documentaries, editorials, reviews, and other messages that take a position on an issue can potentially affect the cognitive system of the consumer. Even news or information that is not strictly intended to bring about change may be used by the consumer as a basis for such change.

The pervasiveness of media in our society and the vast variety of kinds of information and points of view expressed results in an array of choices. Individual audience members use that array as a resource for information necessary in their lives. When persuasion occurs, the consumer, as user of the media, comes as an equal partner to the transaction.

We do not deny that the media are influential, but the nature of that influence is often misunderstood. Although the consumer is faced with a variety of messages, programs, formats and perspectives, the field of choice is not infinite. If one's information is limited, if choices are finite, then information resources are restricted. The society's social institutions determine just what choices will be available. Such institutions as media syndicates, networks, and organizations; governmental bodies; advertisers; educational institutions; and others determine the range of media possibilities.

Further, not all choices are equally available to consumers. A preponderance of certain kinds of journalism, entertainment, and advertising make what the average person will encounter pretty predictable, further limiting the real scope of choice. We do not have the space here to discuss controversies about media ideology, television programming, journalistic practice, and the like, but it is important to note that any society, even ours, never has totally free access to information through the media.[4] The *choice-limiting function* of media institutions may, in reality, be the most powerful aspect of this kind of communication within a society.

Persuasive influence emanating from the media, then, is a conjoint outcome of individual consumer behavior and media productions. Figure 10.1 illustrates this concept. The media provide direction in terms of what is printed and/or aired. From that array of alternatives, the audience member selects certain productions to read or view. Those choices constitute only a portion of the total information resources used by the individual. In the overlap between what the media provides and what the individual selects lies the potential persuasive transaction.[5]

/ The role of the consumer

Let us look more closely now at the individual in the media transaction. In attending to media, people use communication rules, just as they do in all aspects of their social life. Take television viewing, for example.[6] Viewing practices are governed by rules or expectations for how to behave. Almost all families have demonstrable television rules, governing the ways in which the family as individuals and as a unit use the medium. For instance, one of us made the decision several years ago not to have a television set; consequently, our family does not watch television on a daily basis. When something very special is being broadcast, like the Olympics, we will rent a set just for that purpose. Although

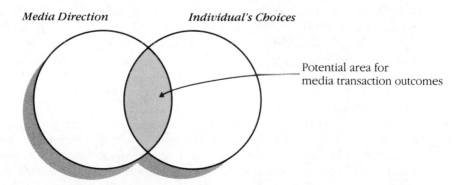

/ **FIGURE 10.1** Choice-making and Choice-limiting within the Media Transaction

our television rules are extreme, they illustrate clearly how people actively manage their viewing behavior. If you ever question whether people are concerned about proper viewing, just observe how parents structure their children's viewing. Even permissiveness about television is itself a kind of rule, stating that easy access to the television set is okay.

Basically, rules for media use are of two types. *Parametric rules* set the limits on what media behaviors are permissible. For example, the periods during the day in which one is allowed to spend time alone to read the newspaper is governed by a parametric rule. The kinds of television shows children are allowed to watch are also established by parametric rules. If you say you wouldn't touch *The National Enquirer,* unless, of course, you were waiting in line at the supermarket, you would be stating a very clear parametric rule.

Tactical rules are the ways in which media may or may not be used to achieve goals. For example, the children in some families are encouraged to watch certain kinds of programs for entertainment. Other forms of entertainment may be proscribed. Many people have the tactical rules of listening to the radio from the time they get out of bed until they leave for work in order to monitor the outside world—news events, weather, and traffic—before leaving their enclave.

One of the most interesting examples in which tactical rules come into play is buying patterns. You would have to be pretty naive to believe that people just jump up in compliance whenever they are confronted with an advertisement. What more typically happens is that, for a variety of reasons, the individual contemplates making a purchase, after which he or she monitors advertising for relevant information on various brands of that product. If the individual needs to make a purchase and is somewhat confused about what to buy, he or she might even open up to be "persuaded" by an effective advertisement.

Recall from our earlier discussion that media communication cannot easily be separated from interpersonal channels. That means we talk to other people about information picked up from media. It also means media rules are largely constructed through social interaction. Where the media are part of the environment of a social relationship, as is television and radio in a family, the partners in the relationship work out their media rules interactionally. Where a person's use of media does not have an impact on others, as would be the case for a single person living alone, rules are still very much influenced by talk with others and observation about how other people use the media. Old media consumption habits developed in an earlier period in one's life may live on, even when one is living alone.

People also work out rules for how and when media are to be directly involved in their social interaction. Many families, for example, actively use television and radio as part of their talk within the family setting. Every evening, we listen to "All Things Considered" on public radio and chat about what we are hearing. That is perhaps a strange-sounding family activity, but it meets three needs in a rather inventive way. First, it gives us a pause in our day, a time to get away from the stresses of work. Second, it provides us with information about current events we could not get from regular television and radio news. Finally, it helps structure our family talk. We find that we can talk to one another with the radio on in a way that television would not permit, probably because we can sit and look at each other when we speak, an arrangement that is conducive to interaction. We certainly wouldn't expect everyone to use the radio in this way, but it works for us. In fact, various media, including television and radio, can just as easily be used to provide a break from social interaction, as the wide use of the "electronic" babysitter well illustrates.

This discussion may seem to imply that people sit around with pencil and paper jotting down all the rules they will follow in using the media. That image, of course, is absurd. Remember from Chapter 2 that although we can usually formulate our rules when called upon to do so, they are usually implicit and out of immediate awareness. When you go off by yourself to read the newspaper after dinner, you do not have to be conscious of following a rule, even though the rule is really there. On the other hand, if your family reserves dinner time for conversation and you decide to read the paper at the dinner table, you will probably hear all kinds of complaints—and they won't be about the food! Again, the rule is very much in operation, even though no one is consciously thinking about it.

So far, we have covered ways in which media are involved in personal change. But what about the other side of the transaction: can consumers influence the media? Indeed, they can, and they do.

/ Audience influence

If media persuasion is a transaction, as we believe it to be, then the direction of influence must flow both ways. It is easy to see how media induce change in individuals; it is perhaps less easy to see how individuals induce change in the media. Media, however, are responsive to the audience. In fact, the outcomes of media persuasion are often unclear: does the audience act in accordance with media direction, or do media act in accord with audience desires? Who is persuading whom? In reality, influence probably flows both ways, as Figure 10.2 illustrates. Let us discuss six ways in which media are affected by the consumer.[7]

First, audience members act as *critics* and fans. The media critic in our society assumes an important role and can influence media change. Likewise, followers of a medium, in providing positive feedback, may be used as a measuring stick of success by a television station, radio network, newspaper, or other media outlet.

Second, our society has established a variety of formal ways in which media institutions are made to be *accountable*. These include legislative hearings, commissions, press councils, and others. Here standards for performance are set, and deviations from those standards are brought into question. This is not to imply that our society keeps a tight rein on its media; certainly, first amendment rights have been powerful in establishing media freedom. However, the factor of accountability does put pressure on the media.

Societal System

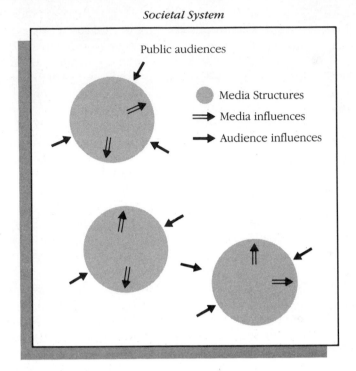

/ FIGURE 10.2 Reciprocal Influences Between Media
Structures and Audiences in the Societal System

There is a fine line between media restriction of choice and audience-induced accountability. The media institutions themselves are part of society and consist of people, like us, who also consume media information. Rather than considering media as separate from audience, it is perhaps more useful to think in system terms, in which society consists of a variety of structures, including media institutions, each part influencing the others.

The third way in which the audience affects the media is through the *market*. Free market advocates believe that this is the best control of all because a medium that is not directly responsive to the market will not survive. Critics of capitalism, on the other hand, believe that the media actually shape the market and its values. Influence in both directions probably occurs.

One kind of media communication especially responsive to the market is advertising. This is, of course, a chicken-and-egg issue. Do people buy because of advertising, or is advertising a response to what people want? Advertisers believe they are using the wants and needs of the audience for persuasive purposes; at the same time, advertising at least reinforces those tendencies and often creates them. Marketing as a field consists not only of selling within existing markets, but also of creating new markets as well. (We discuss advertising at greater length later in this chapter.)

Fourth, people provide the media with *direct feedback*. Letters to the editor, telephone calls to the station, consumer campaigns and demonstrations—all exert some influence on media. This form of influence, however, is rarely considered representative of the market as a whole and may therefore have little influence.

Fifth, the media producers have their own *images* of what the audience is like. These audience images affect in a very direct way what is produced. The images may or may not be accurate, but they do operate. Remember that media producers are themselves members of the audience: they associate with other people, they read, they view, they listen, and, like us, they use their perceptions of what they think is going on in society.

Finally, the media often undertake *formal research* to assess the wants, needs, and tendencies for the audience. Sometimes serious research attempts are made, as in contemplating a program-format change. Other times, such research is viewed by the media with suspicion, if not downright hostility.[8]

Predominant in market research have been social psychological survey techniques which either monitor consumers' selection of media or, through sophisticated interviewing techniques, provide the demographic data discussed in earlier chapters. Considerable controversy exists over the value of such studies. Critics point out that market research only tells advertisers what they know intuitively already: children like toys, the elderly are concerned about their health, and the rich buy expensive automobiles.

Somewhat less vulnerable to the foregoing criticism is qualitative research in the form of the focus group. A *focus group* is a group of consumers who discuss their buying habits with a group leader from a marketing firm. The advantage of this type of research is that it can record more detailed, realistic responses about a product and about how it is perceived in people's cognitive systems. The disadvantage is that, due to the necessarily small number of respondents, generalizing the results to a larger population is difficult. At best, research based on focus groups provides insights and possible hypotheses from which to devise more comprehensive studies or ideas. Most agencies today use a combination of the qualitative focus group research and the more comprehensive quantitative survey techniques.

/ The Persuasive Outcome of Media Transactions

Now that we have discussed the nature of media communication, let us focus more directly on the persuasive outcomes of that process. Because of its societal implications, media persuasion is complex. It is useful to discuss persuasive outcomes in terms of level, degree, and type.[9]

/ Levels of outcome

Persuasive outcomes can occur at a number of levels, including the personal, the group or organization, the institution, the society, or the culture. *Personal* outcomes, of course, may involve personal change. If you make a voting decision on the basis of media information, decide to buy a product because of an advertising campaign, avoid viewing a movie because of a negative review, visit an exotic place after reading about it in the travel section of the Sunday paper, or write a letter of protest to your senator because of a book you have read, you are exhibiting individual persuasive outcomes. However, some of the most important outcomes of media persuasion occur at more inclusive levels than the individual.

The second level is that of the *group or organization.* We were, for quite some time, members of a local anti-nuclear weapons group. That group was almost always involved in one campaign or another as a result of information

/ The Phil Donahue show, which provides a forum for discussions of a wide range of issues, potentially affects persuasive outcomes on the individual, organizational, societal, and cultural levels.

and editorials in the news media, books, articles, motion pictures, and television documentaries. When we think about it, we realize that the group received almost all of its direction from the media. Of course, what the group did affected the individual attitudes, values, and behaviors of its members but the ways in which the group itself found form and substance in response to media is especially important.

Some outcomes affect even larger structures, called *social institutions*. By *institutions* we are referring to major social structures created to fulfill particular functions of importance to a society. Institutions include schools, governmental bureaucracies, political parties, health and medical establishments, and many more. Institutions are hard to change, and such outcomes usually occur very gradually.

An example of an institutional outcome of the New Christian Right is the growth of the "electronic church," the highly popular televised religious programs such as those seen on the Christian Broadcast Network (CBN). As evangelical political concerns developed in the 1970s, the Christian broadcast establishment became increasingly involved in politics. In fact, one of the reasons the Moral Majority enjoyed such fast growth was because it could use mailing lists generated from the audience of Falwell's *Old Time Gospel Hour.* The institution of Christian broadcasting both contributed to and responded to the rise of the New Christian Right.

If institutions can be involved in societal change, then, logically, institutions can affect the entire society, or at least numerous institutions within society. Such outcomes do not occur very frequently, but they are found in the ebb and flow of history, as societies shift values and practices in response to major political, economic, and social developments. Some examples include the effects of the Great Depression of the 1930s, followed by World War II, in shaping the middle American value of materialism; the youth uprising and social turmoil of the 1960s related to the Civil Rights Movement and the Vietnam War; and the shift toward conservatism in the 1980s. The problem with identifying the media with such societal change is that those trends are so wrapped up in the entire social system that the role of the media becomes murky. We can probably fairly conclude, however, that the media act at least as a conduit of information and persuasion from the various groups that speak out during times of social change.

Some outcomes of media persuasion are *cultural*. Surely, the media have something to do with the "acculturation" of many ethnic minorities in this country toward the "middle." Many of our Chicano acquaintances in their forties and fifties, for example, bemoan the fact that their children do not speak Spanish. Many of the traditional customs found among the *Isei* and *Nisei* Japanese Americans in this country are being lost by members of the younger generation (the third generation *Sansei*). The mainstream of American cultural values are indeed affected by the images portrayed in the media. The reverence for youth and beauty, the idolization of the idealized human body, the love affair with the automobile, the extremes of nationalism, the supremacy of utilitarian ethics, and other such cultural tendencies and values are affected, at least in part, by the media transaction.

/ Degrees of outcome

The second way to look at outcome is by their degree of intensity. Outcomes range from major change to intense stability: (1) outcome involves major change; (2) outcome involves minor change; (3) outcome reinforces the status quo; (4) outcome involves extreme rigidity against change.[10]

Major change is not easy to find. Communication outcomes, on a society-wide basis, are usually mild and gradual. There are, of course, exceptions, as the influence of the New Christian Right illustrates. Evangelical Christianity, with a few exceptions, has historically been apolitical in this country. Indeed, politics was even considered off-limits by many leading evangelists. Billy Graham, for example, has often stated his stringent objection to the intrusion of religion into matters of the state. An important tenet of the New Christian Right, however, is activism—the requirement that the good Christian become involved in returning the United States to what the Right believes to be its original values, and to do so in and through the political platform.

More often, minor change is the outcome of media persuasion. Political persuasion is a good example. Numerous election polls demonstrate that the vast majority of voters make up their mind early in a campaign. In fact, media may have little direct influence on the votes of most citizens.[11] The real contention is the usually small, undecided group in the middle. Of course, the ultimate decisions of undecided voters may have a major impact in the outcome of the election but, viewed on a society-wide basis, the actual persuasive influence of the typical media blitz during an election is usually fairly small.

Much of the research on media effects in the 1950s and 1960s led us to realize that media mostly *reinforce* audience attitudes, values, and behaviors.[12] Rather than bring about conversion, media communication normally acts merely to reinforce that which is already in place. There are exceptions, of course, but political advertising, editorials, partisan books, television programming, billboards, and the like tend to make a person more secure in what is already believed. Faced with an array of media choices, most individuals will listen to, view, or read that which supports their own point of view. One of our fathers, whose political views are counter to our own, in the heat of a political argument will remind us that "if you read the *entire* newspaper, you would see things differently." He is right, of course, but we think he is guilty of the same selective perception.

Occasionally, the media function to reinforce the status quo in an extreme way, to the point of creating *rigidity against change*. This is a more probable outcome in societies in which the government exerts heavy control over the media than in our society, but it can occur here too. Political and economic conditions can lead to a coming together of the public on certain issues. War will do that. Patriotism has rarely been higher in this country than during World War II; there was a very strong feeling that our participation in the war was necessary and justified, and the media, in radio news, newspapers, and news reels reinforced that view. Even academicians, who are normally fairly liberal and skeptical about establishment positions, were generally enthusiastic about doing research that would help "save democracy" and overcome international aggression. The intensity of rigid patriotism during the 1940s is highlighted by contrasting it with public attitudes during the Korean and, especially, Vietnam Wars.

/ Functions as outcomes

The third dimension of communication outcomes is function. Here we discuss the kinds of outcome resulting from the media transaction: individual change, fulfillment of goals, agenda setting, the diffusion of innovations, and socio-cultural outcomes.

/ Individual Change.
The subject of the individual effects of media is one of the most researched, yet poorly understood, kinds of communication outcomes. As we saw in Chapter 3, it is very difficult to separate all of the influences on a person's behavior to determine just what effect the media may exert. Yet no subject is more germane to media persuasion than how individuals change their attitudes, beliefs, values, and actions on the basis of media persuasion. As we have already seen, such outcomes, like all others, are a product of transaction. Thus, any explanation of media effects must take the active role of the individual into account. To us, the most sensible theory about the individual effects of media transactions is the Dependency Theory of DeFleur and Ball-Rokeach.[13]

This dependency theory suggests that individual outcomes are a product of the entire social system, consisting of a variety of structures, media organizations, and audiences. Figure 10.3 illustrates the theory.[14] The diagram depicts a society that makes use of its media, along with many other institutions, to accomplish certain functions. The system as a whole exerts some effects on the persons within it, although those effects will be different for each individual, depending on other elements of the environment which exert influence.

According to dependency theory, individuals seek information with which to manage their lives. One source of information is the media. As the individual comes to count on the information obtained from a particular medium, he or she becomes more dependent on that medium. As dependency increases, the effects of the transaction on the person increase. For example, various Christian programs, like the *PTL* ("Praise the Lord") *Club,* the 700 *Club,* the *Old Time Gospel Hour,* and others have large and loyal followings. As is the case with all forms of broadcasting, the audience members of these programs differ in terms of how and why they use Christian television. Many have become quite dependent on these programs to fulfill a variety of functions, including entertainment, information, and inspiration. For those particular viewers, the effects of that programming will be relatively strong.

What kinds of individual effects are we talking about? A quick review of Chapter 3 is useful at this point. Recall that information has an impact on one's cognitive system and its reality, goal, arousal, and relationship dimensions. Any or all of these dimensions of the system may undergo change as a consequence of the media transaction. In one person's case, for example, the emotional intensity of religious belief may be increased by religious programming. Someone

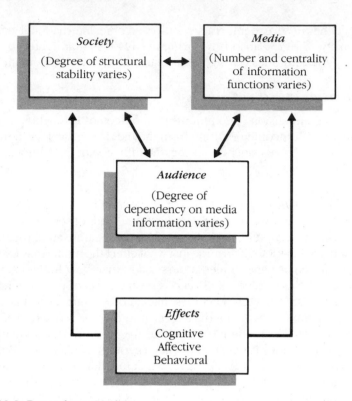

I **FIGURE 10.3** Dependency Model

else might experience a modification in belief as a consequence of information received. Still others may find that they come to value Christian ethics more, or that their relationship with other evangelicals is modified in some way.

I Fulfillment of Societal Functions. The second category of functions of the media transaction include the fulfillment of societal functions.[15] Specifically, four general functions are served by media in our society. The first is *surveillance,* typically accomplished by news reporting. Surveillance involves monitoring the events that affect our lives. It involves getting basic information about our environment—everything from weather to international politics.

The second function of the media is *correlation,* or seeing the relationships among events. A variety of media forms accomplish correlation, the most obvious of which is editorials. Statements of opinion lead people to consider how various parts of the environment affect one another. Correlation can also be fulfilled by other media forms, such as books, documentaries, and even fiction.

The third function for which media are used is *cultural transmission.* Where do we find our cultural roots? Personal contact with our relatives and friends fulfills this function, although family is less important in imparting cultural values than it used to be. Much of what we know about our culture is provided by media depictions. What university professor could not read Malamud's

A New Life, a novel about the experiences of a young professor just out of graduate school, without grinning in recognition? What high school student would not feel some sense of identification with the characters in the award-winning film *Breaking Away?* What student of mass communication would not analyze the spate of T.V. commercials for household cleaning products without gaining a fair idea of our culture's view of women?

The final major function fulfilled by the media is *entertainment.* There is no question that the media, especially in the forms of television, radio, film, and books, provide major outlets for leisure time. Especially in a society which values work, escaping through entertainment is an important human activity.

These four media functions—surveillance, correlation, cultural transmission, and entertainment—are important outcomes of the media transaction. Do not get into the trap of trying to relate each of these functions to a particular medium, format, or message. People mix and match the media in order to accomplish these functions in their lives. Remember, also, that these functions do not occur solely on the individual level; they have societal, cultural, institutional, and group implications as well. To get a fuller picture of these functions of the mass media, peruse Table 10.1[16]

TABLE 10.1

Functions and Dysfunctions of Mass Communication

	Individual	Group	Societal	Cultural
1. Mass communicated activity: surveillance (news)				
Functions (manifest and latent)	Warning: Natural dangers Attack; war	Warning Instrumental	Instrumental: information useful to power	Aids cultural contact Aids cultural growth
	Instrumental: News essential to the economy and other institutions	Adds prestige: Opinion leadership	Detects: Knowledge of subversive and deviant behavior	
	Ethicizing	Status conferral	Manages public opinion: Monitors Controls	
			Legitimizes power: Status conferral	
Dysfunctions (manifest and latent)	Threatens stability: News of "better" societies Fosters panic	Anxiety Privatization Apathy Narcotization	Threatens power: News of reality "Enemy" propaganda Exposes	Permits cultural invasion

(continued)

TABLE 10.1 *(continued)*

Functions and Dysfunctions of Mass Communication

	Individual	*Group*	*Societal*	*Cultural*
2. Mass-communicated activity: correlation (editorial selection, interpretation, and prescription)				
Functions (manifest and latent)	Aids mobilization Impedes threats to social stability Impedes panic	Provides efficiency: Assimilating news Impedes: Overstimulation Anxiety Apathy Privatization	Helps preserve power	Impedes cultural invasion Maintains cultural consensus
Dysfunctions (manifest and latent)	Increases social conformism: Impedes social change if social criticism is avoided	Weakens critical faculties Increases passivity	Increases responsibility	Impedes cultural growth
3. Mass-communicated activity: cultural transmission				
Functions (manifest and latent)	Increases social cohesion: Widens base of common norms, experiences, etc. Reduces anomie Continues socialization: Reaches adults even after they have left such institutions as school	Aids integration: Exposure to common norms Reduces idiosyncrasy Reduces anomie	Extends power: Another agency for socialization	Standardizes Maintains cultural consensus
Dysfunctions (manifest and latent)	Augments "mass" society	Depersonalizes acts of socialization		Reduces variety of subcultures
4. Mass-communicated activity: entertainment				
Functions (manifest and latent)	Respite for masses	Respite	Extends power: Control over another area of life.	
Dysfunctions (manifest and latent)	Diverts public: Avoids social action	Increases passivity Lowers "tastes" Permits escapism		Weakens aesthetics: "Popular culture"

/ Agenda Setting. The third set of outcomes of media transactions involves agenda setting.[17] A good deal of research indicates that the media are effective in establishing the business of the day for the public. In other words, what we pay attention to, what we think is important, and what we seek information about are established, in large measure, by what is depicted in the media—by the editorial process. From all of the ideas submitted for production in any media form, certain ones are selected by the media "bosses" for actual transmission. In news, certain stories are rejected; certain ones are selected. In entertainment, certain pilot programs are chosen; others leave the studio in the editor's wastebasket. In publishing, far more manuscripts are rejected outright than ever see printer's ink. Figure 10.4 illustrates the agenda-setting process as it is manifest in news-making.[18]

The famous journalist Walter Lippman called such agendas the "pseudo-environment," which consists of the "pictures in our heads."[19] He noted the importance of news coverage in shaping this view of what is important in the world beyond our immediate grasp. The most well-known researchers on this subject, Shaw and McCombs, have said, " . . . the mass media may not be successful in telling us what to think, but they are stunningly successful in telling us what to think about."[20] Of course, the agenda is not strictly a media effect; it also requires public interest combined with a lack of information. Remember the concept illustrated in Figure 10.1: only within the overlap between what the media present and what the audience selects can media influence occur.

/ Diffusion of Innovations. The fourth outcome of the media transaction is the diffusion of innovations.[21] How is it that we come to adopt innovations within a society? Where do farmers find new farming techniques? How do physicians learn of new procedures? What was the impetus for the personal computer craze? Why do so many people walk around with stereo headphones on their ears? The diffusion of innovations has undergone considerable study. We know that it is a result of both media information and interpersonal persuasion, as illustrated so well by the changes that happened between 1968 and the present time in the Korean village of Oryu Li. Opinion leaders referred to in the case of innovations as early adopters or innovators, seem important in the diffusion process. The media provide information about the innovation, but the actual persuasion to adopt probably happens interpersonally. Figure 10.5 illustrates the process of the diffusion of innovations.[22]

/ Socio-cultural Outcomes. The final result of the media transaction involves the *socio-cultural definition of reality.*[23] This effect, which is subtler than the other outcomes, is intimately related to all of them. It is perhaps the most important outcome of all. By *socio-cultural definition of reality* we are referring to what the culture perceives as real, to how the world is ordered, to the predominant shape of things within the cognitive systems of the members of the culture. We are dealing with a culture's basic values and assumptions about right and wrong, good and bad, real and imaginary. As we pointed out in Chapter 3,

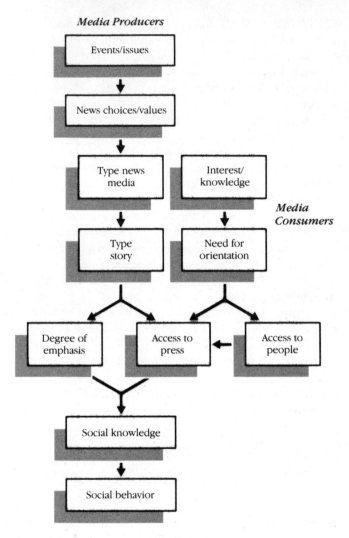

/ FIGURE 10.4 The Agenda-Setting Process

our own culture is characterized by a humanistic and materialistic world view. Most of us place our faith in the products of human beings, including ideas. We believe that problems should be solved rationally, by weighing evidence and examining alternatives. We are therefore very utilitarian in our approach to what is good. People who produce useful products are productive; people who do not are shirkers. A certain segment of our culture values art for its own sake, but the vast majority of people in this country value only those arts that can be considered immediately entertaining. To illustrate the intensity of this world view in our country, consider that natural scientists can take research expenses as a federal tax credit; researchers in the arts, humanities, and social sciences cannot.

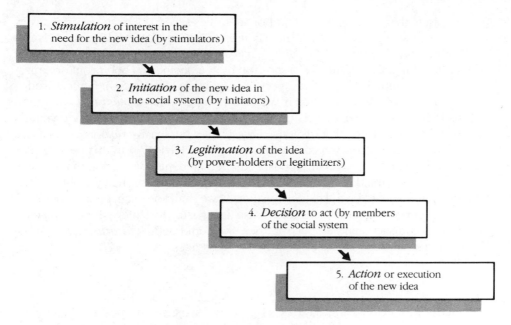

1. *Stimulation* of interest in the need for the new idea (by stimulators)

2. *Initiation* of the new idea in the social system (by initiators)

3. *Legitimation* of the idea (by power-holders or legitimizers)

4. *Decision* to act (by members of the social system

5. *Action* or execution of the new idea

/ FIGURE 10.5 The Diffusion of Innovations

The world view, then, is that which is most valued and considered to constitute the legitimate reality with which one must cope. To what extent do the media participate in shaping this world view? If we look at all media communication together, the total impact is probably great. Any one medium, format, or style, however, probably contributes little. Media advertising may have little effect on your decision to buy "Charlie," "Windsong," or "White Linen," but valuing perfume enough to purchase any brand is itself an important cultural preference, shaped in part by pervasive media forms.

Although this overview touches only the surface of the persuasive role of media in the public arena, it does demonstrate how media communication involve transactions in a complex social system. We now turn to a specific application of persuasion through media: advertising.

/ Advertising

As with any form of communication, *advertising* can be defined from the perspective of the transmitter, message, receiver, or effects. Dunn and Barban define advertising from a transmitter-message perspective when they state:

> Advertising is paid, non-personal communication through various media by business firms, nonprofit organizations, and individuals who are in some way identified in the advertising message and who hope to inform or persuade members of a particular audience.[24]

Note that this common definition identifies several characteristics of advertising. First, advertising is a form of *communication*. Second, advertising is typically *paid for*. When it is not paid for, it is usually donated as if it had commercial value. Third, advertising has a *sponsor*, be it a business, a non-profit organization, or an individual, and the sponsor is typically identified—if not featured—in the ad. Fourth, advertising is typically non-personal or *mediated* communication. Finally, advertising is designed for particular audiences from whom a *response* is desired. That response is typically a persuasive response—that is, a change in the receiver's cognitive system or behavior. From this perspective, advertising is commercially-sponsored, mediated, persuasive communication.

As we pointed out earlier, however, people influence the media as well as being influenced by the media. Further, as we shall soon see, people choose to be influenced by advertising and to use advertising to achieve their own goals. From a transactional perspective, then, we could define *advertising* as mutual influence through mediated commercial messages.

/ Types of advertising

/ General.
Advertising may be classified into two general types. The first is generalized advertising of products, candidates or issues. The most celebrated advertising is aimed at *national* audiences. This type of advertising utilizes nationwide media such as network television, or circulates individual ads on a nationwide basis. We are all familiar with the omnipresent TV ads for soft drinks, automobiles, and toothpaste, or a fund-raising drive for a national charity.

A second type of generalized advertising is that of a *local* dealership, product, or candidate. This type of advertising aims at local or regional audiences and utilizes local newspapers and magazines as well as local television and radio stations, billboards and circulars. Such advertising may be conducted by local automobile dealerships, restaurants, department stores, charities, or political candidates.

/ Specialized.
A second type of advertising is more specialized than the general types. One kind of specialized advertising targets a *particular segment* of the local or national audience or may feature a *specialized product*. Such ads selectively use magazines or radio stations with the desired constituencies as well as more broadly based media—for instance, an advertisement for a particular running shoe or cleaning product. The advertisement of specific products by local businesses or dealerships are combined in newspaper advertising in the form of inserts which contain the pictures and prices of various specific products that a particular store is either featuring or has on "sale." Such advertisements, though not as glamorous or expensive as that through broadcast media, frequently constitutes the backbone of advertising in the print media.

An important kind of specialized advertising, often overlooked by analysts, is the classified advertising which appears in newspapers and some magazines.

A shopper can quickly find the "one-bedroom apartments," "imported automobiles," or "boats and motors" available at any given time in the area covered by the circulation of the local newspaper. In addition, "nickle ads," or publications containing only classified ads, are frequently available in local supermarkets.

/ Functions of advertising

Earlier in this chapter we discussed the broad functions of mass media as surveillance, correlation, cultural transmission, and entertainment. Now we turn to the more specific functions of advertising. We will discuss the societal functions of information dissemination, power/social control, and sales.[25]

/ Information Dissemination.
The first function of advertising is that of providing information to consumers and producers about the marketplace. Based upon the assumption that people are endowed with reason and conscience, the market information function works somewhat like the American judicial system. That is, given comparable advocacy and information on both sides, it is assumed consumers (like members of a jury) will make the best decision for themselves and, ultimately, for society.

From this perspective, advertising serves a useful if not essential function in the economy. In an increasingly complex society, consumers become further removed from the points of production and less acquainted with the quality of workmanship and even availability of products. Mass production makes a greater variety of goods available to most people, with more producers competing for the market. Advertising provides necessary information about products which discriminating consumers could receive in no other way. As James Carey argues,

> One of the fundamental assumptions underlying theoretical analysis of competitive markets, and the whole concept of economic man, is that all entrants into the economic market shall have perfect knowledge, that is, each should be aware of all prices resulting from supply and demand relationships and should have perfect knowledge of alternative forms of satisfying demand. *Caveat emptor*—let the buyer beware—simply means that every individual, being rational, is assumed to possess the ability to exercise correct judgment by basing his directions on available market information.[26]

Since advertising is far less systematized and regulated than our legal system, the idealized model envisioned by Carey is somewhat problematic. That is to say, the assumptions of equally qualified and reliable *sources,* comparable quality and accuracy of *messages,* and the dispassionate and rational weighing of information by *consumers* can at best be only partially realized. Nonetheless, advertising serves the function of providing information to consumers about availability of products, comparative prices, and, to some degree, the quality, or at least characteristics, of products.

/ *Power.* Advertising can exert power economically, politically, and socially. In an address to the American Academy of Advertising,[27] Vincent Norris describes the development of advertising as an *economic* institution in terms of market power. Rather than centralized mass production creating the need for market information in the form of advertising, Norris argues, national advertising arose as a response to the power that suppliers and wholesalers held as the only link between national manufacturers and consumers. Since toothpaste, aspirin, or crackers were generically similar, the wholesaler could set prices by increasing competition among producers in the process of choosing which one would be distributed to retailers. Through national advertising, producers could create brand names and exclusive packaging and reach the consumer directly. By so doing they could create a demand for their specific product, and thereby capture power over the market.

This development had the advantages of shifting control over product packaging, innovation, and, hence, quality from the wholesaler and retailer to the producer. The disadvantage was that competition was no longer determined by product quality and price, nor were resources distributed to the most economically efficient products.

Advertising can also provide power *politically.* Just as manufacturers can reach consumers directly, so political candidates or movements can reach the voting public directly, reducing the power and influence of political parties, labor unions, and other political power brokers. So important has advertising become in political campaigns that we now see candidates "sold" like so much merchandise, and the costs of political campaigns are skyrocketing.

Finally, advertising can create power *socially*—what Potter calls "social control."[28] Like Norris, Potter views advertising as having developed not just from the need to fill an information gap created by mass production or the separation of producers from their consumers. Potter contends that the growth of advertising was driven by the ability of American industry to produce more than consumer demand or *abundance.* In order to create new or expanded markets for this abundance, advertising arose as means not only of meeting existing needs but also of creating new wants. Along with the churches, schools, and industry, advertising became an agency of social control—that is, a means of changing needs, wants, and especially values. In short, a key function of advertising is changing the beliefs, values, and motives of receivers, or what we have called the *cognitive system.*

/ *Product Sales.* Although advertising fulfills other functions, the engine that drives advertising as well as the American economy is product sales. Viewed more broadly, this function of advertising is the influence it has on the buying, voting, giving, and other behaviors of consumers.

When speaking of product sales or behavior change, advertisers themselves stress several mediating processes. We will discuss name recognition, product image, product differentiation, derived need, and commitment.

/ **The image of Air Jordan shoes was carefully created: a striking billboard campaign featuring NBA star Michael Jordan reinforced the image evoked by the shoes' name. In fact, the image was so desirable that, for a time, some stores could not keep up with consumer demands for the product.**
Photo courtesy of NIKE, Inc.

Both advertisers and producers believe that *name recognition* sells. Particularly in the case of impulse buying, a person will reach for the product with the recognizable name over that of other competing products. Likewise in politics, a candidate is said to have the edge if he/she enjoys the best name-recognition. In fact, many candidates new to the political process consider it a moral victory if they are not beaten badly in their first campaign for public office because of the name-recognition they acquire. Many will win on their second or third try.

Product image is also considered an important mediator of consumer behavior. Consider the care with which most politicians nurture their public image, or how manufacturers develop the image of their products. The most dramatic waxing and waning of a politician's public image was that of Richard Nixon, who began in his early years with the image of "Tricky Dicky," developed the image of "The New Nixon" by his election as President in 1968, and whose image finally collapsed amid the revelations of Watergate. Manufactured products also have an image. A "Nova" sounds more exciting and modern than a "Chevy II"—essentially the same car. Soaps, toothpaste, and other products are constantly being advertised as "new and improved" in order to keep their image up to date.

Product differentiation is also considered a necessary mediator of consumer behavior. Particularly in the national advertising of highly similar products such as detergents, cosmetics, toothpaste, soft drinks, pain relievers, or cigarettes, product differentiation is seen as crucial to successful marketing.

The same could be said of a political candidacy, especially in a primary race with several candidates who represent similar beliefs and values.

Creating a *derived need* is another mediating process in consumer behavior. Earlier we discussed the relationship among goal-oriented elements of the cognitive system such as needs, motives, and values. The concept of the goal orientation of individuals fits nicely with advertiser's concept of derived need. Advertisers are fond of pointing out that consumers will frequently satisfy a "want" (say alcohol) over a "need" (for example, food). Furthermore, wants can be elevated to needs as in the case of young people today "needing" designer clothing and electronic toys which their grandparents survived quite nicely without. By contributing substantially to this process of escalating expectations, advertising not only serves the very useful function of fueling the nation's expanding economy, but may profoundly influence social values in the process.

On the other hand, some would argue that the increased reliance on advertising in the political arena has changed the process of choosing public officials in essential ways. First, advertising has made it possible for candidates (who can afford it) to reach an increasing number of people in a rapidly growing population. It has also changed political campaigns from an emphasis on a depth discussion of issues to platitudes and images. Others would argue, however, that platitudes reflect human values and images reflect the character of the individual candidate. Regardless of which side of the issue a person takes, it is clear that advertising serves the function of changing what voters "want" or evaluate in their political candidates.

A final mediating factor in consumer behavior is *commitment* or attitude toward behavior. Much advertising is aimed not at immediate behavior, but at a strengthening of commitment to that behavior which may be realized at a later time. While people may not be in a position to buy, travel, or vote at the moment, it is assumed that increased commitment will increase the possibility of the desired behavior (or resistance to new behavior) at a later date. Such is the function of advertising aimed at preventing defection of political supporters or at a product retaining or expanding its share of the market.

/ Effects of advertising

As in the case of general media effects discussed earlier, the effects of advertising are widely researched and hotly debated. All too often the effects of advertising are inferred after the fact from dramatic increases in the sale of a product or changes in the ratings of politicians in the polls. Advertisers make persuasive arguments about the efficacy of advertising in increasing the sales of Wesson oil, for instance. While such general effects undoubtedly exist in isolated cases, research has suggested that general effects with general audiences are rarely significant. In a review of studies on the effect of alcohol advertising, Strickland claims, "Recent research on the effects of beverage advertising on alcohol consumption has consistently demonstrated very small or negligible effects in a variety of populations."[29]

Recall, however, our earlier discussion of media effects on individuals. Effects on general audiences follows from a transmissional notion of passive, susceptible audiences. The dependency theory of Ball-Rokeach and DeFleur provides a more transactional explanation. Following this theory one would expect that only individuals who are "ready" to interact with an advertisement are potentially susceptible to the persuasive message of the ad. For instance, if the subject of the ad is salient to the viewer, an actor in the ad is perceived as attractive, or the content of the ad identifies with elements in the consumer's cognitive system, the ad might mediate change in the individual. Further, if the advertised message is later reinforced in interpersonal, group, or public persuasive interactions, the impact of the ad may be enhanced.

This individualized influence was supported by Strickland's study of teenagers' viewing of ads and subsequent alcohol consumption. He concludes:

> Teenagers who were highly motivated to attend to advertising for social utility reasons were found to be influenced by exposure to alcoholic beverage advertising. Such a finding is consistent with theoretical models of observational learning of normative social practice, social comparison processes and conformity influences. Likewise, among teenagers who attend to commercials as a means of vicariously identifying with models and life-styles, there is a statistically significant effect of advertising on consumption.[30]

Strickland qualifies his conclusions even further:

> ... given the strong theoretical justification for expecting a significant advertising effect among teenagers who vicariously associate with advertising models (a most 'vulnerable' subgroup), it is difficult to interpret the findings as supporting the contention that advertising is a primary factor in consumption ...[31]

In sum, except in notable, isolated instances the effects of advertising on general audiences can be considered negligible. Specific responses may be effected from individuals who, for a variety of reasons, may identify with the advertised message and have those identifications reinforced in other persuasive communication transactions.

Having looked at a basic definition of advertising as well as its types, functions, and effects, let us turn to some considerations of advertising which concern both advertisers and analysts of advertising.

/ Advertising as process

As we pointed out in our earlier discussion of media, persuasion through advertising is a complex process. This process involves the consumer's cognitive system, considerations of the agency, and message strategies.

/ Understanding the Consumers' Cognitive System.
In his book, *Advertising, The Uneasy Persuasion,*[32] Michael Schudson discusses the consumers' "information environment," roughly analogous to the cognitive system. Schudson insightfully describes consumers' cognitions as well as the sociological

forces which shape those cognitions. Following Schudson, we will discuss the sources of information for consumers as well as describe types of consumers whose cognitive system makes them particularly susceptible to advertising.

Sources of Information. What, then, are the *sources of information* which supplement and rival advertising for a place in consumers' cognitive systems? First and perhaps most important is *direct personal experience*. People who have had personal experience with a type of automobile, a political candidate, or a fast-food franchise will weigh the information received from advertising against beliefs, values, and relationships already established in their cognitive systems through these direct experiences. How often have you heard, "I have owned a Speedy automobile for years and I wouldn't drive anything else," or, "After what Candidate X did to Social Security I'd never vote for X again." Advertising which counters strong dimensions of the cognitive system acquired through personal experience may have little impact, while that which reinforces those same dimensions will probably be quite effective.

A second source of information for consumers is *interpersonal influence*. Conversations with parents, teachers, friends, and others help shape the dimensions of consumers' cognitive systems, which in turn affects how they will respond to advertising. Furthermore, interpersonal interactions which follow exposure to advertising can strengthen or attenuate the effects of the ad. How often have you watched an advertisement on T.V. and said to yourself, "That's the brand my parents use. It looks pretty good to me." Or, conversely, "That is the brand my friend had trouble with; what a dishonest ad." Perhaps after you saw an ad in the newspaper for a political candidate, a friend praised the candidate; the claims and the advertisement were mutually reinforced.

A third source of information for consumers comes through the *media* in forms other than relevant advertising. Newspaper stories and editorials, television documentaries or entertainment programming, magazine articles, and even competing advertisements interact with and affect consumers' beliefs, values, and relationships. News stories on a candidate's corruption or reports of conflict of interest can undermine even the most skillful advertising campaign. Revelations of cost overruns or environmental damage can ruin the image-oriented advertising of a corporation. News stories of dangerous side effects of a particular product can negate the effects of advertising or prompt a costly new advertising campaign. On the other hand, a timely news story or even a sports or entertainment feature can enhance the message of the advertisers. Note, for example, that ads for sporting equipment appear in the sports section of a newspaper.

Other advertising can also have an impact on the cognitive system. Advertisers will sometimes attempt to refute advertising claims of competing products or to poke fun at them, as in *7-Up's* advertising itself as "The Un-cola."

Formal education also affects the cognitive system of consumers and, hence, the way they generate meanings from advertising. Schools and other agencies provide an information pool within the cognitive systems of consumers against which information in advertising is weighed. If you saw an advertisement claiming miraculous medicinal results which violated what you have learned in a basic biology class, you would probably view the ad with great skepticism.

Cognitive components.   In addition to the foregoing sources of consumer information, consumers' interaction with advertising is also affected by two elements of the cognitive system, one in the relationship dimension and the other in the reality dimension.

The element of the relationship dimension of the cognitive system which affects consumers' processing of advertising messages is a *general skepticism* about media generally and advertising in particular. People are becoming more aware of possible bias in the reporting of news stories. Note for instance, the recent attempt by right-wing political groups to take over CBS in order to provide programming, especially news, with a less "liberal" point of view. Further, the use of special effects in television and film, as well as alterations of photographic images used in print media, have made people more cautious of the inferences they draw from such "information."

If people are skeptical about the bias of general media information, they are even more skeptical of advertising itself. Advertising suffers from a general mistrust by consumers, to the point that many consumers simply choose to ignore the ads altogether.

An element of the reality dimension which profoundly affects consumers' cognitive processing of advertising messages is *price*. Most consumers ignore the advertising of Mercedes Benz automobiles or diamond jewelry because the products are simply too expensive. On the other hand, some people will buy things they actually neither need nor want because the product is on sale or the price was "too good" to pass up. Most advertisers are well aware of the significance of the price issue. Accordingly, they target advertising of specific products to specific audiences who are "qualified" to buy certain priced merchandise. Advertising of recreation property or investment programs is frequently mailed directly to people whose professional affiliations or home ownership indicate they may be financially qualified to seriously consider the "offer." Price is an issue in consumers' cognitive system that affects their interaction with and processing of advertised commercial messages.

Types of consumers.   Having discussed the sources of information available to consumers and two salient issues for consumers, let us discuss how this information environment interacts to make some consumers more susceptible to advertising and open to processing mediated commercial messages.

The first type of consumer who is both dependent on advertising and open to its message is the highly *mobile* person or family. In simpler communities and earlier times in U.S. history, people knew the merchants from whom they bought, the quality of products, and the character of political candidates. In modern societies, a large portion of the population moves every few years to a new home and many to a new community. In the absence of personal experience with local merchants, products, and candidates, as well as the absence of an established network of interpersonal influence, mobile people must rely more on advertising to tell them the location of desired products and services as well as the price structure. Whether shopping for a new home, apartment, or automobile, newcomers to a community use the classified ads as a consumers' guide.

Another group reliant on advertising is the extremely *immobile* consumer. Frequently aged or handicapped, these consumers have lost the ability to get around and develop personal experience with new products or candidates, and, in some cases, have become isolated from interpersonal networks. Unable to commute long distances, they rely on advertising for information about products available at reasonable prices and convenient locations.

Still another group dependent on advertising for information and influence is the *poor.* Along with poverty, especially over an extended period of time, comes less formal education, immobility, and limited access to diverse personal experiences. Unable to shop around or wait for a better opportunity, the poor frequently end up paying higher rent and higher prices for goods and services (especially credit) than their more affluent counterparts, thus compounding their problem of poverty. If this situation makes them somewhat more susceptible to advertising, the system provides a built-in counterbalance. As we shall see, advertisers tend not to direct their appeals to people with limited means to respond, thereby insulating the poor, to some degree, from the influence of advertising.

A particularly vulnerable class of potential consumers is the *young*. Not having yet had the opportunity for extensive personal experience or formal education, and being restricted by limited and equally uninformed interpersonal influence, the young have a less developed cognitive system against which to evaluate advertising messages. Furthermore, the young have not had the opportunity to develop skepticism about mediated messages, and price is frequently no object. Of course, naievete does not last long, and we are constantly amazed at some insightful comments made by school children about the poor credibility of some advertising claims. Nonetheless, most children nag their parents to buy products which have just been advertised, with obvious exaggeration, in either the broadcast or print media.

A final group of susceptible consumers of advertising are found in *third world countries*. Although they may possess well-developed and highly-sophisticated cognitive systems which have great survival value in their own cultures, residents of the third world may be unfamiliar with and hence open to advertising techniques developed in other cultures. Furthermore, many third world countries have not developed the regulations against unscrupulous advertising techniques which are illegal in countries with greater experience with commercial advertising.

Do not infer this discussion that we think these groups of people are unintelligent or ignorant. We simply mean that, for the stated demographic reasons, some people have not had sufficient opportunity to develop a sophisticated cognitive system with which to process advertising messages, or (as in the case of the elderly, mobile, and third world residents) that their information environment and cognitive systems are less functional in the situation in which they find themselves.

Remember that consumers are not passive recipients who are buffeted about or manipulated by advertising. At any given time or place, some consumers are simply more or less susceptible to advertised messages, and all consumers transact with different cognitive systems and within different information environments.

/ Considerations of the Agency.

Having considered the consumer's cognitive system, let us turn to considerations important to the advertising agency. Schudson cites four major questions which an advertising agency should consider in the process of mounting a campaign:

1. What is the product, and what, if anything, makes it distinctive?
2. Who is the audience or group of consumers most likely to be interested in the product?
3. Through what media can this target population be most efficiently reached?
4. What kind of advertising appeal will be most effective?[33]

These questions are similar to the discussion of persuasive strategizing in public communication contexts in the previous chapter. Indeed, regardless of context, many of the issues of persuasive strategizing are similar, as well as with issues related to campaigns in general, discussed in the next chapter. We will discuss issues related to constraints of the product, analyzing target audiences and selection of media. In the next section we will discuss in more detail message strategies in advertising campaigns.

Constraints of the product. In any communication situation, the subject or topic places constraints on the communication transaction. In advertising the topic is usually referred to as the "product" even though that may mean a commodity for sale, a politician, an image, or a charity to be supported.

There are obvious differences between *types of products* that consumers buy on a regular basis, such as cleaning products, gasoline, or food, and larger, more durable goods, such as automobiles or homes. Advertisers also distinguish between "search goods" which can be judged on sight (such as jewelry or photographic equipment) and "experience goods" which must be used to be evaluated (such as foods or toothpaste).[34]

One could also classify non-profit institutions as self-help, educational, or care structures. Political candidates are already over-classified as conservative, liberal, independent, or whatever.

Advertisers may also classify goods according to the type of message processing expected from consumers. Foote, Cone & Belding suggest a two-dimensional classification of goods which are either high or low "involvement" with consumers on the one hand and "thinking" or "feeling" products on the other. Their classification system has been presented in a table by Schudson[35] like this:

	Thinking	Feeling
High Involvement	car, house, furniture	jewelry, cosmetics, apparel, motorcycles
Low Involvement	food, household items	cigarettes, liquor, candy

It is interesting to note not only the message implications of this classification but also the development of these possibilities suggested by the reality and arousal dimensions discussed in Chapter 3. We are particularly struck by the possibilities of relating particular products to the various motives and values in the cognitive system. Unfortunately, few of these classification schemes have been supported with scholarly research. They do, however, suggest the importance of considering how the subject or product itself will affect the persuasive communication in advertising.

Another characteristic of products or candidates which may affect the persuasive transaction is what advertisers refer to as *positioning*. This refers to a product's or candidate's image in relation to other products or candidates. For instance, many products appeal to the fact that they are "number one" in volume of sales, implying that they are also the best in quality. Others advertise, "We're number two; we work harder."

Advertisers also need to consider what niche of the market their product may capture. Certainly Oldsmobiles are designed to appeal to a different segment of the market than Cadillacs, Porsches, or Volvos.

Much is said of the political candidate's position on the political spectrum or on particular issues in relation to the position of other candidates. You may hear it said, "Our candidate is trying to attain a position slightly to the left of Reagan but more moderate than Kennedy on this one."

Still another product variable which advertisers consider is its position in the *life cycle* of the product. Advertising strategy is different if the agency is attempting to introduce a new product, expand an existing product into new markets, revitalize the image of an established product, or hold onto a market share in the face of intense competition by new products.

Perhaps the most important constraint placed on advertising by a product or candidate is that of the product's or candidate's *unique features*. Earlier we spoke of product differentiation as a mediator of consumer behavior. One method of product differentiation is what has been called the *unique proposition* or what we have called, in our discussion of public persuasion, *central idea* or *theme*. The question is, "What unique proposition distinguishes a particular product or candidate from all others?" In an attempt to expand its market, the orange juice industry developed the unique proposition, "Orange juice—it's not just for breakfast anymore."

Perhaps one of the most successful unique propositions of all time was the claim of the then-new toothpaste, Crest, that it had been "accepted by the American Dental Association" as an effective decay-prevention product. Although several other toothpaste products soon followed with flouride-based additives, Crest was already differentiated from the pack by its original claim. For the short period that Crest was indeed the only toothpaste "accepted by the American Dental Association," that unique feature of the product provided the basis for an extremely effective persuasive appeal through advertising.

Similarly, a distinctive appeal is usually emphasized with political candidates. In the Democratic Primary of 1984, with eight attractive candidates appearing in joint debates, only Gary Hart was able successfully to break out of the pack and challenge Walter Mondale for the nomination. Even John Glenn's name recognition as a former astronaut was not sufficient. Hart was able to distinguish himself by retaining traditional Democratic values, while repudiating former Democratic solutions and calling for new approaches for old constituencies. Likewise, Jesse Jackson, whom many considered unelectable, was able to hold on until the convention because of his unique appeal to a significant segment of voters.

The target audience.   In addition to the constraints of the product, advertisers are concerned with the types of groups of listeners for whom the advertisement is intended. Although this entire text, especially Chapter 3, should add insight into consumer behavior, we are here interested in what variables advertisers look at when considering their target audience. As in the case of the public persuasion context, there are demographic and topic-specific considerations. Of the variety of demographic variables that could be useful to advertisers, the age, life-style, economic status, and sex of consumers are particularly valuable.

As members of the "baby boom" of the post-World War II era progress in *age,* advertisers will shift the emphasis of their national ads to appeal to that group. Further, different products appeal to different ages, and advertisements are designed to meet that reality.

Life-style is also of concern to advertisers. Earlier we pointed out a shift in families from the traditional nuclear family to a multiplicity of family arrangements, particularly single-parent and single person households, and an increase in both spouses working outside the home. Given these changes in life-style, advertisers and producers may re-evaluate their approach to advertising several kinds of products. Advertising for housing may focus more toward amenities and less on features that require maintenance. Appliances and clothing advertising stresses comfort. Convenience foods, unheard of a generation ago, continue to grow in popularity.

Another audience variable of particular interest to advertisers is *economic status.* The affluent consumer is, of course, more able to respond to a variety of advertising appeals since price is less of an issue. People with money are better "qualified" to buy a larger range of products. Hence, advertisers pay far more attention to the affluent than to the poor.

The fourth, and probably most important, demographic consumer variable for advertisers is *sex.* The primary audience of most advertising is women. Except for such male-dominated markets as certain sporting goods, hardware, and entertainment, women are seen to dominate the marketplace. They not only participate in joint decisions about housing, automobiles, and vacations, but they are the primary purchasers of food, household goods, children's toys and clothing, and even participate heavily in the purchase of men's clothing and toiletries. We shall see in a moment how this may affect advertising messages.

Important as these demographic variables are to advertisers, appeals to *specific audiences* have become even more important. As we pointed out in Chapter 3, not only are cultural values changing, but a greater recognition and acceptance of ethnic minorities and other subcultures is developing. As Yankelovich pointed out, perhaps the most significant change in values generally is the move toward greater heterogeneity. Greater heterogeneity among consumers calls for greater differentiation by advertisers.

For instance, in spite of a general tendency toward convenient and inexpensive products advertisements for Maytag appliances appeal to a segment of the population who either still holds the Puritan value of well-made and lasting products or who is "backlashing" against high repair costs. The advertisements feature a poor, lonely Maytag repairman who seldom gets a call, so well are Maytag appliances constructed. Other ads which are designed to appeal to highly specific segments of the population are those recreational vehicles picturing retired couples, and those for the American Express card urging the specialized group of Americans who travel abroad, "Don't leave home without it."

A special segment of the audience upon which advertisers concentrate is the *heavy user.* A small segment of the population consumes the lion's share of many products. This is true not only of specialized products such as cycling gear, but also of such common products as catsup, soft drinks, and beer.[36]

The "heavy-user" phenomenon applies to the political and social arenas as well as buying behavior. It is not the general public represented in opinion polls that the politician needs to win over, but those who are most likely to appear at the polls. With the voting rate in the U.S. hovering around 50 percent, identifying those most likely to act on their convictions should be of significance to the political advertiser.

Similarly, people who give to one charity are more likely to give to another. It seems that being involved in service to others, whether personally or financially, causes people to image themselves in their cognitive system as caring, involved people.

In an interesting experiment, Freedman and Fraser[37] asked people in an average neighborhood to display a three-inch-square sign on their front lawn that read, "Be a Safe Driver." Two weeks later these same people and a comparable group who had not received the initial request were asked to display a large, unattractive, poorly-lettered sign reading, "Drive Carefully." Among the control group who had made no prior commitment, 83 percent refused. Somewhat surprisingly, among the group who had complied to the previous request (and thereby imaged themselves as involved) 76 percent *agreed* to display the unattractive sign in their front yards.

The well-known saying, "If you want to get something done, ask a busy person," can be extrapolated to, "If you want a purchase, vote, or contribution, solicit the person who already purchases, votes, and gives." In short, advertisers try to target the heavy user.

Not only do advertisers adapt to greater heterogeneity among segments of their audience, but they also adapt to *specific dimensions* of consumers' cognitive systems. In an attempt to alter the perception that Geritol is a diet supplement for the elderly advertisers used testimonials by Evonne Gooligong and Nancy Lopez, young professional athletes, to suggest that Geritol is also for the young. Similarly, Pro Football Hall of Fame defensive tackle Merlin Olsen is featured in advertisements for FTD bouquets, suggesting that even strong, "manly" men appreciate flowers.

Selection of media.   A third important consideration of advertising campaigns is the selection of media. The media vary considerably in their appropriateness to specific products, audiences, and messages within the persuasive transaction.

A primary consideration of advertising agencies in selecting media is the *cost per thousand,* or CPM. The CPM is the ratio of the cost of the ad to the number of potential consumers reached by the ad. Hence, if advertisements costing the same amount of money could be placed in two different media, the agency would probably select the medium that reached the most potential consumers. Conversely, media which reach more consumers can justify higher costs. This is why advertising on network television is more costly during prime time than at hours when the viewing audience is small.

If CPM were the only consideration, media selection would be simple, straightforward, and transmissional. From our transaction perspective, however, selection, of media must be individualized to the specific situation.

Obviously, it would make no sense for a local business or political candidate to advertise on network television. However, even multi-national corporations must decide to what degree they will select international, national, regional, or local media. National airlines such as American, Eastern, United, and Delta choose to devote most of their advertising to local media, especially newspapers.[38] If you wish either to sell or buy an outboard motor, you would probably turn to the classified ads in your newspaper on the "nickle ads" at your supermarket—highly specialized media for individualized transactions.

Generally, media separate naturally into national, regional, or local audiences. Network television as well as magazines and newspapers with wide circulation (such as *Time, Newsweek, The Wall Street Journal* or *The New York Times*) are well suited to nation-wide campaigns, either for brand-name products, candidates for national office, or issues of national interest. Messages about candidates or products of regional or local interest are usually carried in local newspapers, radio stations, local T.V. channels, billboards, or circulars.

However, an agency promoting a newly-released recording could do so by sending a copy to local radio stations all around the country. Conversely, an agency wishing to advertise a national brand-name product on a limited basis could do so by contracting for advertisements in selected local media. Such selective exposure of advertising is called "spot" advertising.

In addition, agencies frequently use a combination of national and local media. You have probably had the experience of seeing an advertisement on network television and hearing the soundtrack of that ad on a local radio station sometime later.

Advertisers must not only select from among national and local media, but consider general and specific audiences as well. Products such as soaps, cosmetics, and gasoline appeal to vitually the entire population and, hence, are well suited to a variety of media, especially the one that can produce the lowest CPM.

On the other hand, many products and their advertising messages are designed to appeal to more specialized audiences. In general, people who travel by commercial airlines tend to be in a higher income bracket than people who travel by bus. Many people who fly regularly do so on business. Hence, an agency handling an advertising campaign for an airline may choose to advertisement in *The Wall Street Journal,* the Business or Travel section of the newspaper, or a radio station which airs business news or classical music (which tend to draw listeners from higher socio-economic brackets). One local radio station we know that plays music popular from the 1940s through 1960s airs advertisements for products that appeal to middle-aged to older people.

Hence, although regional and local media may not be able to boast the lowest general CPM, they may be able to reach more specific potential consumers of specific products, candidates, or issues. This phenomena of specific appeals to specific audiences explains the remarkable effectiveness and increasing popularity of advertising through direct mail to selected mailing lists of highly qualified potential consumers.

/ Message Strategies. Having discussed the consumer's cognitive system and considerations of the agency, including constraints of the product, audience analysis, and media selection, let us now turn to message strategies which result from the interaction of the foregoing considerations. It is not our purpose to explicate a comprehensive analysis of message strategies characteristic of advertising copy. Indeed, the current status of research would not permit such a goal. We will attempt to synthesize some of the most prominent message strategies agreed upon by major media analysts and relate those strategies to the dimensions of people's cognitive systems discussed in Chapter 3. We will discuss message strategies of advertising which interact with the reality, arousal, goal, and relational dimensions of the cognitive system or with combinations of these.

Reality dimension. In our discussion of the reality dimension in Chapter 3, we discussed how beliefs and attitudes are analyzed and organized into arguments. We further pointed out that arguments were based on claims grounded in data or the assertion of data. Further we said that a primary consideration in the use of data was its representativeness, since a communicator could never acquire all of the relevant data, let alone communicate it in limited time and space.

At last we can see the earth as it really is. This small, pale ball floating in the vastness of space. Clearly with limits. Vulnerable, fragile.

For almost 100 years the Sierra Club has been fighting to protect the earth's fragile systems. We have successfully lobbied for laws to limit air and water pollution and to regulate poisonous toxic chemicals. We have won protection for swamps and meadows, rivers and mountains, deserts and prairies. . .those natural places which permit the earth to heal and renew itself. We have consistently been an effective voice for a world healthful for all its inhabitants.

The unique power of the Sierra Club springs from our active grass roots membership. . .volunteers who give freely of their time and expertise. If you want to participate in this work, or share in the satisfaction of it through a supporting membership, please use the membership form attached here.

MEMBERSHIP FORM

☐ YES. I want to join! Please enter a membership in the category checked below:

Name _____

Address _____

City/State _____ Zip _____

MEMBERSHIP CATEGORIES

	Individual	Joint
Regular	☐ $29	☐ $38
Supporting	☐ $50	☐ $58
Contributing	☐ $100	☐ $108
Life	☐ $750	
	(per person)	

SPECIAL CATEGORIES

Senior	☐ $15	☐ $23
Student	☐ $15	☐ $23
Spouse of Life	☐ $15 (annual dues)	

All dues include subscription to *Sierra* ($6) and chapter publications ($1).

SIERRA CLUB

Dept. J-210
P.O. Box 7603
San Francisco,
CA 94120-7603

/ The Sierra Club targets a specific audience that is concerned with environmental issues by advertising in such publications as *Harrowsmith*, *The Country Journal*, *Audubon*, and others.

This problem of communicating large volumes of information in limited time or space is exacerbated in advertising, especially over broadcast media allowing fifteen- to sixty-second spots. Consequently, as Schudson[39] points out, the content of advertising messages tends to *simplify* and *typify* its data and the claims drawn from it. If, as it is frequently claimed, mediated presidential debates of one to three hours oversimplify the issues, how much more will brief advertisements do so?

Slogans such as "It's the real thing" or the bumper sticker "I fight poverty—I work" not only simplify the claim, but omit the data altogether. Unfortunately, complex issues are not well analyzed nor problems solved by clichés.

Not only do advertisements simplify the message, they tend to typify it as well. That is to say, situations selected for advertising are not real nor individualized but are selected to represent a "typical" situation, person, or place. Thus, ads may represent a typical long-distance call, a typical after-work drink, or a typical recreation setting. Furthermore, actors and actresses are selected for ads to represent typical housewives from twenty-five to forty years of age, or typical children, or medical doctors, or whatever category the ad requires. This, of course, not only appeals to consumers' tendency to think in categories and stereotypes but, as some critics claim, even reinforce those categories, stereotypes, and, ultimately, values.

A further characteristic of advertising messages alluded to by Schudson is their *idealization.* That is, the content of advertising messages represents the situation or data, not as it is encountered in real life, but as the advertisers and consumers might wish reality to be. Hence, the actors appearing in ads are usually attractive people in idealized settings engaging in idealized interactions. While the *simplification, typification* and *idealization* of content make advertisements more appealing to consumers, they also make it difficult for the viewer to evaluate advertisements on the reality dimension.

Arousal dimension. In the process of strategizing their messages, advertisers do not neglect the arousal dimension of consumers' cognitive systems. They are conscious not only of the initiation of arousal (more commonly referred to as "grabbing attention"), but also of the listeners' general state of arousal as well. Getting attention has long been a concern not only of advertisers but of salespersons, politicians, and public speakers as well. Without attention, the remainder of the message is certainly superfluous, and in many cases drawing attention to the product may be all a brief ad can accomplish. This depends, of course, on the consumer and the nature of the transaction. For instance, people who are scanning the want ads for inserts in the local newspaper are looking for particular products and their attention is sufficiently aroused to preclude the necessity of elaborate attention-getters. However, advertisements that interrupt compelling radio or TV broadcasts or are isolated in a newspaper or magazine must vie with any number of competing stimuli for people's attention.

In order to attract attention and stimulate arousal in the form of interest, psychologists and rhetoricians emphasize *content* which is vital (or salient), familiar, contains conflict or suspense, arouses curiosity, or provides resolution, release, or humor.[40] An examination of advertisements reveals the use of all of these, especially the vital, conflict, and humor.

Students of communication further recommend as a strategy for arousal the use of *language* which is vivid, contrasting, novel, active, familiar, and concrete. Advertising copy is characterized by all of these adjectives as well as being simple to the point of being ungrammatical at times.

If advertisers are concerned with getting attention and stimulating interest, they have not neglected the *general arousal* or emotions of consumers. Indeed, in an examination of the content of the trade journal *Printers Ink,* from 1888 to the 1950s, Merle Curti found that advertisers' image of consumer behavior shifted from seeing consumers as basically rational to seeing them as basically emotional.[41] This perspective of listeners' cognitive systems may seem overly simplistic in view of the complex interrelationship of dimensions discussed in Chapter 3. However, if advertisers do view consumers as basically emotional, that view should be reflected in the content of advertisements. And indeed it is.

Strong appeals to sex, youth, activity, and other stimulating appeals are evident in modern advertising. So in tune are advertisers with what we have called the arousal dimension of people's cognitive systems that they even "talk of locating 'hot buttons' to sell a new product."[42] Although such manipulative claims perhaps could not be demonstrated by research, and we even doubt that we could recognize a "hot button" if we saw one, at least advertisers seem to believe they exist and attempt to strategize their ads accordingly.

Goal dimension.   Advertisers also place emphasis on motives and values in their message strategies. Appeal to virtually all of Maslow's hierarchy of motives may be found in modern advertising. A variety of ads appeal to consumers' physiological motives for food, sex, and movement. Insurance companies and others appeal to people's goal of safety. A variety of ads for products from soft drinks to greeting cards appeal to our need to belong, while any number of cosmetics, clothing, or automobile ads seemingly promise to build consumer's self-esteem. Appeals to self-actualization are no more subtle: consider the appeal to "Be all that you can be—in the Army."

Advertisers also make appeals to cultural values. Unlike the 1960s when patriotism was openly scorned, increasingly advertising campaigns make unabashed appeals to patriotism, as in Chrysler's slogan, "The Pride Is Back—Born in America."

Relational dimension.   Finally, advertisers appeal to the relational dimension of consumers' cognitive systems in several ways. As we discussed in Chapter 4, people's cognitive systems and particular behavior are influenced by *modeling* the behaviors of respected others.[43] Consider the extensive use of sports, entertainment, and even political celebrities in national advertising. William "The Refrigerator" Perry downs cases of Coca-Cola, Chris Evert Lloyd recommends Lipton Iced Tea Mix, and former Chicago Mayor Jane Byrne sings of reading USA Today "every day." However, as Schudson points out, in creating these role models, the celebrities are representing not themselves but images with which consumers can relate. Thus when actress Sandy Duncan wades through a field of grain for Wheat Thins, she represents not the real person

Sandy Duncan, but a category of sweet, attractive, soft-spoken, and especially slender people who presumably got that way and stay that way by eating Wheat Thins.

A second way advertisers appeal to the relational dimension is by appealing to *authority.* Recall that research has identified authority or competence as one of the major contributors to interpersonal trust or source credibility. Thus you may see a champion auto racer endorse Champion spark plugs or an Olympic gold medal winner endorse Wheaties. Although these "authorities" may not meet the formal tests of reasoning from authority, they do create the semblence of authority and appeal to the cognitive system of consumers on the relational dimension.

Advertisers do not stop there, however. In order to create a further semblance of authority they hire actresses and actors to play roles designed to appeal to consumers' trust derived from an image of competence and integrity.

Perhaps the most widely cited example of this phenomenon is actor Robert Young, the nice guy in *Father Knows Best* and *Marcus Welby, M.D.,* endorsing medical products. Although most people know Young is an actor and not a physician, he does receive serious requests for medical advice and represents the joint authority figure of both parent and physician. In addition, his roles have enhanced his image of character and integrity.

A third way that advertisers appeal to the relational dimension is by casting their product in the role of enhancing highly valued *interpersonal relationships.* Thus, Taster's Choice coffee ads present extremely idealized and typified situations with the unique proposition, "Times like these were made for Taster's Choice."

Combination of dimensions. Perhaps the most powerful ads appeal to a *combination of more than one dimension* of the cognitive system simultaneously. Thus, we see ads which depict highly active work or play situations, picturing highly (usually sexually) attractive people and then advance the unique proposition that it's "Miller time." Not only do these ads emphasize arousal through sex and vitality and attractive interpersonal relationships, but they also appeal simultaneously to the traditional, Puritan value of hard work and the increasingly popular and somewhat hedonistic value of "having fun."

Similarly, Bell Telephone ads urging us to "Reach out and touch someone" appeal to emotional arousal, intimate interpersonal relationships, motives of love or belongingness, and values of family, security, and sometimes patriotism all rolled into a thirty-second TV spot.

/ Advertising and Society

Consumers' active interaction with advertising is affected not only by their cognitive systems, messages, and media but also by the socio-psychological *context* within which the transaction occurs. Schudson discusses several aspects of the social and psychological context that affect the consumer-advertisement transaction.

He first emphasizes the social nature of what he calls "needs" (what we have called motives and values in the goal dimension of people's cognitive systems). Most needs are not physiological, but are socially and culturally produced. As Schudson states, needs are "culturally coded and socially organized."[44] Furthermore, in cultures such as middle class America where physiological needs are readily met with a wider variety of options, media information increases people's choices. This makes the fulfillment of goals even more socially determined.

Of particular interest to Schudson as an aspect of advertising's social context is *gift-giving*. He points out that gift-giving constitutes an important part of interpersonal relationships, cementing relationships between friends and family members.

Although in some cases gifts of utilitarian value are exchanged, the less utilitarian the gift, the more social value it may have. Even the exchange of greeting cards or flowers for Christmas and other special occasions serve to strengthen interpersonal relationships. Schudson goes so far as to place gift-giving "at the heart of the social order."[45] Whether it is that important or not, gift-giving prompts increased buying for holidays like Christmas, Valentine's Day and for special events like weddings and graduation, along with a corresponding increase in advertising.

Another aspect of advertising's social context emphasized by Schudson is the need for people to determine their *place in society*. In more rigid cultures, he points out, a person's status (or casts) may be determined by birth, vocation, or inherited wealth. In more open, democratic societies, status is derived in greater measure from individual achievement which, in a capitalistic society, is usually manifest in acquired income or wealth. Income and wealth are not directly visible but are reflected in the purchase and display of consumer goods such as automobiles, homes, and clothing.

Schudson perceptively points out that what people seek is not status (as Thorstein Veblen and Vance Packard claim) but rather *social membership*. People stretch their budgets to buy a home in a particular neighborhood in order to identify with the kinds of people who live in that neighborhood. They buy a brand of automobile or designer jeans in order to establish similar identifications. According to Schudson, most consumers are not trying to get ahead of their neighbors but just want to be accepted by a social group they respect. Schudson's insightful discussion of the social nature of consumer's "needs" can be expanded beyond what Maslow called "belongingness" to the full spectrum of motives and values discussed in Chapter 3.

I Theory I Practice I Analysis

Theory

1. Societal persuasion is achieved by interaction between the media and interpersonal channels.

2. Media communication involves transaction in which media organizations and consumers are equal partners.

3. Persuasive outcomes of media communication affect individuals, organizations, institutions, the society, and the culture.

4. Outcomes include individual change, fulfillment of needs and goals, agenda settings, socio-cultural reality formation, and diffusion of innovations.

5. Advertisements can range from national brands, candidates, and charities to local dealerships, products, and candidates, as well as specific products and issues to classified advertisements.

6. Commercial advertising can serve the functions of information dissemination, social control, and product sales.

7. The cognitive system of consumers, including other sources of information, skepticism, and price, can influence their interaction with advertising. Certain types of consumers such as the highly mobile, immobile, poor, or young may be particularly susceptible to persuasion by advertising.

8. In creating their campaigns, advertising agencies give serious consideration to specific issues related to the type of product, analysis of the audience, and selection of media.

9. Message strategies appeal to all four dimensions of the cognitive system by such techniques as simplification, typification, idealization, and modeling, as well as appeals to values, motives, arousal, and authority.

Practice

1. Consider some ways in which you could improve your use of media. Actively develop some new media-use rules and try to follow these for a brief period of time. Then decide whether to continue the rules, modify them, or abandon them altogether.

2. Think of some aspect of a television or radio program, newspaper, periodical, or other medium with which you find fault. Think of ways to exert influence to correct that fault. Now carry through on your plan.

3. Think of a personal need or goal that is unfulfilled. How might you use the media to accomplish the goal or meet the need in ways you are not now doing? Make a change in your media consumption habits that will bring about more complete fulfillment of the goal or need.

4. Think of an unattractive behavior that can be done to both a mild and more extreme degree (like the displaying of an unattractive sign on one's front lawn). Clear with your instructor the social acceptability of your proposal. Select a group of people and ask half of them to comply with the mild request. Later, ask both those who complied and those who did not participate the first time to comply with the more undesirable behavior. Compare the results.

Analysis

1. Become an observer in a household to which you have access (other than your own). Over a period of at least three days, carefully observe the media consumption habits of the members of the household. From your observations, infer the media rules used by members of this household. Now interview each member to test your hypothesized rules and to discover how the rules came into existence.

2. Collect several advertisements for the same product or competing products. Analyze their content for appeals to various dimensions of the cognitive system.

Notes

[1]Werner Severin and James W. Tankard, *Communication Theories: Origins, Methods, and Uses* (New York: Hastings House Publishers, 1979), p. 8.

[2]Denis McQuail, *Mass Communication Theory: An Introduction* (Beverly Hills: Sage Publications, 1983), p. 209.

[3]See, for example, Raymond Bauer, "The Obstinate Audience: The Influence Process from the Point of View of Social Communication," *American Psychologist* 19 (1964): 319–28.

[4]James Lull, "A Rules Approach to the Study of Television and Society," *Human Communication Effects: Review and Commentary,* in *Communication Yearbook I,* ed. Brent D. Ruben (New Brunswick: Transaction Books, 1977), p. 65.

[5]Adapted loosely from Nan Lin, "Communication Effects: Review and Commentary," in *Communication Yearbook I,* ed. Brent D. Ruben (New Brunswick: Transaction Books, 1977), p. 65.

[6]This discussion of rules is based on Lull, "Rules."

[7]McQuail, *Mass Communication,* pp. 168–70.

[8]Michael Schudson, *Advertising, The Uneasy Persuasion: Its Dubious Impact on American Society* (New York: Basic Books, Inc., 1984), pp. 56–58.

[9]McQuail, *Mass Communication,* pp. 178–80.

[10]Adapted from McQuail, *Mass Communication,* pp. 178–80.

[11]James A. Anderson and Robert K. Avery, "An Analysis of Changes in Voter Perception of Candidates' Positions," *Communication Monographs* (November 1978): 354–61.

[12]The classical position on this issue is that of Joseph Klapper, *The Effects of Mass Communication* (Glencoe, IL: Free Press, 1960).

[13]Melvin L. DeFleur and Sandra Ball-Rokeach, *Theories of Mass Communication* (New York: Longman, 1982), pp. 232–56.

[14]DeFleur and Ball-Rokeach, *Theories,* p. 243.

[15]This outcome is elaborated in *The Uses of Mass Communication,* ed. Jay Blumler and Elihu Katz (Beverly Hills: Sage, 1974). Specific functions outlined in this section are taken from Charles R. Wright, "Functional Analysis and Mass Communication," *Public Opinion Quarterly* 24 (1960): 605–620.

[16]Wright, "Functional Analysis."

[17]See Donald L. Shaw and Maxwell E. McCombs, *The Emergence of American Political Issues* (St. Paul: West Publishing, 1977).

[18]Shaw and McCombs, *Emergence,* p. 21.

[19]Walter Lippman, *Public Opinion* (New York: MacMillan, 1921).

[20]Shaw and McCombs, *Emergence,* p. 5.

[21]Everett Rogers and F. Floyd Shoemaker, *Communication of Innovations,* 2nd ed. (New York: Free Press, 1971); Everett M. Rogers and D. Lawrence Kincaid, *Communication Networks* (New York: The Free Press, 1981).

[22]Rogers and Shoemaker, *Communication,* p. 276.

[23]This outcome is discussed by Dan Slater and William R. Elliott, "Television's Influence on Social Reality," *Quarterly Journal of Speech* 68 (1982): 69.

[24]S. Watson Dunn and Arnold M. Barban, *Advertising: Its Role in Modern Marketing,* 5th ed. (New York: The Dryden Press, 1982), p. 7.

[25]This discussion is adapted from Kim Rotzoll, James Haefner and Charles Sandage, *Advertising in Contemporary Society* (Columbus, OH: Grid, Inc., 1976).

[26]James W. Carey, "Advertising: An Institutional Approach in *The Role of Advertising,* ed. C. H. Sandage and V. Fryburger (Homewood, IL: Irwin, 1960), p. 13.

[27]Vincent Norris, "Toward the Institutional Study of Advertising," *Occasional Papers in Advertising* 1 (Jan. 1976): 59–73.

[28]David Potter, *People of Plenty* (Chicago: University of Chicago Press, 1954).

[29]Donald Strickland, "Alcohol Advertising: Orientations and Influence," *Journal of Advertising* 1 (1982): 307.

[30]Strickland, "Alcohol," p. 318.

[31]Strickland, "Alcohol," p. 319.

[32]Schudson, *Advertising.*

[33]Schudson, *Advertising,* p. 46.

[34]Schudson, *Advertising,* p. 51.

[35]Schudson, *Advertising,* p. 51.

[36]Dick Tweldt, "How Important to Marketing Strategy is the Heavy User?" *Journal of Marketing* 28 (January 1964): 71–72.

[37]Jonathan L. Freedman and Scott C. Fraser, "Compliance Without Pressure: The Foot-in-the-Door Technique," *Journal of Personality and Social Psychology* 4 (1966): 195–203.

[38]*Advertising Age,* 8 (September 1983): 8.

[39]Schudson, *Advertising,* p. 215.

[40]David M. Jabusch, *Public Speaking: A Transactional Approach* (Boston: Allyn and Bacon, Inc., 1985), p. 104.

[41]Merle Curti, "The Changing Concept of 'Human Nature' in the Literature of American Advertising," *Business History Review* 41 (Winter 1967): 335–57.

[42]Schudson, *Advertising,* p. 58.

[43]See Albert Bandura, *Social Learning Theory* (Englewood Cliffs, NJ: Prentice-Hall, 1977).

[44]Schudson, *Advertising,* p. 131.

[45]Schudson, *Advertising,* p. 136.

11 / Persuasive Communication in Social Movements and Campaigns

For a few years following the Civil War, emancipated blacks in the South began to enjoy their newly acquired political and economic rights. When federal support for this "radical reconstruction" was withdrawn, however, political, economic, and social opportunity for blacks was systematically withdrawn by the white power structure. The situation was institutionalized by the U.S. Supreme Court in 1896 when, in the case of *Plessy vs. Fergerson,* it handed down its "separate but equal" doctrine. Little happened to enhance the human rights of ethnic minorities for six decades thereafter.

In 1954 the United States Supreme Court, in the case of *Brown vs. Board of Education,* set aside the *Plessy* decision and mandated the integration of public schools "with all deliberate speed." A few school districts quietly compiled, but ugly scenes and skirmishes occurred in others. Progress was slow and blacks were still discriminated against at lunch counters, motels, and the working place.

In 1956 a remarkable event occurred in Montgomery, Alabama, which changed the course of history. On her way home from work a weary Rosa Parks refused to relinquish her seat in the back of the bus to a white man. She was arrested and jailed, but an enraged black community, led by a young Baptist minister, boycotted the Montgomery buses until they won a more humane treatment on the public transit system. Martin Luther King, Jr., was catapulted to fame and there followed a variety of marches, sit-ins, and other demonstrations by blacks and whites throughout the country. In 1957 Congress passed the first Civil Rights Act in eighty-two years and ratified the Voting Rights Act of 1964 following the dramatic March on Washington in the summer of 1963. Black leaders such as Malcolm X, Stokley Carmichael, and Medgar Evers emerged. Organizations such as the NAACP, Black Panthers, and the National Urban League mounted campaigns on a variety of race-related issues. The Civil Rights Movement was given new life.

/ Social Movements

One of the most interesting and important phenomena of persuasion is the social movement.[1] Movements not only combine all forms and aspects of persuasion, but are important because of their prevalence and social significance. A *social movement* is an organized and large collectivity that aims to create or oppose fundamental social change. By definition, movements are not part of the establishment: they are uninstitutionalized. In addition, they always encounter opposition and make use of persuasion as an essential part of their action. We will examine in some detail these basic elements of the social movement: organization, scope, social change, lack of institutional status, opposition, and persuasion.

/ Characteristics of social movements

1. Movements are organized collectivities. By definition, social movements are not happenstance or random instances of influence in society. Rather, they are identifiable groups of individuals with similar goals. A movement cannot be identified as a single campaign or organization; rather, the movement consists of a related set of structures, called *social movement organizations.* Although the activities of a movement are diverse and rarely under single, coordinated leadership, there is almost always a loose connection among its various organizations.

In the movement of the New Christian Right, for example, several organizations can be identified, including the Moral Majority, the Christian Voice, the Roundtable, American Citizens for Traditional Values, and others. Each of these organizations acts independently, but there is a good deal of communication among them. They act, if not as a unified voice, as a set of fairly well coordinated voices. That condition is not always found in movements. In the Civil Rights Movement, for example, despite the strong and visible leadership of Martin Luther King, Jr., a variety of organizations emerged, some of which, like the Black Panthers and the Black Muslims, set themselves in opposition to King's message and method. In summary, then, when we talk about the organization of a movement, we are not referring to the kind of planned action found in a single organization.

2. Movements are large in scope. Movements extend over a significant geographic area. Thus, the issue of saving the snail darter is not likely to develop into a social movement, since the focus of the issue is confined to a few miles of a single western river. In contrast, movements related to human rights, arms limitations, or ecology are national, and sometimes international, in scope.

Movements are not only widespread geographically, but usually extend over a long period of time as well. If you think the Women's Movement began in the late 1960s, read some of Susan B. Anthony's speeches of a century earlier or the writings of Elizabeth Cady Stanton or Emma Goldman. Although the Women's

Movement may be unusual in its recurrence at various times throughout history, almost every movement extends over a period of at least several years.

One of the greatest frustrations of movement activists is the fact that, despite the apparent clarity and compelling nature of their aims, change does not happen overnight. For instance, the New Christian Right is a young movement, and we will have to wait and see how it develops. It has roots in nineteenth century Protestant militism and the Populist movement, and for this reason can hardly be regarded as brand new. The contemporary phase of the movement began in the 1970s, as outlined earlier. Some believe this movement is a mere flash in the pan, which would deny its movement status. We think it will endure throughout the 1980s, but a rereading in a few years will tell the tale.

3. Movements aim to create or combat social change. The *sine qua non* of movements is that they are directed toward a general goal of fundamental social change, or of opposition to such change. Movements advocating change are sometimes classified as *reformist.* Movements seeking to restore society to an earlier set of values perceived to be lost are often referred to as *revivalist.* Finally, *resistance* movements arise in opposition to social change itself. The Civil Rights Movement is an example of a reform movement, the New Christian Right represents a revivalist movement, and the counter-movement against the Women's Movement illustrates resistance.

/ **The anti-apartheid movement in South Africa, lead by Bishop Desmond Tutu, among others, is a reformist movement in that it advocates fundamental social change.**

4. Movements lack institutional status. The term *social movement* is reserved for groups that oppose some aspect of the establishment. Of course, the "establishment" is itself multifaceted, so opposition need only counter certain of a society's institutions. The anti-nuclear weapons movement, for example, generally opposes military and foreign policy institutions. Other movements are much broader in their opposition. The Women's Movement and the Civil Rights Movement have acted, at various times and in different ways, against almost all of our society's institutions. The New Christian Right is absolutely clear and focused on what it opposes.

5. Movements always encounter opposition. A movement without opposition is not a movement, according to the standard definition of the term. If movements meet all of the other criteria, then opposition is a natural outcome. Movement opposition typically comes from two sources: establishment opposition and countermovements.

The New Christian Right has met with vociferous and defamatory opposition by liberals in this county. Yale President A. Bartlett Giamatti has called the Moral Majority "dangerous, malicious nonsense."[2] Organizations like the American Civil Liberties Union and the Americans for Democratic Action have taken active stands in opposition. The People for the American Way was established as an organization in direct opposition to the New Christian Right and constitutes a possible core for a countermovement.

6. Movements use persuasion as a primary means of influence. Certainly, a variety of forms of influence may be used in movements, including violence and coercion. In general, movements combine tactics of the "carrot" and the "stick." "Carrot" strategies are inducements; "stick" strategies are threats. The carrot is used to enlist the participation of those who stand to benefit from the movement, and the stick is often used against agencies of power that stand in the way of achieving the movement's goals. Because most movements do not have many sources of power in comparison to establishment institutions, and because they lack the ability to provide material rewards and to harm through punishment, persuasion becomes an important instrument of the movement's activities. In fact, in surveying all of a movement's activities, both practical and symbolic, persuasion becomes an obvious dimension of almost all of them. As Simons has written, "Rather than being an alternative to inducements or constraints, persuasion in conflict situations is either an instrument, an accompaniment, or a consequence of the carrot and the stick."[3]

This is not to suggest that persuasion by itself is what makes the movement successful, or that inadequate persuasion causes a movement to fail. Although persuasion is probably a necessary condition in most movements, it is never sufficient to determine success or failure. That naive view, referred to as *rhetorical determinism,* must be put aside in favor of the more realistic idea that movement outcomes, both positive and negative, are a consequence of a variety of factors, including not only persuasion, but also leadership and access to social and material resources.

/ *The development of social movements*

Although no two movements ever follow exactly the same course, there is a general trend that can be useful in analyzing movements. Basically, movements tend to follow a five-stage course: (1) genesis, (2) social unrest, (3) enthusiastic mobilization, (4) maintenance, (5) termination. These are not discrete chronological steps, but are general phases through which most movements pass. The progress of a movement may waiver, go back and forth among categories, speed up and slow down. Also, different movements go through these stages in different ways; one movement may speed through a stage that takes another movement a very long time to complete. In the long run, however, these five stages fairly capture the general developmental trend.

/ *Genesis.*

Movements arise out of a genesis. The genesis stage of a movement usually occurs long before activists take the stage in a more visible drama. In the beginning, certain individuals feel unhappy about some state of affairs and begin formulating a basic critique and ideas for change. Often these individuals are intellectuals or artists who express discontent through literature, song, or other expressive forms. Slowly, a following develops, one that sows the seeds of activism.

The genesis of the New Christian Right involved four distinct events of the 1970s—the 1973 Supreme Court decision on abortion, the increasingly strong voice of the Gay Rights movement, the proposal to abolish the tax-exempt status of private schools, and the proposed Equal Rights Amendment. The reaction among fundamentalist Christians against these developments, combined with the long-established conservative ideology voiced by leaders such as Senator Barry Goldwater and William F. Buckley, Jr., and the early leadership of certain influentials, catalyzed the movement.

/ *Social Unrest.*

In the second stage, initial discontent and theorizing turns into social unrest. As the movement grows and activists become involved, the quiet discontent of genesis becomes more vocal and public. The first signs of opposition may arise, with members of establishment groups openly recognizing the protesters, but denying their importance or power. During this period arc developed the slogans of the movement and a polarization of attitudes in the form of a "we-they" confrontation.

At this point media attention may be attracted for the first time. Such attention is not strictly a function of planned publicity efforts, but may be shaped in large measure by the news media themselves. While news media may ignore a movement in its incipient phase, it will likely choose fairly innocuous events to cover when it first judges the movement to be newsworthy. Later, as movement activities accelerate, journalists will focus on more substantive issues. What journalists choose to cover determines in part the public perception and the future course of the movement.

The big push in the New Christian Right occurred in 1978, when such concerned Christian businessmen as Richard Viguerie, the mass-mailing expert; Paul Weyrich, the leader of the Committee for the Survival of a Free Congress; Howard Phillips, the leader of the Conservative Caucus; and Terry Dolan, a political activist, began communicating with members of the electronic church like the Reverend Jerry Falwell, who were themselves disenchanted with recent social and moral developments in the country. Falwell, for one, quickly fell into line with the early organizers and became a well-known leader of the New Christian Right.

/ *Enthusiastic Mobilization.*   The third stage of the movement, enthusiastic mobilization, is characterized by confidence and optimism. Membership is growing, publicity is increasing, and, having gotten their feet wet, leaders are putting enthusiastic energy into the movement. As the movement grows in strength, organizational challenges become paramount. Opposition grows, and leaders face new and important obstacles from within and without. There is a tendency in this phase to suppress conflict and build commitment within the movement. These internal objectives, like the external confrontation with opponents, require new forms of persuasion. In this stage, the movement will experience some important victories, and setbacks will be rationalized.

The mobilization stage came quickly for the New Christian Right. The Moral Majority was established in 1979 and became heavily involved in the kind of attention given to details at this point in a movement. During 1980, the movement became increasingly visible. The Christian Roundtable's Political Action Caucus, held in Dallas in June 1980, and Falwell's appearance at the Republican National Convention in Detroit that same summer so captured the nation's attention that the New Christian Right became a major news story on all three networks and in numerous newspapers and magazines throughout the country. At that time, opponents to the movement began to speak out vigorously against the actions of this group, most frequently accusing them of mixing politics and religion. The People for the American Way was established by television producer Norman Lear in 1980 to counteract the movement of the New Christian Right. The mobilization phase of the movement reached its summit with the stunning election of Ronald Reagan in 1980 and the defeat of several notable liberal congress members and senators the same year.

/ *Maintenance.*   The maintenance stage is a crucial turning point. The excitement of the mobilization phase cannot sustain itself indefinitely. There comes a time in the life of most movements when they must prepare to struggle for "the duration." This is a time when many members become disillusioned and drop out or become less active. Fund-raising becomes a bugaboo. The movement, as it becomes old hat to the public, loses its newsworthiness, and publicity begins to fade.

The mobilization period of the New Christian Right probably ended with the 1982 elections, which were not nearly as dramatic as those of 1980. By the

1984 elections, most of the movement's organizations were in place, and systems for communicating and acting were well established. Conservatism seemed the order of the day in American politics. Since 1984 the New Christian Right has been in a holding pattern, clearly implanted in the maintenance phase, and future years will reveal which form of termination the movement experiences.

/ Termination.　Termination can take several forms. Movements may terminate by fading away, disbanding, transforming into new forms, or becoming establishment. Often movements quiet down for a period of time, only to rise again in a new form. That has certainly been the case with the Women's Movement; peace movements, too, have come and gone with each conflict in which this country has been involved.

/ The general aims of social movements

Although each movement has its own objectives, there is a striking similarity in the general aims of most movements. This similarity derives from the common functions that must be fulfilled for any movement to grow and sustain itself.

/ The Aim to Transform.　First, movements aim to transform perceptions of history. Almost always, a movement is driven, in part, by its belief that society's erroneous image of events have led to the conditions of the present day. We are referring here not only to images of past events, but perceptions of the present, and even imaginings about the future. The movement then sets itself the task of changing these images. The Women's Movement, for instance, makes this a major objective, pointing out that the contributions of women exceeded what male-oriented history revealed. The New Christian Right also makes a point about how the historical mandates of the nation's founders have gone astray. In fact, one of the chief objectives of this movement is to return society to what is perceived to be the moral base of earlier times.

/ The Aim to Alter.　Second, movements aim to alter perceptions of society. This aim is two-fold: Movements attempt to change the perception of the opposition, and they try to change the in-group's image of itself. For example, the Civil Rights Movement had to change the public's perception of society's institutions from one of being neutral, or even positive, to inherently racist. The idea of "institutional racism" was used to capture this new image. At the same time, black leaders knew that the self-image of many black people in this country had to be improved. Thus, during the 1960s, slogans such as "Black is beautiful" and "Black Power" were used, setting perceptual transformation on its way. The New Christian Right has defined its enemies as the "secular humanists," defining their activities as "moral insanity," while it has also aimed to make fundamentalists believe that political activism is an important part of being a concerned Christian.

/ *The Aim to Prescribe.* The movement prescribes courses of action. Eventually, the movement must move from theory to practice—specific agendas for action must be proposed. This involves specifying who is to act, what they are to do, and how they are to do it. It means developing political and/or social plans. The anti-nuclear weapons movement quickly captured the idea of a nuclear weapons freeze as one of its chief objectives. Local and statewide initiatives and a congressional bill on the freeze were developed and pushed. Throughout the country, local groups and political action committees were established to promote candidates who supported the freeze and defeat those who did not.

The New Christian Right has made electoral politics a major objective and has established particular ways of bringing pressure to bear. The Christian Voice's congressional "moral report card," which rates each congress member's votes in terms of conservative morality, is an example of a rather specific action planned and carried through.

/ *The Aim to Mobilize.* Mobilization is a natural aim of all movements. The intentions developed by movements cannot be carried out without operational plans to go with them. These involve organizing, soliciting the cooperation of opinion leaders and other influentials, and putting pressure on opponents. The activities of the Civil Rights Movement illustrate this set of functions very well. That movement organized masses of civil rights workers, who staged sit-ins, the Montgomery bus boycott, the march from Selma to Birmingham, the march to Washington and the famous rally at the Lincoln Memorial, and many other events. The New Christian Right has its "Moral Majority Report," its leadership training sessions, its political caucuses, and many other organizing and mobilizing activities.

/ *The Aim to Maintain.* All movements must engage in self-maintenance activities. Setbacks and delays must be justified, if not rationalized. The power of the movement must be kept up, and visibility must be maintained. The anti-nuclear weapons movement has been handed defeat after defeat, as the MX and other new weapons systems have been approved, arms negotiations cancelled, and advocates of military strength elected to office. Maintaining and sustaining the movement has been very difficult. It will be interesting to see the form this movement takes with the conservative landslide in 1984, the start-up of new arms negotiations, and the retirement of Helen Caldicott, one of the movement's most important leaders. Already, new consciousness groups are being developed, and similar activities are being planned to provide a renewed sense of mission and sustenance to the movement.

In direct contrast, the New Christian Right has found the conservative swing of the 1980s to be a fountain of self-justification and renewal. The support of the White House for this movement has provided a legitimacy rarely found in social movements. In 1980, Reagan said at the Dallas Caucus, "I know you cannot support me, but I want you to know that I support you." By 1984, the relationship between the top leadership of the country and the New Christian Right went so far as to include a White House celebration of the establishment of the newest organization in the movement, American Citizens for Tradition Values, with Reagan and Bush in attendance. Such top-level support for a movement has not been seen since President John F. Kennedy's support of civil rights and his warm relationship with Martin Luther King, Jr., in the early 1960s.

These aims point to three kinds of persuasion that all movements must undertake. (1) They must establish a program of internal persuasion to recruit advocates, organize activities, and sustain commitment. (2) They must establish a program of external persuasion to accomplish social goals. (3) They must counteract the persuasion of opponents. The next three sections of the chapter deal with these persuasive actions.

/ Internal persuasion:

/ Persuasion and Ideology.
The ideology of the movement provides its basic foundation. Every movement must be based on a set of ideas or an image of the desirable. Although the term *ideology* has a variety of meanings, we use it here to describe this set of ideas and ideals on which the movement is based. It is, if you will, the movement's theory of the human condition. Such a theory provides a rationale for the mission of the movement.

The ideology of the Civil Rights Movement involves images of undoing years of discrimination and achieving equality through nonviolent resistance. The ideology of the Women's Movement involves equality in law, elimination of sex-role stereotypes, equal access to employment opportunities, and personal freedom. The ideology of the contemporary peace movement has embodied such concepts as nonviolent conflict resolution, disarmament, global security, and human survival. The ideology of the New Christian Right has been one of morality, biblical authority, and political activism. Each of these tenets is elaborated in some detail in the writings and rhetoric of the respective movement. The ideology is set apart from what is believed to be the prevailing ideals of the establishment and seeks to counteract or overcome those establishment ideals.

The ideologies of movements do not spring forth automatically. They must be developed, formulated, negotiated, and promulgated. Persuasion is an important tool in the establishment of a movement's ideological foundation. Ideologies are worked out in the interaction among those who speak on behalf of the movement's organizations.

The ideology of a movement is most often expressed, if not formulated, by its theoreticians. These individuals develop a rationale and philosophy supporting the aims of the movement. Usually theoreticians write their tracts early, often during or before the genesis of the movement, but that is not always the case. The theoreticians of the New Christian Right are conservative theologian Francis Schaeffer and the Baptist minister Tim LaHaye. Schaeffer's primary work on this subject is the *Christian Manifesto,* which provides a theological basis for the new morality in biblical literature and history, setting itself against the well-known *Humanist Manifesto.* Less philosophical in tone and more accessible to the average reader are LaHaye's *Battle for the Mind* and *Battle for the Family,* which set out some of the conceptual bases of the movement. Each of these tracts, like similar works in other movements, are persuasive in nature. They are designed to win converts or reinforce attitudes among believers. In fact, the most important function of such literature is often to provide justification to those who are already sympathetic but who lack an explicit conceptual basis for their feelings. When readers respond to such persuasion with the reaction, "Aha, I knew that all along," an important commitment-building outcome is being realized.

The ideology gives a movement an intellectual core, something that can be pointed to for self-justification. Ideology by itself, however, cannot make a movement. Many organizing activities must be undertaken, which means establishing leadership and garnering resources.

/ Persuasion and Organization.

Persuasion is used to organize a movement. Such organization involves establishing leadership and securing resources. Leadership makes or breaks a movement. Leaders may arise from the grass roots level, emerging in the social unrest period; or they may be professional, being recruited and serving in a paid capacity. Jerry Falwell is a professional leader in the New Christian Right. He was recruited in the early days of the movement to be the organizer and public face of the Moral Majority, and he continues to work in that capacity. Robert Dolan of the National Conservative Political Action Committee is another professional leader of the New Christian Right.

The contemporary Women's Movement is an interesting case in leadership. Because feminist values reject traditional male-oriented hierarchical forms of leadership, many groups in this movement have made concerted attempts to change that pattern. A group called The Feminists, for example, actually restricted the number of comments any member could make at a meeting, so that no one person could emerge as a clear "leader." This movement has leadership, of course, but it is a grass-roots form of leadership in which functions are shared and decisions made more often by consensus than by fiat.[4] This pattern of leadership is quite consistent with the functional approach to leadership discussed in Chapter 6.

The resources of a movement are very important in determining its success or failure. Money plays a significant role. The New Christian Right has been highly successful in fund-raising, especially through the use of direct-mail methods. Other resources are equally important. Movements need access to talent, time, and facilities. The most important resource of any movement is society's influentials. Well-known and respected people who align themselves with the movement usually further the cause. The anti-nuclear weapons movement was materially aided by the involvement of Senators Kennedy and Cranston. The Women's Movement saw progress through involvement of such individuals as Shirley Chisholm, Billy Jean King, Alan Alda, and Marlo Thomas. And, as we have already mentioned, President Reagan's involvement in the New Christian Right gave the movement invaluable support.

Clearly, persuasion functions in garnering all of these kinds of leadership and resources. The direct-mail campaign of the Moral Majority is a prime example of successful persuasion. Jerry Falwell became leader of the Moral Majority in direct response to the persuasive communications of some of his acquaintances, and he uses his persuasive skills to influence others in public appearances and through the mass media.

/ *Persuasion and Commitment.*

Perhaps the most important internal persuasive aim of movements is building commitment. Commitment involves solidarity and loyalty. It also means a willingness on the part of thousands, if not millions, of people to work on behalf of the movement. Economic incentives can be a motivator, but in social movements, symbolic and ideological rewards are usually more powerful. To the extent that individuals perceive that their self-esteem, status, power, and well-being are at stake, they will join the movement. In addition, people fight for cherished beliefs and values. This is one reason why ideology is so important to sustained commitment. Leadership is important, but the intrinsic rewards and motivations of participants depend far more on these symbolic/ideological factors than they do on charismatic leadership.

Such commitment is developed through persuasion. Messages designed to demonstrate the necessity of the movement, communicate how the movement provides opportunities to its members, appeal to one's sense of loyalty, and make use of the sense of responsibility are common in movement persuasion. Remember from our earlier discussion, however, that we are not talking about some all-seeing source communicating to a mass of would-be believers. We are referring to a network of persuasive communications, in which members and leaders talk among themselves.

An important aspect of the internal persuasion in a movement is image-building. Here communication aims to structure the perceptions of the advocates about themselves, the opponents, and the society at large. Four strategies are common: denial, differentiation, bolstering, and transcendence.

Denial involves reassurance about the purity and truth of the ideology. It might, for example, include statements that the movement remains on target, despite setbacks and misgivings. It often impunes the integrity and ethics of the opposition, in order to deny their accusations. The New Christian Right's division of the world into good and evil and its collective image of the moral war illustrates the denial strategy very well.

Differentiation enables the movement to justify its actions and modify images as necessary in order to adapt to change. How do members handle the inevitable shifts and modifications that occur in a movement's ideology and activity? They do so by differentiating what is happening with some outside or ultimate standard. So, for example, much of the persuasive communication in a movement will suggest that shifts are only temporary and are designed to adjust to changing circumstances. Or movement leaders may suggest that tactics are intensified or decelerated for pragmatic purposes, even though the core of belief remains unchanged. There is evidence, for example, that Jerry Falwell began moderating his positions in 1984. He even began to speak of liberating Christian women and providing support for women involved in dangerous pregnancies. Although such changes may appear mild from the outside, they created some adverse reaction from the extreme right, causing a disaffection among the most conservative members of the movement. As of this writing, it is not clear how this problem will be handled, but handled it must be.

The third common image-adjusting strategy is *bolstering*. This involves reaffirmation and collective recall. Bolstering messages prompt the supporters of the movement to remember earlier successes and recall their consistent commitment. One of the most common public statements from representatives of the New Christian Right is a recounting of the various successes achieved—membership increases, election victories, and support from the top.

Finally, *transcendence* appeals to a moral order above and beyond the experience of any person. Appeals to God and divinely-ordained principles are common. The ideology of the New Christian Right is based on such divine authority. Its "moral sanity" is believed simply to be based on God's intentions for human beings.

/ External persuasion

Dividing our discussion of movement persuasion into two sections, internal and external, may imply that persuasive communication is divided cleanly into these two types. That is not the case. Our division only suggests that the aims and dimensions of persuasion in these two fields are different. Actual persuasive messages and strategies often have the effect of accomplishing both internal and external persuasion.

External persuasion is largely a matter of translating ideology into action. Three kinds of activity are commonly found in movements, varying in terms of their use of speech and direct action. *Militant* strategies tend to rely on direct action, including boycotts, demonstrations, blockades, and other sometimes violent means. *Expressivist* strategies tend to be verbal and confrontative. They often involve strident and accusative speech and other forms of invective. *Moderate* strategies are those that try to adapt to the belief structure of the opponent, making use of speech and direct action as necessary. All three of these styles have utility, depending upon the immediate objective and the situation in which the advocate is working. They all involve, in varying degrees, the "carrot" and the "stick."

Simons and his colleagues, after conducting a rather extensive survey of literature on movements, identified ten rhetorical principles of social movements.[5] These are summarized in Table 11.1. This list rather nicely translates many of the observations about movements into communication terms. In so doing, the list presents a summary of social movement persuasion. Not all of these principles are observed by movement activists, but, in the view of Simons and his colleagues, these principles seem to mark successful movements in our society.

TABLE 11.1

Principles of Persuasion in Movements

1. Goals and strategies should be flexible· goals should be adapted to what is feasible, and strategies should be consistent with changing goals.
2. Goals should be written in hierarchical form from most obtainable to least.
3. Movements are most successful if supported by some segment of the society's elite.
4. Public communication should present the appearance that the group is willing to talk and to compromise.
5. Strategies should be developed to present favorable definitions of the group on the part of the larger public.
6. Moderate and more extreme factions should synchronize their efforts.
7. Pressure against adversaries should be persistent.
8. Working within the law or conducting classical nonviolent civil disobedience is usually more effective than acting in violent and offensively illegal ways.
9. Generally, the more change desired, the more militant the actions of the group must be.
10. The more militant the group's actions, the more effort must be expended to guard against backlash.

/ Persuasive Campaigns

On March 22, 1972, the Equal Rights Amendment to the United States Constitution was sent by Congress to the states for ratification. The politics of the rapid ratification by thirty-four states is well documented.[6] With four more states needed for ratification, only Indiana subsequently ratified the amendment and four states voted to rescind their previous ratification. In the face of mounting opposition it became clear the fight to ratify would be a close one.

On October 22, 1976, the Church of Jesus Christ of Latter Day Saints (Mormons) issued a public declaration opposing the E.R.A. The Mormon Church then began working actively to defeat the E.R.A. in unratified states. In the spring of 1978, perhaps in response to the move to extend the deadline for ratification of the E.R.A., the Mormon Church accelerated its activity into what may be called a campaign. In response to this activity, a group of angered members organized the "Mormons for E.R.A." campaign. These opposing Mormon campaigns were only two of many events and campaigns which became part of the continuing Women's Rights Movement.

/ Characteristics of campaigns

A *campaign* can be defined as a sequence of persuasive events which usually is narrower in scope than a movement and can be distinguished by several characteristics. First, a campaign has a *focused purpose*. In contrast to such general goals as "women's liberation" or "peace," a campaign may be focused on the deployment of the MX missile, the closure of a nuclear power plant, or the passage of the E.R.A.

Second, a campaign has an identifiable (although sometimes ineffectual) *organizational structure*. The American Cancer Society, the Buick Division of General Motors, or the Committee to Reelect the President are all identifiable organizations which have conducted campaigns. Further, every private institution and charitable organization has a "development" office specifically charged with conducting fund-raising campaigns.

Campaigns also have an *identifiable leader* or leadership structure. An advertising agency or charitable organization will usually assign a particular campaign to an individual within the organization. Every political campaign has its campaign manager.

Unlike movements, campaigns *need not encounter opposition*. Campaigns to raise funds for such charitable organizations as museums, artistic expression, medical research, and churches rarely encounter opposition. Their primary problems are countering ignorance and apathy, not the active countermovement or campaign of opposing forces. Although political, advertising, and conflicting campaigns on social issues encounter opposition, it is not an inherent characteristic of a campaign.

Like social movements, campaigns are characterized by *persuasive communication*. If political, advertising, or charitable organizations were able to force compliance on the part of voters, buyers, or contributors, campaigns would be unnecessary. Campaigns are by definition sequences of persuasive communication events.

In sum, while movements and campaigns share a common goals-orientation and involve persuasive communication, campaigns have a more focused purpose, organization, and leadership, and may or may not encounter opposition. Indeed, most movements are loose aggregations of smaller campaigns and individual events.

/ Campaign implementation: A functional model[7]

The preparation and execution of a successful campaign involves a complex process which includes a variety of considerations, stages, and functions. Some campaign analysts[8] have claimed that every successful campaign proceeds through a series of stages or specific steps. Other research indicates that while these "steps" seem to occur in most campaigns, they do not necessarily occur in any fixed order.[9] Hence, we will treat these "stages" as *functions* which will be found in most successful campaigns, but which will not always occur in the order that intuition would suggest. For instance, one intuitively would infer that planning and organizing a campaign should precede the mobilization of human and financial resources. However, in a recent race for the U.S. Senate the potential challenger conducted an extensive survey to determine the availability of personal support and financial contributions before deciding to run at all. While in most campaigns these functions will probably occur in roughly the order we discuss them here, individual circumstances may dictate otherwise. We will discuss planning, mobilization, legitimation, case building, and activation.

/ Planning Functions.   Careful planning is found in most successful campaigns. Not only does planning give the campaign direction, but it also lays the foundation for the succeeding functions as well as for the flexible adaptation of those functions to the immediate situation. Let us consider the planning functions of audience analysis, situation analysis, goal-setting, and basic strategy.

Analyzing target audiences.   From a transactional perspective, getting acquainted with the prospective audience or audiences among whom a campaign will be waged is of vital importance. Potential target audiences are first identified and then systematically analyzed for their key characteristics.

Identification of possible target audiences is necessary before they can be specifically analyzed. Campaigns which jump into a flurry of activity before deciding this crucial question may dissipate a great many precious resources. For instance, if you were a church member in favor of the Equal Rights Amendment and your church was actively campaigning against it among unratified state legislators, where would you target your campaign? Would your audiences include the church leadership or its membership? If the latter, which segment of the membership would you target? Would your audiences include specific state legislators, the general public, opinion makers, or the people behind the mass media? Or would you attempt to influence all of these "audiences"? Surely your strategies would vary according to the way you selected from among these diverse target audiences. Hindsight has shown that the Mormon Church, which targeted its own membership as potential campaign workers and specific legislators as its audience, was far more successful in its anti-E.R.A. campaign than were the Mormons for E.R.A., who targeted the general public through the mass media.

Having determined the target audiences, a campaign must *analyze* their *specific characteristics.* The methods selected for doing this depend upon the size and nature of the audience. If the target audience is small and well-defined, such as a sales client, a service club, or a state legislature, campaigners can use *individual contacts* for their analysis. Salespersons frequently work from personal referrals, or a campaign worker may have a personal contact in the targeted organization or legislature who can provide important, specific information about the target audience.

Many campaigns, however, are targeted for larger or less well-defined audiences. In this case, systematic *surveys,* combined with personal contacts, may be necessary. Survey research of target audiences must be conducted with great care, using methodologies well-known to trained professionals. For example, surveys drawn from telephone directories predicted Alf Landon would defeat Franklin Delano Roosevelt in 1936. F.D.R. was provided his margin in a landslide victory by people who did not own telephones! Today a very different segment of the population has unlisted numbers and so would not be reached in a telephone survey.

Survey methods should be designed to give campaign planners data which provide the most representative and clearest view of the target audiences, not data which reinforce preconceived biases. It is deceptively easy for highly committed campaign workers to convince themselves that everyone will look at things the way they do. The resultant false assumptions about audiences destroy the transaction and produce transmissional campaigns which may miss the target audience altogether.

Audience characteristics which a campaign must analyze are those beliefs, attitudes, values, behaviors, emotions, and so on which we discussed in Chapter 3. For small, individualized campaigns, the organization can probably do its own audience analysis. Larger, well-financed campaigns would do well to secure the services of an individual consultant or research organization skilled in survey research.

Analyzing the situation. Not only must the individual characteristics of the audience be analyzed, but so does the particular historical and geographical situation within which the campaign will be conducted. The political, economic, and cultural characteristics of this context are usually considered.

Depending upon the purpose of the campaign, the *political context* can be of pivotal importance. In political campaigns, some congressional districts repeatedly elect candidates from the same political party, and some political years may strongly favor one party or another. However, exceptions exist. Local political issues may override national trends, especially in state and local campaigns. In the Republican landslide of 1984, several Democrats bucked the tide and were elected to Congress as well as to state and local offices on the basis of local political issues.

Political issues can be important in nonpolitical campaigns as well. A trend away from administrative overhead and regulations by a national office, far removed from local control, could profoundly affect campaigns for donations by charitable and religious organizations. What political allegiances and obligations does the target audience have? While some of these political considerations may seem insurmountable, it is better for a campaign to be aware of them so that they can be dealt with if possible.

The *economic context* within which the campaign is waged can also affect the degree of its success or failure. Money may be difficult to raise in hard economic times. On the other hand, hard times also can create a more urgent need, and therefore may strengthen the appeal.

Special economic issues can also impact the campaign. The anti-tax "Proposition 13" wave which started in California and spread throughout the country in the late 1970s made all sorts of campaigns for community development extremely difficult—especially school bond elections. Whether interest rates or unemployment are high or low may influence a campaign to launch a new product or housing development.

In addition to the political and economic context, the *cultural* aspects of the *context* within which the campaign will operate are analyzed. In most cases, the narrower the context, the easier the cultural analysis will be. On the other hand, independent national polls can provide campaigners with data not available on the local level.

An important aspect of the cultural context is the unique *history* of the geo- graphic area to be targeted. In most of his historical novels, and especially in *The Covenant,* James Michener figuratively traces the particular history of an area. In *The Covenant,* he describes the kinds of people who emigrated to South Africa, re-enacts many of their hardships and displacements, and describes the counterproductive policies which were foisted upon the Boers by distant gov- ernments. To the degree that it is accurate, such understanding of the historical heritage of an area helps explain prevalent attitudes, values, and behaviors.

Religion is another cultural variable which bears attention. Very centrally- held religious beliefs can have a great influence on any community which shares them. Understanding of the Mormon belief in "exaltation" by good works on earth goes a long way to explain their opposition to the E.R.A. on the basis of "life-style" issues such as abortion, marriage and divorce laws, and women working outside the home.[10]

Language is another cultural variable which can affect the campaign. While most people in the U.S. speak English as a first language, increasing numbers of people do not. It has been predicted that Spanish may become the dominant lan- guage of the Southwest in the near future. Public notices, signs, and ballots are printed in more than one language in various sections of the country. Further, language is used very differently in various subcultures and geographic areas. An understanding of these linguistic usages can help campaigners relate more effectively with campaign audiences. In analyzing the social situation, then, the political and economic situation should be considered as well as the historical, religious, and linguistic dimensions of the culture.

Goal setting. All forms of persuasive communication depend upon clear, precisely stated goals for their effectiveness. Campaigns are no exception.[11] Goals form the foundation upon which rests everything that is done in the cam- paign. Goals are transactional in that they focus on the ultimate objectives of all participants, from the target audiences to the campaign workers themselves.

Primary and secondary goals. Most campaigns have both *primary and secondary goals.* A fund-raising campaign for the American Cancer Society would have as its primary goal the raising of a specific amount of money for the society's annual operating budget. It might also, however, hope to increase pub- lic consciousness about the causes of cancer as well as increase the name rec- ognition of the society.

Not all campaign goals are as easily decided upon as these, however. Take the case of the Mormons for E.R.A. Their primary purpose was to contribute to the passage of the Equal Rights Amendment by neutralizing the efforts of the Mormon Church against it. But how? Should their goal be to convince the leaders of the church to stop their campaign against the E.R.A. or, failing that, to per- suade church members to pressure the leadership to stop? Or should they design their campaign to influence key, unratified state legislatures by counter- ing the church's lobbyists or by influencing public opinion through exposure in the mass media?

History tells us that the Mormons for E.R.A. failed in their primary purpose. But was their campaign a complete failure? Not necessarily. Considerable evidence suggests that they succeeded in the secondary goal of raising the public consciousness about women's issues in general and about the political and economic power of the Mormon Church in particular.[12]

General goal. In the process of identifying the primary and secondary goals, campaigners usually determine what type of *general goal* or purpose will characterize their campaign. These general classifications have sometimes been treated as "types" of campaigns.[13] However, from our transactional perspective, they are more appropriately viewed as the general response desired from target audiences. We will discuss (1) product sales, (2) charitable contributions, (3) education, (4) image establishment or change, (5) institutional policy change, (6) self-help, (7) community development, and (8) political goals.

A goal with which most people are familiar is *product sales.* This goal can take the form of anything from advertising in the mass media to door-to-door selling. In any case, the primary purpose is to affect the buying behavior of individuals.

Another general goal of campaigns is to raise *charitable contributions.* Thousands of private institutions depend upon fund-raising campaigns. In some instances fund-raising is a primary goal, as in the case of the United Way and the

/ **Former President Jimmy Carter contributes his time and carpentry skills to Habitat for Humanity, a national organization with the general goals of self-help and community development.**

American Cancer Society. In other cases, it is a secondary, though extremely important, goal, as in a political campaign. While the primary goal of fund raising is usually quite clear, the style of the campaign can be profoundly affected by attention to such secondary goals as building the organization's image and goodwill.

Education is yet another general goal of many campaigns. This campaign goal traditionally has been characterized as "indoctrination." From a transactional perspective, the concept of education includes all forms of mutually advantageous information-sharing rather than only the more manipulative notion of indoctrination. Education can be identified as the primary goal of campaigns on energy conservation, anti-smoking, and driver safety. Third-party political candidates, such as John Anderson in 1980, frequently cite "educating the public to the issues" as a significant secondary goal of their campaigns.

Similar to educational campaigns are campaigns designed to create an *image* for an individual or organization or designed to change an existing image. Between his defeat to Edmond G. (Pat) Brown for the governorship of California in 1962 and his nomination for President in 1968, Richard Nixon waged an effective campaign to change his public image from "tricky Dicky" to the "new Nixon." Similarly, oil and utility companies have spent considerable time and money campaigning to alter their images from that of large and uncaring exploiters of the environment to that of warm and concerned partners in protecting the environment.

Still another general goal of a campaign could be *institutional policy change*. You are probably familiar with campaigns on your own campus either to change or retain policies related to grading practices, admission standards, or student evaluations of teaching. On the national scene, campaigns on both sides of the E.R.A. ratification, a nuclear arms freeze, or tax reduction have been fiercely waged. Policy change can take a long time, and its relationship to public opinion makes secondary goals of education and image change potentially very important.

Self-help campaigns have become more common in recent years. The 1970s have sometimes been referred to as the "decade of narcissism." These years witnessed a noticeable shift from the concern for social change which characterized the 1960s to a seeming preoccupation with self-improvement. People's awareness of their diet, blood pressure, interpersonal relationships, stress levels, smoking habits, and other self-related issues were the object of numerous campaigns and continue to be so.

Along with self-help campaigns have come campaigns with the general goal of *community development*. The basic concept behind these campaigns is that people cannot achieve their full human potential in a debilitating environment. Some of the campaigns have resulted in the dramatic restoration of the older, previously decayed sections of larger cities. Old Victorian buildings have been restored, streets beautified, and shopping malls developed in aged warehouses and trolley barns. Private organizations, too, have mounted campaigns to help people help themselves by facilitating the restoration of collapsing community infrastructures.

The arena which often comes to mind when we hear the word *campaign* is *political.* Influencing voting behavior of citizens is a major campaign goal. Millions of people watch every presidential "debate" as well as the national party conventions. Many people's first introduction to the workings of a campaign will be as a volunteer in a campaign for a political candidate.

Specific goal.   Having determined the general goal or purpose of the campaign, planners must then identify the *specific goals,* both primary and secondary. Political campaigns, of course, target the election of a particular candidate, while attempting to create a lasting, positive image for both the candidate and the party. Sales and charitable campaigns may focus not only on a particular product or charity but on a specific audience and volume of sales or contributions as well.

Many campaign organizations will assess the relationship of the campaign to a broader social movement in which it is occurring. Workers campaigning for a nuclear freeze will probably conduct the campaign in such a way as not to impair a broader peace movement. In any case, early in the process very specific primary and secondary goals of the campaign are usually clearly identified. Unlike most of the remaining functions, these goals will probably not change much during the campaign, but will provide a firm foundation upon which the remainder of the campaign is built.

Basic strategizing.   The final planning function in a campaign is that of *basic strategizing.* We will discuss identifying central themes and global strategies.

Although there may be a variety of issues upon which the campaign will capitalize, planners must identify one or a few *central themes* which will characterize the campaign. Prior to the energy crunch in the mid-1970s, oil companies tended to stress the theme of "service" in their advertising campaigns. Since then the central theme has more frequently been "conservation." Similarly, automobile manufacturers have shifted from the theme of "luxury" to "fuel efficiency" and back again to "small luxury."

Sometimes a central theme will involve an image change, even in campaigns which have sales, votes, or contributions as their general purpose. Perhaps the most famous case was the shift from the effeminate image filter cigarettes had in the early 1950s to the "he-man" image Marlboro cigarettes created as a theme for their now-legendary advertising campaign.

It should be apparent that the selection of general themes is a transactional process. A catchy phrase or slogan is not chosen just because it appeals to campaign workers. The campaign theme generally emerges from the exigencies identified by the analysis of the audience and situation.

While the general theme(s) are the images or ideas which characterize the campaign, *global strategies* are the major ways campaigners intend to go about accomplishing the specific goal or purpose. In a recent fund drive, a local office of the American Cancer Society was able to involve a popular TV personality who had been "cured" of cancer himself. The global strategy was a "Walk with Dick Norse," in which volunteers walked through the streets of the city, being "paid" by contributors and relatives. This strategy had the added advantage of making significant media resources available to the campaign at little or no cost.

Early on in political campaigns, the organizers must decide to what extent they will emphasize the strengths of their candidate or attack the opponent. In the 1984 Democratic primaries, Walter Mondale used the global strategy of stressing his own experience and qualifications for the presidency, while Gary Hart stressed a need for new leadership which implied an inadequacy both in the traditional Democratic approach of Mondale and in the presidency of Ronald Reagan. Later Reagan used the global strategy of avoiding as much as possible face-to-face confrontations with Mondale or the press on specific issues while appealing to middle-American values at well-orchestrated rallies and mass media appearances.

Not only do these global strategies depend upon the situation and audience analysis, but they may be altered during the campaign on the basis of a continuing analysis of the success of the campaign as it proceeds.

/ *Mobilization of Resources.*

To a large extent, the success of the campaign will depend on planners' success in mobilizing personnel and material resources to support it. Generally, these types of resources are complementary. That is, money can usually buy the types of services needed in a campaign. Where money is short, personal services and material can be donated.

Personnel resources. No campaign will be successful without competent, dedicated workers in key positions. Of the campaigns we have studied, the quality of the workers has consistently been the single most important variable in the success or lack of success of the campaign. Some years ago a colleague was planning to vacation in Nairobi, Kenya. It was suggested he visit a community development project which was part of a campaign with which he was acquainted. When asked how the project was going, the response was telling: "Fine, and it will continue to prosper as long as the magnificent person who showed me around remains with the project."

Preliminary commitments are usually obtained early in the campaign or even before the campaign is launched. Commitments can be obtained either by personal contacts or by tapping the resources of groups likely to share the goals of the campaign. For instance, groups which are organized to address one issue in the women's movement are likely to support other human rights issues as well.

Recruiting can have a *pyramid effect*. If workers are selected carefully, especially strong leaders and opinion makers, they in turn will recruit additional workers for their segment of the campaign.

Preliminary commitments, however, are just that—preliminary. It is easy for someone to agree to help a campaign in April, but it is quite another matter for a person to spend long hours in meetings or telephoning in September. For sustained mobilization of human resources, contact will need to be renewed throughout the campaign.

Finally, where particular expertise is required the campaign may need to hire a consultant. Reliance on dedicated but unqualified people in key "skill" positions can quickly blunt the effectiveness of a campaign.

Material resources.   Almost as important as personnel resources is the mobilization of material resources. We will discuss monetary, in-kind, and communication resources.

While *fund-raising* can be the goal of an individual campaign, it also constitutes an important function in all other campaigns. During the congressional campaign of 1982, election night reports included not only the voting returns but also the amounts of money spent by some candidates. Several senatorial and gubernatorial candidates spent in excess of a million dollars and a few spent over ten million dollars. With the price of modern mass media, consulting fees, and services of all kinds, few campaigns can be successful without considerable financial resources.

Most campaign managers would prefer contributions of money because it is so convenient and flexible; however, some people find it difficult to ask for money and others find it difficult to give. Perhaps the most overlooked source of material support for a campaign is "in-kind" gifts. These are donations of either goods or services which can be used by the campaign. In one community development campaign, school and office equipment were donated by a school district from its surplus warehouse, a supermarket donated dozens of crates of food with slightly damaged containers (which would have been destroyed otherwise), and a local army post loaned bedding equipment for temporary housing. Literally thousands of dollars of material needs were either donated or loaned. Public agencies frequently have facilities or equipment which either can be loaned or donated out of surplus. Businesses can donate usable material which may or may not be marketable and obtain a tax write-off in the process.

Services can also be donated. Supportive businesses may make available free consulting, printing, and other services. In local United Way campaigns, large corporations often release executives to work on the campaign for several weeks or even months and continue to pay their salaries.

For many reasons, individuals, businesses, and public agencies may find it more convenient to support a campaign with in-kind gifts instead of cash. Before paying for anything, skillful campaign workers ask for it as a donation or loan.

Communication resources constitute a type of material resource which is so important to most campaigns that it merits special emphasis. When considering communication resources, most people will think first of the mass media of communication. Determining what part media will play in the campaign and then setting out to mobilize those media is a primary concern of any campaign. The Mormons for E.R.A. campaign is an interesting case. The attention of the mass media was first attracted by the slogan "Mormons for E.R.A." on a banner during a march in Washington, D.C. A subsequent confrontation between Sonia

Johnson and Senator Orrin Hatch of Utah attracted further attention from the national press.[14] The later excommunication trial of Sonia Johnson captured national headlines. All of these events were not initially intended to mobilize the media, but once curiosity about this conflict within the Mormon Church was manifest, the campaign capitalized on it. Demonstrations at major Mormon events, accompanied by clever airplane trailers, were specifically designed to attract the attention of the national media and were successful in doing so. While the impact of all of this exposure may be open to question, a wide variety of mass media were skillfully exploited by the Mormons for E.R.A. campaign.

Most campaigns, however, do not find the mass media so readily available for little or no expense. Advertising campaigns usually require a substantial budget. Recall, however, that a fund-raising drive for the American Cancer Society mobilized significant amounts of free media coverage by including a prominent TV personality in the campaign. Radio and television stations are obligated to provide a certain amount of "public service" programming, and few meet their quota. Non-profit, charitable, self-help, or community development campaigns may receive significant amounts of media coverage either as public service programming or as in-kind donations. One clever ploy has been to have a corporation sponsor an ad for the campaign. This benefits the campaign not only from the ad but also from the endorsement of the corporation, while the corporation can build its public image and treat the costs as a business expense.

Mobilization of mass media resources is not necessarily so simple as "the more, the better." As we saw in the last chapter, planners must decide which media are best suited to reach the target audiences.

Campaign workers may also consider whether they want to mobilize the mass media at all. In its campaign against the E.R.A., the Mormon Church decided against the use of mass media and concentrated on lobbying specific state legislators by church members who were mobilized by internal church communication and organizational networks.[15]

This example suggests, further, that a wide variety of communication resources should be considered, from mass media to individual word-of-mouth contacts. Important to any campaign could be direct mail, public speeches and symposia, study groups, telephone networks, and the like. As we suggested before, these communication resources should be carefully selected with the transaction with specific target audiences in mind.

/ Legitimation.   Imagine what it would be like to be an American Indian. Your ancestors proudly and freely ranged over the Great Plains and other areas until white settlers began to encroach. Although seldom decisively defeated in battle, your forebearers were ultimately forced to surrender from lack of food, the sources of which had been destroyed by white people. They were herded into concentration camps called reservations and continually relocated when white people found the reservation land contained valuable minerals (such as gold in the revered Black Hills and oil in Oklahoma). Finally, your tribe was settled on a reservation on a pleasant bank of the Missouri River, protected from the harsh

North Dakota winds by a grove of cottonwood trees. The best land within the boundaries of your reservation was leased off to white ranchers by white Bureau of Indian Affairs officials. Then, in the 1960s, your entire village is again relocated to a windy plain above the river to make way for a reservoir which will irrigate white people's farms down stream.

Imagine the derisiveness and suspicion with which you would greet some white "do-gooders" who arrived in your village and announced that you had been selected for a community development project which would be a demonstration to all native American communities of how to improve their situation in life.

Most campaigns do not face this severe problem of legitimizing themselves; however, every campaign must achieve a degree of legitimacy in the eyes of their audiences to be successful. In this discussion, the term *legitimacy* will be used transactionally as that bond of trust between the campaign and its leadership, on the one hand, and the various audiences, on the other. Campaigns can be legitimized by reputation, endorsement, cause, and power.[16]

Reputation.   Reputation is the trust or credibility the organization, product, or candidate presently shares with the audience. The legitimacy of a campaign by the Catholic Church, the Republican Party, the Salvation Army, or a political candidate will be a function of how individual members of the audiences view the campaign on the basis of their prior experience with the organization, product, or candidate.

While reputation is usually built over a number of years, it can be destroyed in a day. The Tylenol tragedy is an interesting case in point. The parent company, Johnson & Johnson, was able to restore quickly both the legitimacy of their product and subsequent campaigns by utilizing their own long and distinguished reputation, disassociating themselves from the cause of the tragedy, and implementing a responsible and costly, albeit temporary, withdrawal of the product.

Endorsement.   If reputation is the trust or credibility the campaign shares with the audience, then *endorsements* constitute, in a sense, borrowed credibility or trust which has been developed over the years by someone else. Great legitimacy may be obtained for the campaign by receiving the endorsement of an individual or group that is highly respected by target audiences. In some cases, endorsements in the form of letters of recommendation or introduction are necessary even to begin the campaign or to gain the admittance or attention of key contributors, workers, or opinion makers.

Endorsements are particularly important to campaigns for an unknown product, candidate, or cause. The credibility of a familiar source is borrowed and used to legitimize the campaign. An important strategy in the campaign of Walter Mondale for the Democratic nomination in 1984 was his successful acquisition of endorsements from the AFL and the NEA, as well as many other national organizations and civic leaders.

From a transactional perspective, people from whom endorsements are solicited should be carefully selected. People with strong trust relationships with a specific target audience are usually sought. Different endorsements may be used with different audiences.

An important consideration is the endorser's ability to produce support. In Chicago politics a few years ago, an endorsement by the late mayor Richard J. Daley was said to have been tantamount to election because of Daley's ability to influence votes, both in political conventions and at the polls. Individuals and organizations with loyal, highly committed followings provide more useful endorsements than those with comparably impressive titles but less influence among their followers.

Cause. A campaign can also be legitimized by the perceived social value of its cause. We all know how difficult it is to turn down the appeal of a stranger who is selling cookies to put a child through school or raising money to fight a dread disease.

Fund-raising campaigns for charitable causes have a natural legitimacy, but product sales and political campaigns can be legitimized by cause as well. Less known candidates can associate themselves with causes such as peace or tax reduction. Product sales can emphasize energy conservation or human development such as weight control, health, and beauty.

Power. A campaign can also be legitimized by associating it with people and groups that exert power over target audiences. The campaign can involve people in positions of leadership, especially in authoritarian organizations, or people who occupy strategic decision-making positions.

In many cases the campaign will be able to involve people who hold positions of power themselves. During its campaign against the E.R.A., the Mormon Church chose to pursue the excommunication of Sonia Johnson. While this act had the disadvantage of attracting some unfavorable publicity, it sent a clear message to church members which in effect said, "While we maintain that opposition to the E.R.A. is not grounds for excommunication, we still hold the power and are not afraid to use it if you go too far." This tactic not only discouraged open support for the E.R.A. within the church, but stimulated support for the church's campaign as well.

Legitimation by power can also be achieved indirectly. Washington, D.C., is full of power brokers. These people may not have power themselves, but have influence with people who do. Former congressional representatives, cabinet members, and bureaucrats, as well as close advisers such as legislative or administrative assistants, often develop lucrative "consulting" careers which capitalize on the influential connections they maintain. Michael Deaver, former Special Counsel to President Reagan, has successfully represented the interests of several foreign countries since leaving the Administration. The cliché, "It's not who you are, but who you know," carries some important implications for legitimizing a campaign by means of power.

Legitimacy, whether by reputation, endorsement, cause, or power, depends transactionally upon the cognitive systems of specific audiences. Some audiences will admire certain qualities or relationships where another audience will not. Audiences will be influenced by different people because of the beliefs, attitudes, or values they represent. Careful audience analysis will reveal what avenues can be most effective as workers attempt to legitimize the campaign.

/ *Case-building.* An important function of any campaign is that of case-building. *Case-building* is the identification of potential issues which are related to the campaign and the selection of arguments to be emphasized with different audiences.

Determining issues. We have defined *issue* as a controversial question upon which two or more positions can be taken. Hence the question, "How old is Candidate X?" is not an issue, but the question, "Is Candidate X too old to execute the responsibilities of the office for which she is a candidate?" is an issue. While this issue may seem to have two basic positions (that is, *yes* or *no*), an individual or audience could take a wide variety of qualified positions on this issue.

Earlier we spoke of *stock issues* as those issues which were so common as to be nearly always a factor in questions related to social change. Here we will show how those stock issues, when applied to the general response of the campaign, will produce *basic issues* which should be explored in most campaigns with a particular general goal.

The most direct application of stock issues is found in campaigns with the goal of institutional policy change. If a campaign is opposed to the deployment of a new missile system, the basic issues might be:

1. Is there a *need* for the missile?
2. Is there a *practical* basing mode for the missile?
3. Will the missile *meet* the Russian challenge?
4. Is the missile the *best* weapons system for this purpose?
5. Will the missile create new and worse *disadvantages?*

In a campaign of institutional policy change, these questions are so universal that one could change not only the name of the weapons system, but the type of policy itself. As we illustrated earlier, these basic issues are somewhat general and will suggest more specific issues which may be more useful as the campaign becomes activated.

In product sales campaigns, the basic issues will be similar but with a slightly different focus. The basic issues for a product sales campaign might be:

1. Is there a *need* for this product?
2. Is the *cost* affordable?
3. What is the *quality* of the product?
4. Is this the *best* product?
5. What are the *disadvantages* of the product (safety factors and so on)?

In campaigns whose goal is charitable contributions, the basic issues might be:

1. What is the *need* for the contribution?
2. Can the potential contributors *afford* the contribution?
3. How much of the contribution gets to the problem and how much is required for *administrative overhead?*
4. Is this charity the most *effective* one for meeting the problem?
5. What are the *disadvantages* to contributing (that is, will giving to this charity damage my reputation)?

In political campaigns, the basic issues are somewhat more individualized and yet roughly follow the stock issues:

1. What *problems* does our society have, and to what extent can they be blamed on the incumbent officers?
2. How is the candidate *qualified* to meet these problems?
3. Are the *policies* the candidate supports likely to solve the problems?
4. Is the candidate the *best* one?
5. Does the candidate have political or personal *liabilities,* and how can they be handled?

In the case of educational or image-oriented campaigns, the basic issues might read like this:

1. What aspects of the audiences' *images* need changing or augmenting?
2. Is there a *feasible* way of doing this?
3. Will this approach bring about the desired *result?*
4. Is there a *better* way to do it?
5. Will it *create new problems,* or will benefits accrue?

Finally, self-help and community-development campaigns are not only similar to one another but also overlap with policy-change campaigns. Basic issues in these campaigns might be:

1. Does the individual or community have a *serious problem(s)* which needs addressing?
2. Is the solution *workable?*
3. Will the solution *actually solve* the problem?
4. Is there a *better* solution?
5. Will the solution have *incidental advantages* or *disadvantages?*

With each of the above type of campaign goals, an application of the stock issues reveals issues basic to each general campaign goal. Although these basic issues have much in common, each type of campaign has basic issues which are unique.

Issues become increasingly specific as they are analyzed in light of the specific situation. *Specific issues* will vary with the specific "product," audience, and context of the campaign.

By *product,* of course, is meant the product, candidate, behavior, or idea which is the object of the campaign. All of these have specific characteristics which may produce specific issues. In most political campaigns the stock "practicality" issue focuses on the candidates' qualifications. One specific issue related to qualifications might be age, but this would not be an issue if the candidate were not unusually young or old. Even then, this issue would be related to health or experience and would be revealed in audience analysis. Recall how Ronald Reagan anticipated and diffused the age issue when he quipped in the 1984 debate, "I won't exploit the age issue by pointing out the youth and inexperience of my opponent."

In the campaign to rehabilitate the image of Tylenol following the random deaths after use of that product, extensive analysis of the issues combined with extensive surveys of public opinion revealed one specific overriding issue: "Will I ever be able to trust Tylenol to be safe?" The entire campaign was designed to meet that one issue head on.

Selecting arguments. Having analyzed the basic and specific issues, campaign planners develop arguments with which each audience can identify. Arguments are the declarative statements which state the campaign's position on the issue. In the Tylenol campaign the arguments could be stated:

I. Main Argument: Tylenol is and always has been a completely safe product.
   A. Supporting Argument: It is produced by a responsible company.
   B. Supporting Argument: It is produced with great care.
   C. Supporting Argument: It has always left the factory in a safe condition.
   D. Supporting Argument: It was made unsafe in an isolated instance by tampering after it left the factory.
   E. Supporting Argument: New packaging will make tampering difficult.

A second series of product tamperings in 1986, which was accomplished despite Tylenol's tamper-resistant packaging, raised the possibility that the tampering was done within the factory and illustrated again the ease with which capsules could be tainted. Johnson & Johnson was faced with another public relations challenge, which they met by discontinuing the manufacturing of Tylenol in capsule form. The arguments in their new campaign thus might now read:

I. Main Argument: Tylenol is once again a completely safe product.
   A. Supporting Argument: It is produced by a responsible company.
   B. Supporting Argument: It is produced with great care.
   C. Supporting Argument: It is produced in tablet and caplet forms, both of which are extremely tamper-resistant.

Arguments do not exist in a vacuum, however. They must be carefully selected to provide transactions with specific cognitive systems of target audiences. We will discuss arguments targeted for campaign workers, opinion makers, the general public, and specific "publics."

Perhaps the first concern is with *campaign workers.* Very early in the process and long before the campaign is taken to the other audiences, there is usually developed a cohesive "case" or line of arguments which will be motivating to campaign workers. While not incompatible with other arguments, these may not be the same arguments which will have the greatest impact on other audiences and may not form the core of the campaign proper.

Consider the arguments used by the Mormon Church in its successful attempt to mobilize members to work against passage of the E.R.A. These arguments related to abortion, homosexual marriage, the draft, and women working outside the home might or might not make sense to uncommitted audiences and would be judged downright irrelevant by strong supporters of E.R.A. However, they made good sense to Mormon audiences because these arguments are firmly grounded in the theology and traditional values of their church. As such they "provided the campaign workers with a remarkably homogeneous doctrine from which to argue their case."[17]

Arguments must also be devised for audiences outside the campaign structure itself. The first group to consider would be *opinion makers.* Opinion makers are professional people like doctors, lawyers, teachers, labor leaders, influential business persons, religious leaders, media and sports personalities, and, above all, civic and political leaders.

If opinion makers can be convinced by the campaign, or better yet be recruited as campaign workers, their contribution can be considerable. Earlier we described diffusion of information as a complex process. Within that process opinion leaders sometimes begin a chain reaction, or *diffusion effect*, in which they influence members of their group, who in turn influence their friends and families, and so on, until the impact becomes considerable.

Opinion leaders tend to be better informed and more competent than the general audience. They are likely to be more intelligent and better read than most people. Arguments for opinion leaders can, therefore, be more detailed and complex. On the other hand, the arguments may need more evidentiary support, especially if they contradict common knowledge.

An interesting case in point is the U.S. government's campaign to mobilize public opinion in favor of the deployment of the MX missile on race-tracks within thousands of square miles of Nevada and Utah real estate. Since Mormons constitute fully two-thirds of the population of Utah and 7 percent in Nevada, the Mormon Church leadership was targeted as important opinion makers in this campaign. In addition, the church had significant influence with two United States senators who were very close to Ronald Reagan. When the Mormon Church finally made a public declaration opposing the Utah-Nevada basing mode, the race-track proposal was quickly withdrawn. It has been suggested that, although the Mormon Church generally assumes a strong defense and high patriotism profile, the decisive argument was that a large influx of "outsiders" would substantially change the theocratic life-style of predominantly Mormon, rural towns—an argument which might be perceived as unimportant by the general population of the U.S.

The *general public* is usually the primary target audience toward which a campaign is directed. The general public is the people who are "qualified" to buy the product, vote for the candidate, or give to the charity, or whose cognitive system is to be influenced. General publics can vary considerably from a voting district or geographic marketing area to the entire geography or population of the U.S. The larger the general public, the more general (or at least universal in appeal), simple, and benign may be the arguments.

In the case of the deployment of the MX, arguments which appealed to audiences throughout the country were the need (or lack of need) for the missile, the adverse impact the extremely high cost would have on taxes, and the economy and the morality (or lack of it) in deploying such a massive weapons system. Careful audience surveys revealed what arguments would provide identification with target audiences on specific issues.

Finally, campaign strategists usually consider selecting arguments for more *specific audiences* within the general public. Specific groups such as people of different ages, group affiliations, geographic areas, vocations, and ethnic minorities may respond to different or more specific arguments in addition to those selected for the general public.

In the case of the MX missile, the people in the small towns which would be affected by the deployment were uneasy about the impact on their life-style, but generally favored deployment because of economic arguments like more jobs and an increase in real estate values. People in some economically depressed towns stood to get very rich. The general populations of the states of Utah and Nevada were generally opposed because they stood to benefit less economically and were not sanguine about being made the ground-zero target in the event of a nuclear holocaust.

Our MX example, then, demonstrates graphically that although arguments are not incompatible or inconsistent, they can be very different depending upon whether they are selected for transactions with campaign workers, opinion makers, the general public, or specific segments of these audiences.

/ Activation Functions.   In order for a campaign to reach fruition, all of the planning, mobilization, legitimation, and case building must be put into action. Although we are discussing activation last, portions of it may begin concurrently with or even before some of the foregoing functions are completed. We will discuss promotion, solidifying preliminary commitments, detailed action plans, penetration, and follow through.

Promotion.   The function of activating or publicizing the legitimacy of the campaign is called *promotion.* It has to do mainly with actively creating a favorable image identity or trust bond with target audiences.

Legitimacy from reputation is difficult to promote over a short period of time since it is usually created through extended personal contact with the product, cause, or campaign workers. Legitimacy from endorsements and cause can effectively be promoted through *media* advertising, direct mail, and personal contacts. Legitimacy from power can be promoted through the same media but is usually handled more subtly and perhaps more privately.

In addition to communicating legitimacy through various media, promotion involves creating an identity for the campaign through favorable *name-recognition*. While favorable name-recognition may be the major goal of image-oriented campaigns, it is an important function of all campaigns. Favorable name-recognition can be promoted through the use of slogans, logos, and even the name itself.

Solidifying preliminary commitments. Earlier we spoke of mobilizing material and personal resources through preliminary commitments. These commitments are useless, however, if they are not solidified and finally collected and used.

Collecting money from people who have made a preliminary commitment or pledge, while usually not too difficult, is not to be taken for granted or ignored. United Way campaigns expect a shrinkage of 5 to 10 percent of pledges with little or no follow-up. Other organizations should expect much greater shrinkage. Pledges can be collected with personal contacts, telephone calls, and letters in roughly that same order of effectiveness and difficulty.

/ **After securing preliminary pledges of support from viewers, public television stations follow up carefully in order to bring in the needed funds.**

Activating workers can be somewhat more difficult than raising money. It is all too easy for people to commit themselves a month or two in advance, only to find their schedules full when their time is needed. Except for announcing organizational meetings, letters rarely suffice. Telephone reminders or, better yet, personal contact are generally the most effective communicative means of activating workers.

Detailed action plans. In order to implement the activation function, a campaign must go beyond basic strategizing to the development and implementation of detailed action plans. Workers will first want to decide upon the *major activities* and events which will constitute the campaign. These would include organizational meetings, public surveys, research, media events, rallies for campaign workers, speaking events, interviews with power brokers, fund raising, production of campaign materials (t-shirts, bumper-stickers, posters), and the many other specific functions mentioned earlier. Major activities can be decided upon in a meeting of the central campaign committee and, taken together, constitute the master plan for the campaign.

Having decided upon a master plan composed of all major activities, planners then decide upon the specific steps required to implement each activity. The development of *specific implementaries* can be assigned to subcommittees or even individuals with the necessary expertise.

For more elaborate campaigns, major activities can be delegated to subcommittees which in turn will need to develop their own detailed action plans. Coordination is usually maintained by the central committee, however, in order to avoid conflicts in scheduling and duplication of effort. In any case, the more detailed the plans, the less likely it will be that some significant person, arrangement, or piece of equipment will be overlooked.

When the responsible committees and individuals have decided upon the major activities and detailed implementaries, a detailed *campaign calendar* is usually constructed. The building of a campaign calendar not only insures that every detail will be accomplished, but it helps remind workers of details which may have been overlooked as the campaign progresses, and these details can be added to the calendar as the need arises. Implementation of detailed action plans becomes simple, clear, and flexible, while the "big picture" of how the campaign is proceeding is maintained.

Penetration. Penetration is the domino or mushrooming effect without which few campaigns can achieve maximum impact. It is accomplished by campaign workers compounding their influence by recruiting either other campaign workers or non-official opinion makers who in turn advance the goals of the campaign.

Most insurance and investment sales persons are encouraged to solicit from clients who have just purchased the product the names of at least five other people "who would be interested in the advantages of this product." The Amway Corporation has expanded rapidly because sales persons are encouraged to become managers by recruiting friends to become sales persons. One person influences five, which grows to twenty-five, 125, 625, and so on. Thus, the pyramid builds, influence is compounded, and the population is "penetrated."

When the campaign has started well and is expanding, it is easy for campaign organizers and workers alike to let down. Yet it is precisely at this point that extra effort is required if penetration is to accelerate successfully.

Follow-through. A final function in the activation of the campaign is follow-through. No campaign organization is perfectly efficient. Furthermore, workers need encouragement and sometimes reminding. A district manager in a political campaign may assign each worker fifty names to call in their neighborhoods the week before elections. Follow-through might involve calling each worker a day or two before the election "just to see how it's going."

A fund-raiser should be instructed to note which pledgers might need a call later to remind them to send in the check. In a pyramidal structure such as we described earlier, if a person on one of the middle levels of the pyramid fails to do the job, an entire section of the pyramid can become disfunctional.

Of particular importance is follow-through even after the specific campaign is completed. Workers and organizers can be rewarded with at least a "thank-you." A particularly effective technique is a brief letter of thanks acknowledging specifically what the individual contributed to the campaign. A copy of the letter can be sent to the worker's employer or superior in an organization of importance to the worker. There are few supervisors who are not pleased to find a person in their organization who is competent and motivated. Frequently, the individual will be rewarded by the organization with increased status or even monetary rewards at no cost to the campaign. Further, a willing worker or supporter is created for any subsequent campaign.

/ The campaign organization

While each of the foregoing functions is important in varying degrees to most campaigns, few campaigns will be successful without a campaign organization to implement those functions. Here we are concerned with the basic organization that most campaigns will require, which includes a campaign manager, a central committee, district and subdistrict chairpersons, and grassroots workers.

/ Campaign Manager.
The most important person in the campaign organization is the campaign manager. In most cases this is the person who runs the campaign but is not the principal sponsor. A political candidate rarely serves as his or her own campaign manager, nor does a minister typically manage the annual fund-raising campaign for a church. Delegation of authority is important to all levels of the campaign and it begins with the selection of a campaign manager.

A good campaign manager should, above all else, be dedicated to the cause of the campaign, be a generally well-organized person, and possess proven management experience, preferably in campaigns similar to the one being managed. The campaign manager will participate with the sponsoring individual or organization in top-level strategy decisions, but will also work with the central committee and key subcommittee chairpersons and directors in the coordination of the campaign as it proceeds.

/ *Central Committee.*   The central committee is composed of that group of leaders who supervise the day-to-day implementation of the campaign. It can be organized in two ways.

One common approach to organizing the central committee is by *functions* which are required by the campaign. Hence, the central committee would be composed of a personnel coordinator, development director, media coordinator, administrative assistant, and such specific directors as individual campaigns may require.

The *personnel coordinator* is responsible for the recruitment, training, assignment, and continued motivation of campaign workers. You will recall the importance placed earlier on having dedicated, competent campaign workers. By sitting on the central committee the personnel coordinator will know of the expertise which may or may not be available to the campaign.

The *development director* is responsible for the mobilization of material resources. Like the personnel coordinator, the development director should be a member of the central committee in order to understand more clearly the needs of the campaign and to provide realistic appraisals for the committee of the availability of monetary and in-kind resources.

If it is anticipated that the campaign will make extensive use of the mass media, a *media coordinator* is usually made a part of the central committee. Media can consume such huge amounts of the financial and material resources that direct supervision by the central committee is desirable. Further, coordination of media events, or the lack of it, can have such profound effects on the success of the campaign that the use of media should be of concern to the central committee.

In large campaigns, an *administrative assistant* is necessary to organize the campaign headquarters, provide careful accounting of funds, supervise workers, and plan communication among various segments of the campaign. This person needs to have the "big picture" of the campaign provided by membership on the central committee.

In addition to these individuals who sit on the central committee because they represent common campaign functions, campaigns may have individuals who perform specific functions so important to the campaign that membership on the central committee is desirable. For instance, in an advertising campaign, the person in charge of producing media advertisements would be on the central committee in order to provide input on the practical possibilities or limitations imposed by the production process. In a campaign designed to influence legislative bodies on an issue such as the E.R.A., a legislative liaison director might be on the central committee. In any case, the central committee can be organized according to the campaign functions the members represent.

A second way of organizing the central committee is by geography. Sales and political campaigns, where geographic coverage can be important, are particularly amenable to this type of organization. A central committee organized by this scheme would simply include the chairpersons or supervisors of the major areas or districts into which the campaign organization is divided.

Most central committees, depending upon their size, are organized in a combination of the functional and geographic approaches. That is, the functional directors and the major district managers would serve on the central committee. This organization has the advantage of providing functional input as well as geographic coordination by the central committee. However, every campaign is unique and individual adjustments may be made in the executive committee on the basis of the size, complexity, context, and specific content of each campaign.

/ Workers. Every successful campaign rests on the shoulders of dedicated workers. With the possible exception of advertising, self-help, or education campaigns which can be implemented by small, professional organizations, most campaigns require that large numbers of workers be organized—usually by geographic area. Materials need to be distributed, telephone contacts made, and doorbells rung. The objective of this organization is to cover the territory completely without unnecessary duplication or wasted effort. Some campaign leaders will call workers in their area three or four times to remind them of a meeting or to check on their progress. Further, on occasion a worker may accomplish a task, only to find that a task someone else did negated his or her effort. Had the tasks been coordinated, both could have accomplished their purpose. Workers can rapidly lose their commitment if they feel their efforts are wasted, either by not being given enough to do, by being assigned tasks significantly above or below their level of expertise, or by having their efforts negated by subsequent actions or decisions. Chairpersons and managers are usually selected at every level of the pyramidal organization who will have not only the drive to follow through, but also the organizational savvy to efficiently use the time and abilities of the campaign workers.

/ Theory / Practice / Analysis

Theory

1. Social movements are uninstitutionalized collectivities that attempt to promote or resist fundamental social change.

2. Movements tend to progress through the stages of genesis, social unrest, mobilization, maintenance, and termination.

3. Movements aim to transform the perceptions of history, alter the perceptions of society, prescribe courses of action, mobilize for action, and engage in self-maintenance activities.

4. Movement rhetoric accomplishes both internal organizational and commitment-building functions and external communication.

5. Movements necessarily encounter opposition from within, from counter-movements, and from the establishment.

6. Campaigns are sequential persuasive events which have an identifiable purpose, organization, and leadership.

7. Campaigns can best be implemented and analyzed by understanding their functions. The planning function involves analyzing target audiences, as well as the political, economic, and social dimensions of the situational context.

8. Setting primary and secondary goals is another planning function. General campaign goals include product sales, charitable contributions, education, image creation or change, institutional policy change, self-help, community development, and political support. Basic strategizing involves identifying central themes and determining global strategies.

9. A second function is mobilizing resources. Personnel resources can be mobilized through personal contacts, supporting groups, and the pyramid effect. Material resources can be mobilized through fund-raising, in-kind contributions, and communication resources.

10. Legitimation of the campaign may be accomplished through exploiting reputation, endorsement, cause, or power.

11. Case building can be accomplished by analyzing basic and specific issues to form the foundation of the argumentative case. Specific arguments are selected for specific target audiences such as campaign workers, opinion makers, and general and specific publics.

12. Campaigns are activated by promoting favorable name recognition, publicizing endorsements and cause, and exploiting reputation and power. Further activation is accomplished by solidifying preliminary commitments, devising detailed action plans, achieving penetration, and following through.

13. Campaign organization is a key determinant of a successful campaign.

Practice

1. Become involved in a social movement. As you work for the movement, take note of its stages, functions, and persuasion. As part of your role, make a concerted effort to plan communications designed to counteract opposition.

2. Join a campaign as a volunteer or paid worker. It can be a fund-raising campaign for a charity or church, a political campaign, an advertising

campaign, or any of the other goals cited in this chapter. Keep a journal of your observations and experiences.

3. Organize your class into a campaign to change some policy at your college or university. Identify a common dissatisfaction with parking, food services, grading, admissions, or other policy. Work to get the policy changed. Keep a journal.

4. Mount a fund-raising campaign for a scholarship fund in the communication department.

Analysis

1. Select a major media campaign—political, advertising, or other. Conduct research in the form of library reading, observations, and interviewing to determine the levels, intensities, and types of outcomes of the campaign.

2. Select a contemporary social movement of interest. Collect several examples of persuasive messages produced by participants in the movement. Examine these specimens in terms of their tactics for transforming perceptions of history, altering images of society, or engaging in self-maintenance.

3. Using the social movement you selected in Analysis item 2, write a brief paper describing what you believe the movement's ideology to be and how you think that ideology came into being. Examine also the ways in which the ideology seems to have affected the behavior of the movement's participants.

4. Select a movement from history on which you can find written material in the library. Study how the movement changed over time. Write a paper contrasting the rhetorical techniques of the movement during a period in which members' commitment was on the rise to a period in which that commitment seemed to be declining. What do you think are the essential differences, in this movement, between the two bodies of persuasive discourse? How do you explain the difference? What forms of control were used? How effective do they appear to have been?

5. Examine the social control measures used against the movement you studied in Analysis item 4.

6. Compare a social movement (for example, civil rights, women's liberation) with a campaign within that movement (for example, to pass the Civil Rights Bill of 1964 or the E.R.A.) according to the distinguishing characteristics discussed in this chapter.

7. Write a brief argument supporting the notion that planning, mobilization, legitimation, and activation are functions rather than steps in a campaign.

8. Analyze a campaign. Using the journal you kept in the campaign you worked on, evaluate how skillfully the campaign accomplished the functions discussed in this chapter. What techniques or innovations were used?

Notes

[1]Material for this section was taken primarily from Charles Stewart, Craig Smith, and Robert E. Denton, *Persuasion and Social Movements* (Prospect Heights, IL: Waveland Press, 1984), and Herbert W. Simons, Elizabeth W. Mechling, and Howard N. Schreier, "The Functions of Human Communication in Mobilizing for Action from the Bottom Up: The Rhetoric of Social Movements," in *Handbook of Rhetorical and Communication Theory,* ed. Carroll C. Arnold and John W. Bowers (Boston: Allyn and Bacon, 1984), pp. 792–868. See also John W. Bowers and Donovan J. Ochs, *The Rhetoric of Agitation and Control* (Reading, MA: Addison-Wesley, 1971).

[2]A. Bartlett Giamatti, "The Moral Majority is a Threat to the Freedom of Americans," *Pittsburgh Post-Gazette,* 5 September 1981, p. 8.

[3]Simons, Mechling, and Schreier, "Functions," p. 798.

[4]The nature of leadership in the Women's Movement is discussed in some detail by Karen A. Foss, "Ideological Manifestations in the Discourse of Contemporary Feminism," unpublished doctoral dissertation, University of Iowa, 1976

[5]Simons, Mechling, and Schreier, "Functions," pp. 828–29.

[6]The politics of this fight up to 1975 is described and documented by Janet K. Boles, *The Politics of the Equal Rights Amendment* (New York: Longman, 1979).

[7]This model is adapted from the "stages" of Herbert W. Simons' developmental model in *Persuasion: Understanding, Practice and Analysis* (Reading, MA: Addison-Wesley, 1976), Chapter 12.

[8]Simons, *Persuasion.*

[9]David M. Jabusch, "Social Demonstration: A Campaign for Community Development," paper delivered at a colloquium of the Communication Department, University of Utah, October 1979.

[10]See David M. Jabusch, "Mormon Anti-E.R.A. Rhetoric: An Exercise in Piety," paper delivered to the Speech Communication Association, Anaheim, California, November 1981.

[11]Simons, *Persuasion,* p. 250.

[12]David M. Jabusch, "Sonia Johnson and the Mormons for E.R.A. Campaign, paper delivered to the Speech Communication Association, New York City, November 1980.

[13]Simons, *Persuasion,* p. 226.

[14]Sonia Johnson, *From Housewife to Heretic* (Garden City, NY: Doubleday & Company, Inc., 1981).

[15]David M. Jabusch, "The L.D.S. Church Campaign Against the E.R.A.," paper delivered to the Speech Communication Association, 1982.

[16]Simons, *Persuasion,* pp. 234–36.

[17]Jabusch, "Mormon Anti-E.R.A. Rhetoric."

Author Index

Author Index

Adorno, T., 83, 112
Agarwala-Rogers, R., 173
Ajzen, I., 75, 111
Alderton, S. M., 173
Alexander, D., 62, 67, 74
Allport, G., 74
Anderson, J. A., 281
Aristotle, 51
Averill, J. R., 74
Avery, R. K., 281

Bales, R. F., 173
Ball-Rokeach, S., 253, 281
Bandura, A., 87, 112, 282
Baraclough, R., 23, 139
Barban, A. M., 259, 282
Barnard, C., 173
Barnlund, D. C., 23
Bauer, R., 281
Beavin, J., 139
Berger, C. R., 43
Blumler, J., 281
Bohn, E., 90, 112
Bormann, E. G., 217
Bostrom, R., 55, 74
Bowers, J., 242
Bradac, J., 242
Bradley, P. H., 173
Brock, T., 43
Burgoon, J. K., 23, 242
Burgoon, M., 23, 113
Burleson, B. R., 140

Cacioppo, J. T., 55, 74, 111, 242
Campbell, D., 241
Carey, J., 261, 282
Cialdini, R. B., 23

Cody, M. J., 139
Collins, B., 173
Cormick, G., 198
Courtright, J., 242
Cronen, V., 43, 73
Curti, M., 277, 282
Cusella, L. P., 173

Dance, F. E. X., 23
Davis, A., 198
DeFleur, M., 253, 281
Delia, J. G., 75, 140
Denton, R. E., 320
Dewey, J., 241
Diez, M. E., 197
Donohue, W. A., 197, 198
Doob, L., 85, 112
Driver, M. S., 43
Dunn, S. W., 259, 282

Ehninger, D., 242
Elliott, W. R., 282
Elms, A. C., 112

Farace, R. V., 172
Faules, D. F., 62, 67, 74
Festinger, L., 101, 113
Field, P. B., 82, 112
Fishbein, M., 75, 111
Fisher, W. R., 242
Foss, K. A., 217, 320
Fotheringham, W. C., 4
Fraser, S. C., 272, 282
Freedman, J. L., 272, 282
Frenkel-Brunswick, E., 112

Frey, L. R., 173
Frost, J. H., 140

Garreau, J., 241
Georgacarakos, G. N., 140
Giffin, K., 139
Greenwald, A., 79, 111
Gronbeck, B. E., 242
Guetzkow, H., 173
Gulliver, P. H., 198

Haefner, J., 282
Harre, R., 24, 74
Harris, L., 73
Hart, R. P., 217
Hawes, L., 23
Heider, F., 94, 98, 112
Hovland, C. I., 85, 241, 111

Jablin, F. M., 173
Jabusch, D. M., 23, 24, 67, 74, 75, 90, 112, 139, 173, 242, 282, 320
Jacklin, C. N., 112
Jackson, D., 139
James, W., 96
Janis, I. L., 64, 65, 74, 82, 111, 112, 241
Johnson, B. M., 172
Jones, T. S., 140
Jordan, W. J., 139

Kahn, R., 172
Katz, D., 172
Katz, E., 281

323

Subject Index

Subject Index

Acknowledgments

P. 258 Fig. 10.4, Reprinted by permission from *The Emergence of American Political Issues* by Donald L. Shaw and Maxwell E. McCombs; Copyright © 1977 by West Publishing Company. All rights reserved. Page 21. **P. 259** Fig. 10.5, Adapted with permission of the Free Press, a Division of Macmillan, Inc. from *Communication of Innovations,* Second Edition, by Everett M. Rogers with F. Floyd Shoemaker. Copyright © 1971 by The Free Press. **P. 264, 265** From "Alcohol Advertising: Orientations and Influence" by Donald Strickland from *Journal of Advertising* Vol. 1, 1982. Reprinted by permission. **P. 270** From *Advertising, The Uneasy Persuasion: Its Dubious Impact on American Society* by Michael Schudson, Copyright © 1984 by Michael Schudson. Reprinted by permission of Basic Books, Inc., Publishers.

Photo Credits